THE
INTELLECTUAL ADVENTURE
OF ANCIENT MAN

THE
INTELLECTUAL ADVENTURE
OF ANCIENT MAN

AN ESSAY ON SPECULATIVE THOUGHT

IN THE ANCIENT NEAR EAST

By

H. *and* H. A. FRANKFORT · JOHN A. WILSON

THORKILD JACOBSEN · WILLIAM A. IRWIN

THE UNIVERSITY OF CHICAGO PRESS · CHICAGO

AN ORIENTAL INSTITUTE ESSAY

THE UNIVERSITY OF CHICAGO PRESS, CHICAGO 37
Cambridge University Press, London, N.W. 1, England
The University of Toronto Press, Toronto 5, Canada

PREFACE

THIS volume contains lectures given as a public course in the Division of the Humanities of the University of Chicago. Except for minor changes, they are published in the form in which they were delivered, not in order to avoid transforming them into scientific treatises but because we believe that the direct expository method involves something of a challenge. In effect, we are presenting Webster's definition of an essay—"a literary composition, analytical or interpretative in nature, dealing with its subject from a more or less limited or personal standpoint and permitting a considerable freedom of style and method." We believe that the essay form possesses potentialities, even in dealing with our fragmentary and intricate sources which impose attention to detail as a first duty on every worker in the field. Such essays may claim a new freedom of method; they may have to cut across a historical approach for the sake of a new perspective; they may have to ignore the many-sidedness of a problem for the sake of a single aspect of it; sometimes their aim must be to evoke rather than to prove or argue. But, however varied their treatment may be, the essayists will have one characteristic in common. Bent on discovering the meaning of cultural and historical phenomena, their approach will be humanistic, and they will express themselves in terms understood by the educated layman.

Since these lectures address themselves primarily to a lay audience, the critical and documentary apparatus has been cut to a minimum and placed at the ends of the chapters. Our professional colleagues, however, will have little difficulty in distinguishing where we propound accepted views and where we offer new interpretations. We intend to defend some of the latter with all necessary documentation in future publications. Unless otherwise indicated, the translations in the present volume are those of the individual author, except in the case of biblical quotations, a large number of which are taken from the American Standard Version (used

v

with permission of the International Council of Religious Education).

The four main contributions in these lectures have been integrated through continued discussions and the exchange of preliminary manuscripts over a series of several months in advance of delivery. The result has been agreement on a unified point of view, which binds together divergent methods of presentation. Mrs. H. A. Groenewegen Frankfort, who was the first to suggest the subject of these lectures and who has contributed her special knowledge as a student of philosophy, serves with her husband as the author of the first and last chapters. She is also responsible for the poetical rendering of the translations from the Sumerian and Akkadian in chapters v–vii.

ORIENTAL INSTITUTE
UNIVERSITY OF CHICAGO
March 1946

TABLE OF CONTENTS

INTRODUCTION
By H. *and* H. A. FRANKFORT

EGYPT
By JOHN A. WILSON

MESOPOTAMIA
By THORKILD JACOBSEN

THE HEBREWS
By WILLIAM A. IRWIN

CONCLUSION
By H. *and* H. A. FRANKFORT

INDEX

INTRODUCTION
H. *and* H. A. FRANKFORT

CHAPTER I

MYTH AND REALITY

IF WE look for "speculative thought" in the documents of the ancients, we shall be forced to admit that there is very little indeed in our written records which deserves the name of "thought" in the strict sense of that term. There are very few passages which show the discipline, the cogency of reasoning, which we associate with thinking. The thought of the ancient Near East appears wrapped in imagination. We consider it tainted with fantasy. But the ancients would not have admitted that anything could be abstracted from the concrete imaginative forms which they left us.

We should remember that even for us speculative thought is less rigidly disciplined than any other form. Speculation—as the etymology of the word shows—is an intuitive, an almost visionary, mode of apprehension. This does not mean, of course, that it is mere irresponsible meandering of the mind, which ignores reality or seeks to escape from its problems. Speculative thought transcends experience, but only because it attempts to explain, to unify, to order experience. It achieves this end by means of hypotheses. If we use the word in its original sense, then we may say that speculative thought attempts to *underpin* the chaos of experience so that it may reveal the features of a structure—order, coherence, and meaning.

Speculative thought is therefore distinct from mere idle speculation in that it never breaks entirely away from experience. It may be "once removed" from the problems of experience, but it is connected with them in that it tries to explain them.

In our own time speculative thought finds its scope more severely limited than it has been at any other period. For we possess in science another instrument for the interpretation of experience, one that has achieved marvels and retains its full fascination. We do not allow speculative thought, under any circumstances, to en-

3

croach upon the sacred precincts of science. It must not trespass on the realm of verifiable fact; and it must never pretend to a dignity higher than that of working hypotheses, even in the fields in which it is permitted some scope.

Where, then, is speculative thought allowed to range today? Its main concern is with man—his nature and his problems, his values and his destiny. For man does not quite succeed in becoming a scientific object to himself. His need of transcending chaotic experience and conflicting facts leads him to seek a metaphysical hypothesis that may clarify his urgent problems. On the subject of his "self" man will, most obstinately, speculate—even today.

When we turn to the ancient Near East in search of similar efforts, two correlated facts become apparent. In the first place, we find that speculation found unlimited possibilities for development; it was not restricted by a scientific (that is, a disciplined) search for truth. In the second place, we notice that the realm of nature and the realm of man were not distinguished.

The ancients, like the modern savages, saw man always as part of society, and society as imbedded in nature and dependent upon cosmic forces. For them nature and man did not stand in opposition and did not, therefore, have to be apprehended by different modes of cognition. We shall see, in fact, in the course of this book, that natural phenomena were regularly conceived in terms of human experience and that human experience was conceived in terms of cosmic events. We touch here upon a distinction between the ancients and us which is of the utmost significance for our inquiry.

The fundamental difference between the attitudes of modern and ancient man as regards the surrounding world is this: for modern, scientific man the phenomenal world is primarily an "It"; for ancient—and also for primitive—man it is a "Thou."

This formulation goes far beyond the usual "animistic" or "personalistic" interpretations. It shows up, in fact, the inadequacies of these commonly accepted theories. For a relation between "I" and "Thou" is absolutely *sui generis*. We can best explain its unique quality by comparing it with two other modes of cognition: the relation between subject and object and the relation that exists when I "understand" another living being.

The correlation "subject-object" is, of course, the basis of all scientific thinking; it alone makes scientific knowledge possible. The second mode of cognition is the curiously direct knowledge which we gain when we "understand" a creature confronting us— its fear, let us say, or its anger. This, by the way, is a form of knowledge which we have the honor of sharing with the animals.

The differences between an I-and-Thou relationship and these two other relationships are as follows: In determining the identity of an object, a person is active. In "understanding" a fellow-creature, on the other hand, a man or an animal is essentially passive, whatever his subsequent action may turn out to be. For at first he receives an impression. This type of knowledge is therefore direct, emotional, and inarticulate. Intellectual knowledge, on the contrary, is emotionally indifferent and articulate.

Now the knowledge which "I" has of "Thou" hovers between the active judgment and the passive "undergoing of an impression"; between the intellectual and the emotional, the articulate and the inarticulate. "Thou" may be problematic, yet "Thou" is somewhat transparent. "Thou" is a live presence, whose qualities and potentialities can be made somewhat articulate—not as a result of active inquiry but because "Thou," as a presence, reveals itself.

There is yet another important difference. An object, an "It," can always be scientifically related to other objects and appear as part of a group or a series. In this manner science insists on seeing "It"; hence, science is able to comprehend objects and events as ruled by universal laws which make their behavior under given circumstances predictable. "Thou," on the other hand, is unique. "Thou" has the unprecedented, unparalleled, and unpredictable character of an individual, a presence known only in so far as it reveals itself. "Thou," moreover, is not merely contemplated or understood but is experienced emotionally in a dynamic reciprocal relationship. For these reasons there is justification for the aphorism of Crawley: "Primitive man has only one mode of thought, one mode of expression, one part of speech—the personal." This does not mean (as is so often thought) that primitive man, in order to explain natural phenomena, imparts human characteristics to an inanimate world. Primitive man simply does not know an inanimate world. For this very reason he does not "personify" inanimate phenomena nor does he fill an empty world with the ghosts of the dead, as "animism" would have us believe.

The world appears to primitive man neither inanimate nor empty but redundant with life; and life has individuality, in man and beast and plant, and in every phenomenon which confronts man—the thunderclap, the sudden shadow, the eerie and unknown clearing in the wood, the stone which suddenly hurts him when he stumbles while on a hunting trip. Any phenomenon may at any time face him, not as "It," but as "Thou." In this confrontation, "Thou" reveals its individuality, its qualities, its will. "Thou" is not contemplated with intellectual detachment; it is experienced as life confronting life, involving every faculty of man in a reciprocal relationship. Thoughts, no less than acts and feelings, are subordinated to this experience.

We are here concerned particularly with thought. It is likely that the ancients recognized certain intellectual problems and asked for the "why" and "how," the "where from" and "where to." Even so, we cannot expect in the ancient Near Eastern documents to find speculation in the predominantly intellectual form with which we are familiar and which presupposes strictly logical procedure even while attempting to transcend it. We have seen that in the ancient Near East, as in present-day primitive society, thought does not operate autonomously. The whole man confronts a living "Thou" in nature; and the whole man—emotional and imaginative as well as intellectual—gives expression to the experience. All experience of "Thou" is highly individual; and early man does, in fact, view happenings as individual events. An account of such events and also their explanation can be conceived only as action and necessarily take the form of a story. In other words, the ancients told myths instead of presenting an analysis or conclusions. We would explain, for instance, that certain atmospheric changes broke a drought and brought about rain. The Babylonians observed the same facts but experienced them as the intervention of the gigantic bird Imdugud which came to their rescue. It covered the sky with the black storm clouds of its wings and devoured the Bull of Heaven, whose hot breath had scorched the crops.

In telling such a myth, the ancients did not intend to provide entertainment. Neither did they seek, in a detached way and without ulterior motives, for intelligible explanations of the natural phenomena. They were recounting events in which they were involved to the extent of their very existence. They experienced, directly, a conflict of powers, one hostile to the harvest upon which they depended, the other frightening but beneficial: the thunderstorm reprieved them in the nick of time by defeating and utterly destroying the drought. The images had already become traditional at the time when we meet them in art and literature, but originally they must have been seen in the revelation which the experience entailed. They are products of imagination, but they are not mere fantasy. It is essential that true myth be distinguished from legend, saga, fable, and fairy tale. All these may retain elements of the myth. And it may also happen that a baroque or frivolous imagination elaborates myths until they become mere stories. But true myth presents its images and its imaginary actors, not with the playfulness of fantasy, but with a compelling authority. It perpetuates the revelation of a "Thou."

The imagery of myth is therefore by no means allegory. It is nothing less than a carefully chosen cloak for abstract thought. The imagery is inseparable from the thought. It represents the form in which the experience has become conscious.

Myth, then, is to be taken seriously, because it reveals a significant, if unverifiable, truth—we might say a metaphysical truth. But myth has not the universality and the lucidity of theoretical statement. It is concrete, though it claims to be inassailable in its validity. It claims recognition by the faithful; it does not pretend to justification before the critical.

The irrational aspect of myth becomes especially clear when we remember that the ancients were not content merely to recount their myths as stories conveying information. They dramatized them, acknowledging in them a special virtue which could be activated by recital.

Of the dramatization of myth, Holy Communion is a well-known example. Another example is found in Babylonia. During each New Year's festival the Babylonians re-enacted the victory which Marduk had won over the powers of chaos on the first New

Year's Day, when the world was created. At the annual festival the Epic of Creation was recited. It is clear that the Babylonians did not regard their story of creation as we might accept the theory of Laplace, for instance, as an intellectually satisfying account of how the world came to be as it is. Ancient man had not thought out an answer; an answer had been revealed to him in a reciprocal relationship with nature. If a question had been answered, man shared that answer with the "Thou" which had revealed itself. Hence, it seemed wise that man, each year, at the critical turn of the seasons, should proclaim the knowledge which he shared with the powers, in order to involve them once more in its potent truth.

We may, then, summarize the complex character of myth in the following words: Myth is a form of poetry which transcends poetry in that it proclaims a truth; a form of reasoning which transcends reasoning in that it wants to bring about the truth it proclaims; a form of action, of ritual behavior, which does not find its fulfilment in the act but must proclaim and elaborate a poetic form of truth.

It will now be clear why we said at the beginning of this chapter that our search for speculative thought in the ancient Near East might lead to negative results. The detachment of intellectual inquiry is wanting throughout. And yet, within the framework of mythopoeic thought, speculation may set in. Even early man, entangled in the immediacy of his perceptions, recognized the existence of certain problems which transcend the phenomena. He recognized the problem of origin and the problem of *telos*, of the aim and purpose of being. He recognized the invisible order of justice maintained by his customs, mores, institutions; and he connected this invisible order with the visible order, with its succession of days and nights, seasons and years, obviously maintained by the sun. Early man even pondered the hierarchy of the different powers which he recognized in nature. In the Memphite Theology, which will be discussed in chapter ii, the Egyptians, at one point, reduced the multiplicity of the divine to a truly monotheistic conception and spiritualized the concept of creation. Nevertheless, they spoke the language of myth. The teachings of such documents can be termed "speculative" in recognition of their intention, if not of their performance.

To give an example, let us anticipate our colleagues and consider various possible answers to the question of how the world came into being. Some modern primitives, the Shilluk, in many respects related to the ancient Egyptians, give the following answer to this question: "In the beginning was Ju-ok the Great Creator, and he created a great white cow who came up out of the Nile and was called Deung Adok. The white cow gave birth to a man-child whom she nursed and named Kola."[1] Of such a story (and there are many of this type) we can say that apparently any form which relates the coming into being as a concretely imagined event satisfies the inquirer. There is no shadow of speculative thought here. Instead there is immediacy of vision—concrete, unquestioned, inconsequential.

We move one step farther if the creation is imagined, not in a purely fantastic manner, but by analogy with human conditions. Creation is then conceived as birth; and the simplest form is the postulate of a primeval couple as the parents of all that exists. It seems that for the Egyptians, as for the Greeks and the Maoris, Earth and Sky were the primeval pair.

The next step, this time one which leads in the direction of speculative thought, is taken when creation is conceived as the action of one of the parents. It may be conceived of as birth by a Great Mother, either a goddess, as in Greece, or a demon, as in Babylonia. Alternatively it is possible to conceive creation as the act of a male. In Egypt, for instance, the god Atum arose unaided from the primeval waters and started the creation of cosmos out of chaos by begetting on himself the first pair of gods.

In all these creation stories we remain in the realm of myth, even though an element of speculation can be discerned. But we move into the sphere of speculative thought—albeit mythopoeic speculative thought—when it is said that Atum was the Creator; that his eldest children were Shū and Tefnūt, Air and Moisture; that their children were Geb and Nūt, Earth and Sky; and their children, again, the four gods of the Osiris cycle through whom (since Osiris was the dead king as well as god) society is related to the cosmic powers. In this story of creation we find a definite cosmological system as the outcome of speculation.

Nor does this remain an isolated instance in Egypt. Even chaos itself became a subject of speculation. It was said that the primeval waters were inhabited by eight weird creatures, four frogs and four snakes, male and female, who brought forth Atum the sun-god and creator. This group of eight, this Ogdoad, was part, not of the created order, but of chaos itself, as the names show. The first pair was Nūn and Naunet, primeval, formless Ocean and primeval Matter; the second pair was Hūh and Hauhet, the Illimitable and the Boundless. Then came Kūk and Kauket, Darkness and Obscurity; and, finally, Amon and Amaunet, the Hidden and Concealed ones—probably the wind. For the wind "bloweth where it listeth and thou hearest the sound thereof but canst not tell whence it cometh and whither it goeth" (John 3 : 8). Here, surely, is speculative thought in mythological guise.

We also find speculative thought in Babylonia, where chaos is conceived, not as a friendly and co-operative Ogdoad which brings forth the creator, Sun, but as the enemy of life and order. After Ti'amat, the Great Mother, had given birth to countless beings, including the gods, the latter, under the guidance of Marduk, fought a critical battle in which she was overcome and destroyed. And out of her the existing universe was constructed. The Babylonian placed that conflict at the basis of existence.

Throughout the ancient Near East, then, we find speculative thought in the form of myth. We have seen how the attitude of early man toward the phenomena explains his mythopoeic form of thought. But, in order to understand its peculiarities more fully, we should consider the form it takes in somewhat greater detail.

THE LOGIC OF MYTHOPOEIC THOUGHT

We have hitherto been at pains to show that for primitive man thoughts are not autonomous, that they remain involved in the curious attitude toward the phenomenal world which we have called a confrontation of life with life. Indeed, we shall find that our categories of intellectual judgment often do not apply to the complexes of cerebration and volition which constitute mythopoeic thought.

And yet the word "logic" as used above is justified. The ancients expressed their "emotional thought" (as we might call it) in terms of cause and effect; they explained phenomena in terms of time and space and number. The form of their reasoning is far less alien to ours than is often believed. They could reason logically; but they did not often care to do it. For the detachment which a purely intellectual attitude implies is hardly compatible with their most significant experience of reality. Scholars who have proved at length that primitive man has a "prelogical" mode of thinking are likely to refer to magic or religious practice, thus forgetting that they apply the Kantian categories, not to pure reasoning, but to highly emotional acts.

We shall find that if we attempt to define the structure of mythopoeic thought and compare it with that of modern (that is, scientific) thought, the differences will prove to be due rather to emotional attitude and intention than to a so-called prelogical mentality. The basic distinction of modern thought is that between *subjective* and *objective*. On this distinction scientific thought has based a critical and analytical procedure by which it progressively reduces the individual phenomena to typical events subject to universal laws. Thus it creates an increasingly wide gulf between our perception of the phenomena and the conceptions by which we make them comprehensible. We see the sun rise and set, but we think of the earth as moving round the sun. We see colors, but we describe them as wave-lengths. We dream of a dead relative, but we think of that distinct vision as a product of our own subconscious minds. Even if we individually are unable to prove these almost unbelievable scientific views to be true, we accept them, because we know that they can be proved to possess a greater degree of objectivity than our sense-impressions. In the immediacy of primitive experience, however, there is no room for such a critical resolution of perceptions. Primitive man cannot withdraw from the presence of the phenomena because they reveal themselves to him in the manner we have described. Hence the distinction between subjective and objective knowledge is meaningless to him.

Meaningless, also, is our contrast between reality and appearance. Whatever is capable of affecting mind, feeling, or will has thereby established its undoubted reality. There is, for instance, no reason why dreams should be considered less real than impressions received while one is awake. On the contrary, dreams often affect one so much more than the humdrum events of daily life that they appear to be more, and not less, significant than the usual perceptions. The Babylonians, like the Greeks, sought divine guidance by passing the night in a sacred place hoping for a revelation in dreams. And pharaohs, too, have recorded that dreams induced them to undertake certain works. Hallucinations, too, are real. We find in the official annals of Assarhaddon of Assyria[2] a record of fabulous monsters—two-headed serpents and green, winged creatures—which the exhausted troops had seen in the most trying section of their march, the arid Sinai Desert. We may recall that the Greeks saw the Spirit of the Plain of Marathon arisen in the fateful battle against the Persians. As to monsters, the Egyptians of the Middle Kingdom, as much horrified by the desert as are their modern descendants, depicted dragons, griffins, and chimeras among gazelles, foxes, and other desert game, on a footing of perfect equality.

Just as there was no sharp distinction among dreams, hallucinations, and ordinary vision, there was no sharp separation between the living and the dead. The survival of the dead and their continued relationship with man were assumed as a matter of course, for the dead were involved in the indubitable reality of man's own anguish, expectation, or resentment. "To be effective" to the mythopoeic mind means the same as "to be."

Symbols are treated in the same way. The primitive uses symbols as much as we do; but he can no more conceive them as signifying, yet separate from, the gods or powers than he can consider a relationship established in his mind—such as resemblance—as connecting, and yet separate from, the objects compared. Hence there is coalescence of the symbol and what it signifies, as there is coalescence of two objects compared so that one may stand for the other.

In a similar manner we can explain the curious figure of thought *pars pro toto*, "a part can stand for the whole"; a name, a lock of hair, or a shadow can stand for the man because at any moment the lock of hair or shadow may be felt by the primitive to be pregnant with the full significance of the man. It may confront him with a "Thou" which bears the physiognomy of its owner.

An example of the coalescence of a symbol and the thing it stands for is the treating of a person's name as an essential part of him— as if it were, in a way, identical with him. We have a number of pottery bowls which Egyptian kings of the Middle Kingdom had inscribed with the names of hostile tribes in Palestine, Libya, and Nubia; the names of their rulers; and the names of certain rebellious Egyptians. These bowls were solemnly smashed at a ritual, possibly at the funeral of the king's predecessor; and the object of this ritual was explicitly stated. It was that all these enemies, obviously out of the pharaoh's reach, should die. But if we call the ritual act of the breaking of the bowls symbolical, we miss the point. The Egyptians felt that *real* harm was done to the enemies by the destruction of their names. The occasion was even used to cast a propitious spell of wider scope. After the names of the hostile men, who were enumerated "that they should die," were added such phrases as: "all detrimental thought, all detrimental talk, all detrimental dreams, all detrimental plans, all detrimental strife," etc. Mentioning these things on the bowls to be smashed diminished their actual power to hurt the king or lessen his authority.

For us there is an essential difference between an act and a ritual or symbolical performance. But this distinction was meaningless to the ancients. Gudea, a Mesopotamian ruler, describing the founding of a temple, mentions in one breath that he molded a brick in clay, purified the site with fire, and consecrated the platform with oil. When the Egyptians claim that Osiris, and the Babylonians that Oannes, gave them the elements of their culture, they include among those elements the crafts and agriculture as well as ritual usages. These two groups of activities possess the same degree of reality. It would be meaningless to ask a Babylonian whether the success of the harvest depended on the skill of the farmers or on the correct performance of the New Year's festival. Both were essential to success.

Just as the imaginary is acknowledged as existing in reality, so concepts are likely to be substantialized. A man who has courage or eloquence possesses these qualities almost as substances of which he can be robbed or which he can share with others. The concept of "justice" or "equity" is in Egypt called *ma͑at*. The king's mouth is the temple of *ma͑at*. *Ma͑at* is personified as a goddess; but at the same time it is said that the gods "live by *ma͑at*." This concept is represented quite concretely: in the daily ritual the gods are offered a figure of the goddess, together with the other material offerings, food and drink, for their sustenance. Here we meet the paradox of mythopoeic thought. Though it does not know dead matter and confronts a world animated from end to end, it is unable to leave the scope of the concrete and renders its own concepts as realities existing per se.

An excellent example of this tendency toward concreteness is the primitive conception of death. Death is not, as for us, an event —the act or fact of dying, as Webster has it. It is somehow a substantial reality. Thus we read in the Egyptian Pyramid Texts a description of the beginning of things which runs as follows:

> When heaven had not yet come into existence,
> When men had not yet come into existence,
> When gods had not yet been born,
> When death had not yet come into existence. . . . .[3]

In exactly the same terms the cupbearer Siduri pities Gilgamesh in the Epic:

> Gilgamesh, whither are you wandering?
> Life, which you look for, you will never find.
> For when the gods created men, they let
> death be his share, and life
> withheld in their own hands.

Note, in the first place, that life is opposed to death, thus accentuating the fact that life in itself is considered endless. Only the intervention of another phenomenon, death, makes an end to it. In the second place, we should note the concrete character attributed to life in the statement that the gods withheld life in their hands. In case one is inclined to see in this phrase a figure of speech, it is well to remember that Gilgamesh and, in another myth, Adapa are given a chance to gain eternal life simply by eating life as a substance. Gilgamesh is shown the "plant of life," but a ser-

pent robs him of it. Adapa is offered bread and water of life when
he enters heaven, but he refuses it on the instruction of the wily
god Enki. In both cases the assimilation of a concrete substance
would have made the difference between death and immortality.

We are touching here on the category of *causality*, which is as
important for modern thought as the distinction between the subjective and the objective. If science, as we have said before, reduces the chaos of perceptions to an order in which typical events
take place according to universal laws, the instrument of this conversion from chaos to order is the postulate of causality. Primitive
thought naturally recognized the relationship of cause and effect,
but it cannot recognize our view of an impersonal, mechanical, and
lawlike functioning of causality. For we have moved far from the
world of immediate experience in our search for true causes, that
is, causes which will always produce the same effect under the
same conditions. We must remember that Newton discovered the
concept of gravitation and also its laws by taking into account three
groups of phenomena which are entirely unrelated to the merely
perceptive observer: freely falling objects, the movements of the
planets, and the alternation of the tides. Now the primitive mind
cannot withdraw to that extent from perceptual reality. Moreover,
it would not be satisfied by our ideas. It looks, not for the "how,"
but for the "who," when it looks for a cause. Since the phenomenal
world is a "Thou" confronting early man, he does not expect to
find an impersonal law regulating a process. He looks for a pur-
poseful will committing an act. If the rivers refuse to rise, it is not
suggested that the lack of rainfall on distant mountains adequately
explains the calamity. When the river does not rise, it has *refused*
to rise. The river, or the gods, must be angry with the people who
depend on the inundation. At best the river or the gods intend to
convey something to the people. Some action, then, is called for.
We know that, when the Tigris did not rise, Gudea the king went
to sleep in the temple in order to be instructed in a dream as to the
meaning of the drought. In Egypt, where annual records of the
heights of the Nile flood were kept from the earliest historical
times, the pharaoh nevertheless made gifts to the Nile every year
about the time when it was due to rise. To these sacrifices, which

were thrown into the river, a document was added. It stated, in the form of either an order or a contract, the Nile's obligations.

Our view of causality, then, would not satisfy primitive man because of the impersonal character of its explanations. It would not satisfy him, moreover, because of its generality. We understand phenomena, not by what makes them peculiar, but by what makes them manifestations of general laws. But a general law cannot do justice to the individual character of each event. And the individual character of the event is precisely what early man experiences most strongly. We may explain that certain physiological processes cause a man's death. Primitive man asks: Why should *this* man die *thus* at *this* moment? We can only say that, given these conditions, death will always occur. He wants to find a cause as specific and individual as the event which it must explain. The event is not analyzed intellectually; it is experienced in its complexity and individuality, and these are matched by equally individual causes. Death is *willed*. The question, then, turns once more from the "why" to the "who," not to the "how."

This explanation of death as willed differs from that given a moment ago, when it was viewed as almost substantialized and especially created. We meet here for the first time in these chapters a curious multiplicity of approaches to problems which is characteristic for the mythopoeic mind. In the Gilgamesh Epic death was specific and concrete; it was allotted to mankind. Its antidote, eternal life, was equally substantial: it could be assimilated by means of the plant of life. Now we have found the view that death is caused by volition. The two interpretations are not mutually exclusive, but they are nevertheless not so consistent with each other as we would desire. Primitive man, however, would not consider our objections valid. Since he does not isolate an event from its attending circumstances, he does not look for one single explanation which must hold good under all conditions. Death, considered with some detachment as a state of being, is viewed as a substance inherent in all who are dead or about to die. But death considered emotionally is the act of hostile will.

The same dualism occurs in the interpretation of illness or sin. When the scapegoat is driven into the desert, laden with the sins of the community, it is evident that these sins are conceived as having substance. Early medical texts explain a fever as due to "hot" matter's having entered a man's body. Mythopoeic thought substantializes a quality and posits some of its occurrences as causes, others as effects. But the heat that caused the fever may also have been "willed" upon the man by hostile magic or may have entered his body as an evil spirit.

Evil spirits are often no more than the evil itself conceived as substantial and equipped with will-power. In a vague way they may be specified a little further as "spirits of the dead," but often this explanation appears as a gratuitous elaboration of the original view, which is no more than the incipient personification of the evil. This process of personification may, of course, be carried much further when the evil in question becomes a focus of attention and stimulates the imagination. Then we get demons with pronounced individuality like Lamashtu in Babylonia. The gods also come into being in this manner.

We may even go further and say that the gods as personifications of power among other things fulfil early man's need for causes to explain the phenomenal world. Sometimes this aspect of their origin can still be recognized in the complex deities of later times. There is, for instance, excellent evidence that the great goddess Isis was, originally, the deified throne. We know that among modern Africans closely related to the ancient Egyptians the enthroning of the new ruler is the central act of the ritual of the succession. The throne is a fetish charged with the mysterious power of kingship. The prince who takes his seat upon it arises a king. Hence the throne is called the "mother" of the king. Here personification found a starting-point; a channel for emotions was prepared which, in its turn, led to an elaboration of myth. In this way Isis "the throne which made the king" became "the Great Mother," devoted to her son Horus, faithful through all suffering to her husband Osiris—a figure with a powerful appeal to men even outside Egypt and, after Egypt's decline, throughout the Roman Empire.

The process of personification, however, only affects man's attitude to a limited extent. Like Isis, the sky-goddess Nūt was considered to be a loving mother-goddess; but the Egyptians of the New Kingdom arranged for their ascent to heaven without reference to her will or acts. They painted a life-sized figure of the goddess inside their coffins; the dead body was laid in her arms; and the dead man's ascent to heaven was assured. For resemblance was a sharing of essentials, and Nūt's image coalesced with its prototype. The dead man in his coffin rested already in heaven.

In every case where we would see no more than associations of thought, the mythopoeic mind finds a causal connection. Every resemblance, every contact in space or time, establishes a connection between two objects or events which makes it possible to see in the one the cause of changes observed in the other. We must remember that mythopoeic thought does not require its explanation to represent a continuous process. It accepts an initial situation and a final situation connected by no more than the conviction that the one came forth from the other. So we find, for instance, that the ancient Egyptians as well as the modern Maori explain the present relation between heaven and earth in the following manner. Heaven was originally lying upon earth; but the two were separated, and the sky was lifted up to its present position. In New Zealand this was done by their son; in Egypt it was done by the god of the air, Shū, who is now between earth and sky. And heaven is depicted as a woman bending over the earth with outstretched arms while the god Shū supports her.

Changes can be explained very simply as two different states, one of which is said to come forth from the other without any insistence on an intelligible process—in other words, as a transformation, a metamorphosis. We find that, time and again, this device is used to account for changes and that no further explanation is then required. One myth explains why the sun, which counted as the first king of Egypt, should now be in the sky. It recounts that the sun-god Rē became tired of humanity, so he seated himself upon the sky-goddess Nūt, who changed herself into a huge cow standing four square over the earth. Since then the sun has been in the sky.

The charming inconsequentiality of this story hardly allows us to take it seriously. But we are altogether inclined to take explanations more seriously than the facts they explain. Not so primitive man. He knew that the sun-god once ruled Egypt; he also knew that the sun was now in the sky. In the first account of the relation between sky and earth he explained how Shū, the air, came to be between sky and earth; in the last account he explained how the sun got to the sky and, moreover, introduced the well-known concept of the sky as a cow. All this gave him the satisfaction of feeling that images and known facts fell into place. That, after all, is what an explanation should achieve (cf. p. 16).

The image of Rē seated on the cow of heaven, besides illustrating a nonspeculative type of causal explanation which satisfies the mythopoeic mind, illustrates a tendency of the ancients which we have discussed before. We have seen that they are likely to present various descriptions of identical phenomena side by side even though they are mutually exclusive. We have seen how Shū lifted the sky-goddess Nūt from the earth. In a second story Nūt rises by herself in the shape of a cow. This image of the sky-goddess is very common, especially when the accent lies on her aspect as mother-goddess. She is the mother of Osiris and, hence, of all the dead; but she is also the mother who gives birth each evening to the stars, each morning to the sun. When ancient Egyptian thought turned to procreation, it expressed itself in images derived from cattle. In the myth of sun and sky the image of the sky-cow does not appear with its original connotation; the image of Nūt as a cow evoked the picture of the huge animal rising and lifting the sun to heaven. When the bearing of the sun by Nūt was the center of attention, the sun was called the "calf of gold" or "the bull." But it was, of course, possible to consider the sky, not predominantly in its relation to heavenly bodies or to the dead who are re-born there, but as a self-contained cosmic phenomenon. In that case Nūt was described as a descendent of the creator Atum through his children, Shū and Tefnūt, Air and Moisture. And she was, furthermore, wedded to the earth. If viewed in this manner, Nūt was imagined in human form.

We see, again, that the ancients' conception of a phenomenon differed according to their approach to it. Modern scholars have reproached the Egyptians for their apparent inconsistencies and have doubted their ability to think clearly. Such an attitude is sheer presumption. Once one recognizes the processes of ancient thought, their justification is apparent. After all, religious values are not reducible to rationalistic formulas. Natural phenomena, whether or not they were personified and became gods, confronted ancient man with a living presence, a significant "Thou," which, again, exceeded the scope of conceptual definition. In such cases our flexible thought and language qualify and modify certain concepts so thoroughly as to make them suitable to carry our burden of expression and significance. The mythopoeic mind, tending toward the concrete, expressed the irrational, not in our manner, but by admitting the validity of several avenues of approach at one and the same time. The Babylonians, for instance, worshiped the generative force in nature in several forms: its manifestation in the beneficial rains and thunderstorms was visualized as a lion-headed bird. Seen in the fertility of the earth, it became a snake. Yet in statues, prayers, and cult acts it was represented as a god in human shape. The Egyptians in the earliest times recognized Horus, a god of heaven, as their main deity. He was imagined as a gigantic falcon hovering over the earth with outstretched wings, the colored clouds of sunset and sunrise being his speckled breast and the sun and moon his eyes. Yet this god could also be viewed as a sun-god, since the sun, the most powerful thing in the sky, was naturally considered a manifestation of the god and thus confronted man with the same divine presence which he adored in the falcon spreading its wings over the earth. We should not doubt that mythopoeic thought fully recognizes the unity of each phenomenon which it conceives under so many different guises; the many-sidedness of its images serves to do justice to the complexity of the phenomena. But the procedure of the mythopoeic mind in expressing a phenomenon by manifold images corresponding to unconnected avenues of approach clearly leads away from, rather than toward, our postulate of causality which seeks to discover identical causes for identical effects throughout the phenomenal world.

We observe a similar contrast when we turn from the category of *causality* to that of *space*. Just as modern thought seeks to establish causes as abstract functional relations between phenomena, so it views space as a mere system of relations and functions. Space is postulated by us to be infinite, continuous, and homogeneous—attributes which mere sensual perception does not reveal. But primitive thought cannot abstract a concept "space" from its experience

of space. And this experience consists in what we would call quali-
fying associations. The spatial concepts of the primitive are concrete orientations; they refer to localities which have an emotional
color; they may be familiar or alien, hostile or friendly. Beyond
the scope of mere individual experience the community is aware
of certain cosmic events which invest regions of space with a particular significance. Day and night give to east and west a correlation with life and death. Speculative thought may easily develop in
connection with such regions as are outside direct experiences, for
instance, the heavens or the nether world. Mesopotamian astrology
evolved a very extensive system of correlations between heavenly
bodies and events in the sky and earthly localities. Thus mythopoeic thought may succeed no less than modern thought in establishing a co-ordinated spatial system; but the system is determined,
not by objective measurements, but by an emotional recognition
of values. The extent to which this procedure determines the primitive view of space can best be illustrated by an example which will
be met again in subsequent chapters as a remarkable instance of
ancient speculation.

In Egypt the creator was said to have emerged from the waters
of chaos and to have made a mound of dry land upon which he
could stand. This primeval hill, from which the creation took its
beginning, was traditionally located in the sun temple at Heliopolis, the sun-god being in Egypt most commonly viewed as the creator. However, the Holy of Holies of each temple was equally sacred; each deity was—by the very fact that he was recognized as
divine—a source of creative power. Hence each Holy of Holies
throughout the land could be identified with the primeval hill.
Thus it is said of the temple of Philae, which was founded in the
fourth century B.C.: "This [temple] came into being when nothing
at all had yet come into being and the earth was still lying in darkness and obscurity." The same claim was made for other temples.
The names of the great shrines at Memphis, Thebes, and Her-
monthis explicitly stated that they were the "divine emerging
primeval island" or used similar expressions. Each sanctuary possessed the essential quality of original holiness; for, when a new
temple was founded, it was assumed that the potential sacredness
of the site became manifest. The equation with the primeval hill

received architectural expression also. One mounted a few steps or followed a ramp at every entrance from court or hall to the Holy of Holies, which was thus situated at a level noticeably higher than the entrance.

But this coalescence of temples with the primeval hill does not give us the full measure of the significance which the sacred locality had assumed for the ancient Egyptians. The royal tombs were also made to coincide with it. The dead, and, above all, the king, were reborn in the hereafter. No place was more propitious, no site promised greater chances for a victorious passage through the crisis of death, than the primeval hill, the center of creative forces where the ordered life of the universe had begun. Hence the royal tomb was given the shape of a pyramid which is the Heliopolitan stylization of the primeval hill.

To us this view is entirely unacceptable. In our continuous, homogeneous space the place of each locality is unambiguously fixed. We would insist that there must have been one single place where the first mound of dry land actually emerged from the chaotic waters. But the Egyptian would have considered such objections mere quibbles. Since the temples and the royal tombs were as sacred as the primeval hill and showed architectural forms which resembled the hill, they shared essentials. And it would be fatuous to argue whether one of these monuments could be called the primeval hill with more justification than the others.

Similarly, the waters of chaos from which all life emerged were considered to be present in several places, sometimes playing their part in the economy of the country, sometimes necessary to round out the Egyptian image of the universe. The waters of chaos were supposed to subsist in the form of the ocean surrounding the earth, which had emerged from them and now floated upon them. Hence these waters were also present in the subsoil water. In the cenotaph of Seti I at Abydos the coffin was placed upon an island with a double stair imitating the hieroglyph for the primeval hill; this island was surrounded by a channel filled always with subsoil water. Thus the dead king was buried and thought to rise again in the locality of creation. But the waters of chaos, the Nūn, were also the waters of the nether world, which the sun and the dead have to cross. On the other hand, the primeval waters had once contained all the potentialities of life; and they were, therefore, also the waters of the annual inundation of the Nile which renews and revives the fertility of the fields.

The mythopoeic conception of *time* is, like that of space, qualitative and concrete, not quantitative and abstract. Mythopoeic thought does not know time as a uniform duration or as a succession of qualitatively indifferent moments. The concept of time as it is used in our mathematics and physics is as unknown to early man as that which forms the framework of our history. Early man does not abstract a concept of time from the experience of time.

It has been pointed out, for example, by Cassirer, that the time experience is both rich and subtle, even for quite primitive people. Time is experienced in the periodicity and rhythm of man's own life as well as in the life of nature. Each phase of man's life—childhood, adolescence, maturity, old age—is a time with peculiar qualities. The transition from one phase to another is a crisis in which man is assisted by the community's uniting in the rituals appropriate to birth, puberty, marriage, or death. Cassirer has called the peculiar view of time as a sequence of essentially different phases of life "biological time." And the manifestation of time in nature, the succession of the seasons, and the movements of the heavenly bodies were conceived quite early as the signs of a life-process similar, and related, to that of man. Even so, they are not viewed as "natural" processes in our sense. When there is change, there is a cause; and a cause, as we have seen, is a will. In Genesis, for instance, we read that God made a covenant with the living creatures, promising not only that the flood would not recur but also that "while the earth remaineth, seedtime and harvest, cold and heat, summer and winter, day and night shall not cease" (Gen. 8 : 22). The order of time and the order of the life of nature (which are one) are freely granted by the God of the Old Testament in the fulness of his power; and when considered in their totality, as an established order, they are elsewhere, too, thought to be founded upon the willed order of creation.

But another approach is also possible, an approach not toward the sequence of phases as a whole but toward the actual transition from one phase to another—the actual succession of phases. The varying length of the night, the ever changing spectacles of sunrise and sunset, and the equinoctial storms do not suggest an automatic smooth alternation between the "elements" of mythopoeic time. They suggest a conflict, and this suggestion is strengthened by the anxiety of man himself, who is wholly dependent upon weather and seasonal changes. Wensinck has called this the "dramatic conception of nature." Each morning the sun defeats darkness and chaos, as he did on the day of creation and does, every year, on New Year's Day. These three moments coalesce; they are felt to be essentially the same. Each sunrise, and each New Year's Day, repeats the first sunrise on the day of creation; and for the mythopoeic mind each repetition coalesces with—is practically identical with—the original event.

We have here, in the category of time, a parallel to the phenomenon which we recognized in the category of space when we learned that certain archetypal localities, like the primeval hill, were thought to exist on several sites throughout the land because these sites shared with their prototype some of its overwhelmingly important aspects. This phenomenon we called coalescence in space. An example of coalescence in time is an Egyptian verse which curses the enemies of the pharaoh. It must be remembered that the sun-god Rē had been the first ruler of Egypt and that the pharaoh was, to the extent that he ruled, an image of Rē. The verse says of the enemies of the king: "They shall be like the snake Apōphis on New Year's morning."[4] The snake Apōphis is the hostile darkness which the sun defeats every night on his journey through the nether world from the place of sunset in the west to the place of sunrise in the east. But why should the enemies be like Apōphis on New Year's morning? Because the notions of creation, daily sunrise, and the beginning of the new annual cycle coalesce and culminate in the festivities of the New Year. Hence the New Year is invoked, that is, conjured up, to intensify the curse.

Now this "dramatic conception of nature which sees everywhere a strife between divine and demoniac, cosmic and chaotic powers" (Wensinck), does not leave man a mere spectator. He is too much involved in, his welfare depends too completely upon, the victory of the beneficial powers for him not to feel the need to participate on their side. Thus we find, in Egypt and Babylonia, that man—that is, man in society—accompanies the principal changes in nature with appropriate rituals. Both in Egypt and in Babylonia the New Year, for instance, was an occasion of elaborate celebrations in which the battles of the gods were mimed or in which mock-battles were fought.

We must remember again that such rituals are not merely symbolical; they are part and parcel of the cosmic events; they are man's share in these events. In Babylonia, from the third millennium down to Hellenistic times, we find a New Year's festival which lasted several days. During the celebration the story of creation was recited and a mock-battle was fought in which the king impersonated the victorious god. In Egypt we know mock-battles in several festivals which are concerned with the defeat of death and rebirth or resurrection: one took place at Abydos, during the annual Great Procession of Osiris; one took place on New Year's Eve, at the erection of the Djed pillar; one was fought, at least in the time of Herodotus, at Papremis in the Delta. In these festivals man participated in the life of nature.

Man also arranged his own life, or at least the life of the society to which he belonged, in such a manner that a harmony with nature, a co-ordination of natural and social forces, gave added impetus to his undertakings and increased his chances for success. The whole "science" of omens aims, of course, at this result. But there are also definite instances which illustrate the need of early man to act in unison with nature. In both Egypt and Babylon a king's coronation was postponed until a new beginning in the cycle of nature provided a propitious starting-point for the new reign. In Egypt the time might be in the early summer, when the Nile began to rise, or in the autumn, when the inundation receded and the fertilized fields were ready to receive the seed. In Babylonia the king began his reign on New Year's Day; and the inauguration of a new temple was celebrated only at that time.

This deliberate co-ordination of cosmic and social events shows most clearly that time to early man did not mean a neutral and abstract frame of reference but rather a succession of recurring phases, each charged with a peculiar value and significance. Again, as in dealing with space, we find that there are certain "regions" of time which are withdrawn from direct experience and greatly stimulate speculative thought. They are the distant past and the future. Either of these may become normative and absolute; each then falls beyond the range of time altogether. The absolute past does not recede, nor do we approach the absolute future gradually. The "Kingdom of God" may at any time break into our present. For the Jews the future is normative. For the Egyptians, on the other hand, the past was normative; and no pharaoh could hope to achieve more than the establishment of the conditions "as they were in the time of Rē, in the beginning."

But here we are touching on material which will be discussed in subsequent chapters. We have attempted to demonstrate how the "logic," the peculiar structure, of mythopoeic thought can be derived from the fact that the intellect does not operate autonomously because it can never do justice to the basic experience of early man, that of confrontation with a significant "Thou." Hence when early man is faced by an intellectual problem within the many-sided complexities of life, emotional and volitional factors are never debarred; and the conclusions reached are not critical judgments but complex images.

Nor can the spheres which these images refer to be neatly kept apart. We have intended in this book to deal successively with speculative thought concerning (1) the nature of the universe; (2) the function of the state; and (3) the values of life. But the reader will have grasped that this, our mild attempt to distinguish the spheres of metaphysics, politics, and ethics, is doomed to remain a convenience without any deep significance. For the life of man and the function of the state are for mythopoeic thought imbedded in nature, and the natural processes are affected by the acts of man no less than man's life depends on his harmonious integration with nature. The experiencing of this unity with the utmost intensity was the greatest good ancient oriental religion could bestow. To conceive this integration in the form of intuitive imagery was the aim of the speculative thought of the ancient Near East.

NOTES

1. Seligmann, in *Fourth Report of the Wellcome Tropical Research Laboratories at the Gordon Memorial College, Khartoum* (London, 1911), Vol. B: *General Science*, p. 219.

2. D. D. Luckenbill, *Ancient Records of Assyria and Babylonia*, Vol. II, par. 558.

3. Sethe, *Die altaegyptischen Pyramidentexte nach den Papierabdrücken und Photographien des Berliner Museums* (Leipzig, 1908), par. 1466.

4. Adolf Erman, *Aegypten und aegyptisches Leben im Altertum*, ed. Hermann Ranke (Tübingen, 1923), p. 170.

SUGGESTED READINGS

CASSIRER, ERNST. *Philosophie der symbolischen Formen II: Das mythische Denken.* Berlin, 1925.

FRANKFORT, HENRI. *Kingship and the Gods: A Study of Ancient Near Eastern Religion as the Integration of Society and Nature.* Chicago, 1948.

LEEUW, G. VAN DER. *Religion in Essence and Manifestation: A Study in Phenomenology.* New York, 1938.

LÉVY-BRUHL, L. *How Natives Think.* New York, 1926.

OTTO, RUDOLF. *The Idea of the Holy: An Inquiry into the Non-rational Factor in the Idea of the Divine and Its Relation to the Rational.* London, 1943.

RADIN, PAUL. *Primitive Man as Philosopher.* New York, 1927.

EGYPT

JOHN A. WILSON

CHAPTER II

EGYPT: THE NATURE OF THE UNIVERSE

GEOGRAPHIC CONSIDERATIONS

THE separation of these chapters into the fields of Egypt, Mesopotamia, and the Hebrews is a necessary separation, because the three cultures exhibited their general uniformity in individual terms and with distinctly different developments. As the case was presented in the introductory chapter, the common attitude of mind toward the phenomena of the universe was governing for each of the three separate treatments. It is no thesis in our material that the Egyptian phenomena were unique, even though our exclusive preoccupation with Egypt may seem to ignore the many elements common to Egypt and her neighbors. The common ground is the important consideration for those who wish to know something about the developing human mind rather than the mind of the Egyptian alone. We consider, then, that our documentary material illustrates the early and preclassical mind with examples from one of the three cultures.

Within that uniformity of viewpoint the cultures were different, as British culture differs from that of continental Europe or from that of the United States. Geography is not the sole determinant in matters of cultural differentiation, but geographic features are subject to description which is practically incontrovertible, so that a consideration of the geographic uniqueness of Egypt will suggest easily some of the factors of differentiation. Throughout the Near East there is a contrast between the desert and the sown land; Egypt had and still has a concentration of that contrast.

The essential part of Egypt is a green gash of teeming life cutting across brown desert wastes. The line of demarcation between life and nonlife is startlingly clear: one may stand at the edge of the cultivation with one foot on the irrigated black soil and one foot on the desert sands. The country is essentially rainless; only

31

the waters of the Nile make life possible where otherwise there would be endless wastes of sand and rock.

But what a life the Nile makes possible! The little agricultural villages contract themselves within smallest compass, in order not to encroach upon the fertile fields of rice, cotton, wheat, or sugar cane. When properly cared for, the land can yield two crops a year. Normally Egypt has a very comfortable surplus of agricultural produce for export.

This richness is confined to the green Nile Valley. Only 3.5 per cent of the modern state of Egypt is cultivable and habitable. The remaining 96.5 per cent is barren and uninhabitable desert. Today perhaps 99.5 per cent of the population lives on the 3.5 per cent of the land which will support population. That means an even greater contrast between the desert and the sown, and it means that on the cultivable land there is a concentration of people close to the saturation point. Today *habitable* Egypt has over 1,200 persons to the square mile. The figures for Belgium, the most densely populated country of Europe, are about 700 to the square mile; for Java, about 900 to the square mile. The density of population in modern Egypt is therefore so great that the concentration approaches that of an industrial and urban country rather than that of an agricultural and rustic country. Yet Egypt, with her fertile soil, is always essentially agricultural.

No figures are available for ancient Egypt, of course, and the population could not have been as great as today; but the main features were surely the same as at the present: a hermetically sealed tube containing a concentration of life close to the saturation point. The two features of isolation and semiurban population combine to make Egypt different from her neighbors. At the present day the Arabs of Palestine and of Iraq concede the general cultural leadership of Egypt, as being the most sophisticated of the Arab countries; and yet they do not feel that the Egyptians are truly Arabs. The Egyptians are not subject to the great conservative control of the Arabian Desert. The deserts adjacent to Palestine and Iraq are potential breeding-grounds for fierce and puritanical elements in the populations of those countries. Egypt, with her agricultural wealth and with her people lying cheek by jowl, developed an early sophistication, which expressed itself intellectually in tendencies toward catholicity and syncretism. Within Egypt the most divergent concepts were tolerantly accepted and woven together into what we moderns might regard as a clashing philosophical lack of system, but which to the ancient was inclusive. The way of the Semite, who held a contact with the desert, was to cling fiercely to tradition and to resist innovations, which changed the purity and simplicity of life. The way of the Egyptian was to accept innovations and to incorporate them into his thought, without discarding the old and outmoded. This means that it is impossible to find in ancient Egypt a system in our sense, orderly and consistent. Old and new lie blandly together like some surrealist picture of youth and age on a single face.

However, if the ancient Egyptian was tolerant of divergent concepts, it does not necessarily follow that he was tolerant of other peoples. He was semiurban and sophisticated of mind and felt foreigners to be rustic and uninitiated. He was cut off from his neighbors by sea and desert and felt that he could afford a superior isolationism. He made a distinction between "men," on the one hand, and Libyans or Asiatics or Africans, on the other.[1] The word "men" in that sense meant Egyptians: otherwise it meant "humans" in distinction to the gods, or "humans" in distinction to animals. In other words, the Egyptians were "people"; foreigners were not. At a time of national distress, when the stable old order had broken down and social conditions were upside-down, there was a complaint that "strangers from outside have come into Egypt. . . . . Foreigners have become people everywhere."[2] The concept that only our group is "folks," that outsiders lack something of humanity, is not confined to the modern world.

However, the Egyptian isolationist or nationalist feeling was a matter of geography and of manners rather than of racial theory and dogmatic xenophobia. "The people" were those who lived in Egypt, without distinction of race or color. Once a foreigner came to reside in Egypt, learned to speak Egyptian, and adopted Egyptian dress, he might finally be accepted as one of "the people" and was no longer the object of superior ridicule. Asiatics or Libyans or Negroes might be accepted Egyptians of high position when they had become acclimatized—might, indeed, rise to the highest position of all, that of the god-king who possessed the nation. The same Egyptian word means the "land" of Egypt and the "earth." It is correct to say that, when any element was within this land, it merited full and tolerant acceptance.

The ancient Egyptian's sense that his land was the one land that really mattered was fostered by a knowledge that those other countries with which he had immediate contact were not so fully developed in culture as his own. Babylonia and the Hittite region were too distant for proper comparison, but the near-by lands of the Libyans, the Nubians, and the Asiatic Bedouins were clearly inferior in cultural development. Palestine and Syria were sometimes colonized by Egypt, or were sometimes under Egyptian cultural and commercial leadership. Until the Assyrians and Persians and Greeks finally came in conquering domination, it was possible for the Egyptian to feel a comforting sense that his civilization was superior to all others. An Egyptian story puts into the mouth of a Syrian prince this sweeping statement to an envoy who had come to him from the land of the Nile: "For (the imperial god) Amon founded all lands. He founded them, but first he founded the land of Egypt, from which thou hast come. For skilled work came forth from it to reach this place where I am, and teaching came from it to reach this place where I am."[3] Because the source is Egyptian, we cannot be sure that a prince of Syria actually did say such words, acknowledging Egyptian leadership in learning and craftsmanship, but this story from Egypt carries the assurance that it was a comforting doctrine to those who believed themselves to live at the center of the world.

Thus it may be claimed that the physical isolation of Egypt from other lands produced a self-centered feeling of separateness, within which Egypt had an intellectual development of diverse elements in admixture. It is our part to try to resolve some of these seeming incongruities into a semblance of order which the reader will be able to grasp. To be sure, it is unjust to leave an impression that there was anarchical chaos; no people could maintain a way of life for two thousand visible years without established foundations. We shall find foundation stones and a sensible structure rising from those stones; but it is sometimes puzzling to a visitor to find a front door on each of four sides of a building.

Let us return again to the geography of Egypt. We have the picture of the green gash of life cutting through the brown stretches of nonlife. Let us examine the mechanics of the Egyptian scene. The Nile cuts north out of Africa, surmounts five rocky cataracts, and finally empties into the Mediterranean. These cataracts form the barriers of Egypt against the Hamitic and Negro peoples to the south just as effectively as the deserts and the sea bar Libyan and Semitic peoples to the north, east, and west. In the morning the sun rises in the east, it crosses the sky by day, and it sets in the west in the evening. Of course, you know that; but it is important enough in Egypt to deserve repeated mention, because the daily birth, journey, and death of the sun were dominating features of Egyptian life and thought. In a country essentially rainless, the daily circuit of the sun is of blazing importance. We might think that there was too much sun in Egypt, that shade was a welcome necessity; but the Egyptian hated the darkness and the cold and stretched himself happily to greet the rising sun. He saw that the sun was the source of his life. At night "the earth is in darkness, as if it were dead."[4] So the personification of the sun's power, the sun-god, was the supreme god and the creator-god.

It is curious that the Egyptians gave relatively little credit to another force—the wind. The prevailing wind in Egypt comes from the north, across the Mediterranean and then down the trough of the Nile Valley. It mitigates the unceasing heat of the sun and makes Egypt an easier place in which to live; it contrasts with those hot dry winds of late spring, which bring sandstorms and a brittle heat out of Africa to the south. This north wind was good, and the Egyptians expressed their appreciation and made it into a minor divinity; but, relative to the all-pervading power of the sun, the wind was practically ignored.

It is somewhat different in the case of the Nile. The river was so obvious a source of life that it had its appreciated place in the scheme of things, even though it also could not compete with the sun for position. The Nile had a cycle of birth and death on an annual basis, which corresponded to the daily birth and death of the sun. In the summer the river lies quiet and slow between its shrunken banks, while the fields beside it parch and turn to dust and blow away toward the desert. Unless water can be raised by a series of lifts from the river or from very deep wells, agricultural growth comes to a standstill, and people and cattle grow thin and torpidly look upon the face of famine.

Then, just as life is at its lowest ebb, the Nile River stirs sluggishly and shows a pulse of power. Through the summer it swells slowly but with increasing momentum until it begins to race with mighty waters, burst its banks, and rush over the miles of flat land lying on each side. Great stretches of moving, muddy water cover the land. In a year of a high Nile they encroach upon the little village islands standing up out of the fields, nibble at the mud-brick houses, and bring some of them tumbling down. From inert, dusty wastes, the land has turned to a great shallow stream, which carries a refertilizing load of silt. Then the peak of the flood passes, and the waters become more sluggish. Out of the flooded stretches there appear little peaks of soil, refreshed with new, fertile mud. The torpor of men disappears; they wade out into the thick mud and begin eagerly sowing their first crop of clover or grain. Life has come again to Egypt. Soon a broad green carpet of growing fields will complete the annual miracle of the conquest of life over death.

These, then, were the two central features of the Egyptian scene: the triumphant daily rebirth of the sun and the triumphant annual rebirth of the river. Out of these miracles the Egyptians drew their assurance that Egypt was the center of the universe and their assurance that renewed life may always be victorious over death.

It is necessary to make some qualification to a picture which has been presented in terms of a free gift of life and fertility. Egypt was rich but not prodigal: the fruit did not drop from the trees for indolent farmers. The sun and the Nile did combine to bring forth renewed life, but only at the cost of a battle against death. The sun warmed, but in the summer it also blasted. The Nile brought fertilizing water and soil, but its annual inundation was antic and unpredictable. An exceptionally high Nile destroyed canals, dams, and the homes of men. An exceptionally low Nile brought famine. The inundation came quickly and moved on quickly; constant, back-breaking work was necessary to catch, hold, and dole out the waters for the widest and longest use. The desert was always ready to nibble away at the cultivation and turn fertile silt into arid sand. The desert in particular was a terrible place of venomous serpents, lions, and fabulous monsters. In the broad muddy stretches of the Delta, jungle-like swamps had to be drained and cleared to make arable fields. For more than a third of every year the hot desert winds, the blasting sun, and the low Nile brought the land within sight of death, until the weather turned and the river brought abundant waters again. Thus Egypt was rich and blessed in contrast with her immediate neighbors, but within her own territory she experienced struggle, privations, and dangers which made the annual triumph real. There was a sense that the triumph was not an automatic privilege but that it must be earned at some cost.

We have already suggested that the Egyptians were self-centered and had their own satisfied kind of isolationism. We have said that they used the word "humans" to apply to Egyptians in distinction from foreigners. The concept that Egypt was the focal center of the universe set the standard for what was right and normal in the universe in terms of what was normal in Egypt. The central feature of Egypt is the Nile, flowing north and bringing the necessary water for life. They therefore looked at other peoples and other existences in terms of their own scene. The Egyptian word "to go north" is the Egyptian word "to go downstream," and the word "to go south" is the word "to go upstream," against the current. When the Egyptians met another river, the Euphrates, which flowed south instead of north, they had to express the sense of contrast by calling it "that circling water which goes downstream in going upstream," which may also be translated "that inverted water which goes downstream by going south."[5]

Navigation on the Nile employed the power of the current in moving north. In moving south, boats raised the sail in order to take advantage of the prevailing north wind, which would push them against the current. Since this was normal, it became the ideal for any world, including the afterlife. Into their tombs the Egyptians put two model boats, which might be projected by magic into the next world for navigation there. One boat had the sail down, for sailing north with the current on the waters of the other world;

one boat had the sail up for sailing south with that north wind which must be normal in any proper existence, here or hereafter.

So, too, rain could be understood only in terms of the waters which came to Egypt. Addressing the god, the Egyptian worshiper acknowledged his goodness to Egypt: "Thou makest the Nile in the lower world and bringest it whither thou wilt, in order to sustain mankind, even as thou hast made them." Then, in an unusual interest in foreign lands, the worshiper went on: "Thou makest that whereon all distant countries live. Thou hast put (another) Nile in the sky, so that it may come down for them, and may make waves upon the mountains like a sea, in order to moisten their fields in their townships. . . . . The Nile in the sky, thou appointest it for the foreign peoples and (for) all the beasts of the highland which walk upon feet, whereas the (real) Nile, it comes from the lower world for (the people of) Egypt."[6] If we reverse our concept that water normally falls from the skies and accept as appropriate a system in which water comes up from caverns below to be the only proper sustainer of life, then we will refer to rain in our own terms. It is then not the case that Egypt is a rainless country but rather it is the case that other countries have their Nile falling from the skies.

In the quotation just given there is a significant grouping of foreign peoples and the beasts of the highland. I do not mean that it is significant in coupling barbarians with cattle, although that has a minor implication. It is rather that these two had their habitat in regions which were similarly conceived in their contrast to the Nile Valley. Egypt was a flat pancake of fertile black soil ($\Longleftrightarrow$). Every foreign country consisted of corrugated ridges of red sand. The same hieroglyphic sign was used for "foreign country" that was used for "highland" or for "desert" ($\bowtie$); a closely similar sign was used for "mountain" ($\bowtie$), because the mountain ridges which fringed the Nile Valley were also desert and also foreign. Thus the Egyptian pictorially grouped the foreigner with the beast of the desert and pictorially denied to the foreigner the blessings of fertility and uniformity.

Just as people from our own western plains feel shut in if they visit the hills of New England, so the Egyptian had a similar claustrophobia about any country where one could not look far across the plain, where one could not see the sun in all its course. One Egyptian scribe wrote to another: "Thou hast not trodden the road to Meger (in Syria), in which the sky is dark by day, which is overgrown with cypresses, oaks, and cedars that reach the heavens. There are more lions there than panthers or hyenas, and it is surrounded by Bedouin on (every) side. . . . . Shuddering seizes thee, (the hair of) thy head stands on end, and thy soul lies in thy hand. Thy path is filled with boulders and pebbles, and there is no passable track, for it is overgrown with reeds, thorns, brambles, and wolf's pad. The ravine is on one side of thee, while the mountain rises on the other."[7]

A similar sense that a land of mountains, rain, and trees is a dismal place comes out in the words: "The miserable Asiatic, it goes ill with the land where he is, (a land) troubled with water, inaccessible because of the many trees, with its roads bad because of the mountains." Just as this land was wrong in every respect, so the miserable Asiatic was unaccountable: "He does not live in a single place, but his feet wander. He has been fighting since the time of Horus, but he conquers not, nor is he conquered, and he never announces the day in fighting. . . . . He may plunder a lonely settlement, but he will not take a populous city. . . . . Trouble thyself not about him: he is (only) an Asiatic."[8] Our own standard of life is the one which we apply to others, and on the basis of this standard we find them wanting.

There is another topographical feature of the Nile Valley which finds its counterpart in the Egyptian psychology. That is the uniformity of landscape. Down the center of the land cuts the Nile. On each bank the fertile fields stretch away, with the west bank the counterpart of the east. Then comes the desert, climbing up into two mountain fringes lining the valley. Again, the western mountain desert is the counterpart of the eastern. Those who live on the black soil look out through the clear air and see practically the same scene everywhere. If they travel a day's journey to the south or two days' journey to the north, the scene is much the same. Fields are broad and level; trees are rare or small; there is no exceptional break in the vista, except where some temple has been erected by man, or except in the two mountain ranges, which are really the outer limits of Egypt.

In the broad reaches of the Delta the uniformity is even more striking. There the flat stretches of fields move on monotonously without feature. The only land which matters in Egypt has uniformity and it has symmetry.

The interesting result of uniformity is the way in which it accentuates any exceptional bit of relief that happens to break the monotonous regularity. Out in the desert one is conscious of every hillock, of every spoor of an animal, of every desert duststorm, of every bit of movement. The rare irregular is very striking in an environment of universal regularity. It has animation; it has life within the dominating pattern of nonlife. So also in Egypt the prevailing uniformity of landscape threw into high relief anything which took exception to that uniformity. A solitary tree of some size, a peculiarly shaped hill, or a storm-cut valley was so exceptional that it took on individuality. Man who lived close to nature endowed the exceptional feature with animation; it became inspirited to his mind.

The same attitude of mind looked upon the animals which moved through the scene: the falcon floating in the sky with no more apparent motive power than the sun; the jackal flitting ghostlike along the margin of the desert; the crocodile lurking lumplike on the mudflats; or the powerful bull in whom was the seed of procreation. These beasts were forces going beyond the normality of landscape; they were forces which transcended the minimal observed natures of animals. They therefore took on high relief in the scene and were believed to be vested with mysterious or inscrutable force related to an extra-human world.

This may be an oversimplification of ancient man's animistic outlook on nature. Of course, it is true that any agricultural people has a feeling for the force that works in nature and comes to personalize each separate force. And before there were naturalists to explain the mechanism of plants and animals, to reason out the chain of cause and effect in the behavior of other things in our world, man's only yardstick of normality was humanity: what he knew in himself and in his own experience was human and normal; deviations from the normal were extra-human and thus potentially superhuman. Therefore, as was pointed out in the opening chapter, the human came to address the extra-human in terms of human intercourse. The phenomenal world to him was not "It" but "Thou." It was not necessary that the object become finally super-human and be revered as a god before it might be conceived in terms of "Thou." As extra-human, but not of divine nature, it was accorded the "Thou" rather than the "It" by man. The Egyptians might—and did—personify almost anything: the head, the belly, the tongue, perception, taste, truth, a tree, a mountain, the sea, a city, darkness, and death. But few of these were personified with regularity or with awe; that is, few of them reached the stature of gods or demigods. They were forces with which man had the "Thou" relation. And it is a little difficult to think of anything in the phenomenal world with which he might not have that relation as indicated in scenes and texts. The answer is that he might have the "Thou" relation with anything in the phenomenal world.

Another aspect of the uniform landscape of Egypt was its sym-metry: east bank balancing west bank, and eastern mountain range balancing western mountain range. Whether this bilateral sym-metry of landscape was the reason or not, the Egyptian had a strong sense of balance, symmetry, and geometry. This comes out clearly in his art, where the best products show a fidelity of proportion and a careful counterpoising of elements in order to secure a har-monious balance. It comes out in his literature, where the best products show a deliberate and sonorous parallelism of members, which achieve dignity and cadence, even though it seems monot-onous and repetitive to modern ears.

Let us illustrate this literary balance by quotations from a text giving a statement of one of the Egyptian kings:

> Give heed to my utterances / hearken to them.
> I speak to you / I make you aware
> That I am the son of Rē / who issued from his body.
> I sit upon his throne in rejoicing / since he established me
>   as king / as lord of this land.
> My counsels are good / my plans come to pass.
> I protect Egypt / I defend it.[9]

The balance sought by the artist could be illustrated by Egyptian sculptures or paintings. Instead, we shall quote from the inscription of a "chief craftsman, painter, and sculptor," who went into con-siderable detail with regard to his technical abilities. Of his modeling, he said: "I know how to work up clay, how to proportion (it) according to rule, how to mold or introduce (it) by taking away or adding to it so that (each) member comes to its (proper) place." Of his drawing, he said: "I know (how to express) the movement of a figure, the carriage of a woman, the pose of a single instant, the cowering of the isolated captive, or how one eye looks at the other."[10] The emphasis of his claimed skill lies in proportion, balance, and poise.

The same balance comes out in the Egyptian's cosmology and his theology, where he sought for a counterpoise to each observed phenomenon or each supernatural element. If there is a sky above, there must be a sky below; each god must have his goddess consort, even though she has no separate divine function but is simply a feminine counterpart of himself. Some of this striving for bilateral symmetry seems to us strained, and undoubtedly artificial concepts did arise in the search to find a counterpoise for anything observed or conceived. However, the psychological desire for balance which drew forth the artificial concept was not itself artificial but was a deeply engrained desire for symmetric poise.

That deep desire for balance will appear to the reader as contradictory to the lack of order which we deplored in the Egyptians' bland acceptance of any new concept, whether it conformed to an old concept or not, and their maintenance of apparently conflicting concepts side by side. There is a contradiction here, but we believe that it can be explained. The ancient Egyptian had a strong sense of symmetry and balance, but he had little sense of incongruity: he was perfectly willing to balance off incompatibles. Further, he had little sense of causation, that A leads sequentially to B and B leads sequentially to C. As remarked in the introductory chapter, the ancient did not recognize causality as impersonal and binding. It is an oversimplification to say that the Egyptian's thinking was in terms of geometry rather than in terms of algebra, but that statement may give some idea of his limited virtues. The order in his philosophy lay in physical arrangement rather than in integrated and sequential systematization.

COSMOLOGY

It is now time to consider the terms in which the Egyptian viewed the physical universe, of which his own land was the focal center. First of all, he took his orientation from the Nile River, the source of his life. He faced the south, from which the stream came. One of the terms for "south" is also a term for "face"; the usual word for "north" is probably related to a word which means the "back of the head." On his left was the east and on his right the west. The word for "east" and "left" is the same, and the word for "west" and "right" is the same.

We were technically incorrect in stating that the Egyptian's orientation was to the south; more precisely we should say that the Egyptian "australized" himself toward the source of the Nile. It is significant that he did not take his primary direction from the east, the land of the rising sun, the region which he called "God's Land." As we shall see, the formulated theology did emphasize the east. But back in the prehistoric days before theology had crystallized, when the terms of the Egyptian language were forming, the dweller on the Nile faced toward the south, the source of the annual re-fertilization of his land. The theological priority of the sun seems thus to be a later development.

It may be that we are dealing with two separate searchings for direction. In the trough of Upper Egypt, where the Nile so clearly flows from the south as the dominating feature of the land, the compass of man's attention swung to the south. In the Delta, where the broad stretches had no such magnetic pull of direction, the rising of the sun in the east was a more important phenomenon. The worship of the sun may thus have been more important in the north and may have been transferred to the entire land as state theology in some prehistoric conquest of the south by the north. Such a conquest would have established the theological primacy of the sun and made the east, which was the region of the sun's rebirth, the area of religious importance, but it would not affect the words which showed that man's polarity was originally to the south.

The crystallized theology, as we know it in historic times, made the orient, the land of the sun's rising, the region of birth and re-birth, and made the occident, the land of the sun's setting, the region of death and life after death. The east was *ta-netjer*, "God's Land," because the sun rose there in youthly glory. This general term for the east was even used for specific foreign countries, which were otherwise despised. Syria, Sinai, and Punt, all lying to the east, might be afflicted with mountains, trees, and rain, might be inhabited by "miserable Asiatics," but they belonged to the youthful sun-god, so that they were designated also as "God's Land" and enjoyed a reflected glory through geographical accident and not through inner merit. Implicitly the good produce of these eastern countries was ascribed to the sun-god rather than to the inhabitants: "All good woods of God's Land: heaps of myrrh gum, trees of fresh myrrh, ebony, and clean ivory, ... baboons, apes, greyhounds, and panther skins"[11] or "cedar, cypress, and juniper, ... all good woods of God's Land."[12]

In the dogma that arose in magnification of the rising sun the grateful joy of all creation at the renewed appearance of the morning sun was expressed again and again. The contrast between evening and morning was a contrast between death and life. "When thou settest on the western horizon, the land is in darkness in the manner of death . . . . (but) when the day breaks, as thou risest on the horizon, ... they awake and stand upon their feet, ... they live because thou hast arisen for them."[13] Not only does mankind join in this renewal of life, but "all beasts prance upon their feet, and everything that flies or flutters,"[14] and "apes worship him; 'Praise to thee!' (say) all beasts with one accord."[15] The Egyptian pictures show this morning worship of the sun by animals: the apes stretching out limbs which had been cooled at night, in apparent salutation to the warmth of the sun, or the ostriches limbering up at dawn by dancing a stately pavan in the first rays of the sun. Such observed phenomena were visible proofs of the communion of men, beasts, and the gods.

But to return to the Egyptian's concept of the world in which he lived. We are going to try to give this in a single picture, which will have only partial justification. In the first place, we are concerned with something like three thousand years of observed history, with the vestiges of prehistoric development partially visible; and there was constant slow change across this long stretch of time. In the second place, the ancient Egyptian left us no single formulation of his ideas which we may use as nuclear material; when we pick and choose scraps of ideas from scattered sources, we are gratifying our modern craving for a single integrated system. That is, our modern desire to capture a single picture is photographic and static, whereas the ancient Egyptian's picture was cinematic and fluid. For example, we should want to know in our picture whether the sky was supported on posts or was held up by a god; the Egyptian would answer: "Yes, it is supported by posts or held up by a god— or it rests on walls, or it is a cow, or it is a goddess whose arms and feet touch the earth." Any one of these pictures would be satisfactory to him, according to his approach, and in a single picture he might show two different supports for the sky: the goddess whose arms and feet reach the earth, and the god who holds up the sky-goddess. This possibility of complementary viewpoints applies to other concepts. We shall therefore pick a single picture, in the knowledge that it tells a characteristic story, but not the only story.

The Egyptian conceived of the earth as a flat platter with a corrugated rim. The inside bottom of this platter was the flat alluvial plain of Egypt, and the corrugated rim was the rim of mountain countries which were the foreign lands. This platter floated in water. There were the abysmal waters below, on which the platter rested, called by the Egyptian "Nūn." Nūn was the waters of the underworld, and, according to one continuing concept, Nūn was the primordial waters out of which life first issued. Life still issued from these underworld waters, for the sun was reborn every day out of Nūn, and the Nile came pouring forth from caverns which were fed from Nūn. In addition to being the underworld waters, Nūn was the waters encircling the world, the Okeanos which formed the outermost boundary, also called the "Great Circuit" or the "Great Green." Thus it was clear that the sun, after its nightly journey under the world, must be reborn beyond the eastern horizon out of those encircling waters, just as all the gods had originally come forth out of Nūn.

Above the earth was the inverted pan of the sky, setting the outer limit to the universe. As we have already said, the craving for symmetry, as well as a sense that space is limited, called forth a counterheaven under the earth, bounding the limits of the underworld. This was the universe within which man and the gods and the heavenly bodies operated.

Various qualifications to this picture are immediately necessary. Our picture gives the vault of heaven as suspended by apparent levitation above the earth. That would appeal to the ancient Egyptian as dangerous, and he would ask for some visible means of support. As we have already said, he provided various means of support in various concepts, the incompatibility of which he cheerfully ignored. The simplest mechanism was four posts set on earth to carry the weight of heaven. These were at the outer limits of the

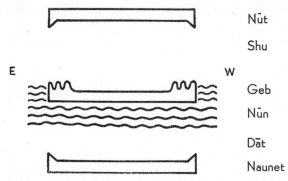

earth, as is indicated by such texts as: "I have set . . . . the terror of thee as far as the four pillars of heaven,"[16] and the number four suggests that they were placed at the four points of the compass. Fortunately, this arrangement appealed to the Egyptian as being both strong and permanent: "(As firm) as heaven resting upon its four posts" is a simile used more than once.[17]

But heaven might have other support. Between heaven and earth there was Shū, the air-god, and it was his function to stand firmly on earth and carry the weight of heaven. In the Pyramid Texts (1101) it is said: "The arms of Shū are under heaven, that he may carry it." Significantly, another version of this text gives a variant: "The arms of Shū are under Nūt, that he may carry her," for heaven was, of course, personified as a deity, the sky-goddess Nūt. She is represented as crouching over earth, with her fingers and toes touching the ground, while the sun, moon, and stars adorn her body. She may carry her own weight in this pose, or the air-god Shū may take some of her weight on his uplifted hands.

Again, the vault of heaven might be represented as the underbelly of a celestial cow, studded with stars, and providing the Milky Way along which the boat of the sun might make its heavenly course. That these concepts are essentially alternatives did not seem to bother the Egyptian. In the course of a single text he might use these differing ideas about heaven; each concept pleased him and had its pertinent value in a universe which was fluid and in which almost all things were possible to the gods. Within his own standards of what is credible and convincing, he had his own consistency. All his concepts of heaven and its supports gave him assurance instead of uncertainty, because they were all stable and enduring and because one concept could be taken as complementing another instead of contradicting it.

Under the vault of heaven were the heavenly bodies, the stars hanging from the inverted pan or else spangling the belly of the cow or of the goddess, and the moon similarly treated. The moon has curiously little weight in Egyptian mythology, or, rather, we should say that it has little weight in the evidence which has descended to us. There are traces that there had been early important centers of moon worship, but this worship became diverted into less cosmic directions in historic times. Thus the moon-god Thoth was more important as a god of wisdom and a divine judge than he was through his heavenly activity. The waning and waxing moon disk as one of the two celestial eyes became a rather formal part of the Osiris story, serving as the injury suffered by Horus in fighting for his father, an injury which was restored every month by the moon-god. Conceivably this idea was taken over from some earlier myth in which the moon had had an importance comparable to that of the sun, the other celestial eye. In historical times there was little comparison between the two bodies.

Similarly, the stars had their importance in the measuring of time, and two or three of the major constellations were deities of some weight; but only one group of stars achieved lasting importance in the Egyptian scene. Again, this importance had to do with triumph over death. In the clear Egyptian air the stars stand out with brilliance. Most of the stars swing across the sky with a scythe-like sweep and disappear below the horizon. But one section of the skies employs a smaller orbit, and there the stars may dip toward the horizon but never disappear. Those are the circumpolar stars swinging around the North Star, stars which the Egyptians called "those that know no destruction" or "those that know no weariness." These undying stars they took as the symbol of the dead who triumphed over death and went on into eternal life. That north section of heaven was in early times an important part of the universe. Visibly there was no death there; therefore, it must be the place of the eternal blessedness for which Egyptians longed. In the early mortuary texts, which we moderns call the Pyramid Texts, the goal of the deceased was the region of Dāt in the northern part of heaven, where he would join the circumpolar stars "which know no destruction" and thus live forever himself. There were located their Elysian Fields, the "Field of Reeds" and the "Field of Offerings," in which the dead would live as an *akh*, an "effective" spirit.

As time went on, and as the dominant mythology of the sun spread its weight over the nation, the region of Dāt shifted from the northern part of the sky to the underworld. The old texts which tried every conceivable method of boosting the dead into heaven were still reiterated with solemn fervor, but the entryway into the next world was now in the west, and the two Elysian Fields were below the earth. This was clearly because the sun died in the west, had its spiritual course under the earth, and gloriously was reborn in the east. So, too, the dead must share in this promise of constantly continued life, must be shifted to the proximity of the sun in order to participate in his fate. Thus our picture of the universe must recognize Dāt, the area between earth and the counterheaven as the realm of the immortal dead.

Enough has already been said about the central importance of the sun in this scene. Something must be said about his motive power on his daily journey. Most commonly he is depicted as moving by boat, and the bilateral symmetry which the Egyptian loved gave him a boat for the day and another boat for the night. Various important gods formed the crews of these two boats. This journey might not be all stately and serene: there was a serpent lurking along the way to attack the boat and presumably swallow the sun; battle was necessary to conquer this creature. This is, of course, the common belief in many lands that eclipses occur when a snake or dragon swallows up the sun. But a true eclipse was not the only phenomenon involved; every night an attempt to swallow up the sun was met and conquered in the underworld.

The sun might have other motive power. It seemed to be a rolling ball, and the Egyptians knew a rolling ball in that pellet which the dung beetle pushed across the sand. So a beetle, a scarab, became a symbol for the morning sun, with an afternoon counterpart in an old man wearily moving toward the western horizon. Again, the symbol of the falcon soaring in apparent motionlessness in the upper air suggested that the sun disk also might have falcon wings for its effortless flight. As before, these concepts were felt to be complementary and not conflicting. The possession of many manifestations of being enlarged the glory of the god.

To move the concept of the sun even farther from the physical, from the notion of a fiery disk which swung around the earth every twenty-four hours, we must here note other aspects of the sun-god, Rē. As supreme god, he was a divine king, and legend said that he had been the first king of Egypt in primordial times. He was thus represented in the form of a bearded deity with a disk as his crown. As supreme god, he loaned himself to other gods, in order to enlarge them and give them a primacy within geographical or functional limits. Thus he was both Rē and Rē-Atum, the creator god, at Heliopolis. He was Rē-Harakhte, that is, Rē-Horus-of-the-Horizon, as the youthful god on the eastern horizon. At various localities he became Montu-Rē, a falcon-god, Sobek-Rē, a crocodile-god, and Khnum-Rē, a ram-god. He became Amon-Rē, King of the Gods, as the imperial god of Thebes. As we have said, these separate manifestations enlarged him. He was not simply a solar disk. He had personality as a god. Here we revert again to the distinction between the scientific concept of a phenomenon as "It" and the ancient concept of a phenomenon as "Thou" given in chapter i. There it was said that science is able to comprehend the "It" as ruled by laws which make its behavior relatively predictable, whereas the "Thou" has the unpredictable character of an individual, "a presence known only in so far as it reveals itself." In these terms the apparently antic and protean character of the sun becomes simply the versatile and ubiquitous reach possible to a very able individual. Surprise at this being's many-sided personality may ultimately give way to an expectation that he will be able to participate in any situation with specialized competence.

COSMOGONY

Now we shall examine some of the Egyptian creation stories. It is significant that a plural should be necessary, that we cannot settle down to a single codified account of the beginnings. The Egyptian accepted various myths and discarded none of them. It is further to be noted that it is easier to observe close parallels between the Babylonian and Hebrew accounts of the genesis than it is to relate the Egyptian accounts to the other two. Within the broad area of general developmental similarity in the ancient Near East, Egypt stood slightly apart.

We have already noted that Nūn, the primordial abyss, was the region out of which life first came. This is, of course, particularly true of the sun, because of his daily re-emergence from the depths, and of the Nile, because it consists of ground waters. But the phrase "who came forth from Nūn" is used of many other individual gods and of the council of the gods as a group. In large part, we need not seek too seriously for a myth for this idea. The depths or the primordial waters are a concept needing no teleological story; Tennyson's reference to life as "that which drew from out the boundless deep" needs no explanation.

However, we must give closer attention to one account of life appearing out of the waters, and that has the location of creation on a "primeval hillock." We have mentioned how broad sheets of water cover Egypt when the Nile inundation is at its height and how the sinking of the waters brings into view the first isolated peaks of mud, refreshed with new fertile silt. These would be the first islands of promise for new life in a new agricultural year. As these first hillocks of slime lift their heads out of the floodwaters into the baking warmth of the sun, it is easy to imagine that they sputter and crackle with new life. The modern Egyptians believe that there is special life-giving power in this slime, and they are not alone in this belief. A little less than three centuries ago there was a scientific controversy about spontaneous generation, the ability of apparently inorganic matter to produce living organisms. One Englishman wrote that if his scholarly opponent doubted that life came into being through putrefaction which went on in mud or slime, "let him go to Egypt, and there he will find the fields swarming with mice begot of the mud of Nylus, to the great calamity of the inhabitants."[18] It is not hard to believe that animal life may come out of this highly charged mud.

The evidence on the Egyptian myth of the origin of life on the primeval hillock is scattered and allusive. The essential point is that the creator-god made his first appearance on this solitary island. At least two different theological systems claimed primacy through the possession of a primeval hillock, and indeed ultimately every temple which had a high place for its god probably considered that high place to be the place of creation. The pyramids themselves borrow this idea of a rising hill as a promise to the deceased Egyptian buried within the pyramid that he will emerge again into new being. As pointed out in chapter i, the concept of the creation hillock is the essential, and its location in space, whether Heliopolis or Hermopolis, was of no concern to the Egyptian.

Let us take a passage from the Book of the Dead, which states this first solitary appearance of Rē-Atum, the creator-god. The text is provided with explanatory glosses.

I am Atum when I was alone in Nūn (the primordial waters); I am Rē in his (first) appearances, when he began to rule that which he had made. What does that mean? This "Rē when he began to rule that which he had made" means that Rē began to appear as a king, as one who existed before (the air-god) Shū had (even) lifted (heaven from earth), when he (Rē) was on the primeval hillock which was in Hermopolis.[19]

The text then goes on to emphasize the fact that the god was self-created and that he proceeded to bring into being "the gods who are in his following."

The Egyptian hieroglyph which means the primeval "hillock of appearance" means also "to appear in glory." It shows a rounded mound with the rays of the sun streaming upward from it (⊜), graphically portraying this miracle of the first appearance of the creator-god.

The text which we have cited placed the creation on a mound in the town of Hermopolis, the home of certain gods who were in being before the creation. However, that anomaly of pre-creation existence need not worry us too seriously, for the names of these gods show that they represent the formless chaos which existed before the creator-god brought order out of disorder. We should qualify the term "chaos" slightly, as these pre-creation gods are neatly paired off into four couples, a god and a goddess for each quality of chaos. That is another example of the love of symmetry. These four pairs of gods persisted in mythology as the "Eight" who were before the beginning. They were Nūn, the primordial waters, and his consort, Naunet, who came to be the counter-heaven; Hūh, the boundless stretches of primordial formlessness, and his consort, Hauhet; Kūk, "darkness," and his consort, Kauket; and Amūn, that is, Amon, "the hidden," representing the intangibility and imperceptibility of chaos, with his consort, Amaunet. All this is a way of saying what the Book of Genesis says—that, before creation, "the earth was waste and void; and darkness was upon the face of the deep." Hūh and Amūn, boundlessness and imperceptibility, are rough parallels to the Hebrew *tohu wavohu*, "waste and void"; while Kūk, darkness, and Nūn, the abyss, are clearly similar to the Hebrew *hoshek al-penei tehom*, "darkness upon the face of the deep waters." This similarity is interesting but not too alluring, because the Egyptian story and the Hebrew diverge immediately when one comes to the episodes of creation, with Egypt emphasizing the self-emergence of a creator-god, whereas the creator-god of Genesis existed alongside the chaos. You have to begin with some concept, so that primitive man everywhere would try to conceive of a formlessness before form was made. This formlessness might have much the same terms anywhere. We shall revert to the Genesis story later.

At this point we cannot pursue the other emergences of a primeval hillock in other cult centers or the implications of this thought in the beliefs and iconography of Egypt. We wish instead to plunge on to a more developed mythological phenomenon which has its importance in the creation stories.

In early times the sun-god had his own family of gods, which was also the supreme council of the gods. This group, which had its chief center at the temple of the sun at Heliopolis, was the Ennead, "the Nine," consisting of four interrelated couples surmounted by one common ancestor. This Ennead or "Nine" may be placed in contrast to the "Eight," which we have already discussed, for the "Eight" comprised elements of cosmic disorder, whereas this "Nine" contained only progressive steps of cosmic order: air and moisture; earth and sky; the beings on the earth. This says clearly that the creation marks the dividing-line between preceding confusion and present order. It is not implied that the creator-god conquered and annihilated the elements of chaos and set the elements of order in their place. On the contrary, it is obvious that such pre-creation gods as Nūn, the underworld waters, and Kūk, darkness, continued after the creation; but they continued in their proper places and not in universal and formless disorder. In that sense, this creation has similarities with the creation in Genesis: a separation of light from darkness and a separation of waters below from waters above.

The sun-god Atum, as he perched on the primeval hillock, was self-created; as the Egyptian puts it, he "became, by himself." Now the name Atum means "everything" and it means "nothing." This is not as paradoxical as it sounds, for the word means "what is finished, completed, perfected," and all these terms have their positive and their negative. "Finis," written at the end of a book, means: "That's all. There isn't any more." So, too, Atum means all-inclusiveness and it means emptiness, at the beginning rather than at the end. Atum is the inchoation of all. He is like that pregnant stillness which precedes a hurricane.

There are varying accounts of the creation itself. The Book of the Dead (17) states that the sun-god created his names, as the ruler of the Ennead. This is explained as meaning that he named the parts of his body and that "thus arose these gods who are in his following." That is delightfully primitive and has a consistency of its own. The parts of the body have separate existence and separate character, so that they may have relation to separate deities. The name is a thing of individuality and of power; the act of speaking a new name is an act of creation. Thus we have the picture of the creator squatting on his tiny island and inventing names for eight parts of his body—or four pairs of parts—with each utterance bringing a new god into existence.

The Pyramid Texts present a different picture. Addressing Atum and recalling the occasion when the god was high upon the primeval hillock, the inscription goes on: "Thou didst spit what was Shū; thou didst sputter out what was Tefnūt. Thou didst put thy arms about them as the arms of a *ka*, for thy *ka* was in them"

(1652–53). This has the creation as a rather violent ejection of the first two gods. Perhaps it was as explosive as a sneeze, for Shū is the god of air, and his consort, Tefnūt, is the goddess of moisture. The reference to the *ka* needs explanation. We shall discuss the *ka* or other personality of an individual later. The concept of the *ka* has something of the alter ego in it and something of the guardian spirit with the protecting arms. That is why Atum puts his arms protectingly around his two children, for his *ka* was in them, an essential part of himself.

Another, more earthy, text makes the production of Shū and Tefnūt an act of self-pollution on Atum's part.[20] This is clearly an attempt to surmount the problem of generation by a god alone, without an attending goddess.

The couple Shū and Tefnūt, air and moisture, gave birth to earth and sky, the earth-god Geb and the sky-goddess Nūt. Or, according to another concept, the air-god Shū lifted and tore asunder earth and sky. Then in their turn Geb and Nūt, earth and sky, mated and produced two couples, the god Osiris and his consort Isis, the god Seth and his consort Nephthys. These represent the creatures of this world, whether human, divine, or cosmic. I shall not take time to argue the exact original significance of these four beings, as we are not precisely certain of any of them.

Atum
Shū—Tefnūt
Geb—Nūt
Osiris—Isis   Seth—Nephthys

Thus in this ruling family of the gods we have a creation story implicitly. Atum, the supercharged vacuum, separated into air and moisture. As if in the operation of the nebular hypothesis, air and moisture condensed into earth and sky. Out of earth and sky came the beings that populate the universe.

We do not here wish to go into some of the other creation stories, such as the god who was himself the "rising land" on which the miracle took place. It is interesting that we lack a specific account of the creation of mankind, except in the most allusive way. A ram-god, Khnum, is referred to as forming mankind on his potter's wheel, or the sun-god is called the "discoverer of mankind."[21] But no story of separate creation of man is necessary, for a reason which we shall discuss more fully later; that reason is that there was no firm and final dividing-line between gods and men. Once a creation was started with beings, it could go on, whether the beings were gods, demigods, spirits, or men.

One of the texts which comments incidentally on creation states that mankind was made in the image of god. This text emphasizes the goodness of the creator-god in caring for his human creatures. "Well tended are men, the cattle of god. He made heaven and earth according to their desire, and he repelled the water monster (at creation). He made the breath (of) life (for) their nostrils. They are his images that have issued from his body. He arises in heaven according to their desire. He made for them plants and animals, fowl and fish, in order to nourish them. He slew his enemies and destroyed (even) his (own) children when they plotted rebellion (against him)."[22] The text is interesting and unusual in making the purposes of creation the interests of humans; normally the myth recounts the steps of creation without indication of purpose. But this particular text happens to have strong moral purpose. Note, for example, the reference to the god's destroying mankind when they rebelled against him. We shall return to this remote parallel to the biblical Flood story in the next chapter.

We must examine at length one final document bearing on the creation. This is an inscription called the Memphite Theology, a context so strange and different from the material we have been discussing that it seems, at first glance, to come from another world. And yet closer examination assures us that the difference is a matter of degree and not of kind, because all the strange elements in the text of the Memphite Theology were present in other Egyptian texts in isolated instances; only in this text were they brought together into a broad philosophical system about the nature of the universe.

The document in question is a battered stone in the British Museum, bearing the name of an Egyptian pharaoh who ruled about 700 B.C.[23] However, this pharaoh claimed that he had simply copied an inscription of the ancestors, and his claim is borne out by the language and typically early physical arrangement of the text. We are dealing with a document which comes from the very beginning of Egyptian history, from the time when the first dynasties made their new capital at Memphis, the city of the god Ptah. Now, Memphis as the center of a theocratic state was an upstart; it had had no national importance before. To make matters worse, Heliopolis, a traditional religious capital of Egypt, the home of the sun-god Rē and of the creator-god Rē-Atum, was only twenty-five miles from Memphis. It was necessary to justify a new location of the center of the world. The text in question is part of a theological argument of the primacy of the god Ptah and thus of his home, Memphis.

The creation texts which we have discussed earlier have been more strictly in physical terms: the god separating earth from sky or giving birth to air and moisture. This new text turns as far as the Egyptian could turn toward a creation in philosophical terms: the thought which came into the heart of a god and the commanding utterance which brought that thought into reality. This creation by thought conception and speech delivery has its experiential background in human life: the authority of a ruler to create by command. But only the use of physical terms such as "heart" for thought and "tongue" for command relate the Memphite Theology to the more earthy texts which we have been considering. Here, as Professor Breasted has pointed out, we come close to the background of the Logos doctrine of the New Testament: "In the beginning was the Word, and the Word was with God, and the Word was God."

Before undertaking this difficult text itself, we should lay out for ourselves the known factors that play into the interpretation of the text. First, the Memphite text takes off from the creation stories which I have already recounted: Atum coming into being out of Nūn, the primeval waters, and Atum bringing his Ennead of gods into existence. The Memphite text is aware that these were prevailing concepts in Egypt. In place of discarding them as competitive, it wishes to subsume them into a higher philosophy, to take advantage of them by pointing out that they belong to a higher system.

That higher system employs *invention* by the cognition of an idea in the mind and *production* through the utterance of a creating order by speech. Now thought and speech are ancient attributes of power in Egypt, personified as deities in our earliest literature.

They occur normally as a pair of related attributes of the sun-god: Hū, "authoritative utterance," that speech which is so effective that it creates, and Sia, "perception," the cognitive reception of a situation, an object, or an idea. Hū and Sia were attributes that carried governing authority. In the Pyramid Texts the ruling god leaves his shrine and surrenders his office to the deceased king, because the latter "has captured Hū, has control of Sia" (300). In our Memphite text these two attributes of power are taken in material terms: the heart is the organ which conceives thought, and the tongue is the organ which creates the conceived thought as a phenomenal actuality. All this is credited to the activity of the Memphite god Ptah, who is himself thought and speech in every heart and on every tongue, and thus was the first creative principle, just as he remains now.

The part of the text in which we are interested begins by equating Ptah with Nūn, the primeval waters out of which came Atum, the normally accepted creator-god. This in itself makes Ptah antecedent to the sun-god, and that priority occurs in passing references in other texts. But our text does not leave the priority implicit; it states the mechanism by which Ptah produced Atum.

"Ptah, the Great One; he is the heart and tongue of the Ennead of gods . . . . who begot the gods. . . . . There came into being in the heart, and there came into being on the tongue (something) in the form of Atum." This is the invention and production of Atum. Out of nothing, there came into existence the idea of an Atum, of a creator-god. That idea "became, in the heart" of the divine world, which heart or mind was Ptah himself; then that idea "became, upon the tongue" of the divine world, which tongue or speech was Ptah himself. The Egyptian uses pictorial, physical language; it says elliptically: "in-the-form-of-Atum became, in the heart, and became, on the tongue," but there is no question of the meaning. Conception and parturition reside in these terms.

But Ptah's creative power does not stop with the production of the traditional creator-god. "Great and mighty is Ptah, who has transmitted [power to all gods], as well as their spirits, through this (activity of the) heart and this (activity of the) tongue." Nor does the creative principle stop with the gods. "It has come to pass that the heart and tongue control [every] member (of the body) by teaching that he (Ptah) is throughout every body (in the form of the heart) and throughout every mouth (in the form of the tongue), of all gods, of all men, of [all] animals, of all creeping things, and of what(ever) lives, by (Ptah's) thinking (as the heart) and commanding (as the tongue) anything that he wishes." In other words, we have no single miracle of thought conception and articulation, but the same principles of creation which were valid in the primeval waters to bring forth Atum are still valid and operative. Wherever there is thought and command, there Ptah still creates.

The text even draws an invidious distinction between the traditional creation by which Atum brought forth Shū and Tefnūt and that creation whereby Ptah spoke Shū and Tefnūt and thus brought them into being. Ptah's teeth and lips are the articulating organs of the productive speech. As we mentioned earlier, one version of the Atum story makes Shū and Tefnūt products of the self-pollution of the creator-god. Thus teeth and lips in the case of Ptah are brought into parallelism with the semen and hands of Atum. To our modern prejudice, this makes the Ptah creation a nobler activity; but it is not certain that the ancient meant to belittle the more physical story. Perhaps he was simply expressing the correspondence of alternative myths when he said: "Now the Ennead of Atum came into being from his seed and by his fingers; but the Ennead (of Ptah) is the teeth and the lips in this mouth which uttered the name of everything and (thus) Shū and Tefnūt came forth from it." We have already seen how the utterance of a name is in itself an act of creation.

That text goes on to specify in detail the products of the activity of the conceptive heart and creative tongue, without adding anything essentially new. It explains the mechanistic relation of the various senses to the heart and tongue by stating that the function of the sight of the eyes, the hearing of the ears, and the smelling of the nose is to report to the heart. On the basis of this sensory information, the heart releases "everything which is completed," that is, every established concept, and then "it is the tongue which announces what the heart thinks."

Then the text summarizes the range of this creative power of Ptah as heart and tongue. Thus were the gods born; thus came into being all of the divine order; thus were made the directive des-

tinies which supply mankind with food and provisions; thus was
made the distinction between right and wrong; thus were made all
arts, crafts, and human activities; thus Ptah made provinces and
cities and set the various local gods in their governing places.
Finally: "Thus it was discovered and understood that his (Ptah's)
power is greater than (that of the other) gods. And so Ptah rested
after he had made everything, as well as the divine order." Admittedly the word "rested" introduces a parallel to the Genesis story
of God's resting on the seventh day. The translation "rested" is
defensible, but it is probably safer to render: "And so Ptah was
satisfied, after he had made everything."

It is clear that there is some special pleading in this text, the attempt of an upstart theology to establish itself as national and universal against older, traditional ways of thinking. That comes out
in a quotation which we have just given, which might be para-
phrased: For these reasons, all right-thinking men have come to
the conclusion that Ptah is the most powerful of all gods. Undoubtedly that special interest does lie in this text, but that fact need not
concern us much. As we have said, the Memphite Theology did
not wish to conquer and annihilate the theology of Heliopolis but
to conquer and assimilate it. And, after all, we are more interested
in the possibility of a developed speculative thought as given in this
text than in any controversy between two important shrines.

Perhaps it would be better to call our rendering of the words
"the word of the god" by "the divine order" a free paraphrase.
But we should still justify it. "The word of the god" can and does
mean "concern of the gods" or what we might call "divine interests." But the phrase "the divine order" implies that the gods have
a system into which all the created elements should fit as soon as
created. The context enumerates the created elements: gods, fortunes, food, provisions, towns, districts, etc. These are summed
up in the term "everything," after which we have "as well as the
word of the god." What can this mean other than the directive
order?

One can argue this same sense in other Egyptian contexts. For
example, an assertion that the righteous man is not wiped out by
death but has an immortality because of his goodly memory is indorsed with the words: "That is the method of reckoning of the

word of god"; in freer sense: "That is the principle of the divine order."[24]

Because the Egyptians thought of the word in physical, concrete terms and because the priesthood was the interpreter of what was divine, this "word of god" came to be treated as a body of literature, the sacred writings, but it was still the directive speech given by the gods. A dead noble was promised "every good and pure thing, in conformance to that writing of the word of god which (the god of wisdom) Thoth made."[25] In another passage one scribe chides another for the impious presumption of his boasting: "I am astonished when thou sayest: 'I am more profound as a scribe than heaven, or earth, or the underworld!' . . . . The house of books is concealed and invisible; the council of its gods is hidden and distant. . . . . Thus I answer thee: 'Beware lest thy fingers approach the word of god!' "[26] What the gods have said is in itself directive and controlling; it sets an order within which man and the other elements of the universe operate.

Thus the "word of the god" is nothing so simple in these contexts as "divine writing" or hieroglyphic. It is the word or concern or business of the gods which applies to the elements which the gods have created. Not only were material elements created, but there was created for them a "word," which applied to them and which put them into their appropriate places in the god's scheme of things. Creation was not the irresponsible production of oddly assorted pieces, which might be shaken down in a vast impersonal lottery wheel. Creation was accompanied and directed by a word which expressed some kind of a divine order in order to comprehend the created elements.

In summary, the ancient Egyptian was self-conscious about himself and his universe; he produced a cosmos in terms of his own observation and his own experience. Like the Nile Valley, this cosmos had limited space but reassuring periodicity; its structural framework and mechanics permitted the reiteration of life through the rebirth of life-giving elements. The creation stories of the ancient Egyptian were also in terms of his own experience, although they bear loose general similarity to other creation stories. The most interesting advance lies in a very early attempt to relate creation to the processes of thought and speech rather than to mere physical activity. Even this "higher" philosophy is given in pictorial terms arising out of Egyptian experience.

NOTES

1. Champollion, *Mon.*, 238–40.
2. Admon., 3:1; 1:9.
3. Wenamon, 2:19–22.
4. Aton Hymn, 3.
5. Tombos, l. 13.
6. Aton Hymn, 9–10.
7. Anast. I, 19:2–4; 24:1–4.
8. Merikarē, 91–98.
9. Med. Habu II, 83, ll. 57–58.
10. Louvre, C 14, 8–10.
11. Urk. IV, 329.
12. *Ibid.*, 373.
13. Aton Hymn, 3–6.
14. Aton Hymn, 5.
15. BD, Introductory Hymn.
16. Urk. IV, 612.
17. *Ibid.*, 183, 843.
18. *Encyclopaedia Britannica* (11th ed.).
19. Urk. V, 6 = BD, 17.
20. Pyr. 1248.
21. In Beatty I, p. 24.
22. Merikarē, 130–34.
23. Kurt Sethe, *Dramatische Texte zu altägyptischen Mysterienspieen.*
24. Peasant, B1, 307–11.
25. Cairo 28085; Lacau, *Sarc. ant.*, p. 206.
26. Anast. I, 11:4–7.

CHAPTER III
EGYPT: THE FUNCTION OF THE STATE

THE UNIVERSE AND THE STATE

THE first two chapters have attempted to establish the attitude of mind with which ancient man viewed the world around him. Before moving directly to a consideration of the state and its place in the Egyptian scene, we should consider two questions which provide a setting for that consideration. Did the ancient Egyptian see an essential difference in substance between man, society, the gods, plants, animals, and the physical universe? Did he believe the universe to be benevolent, hostile, or indifferent to him? These questions have bearing on the relation of the state to the universe and on the functioning of the state for the benefit of man.

Let us take first the question about difference of substance among men, gods, and other elements of the universe. This problem has vexed Christian theologians for centuries. We can give only a personal answer with reference to ancient Egypt. To be sure, a man seems to be one thing, and the sky or a tree seems to be another. But to the ancient Egyptian such concepts had a protean and complementary nature. The sky might be thought of as a material vault above earth, or as a cow, or as a female. A tree might be a tree or the female who was the tree-goddess. Truth might be treated as an abstract concept, or as a goddess, or as a divine hero who once lived on earth. A god might be depicted as a man, or as a falcon, or as a falcon-headed man. In one context the king is described as the sun, a star, a bull, a crocodile, a lion, a falcon, a jackal, and the two tutelary gods of Egypt—not so much in simile as in vital essence.[1] There was thus a continuing substance across the phenomena of the universe, whether organic, inorganic, or abstract. It is not a matter of black being antipodal to white but rather that the universe is a spectrum in which one color blends off into another without line of demarcation, in which, indeed, one color may become another under alternating conditions.

We wish to argue this point further. Our line of argument will be that to the ancient Egyptian the elements of the universe were consubstantial. If that be true, the terms which he knew best—human behavior—would be the frame of reference for nonhuman phenomena. It would then be idle to argue whether the universe, or the gods of the universe, were believed to be benevolent, malevolent, or indifferent. They would be just like humans: benevolent when they were benevolent, malevolent when malevolent, and indifferent when indifferent. To put it in active terms, they would be benevolent when benevolence was their stated business and malevolent when malevolence was their stated business. That conclusion would have relation to the business of the state and the forces responsible for the state.

The first claim for the argument that the elements of the universe were of one substance is in the principle of free substitution, interchange, or representation. It was very easy for one element to take the place of another. The deceased wanted bread, so that he might not be hungry in the next world. He made contractual arrangements whereby loaves of bread were presented regularly at his tomb, so that his spirit might return and eat of the bread. But he was aware of the transitory nature of contracts and of the greed of hired servants. He supported his needs by other forms of bread. A model loaf made of wood and left in the tomb would be an adequate representative of an actual loaf. The picture of loaves of bread on the tomb wall would continue to feed the deceased by representation. If other means of presentation were lacking, the word "bread," spoken or written with reference to his nourishment, might be an effective substitute. This is an easy concept: the physical man was formerly here; now the spiritual man is over there; we must project over to him spiritual, not physical, bread, so that the absolute is not necessary; the name or the idea or the representation will be enough.

Let us carry representation into another area. A god represented something important in the universe: the sky, a district of Egypt, or kingship. In terms of his function that god had extensiveness and intangibility. But he might have a localization in our world, in a place where he might feel at home; that is, a shrine might be specified for him. In that shrine he might have a place of manifestation in an image. This image was not the god; it was merely a mechanism of stone or wood or metal to permit him to make an appearance. This is stated by the Egyptians in one of the creation accounts. The creator-god acted for the other gods, and "he made their bodies like that with which their hearts were satisfied. So the gods entered into their bodies of every (kind of) wood, of every (kind of) stone, or every (kind of) clay . . . . in which they had taken form."² These images were provided for them so that they might have places in which to take visible form. Thus the god Amon might be at home in a stone statue of human form, in a specially selected ram, or in a specially selected gander. He remained himself and did not become identical with this form of appearance, and yet he had a different form of appearance for a different purpose, just as humans might maintain different homes or might have different garments.

Of course, we rationalize the image or the sacred animal as being an empty shell of divinity unless divinity were manifest in the shell. However, in another sense the image or the animal was a representative of divinity or was divinity itself. I mean that divinity would be present in his place of manifestation whenever his business placed him there, and his business placed him there when the act of worship before the image called him into residence. So that the image did act for and as the god whenever the worshiper addressed himself to the image. In that sense, the image was the god *for all working purposes.*

There were other substitutes for the gods. The king of Egypt was himself one of the gods and was the land's representative among the gods. Furthermore, he was the one official intermediary between the people and the gods, the one recognized priest of all the gods. Endowed with divinity, the pharaoh had the protean character of divinity; he could merge with his fellow-gods and could become any one of them. In part this was symbolic, the acting of a part in religious drama or the simile of praise. But the Egyptian did not distinguish between symbolism and participation; if he said that the king was Horus, he did not mean that the king was playing the part of Horus, he meant that the king *was* Horus, that the god was effectively present in the king's body during the particular activity in question.

How can the king be the god-king unless the god-king is present in him, so that the two become one? A single text magnifying the king equates him with a series of deities: "He is Sia," the god of perception; "he is Rē," the sun-god; "he is Khnum," the god who brings mankind into being on his potter's wheel; "he is Bastet," the goddess who protects; and "he is Sekhmet," the goddess who punishes.[3] Understanding, supreme rule, building-up of the populace, protection, and punishment were all attributes of the king; the king *was* each of them; each of these attributes was manifest in a god or goddess; the king *was* each of these gods or goddesses.

Carrying the principle of substitution one step further, if the king could represent a god, it is also true that the king could be represented by a man. The business of kingship was too detailed for absolute rule by a single individual, so that certain responsibilities must be deputized, even though state dogma said that the king did all. Similarly, state dogma might insist that the king was the sole priest for all the gods; but it was impossible for him to function every day in all the temples; that activity must also be deputized. Here we must admit that there is some difference of representation; the priest or official acted *for* the king, not *as* the king. It was deputizing rather than participating in the nature of the other being. This is an acknowledged difference, but even this difference is not absolute. Those who act in the place of another share somewhat in the personality of that other. Simply the physical grouping of the tombs of Old Kingdom courtiers around the pyramid of pharaoh shows that they wished to share in his divine glory by belonging to him and thus participating in him. Even here they belonged to some portion of the same spectrum and had an ultimate consubstantiality with him, which was partially derived and partially innate. Between god and man there was no point at which one could erect a boundary line and state that here substance changed from divine, superhuman, immortal, to mundane, human, mortal.

The fluidity of Egyptian concepts and the tendency to synthesize divergent elements have led some Egyptologists to believe

that the Egyptians were really monotheistic, that all gods were sub-
sumed into a single god. In a moment we shall present a text that
would seem to be a prime document for this thesis of essential
monotheism, but we wish to preface it by insisting that it is not a
matter of single god but of single nature of observed phenomena
in the universe, with the clear possibility of exchange and substitution. With relation to gods and men the Egyptians were monophysites: many men and many gods, but all ultimately of one nature.

The text that we mentioned presents an ancient Egyptian trinity:
the three gods who were supremely important at one period of history all taken up into a single divinity. The purpose was to enlarge
the god Amon by incorporating the other two gods into his being.
"All gods are three—Amon, Rē, and Ptah—and they have no second." Amon is the name of this single being, Rē is his head, and
Ptah is his body. "Only he is: Amon and Rē [and Ptah], together
three."[4] Three gods are one, and yet the Egyptian elsewhere insists on the separate identity of each of the three.

In another group of hymns which has been called monotheistic[5]
the god is addressed as a single personage of composite form,
Amon-Rē-Atum-Harakhte, that is, the several sun-, supreme-, and
national-gods rolled up into one. The text goes on to break this
being down into his several facets as Amon, Rē, Atum, Horus, and
Harakhte, and also to equate him with Khepri, Shū, the moon, and
the Nile. Whether this is monotheistic or not depends upon one's
definition. It may be hair-splitting, but we prefer to invoke the
principles of consubstantiality and free interchange of being and
claim that the Egyptians were monophysite instead of monotheistic. They recognized different beings but felt those beings to be
of a single essential substance, a rainbow, in which certain colors
were dominant under certain conditions and others dominant when
the conditions altered. A complete personality includes many different aspects of personality.

One element of consubstantiality lies in the fact that the Egyptian gods were very human, with human weaknesses and varying
moods. They could not remain on a high and consistent plane of in-
fallibility. And no god was single-mindedly devoted to a single
function. For example, the god Seth is well known as the enemy

of the "good" gods Osiris and Horus; therefore, Seth was the enemy of good; he was roughly like the devil. Yet throughout Egyptian history Seth appeared also as a good god, who functioned beneficently for the dead at times, who fought on behalf of the sun-god, and who acted positively for the enlargement of the Egyptian state. Horus, the good son throughout Egyptian history, once flew into a rage at his mother Isis and chopped off her head, so that the poor goddess was forced to take the form of a headless statue.[6]

The Egyptians apparently delighted in the humanness of their gods. A well-known story tells how Rē, the creator-god, repented that he had created mankind, which had devised evil against him. He decided to destroy them and sent Sekhmet, the "Powerful," against them. This goddess slew mankind, waded in their blood, and exulted in their destruction. Then Rē relented and regretted his desire to obliterate. Instead of ordering Sekhmet to stop the slaughter, he resorted to a stratagem. Seven thousand jars of red-colored beer were poured out in Sekhmet's path, so that she might believe that it was blood. She waded lustily into it, became drunken, and stopped her slaughtering.[7]

This childish tale, so different from the biblical story of the Flood because of its lack of moral motivation, is told here only to emphasize the frequent littleness of the Egyptian gods. They changed their minds, and they resorted to tricks to accomplish their ends. And yet—in a neighboring text—they may be portrayed as noble and consistent.

Another, more sophisticated story tells of a trial in the divine tribunal. A minor deity rose and shouted an insult at the supreme, presiding god; he cried: " 'Thy shrine is empty!' Then Rē-Harakhte was pained at this retort which had been made to him, and he lay down on his back, and his heart was very, very sore. Then the Ennead went out . . . . to their tents. And so the great god spent a day lying on his back in his arbor, alone, while his heart was very, very sore." In order to cure his sulks, the other gods sent the goddess of love to him, and she exhibited to him her charms. "Then the great god laughed at her; and so he arose and sat down (again) with the great Ennead," and the trial was resumed.[8] This is admittedly a lusty tale for entertainment, but its characterization of the gods accords with the picture given in more sober contexts.

If the gods were so human, it will not be surprising that humans could address them in brusque terms. Not infrequently there are texts in which the worshiper recalls the nature of his services to the gods and threatens those gods who fail to return service for service. One of the famous passages in Egyptian literature is called the "Cannibal Hymn," because the deceased expresses his intention of devouring those whom he meets in his path, human or divine. It was originally written for the deceased king but was later taken over by commoners. "The sky is overcast, the stars are be-clouded, ... the (very) bones of the earth-god tremble, ... when they see (this dead man) appear animated as a god who lives on his fathers and feeds on his mothers. . . . . (He) is the one who eats men and lives on gods. . . . . (He) is the one who eats their magic and devours their glory. The biggest of them are for his breakfast; their middle-sized are for his dinner; and the smallest of them are for his supper. Their old males and females (serve only) for his fuel."[9]

The effective continuation of that concept is that any human might become so magically potent that he could consume the greatest of the gods and, by consuming them, take their magic and their glory into his own being. That is the ultimate statement of consubstantiality from highest to lowest in the universe. It may sound childish, like the mighty imaginings of a small boy who dreams of becoming Superman and conquering the world. But the small boy is not yet grown up, and it is not beyond the range of his dreams for his future that he may be incredibly great some day. The same range of possibility was present for the Egyptian through the single substance which extended from him up into the vast unknown.

This statement which we are making about the single substance of the Egyptian universe is true of the earlier long period of Egyptian thinking, down to perhaps 1300 B.C. Involved in this concept of consubstantiality is the feeling that there is no ultimate difference between men and gods. It is necessary to make a reservation, however, about the later period of Egyptian history. As shall be seen in the next chapter, there came a time when a gulf developed between weak, little man, and powerful god. In that later period a difference was felt, and the two were no longer of the same substance. For the present, however, we do not wish to stress the later change but rather the earlier unity.

Indeed, the more one examines this hypothesis of consubstantiality, the more exceptions or qualifications one must admit. We gave one in the last chapter when we said that the Egyptians did not accept foreigners as being like themselves. We shall give another later in this chapter, when we point out a difference in administrative freedom between the king, who was a god, and his ministers, who were humans. It is a question whether one is talking about difference qualitatively (difference of substance) or quantitatively (variations of the same substance). We take it to be a quantitative difference of the same substance. In contrast to ourselves and to other peoples, the Egyptians took the universe as being of one continuous substance, without any definite line of demarcation between part and part.

To return, then, to the question about the disposition of the universe toward the Egyptian, whether friendly, hostile, or indifferent. Since there is but one substance reaching from man off into the unknowns, the world of the dead, the world of gods and spirits, the world of organic and inorganic nature, this means that the frame of reference must be human behavior itself. Are other men friendly, hostile, or indifferent to us? The answer must be that they are not exclusively any of these three dispositions but that interested beings are benevolent or malevolent, according to whether their interests are complementary or competitive, and uninterested beings are indifferent. It becomes a matter of the stated concern of the force in question, as well as the particular disposition of the force at a stated time. The sun gives life by warming; but it may destroy life by blasting, or it may destroy life by withdrawing itself and chilling. The Nile brings life, but an unusually low or an unusually high Nile may bring destruction and death.

The modern Egyptian feels himself to be surrounded by unseen personalized forces, the *ginn*, each of them concerned with some phenomenon: a child, a sheep, a house, a tree, running water, fire, etc. Some are friendly, some unfriendly; but most are static unless one offends them, when they become malevolent, or unless one invokes them to benevolence. The ancient Egyptian had a similar sense of a surrounding world of forces. A mother had to croon a protective song over her sleeping child: "Thou flowing thing that comes in darkness and enters furtively in, with her nose behind her and her face twisted around, who fails in that for which she came— hast thou come to kiss this child? I will not let thee kiss him! Hast thou come to strike dumb? I will not let thee strike dumbness into him! Hast thou come to injure him? I will not let thee injure him! Hast thou come to carry him away? I will not let thee carry him away from me! I have made his magical protection against thee out of clover . . . . onions . . . . honey. . . . ."[10] In an incantation against disease, the malevolent forces which may bring sickness include "every blessed male, every blessed female, every dead male, and every dead female," that is, the dead who have attained a state of eternal glory, as well as those who have died without certainty of immortality.[11]

However, despite this surrounding world of uncertain spiritual forces, the general rule was that certain beings had a stated function or activity, and that activity was either friendly or hostile. Thus the generally beneficent functions of the sun, the Nile, the north wind, Osiris, or Isis were established; just as the generally dangerous or hostile functions of the Apōphis-demon, Seth, or Sekhmet were established. These functions were general, and at times it might be necessary to protect an individual from the "good" Osiris or to intrust an individual to the helpful activity of the "bad" Seth, just as humans in this world have more than one side to their characters.

If this functional authority and responsibility are clear, then we must seek our answer to the functions of the state in those forces which had authority over and responsibility for the state. The speculative thought of the ancient Egyptians will provide no treatise on the philosophy of statecraft or the relation of government to the governed, but their speculative thought will play upon the powers, attributes, and interests of those gods who were primarily concerned with Egypt as a going concern. Ultimately our attention focuses on statements concerning the "good god" who was king of Egypt. We can best discover the functions of the state by determining the ideals laid down in scattered sources for the one individual responsible for government—the king.

THE KING

The Egyptian's love of symmetrical balance produced an ideal ruler who was nicely composed of graciousness and terror, because rule is nurture and rule is control. Again and again this balance appears in close juxtaposition in the texts. The king is "that beneficent god, the fear of whom is throughout the countries like (the fear of) Sekhmet in a year of plague."[12] Poems of praise emphasize the two aspects of his being with bewilderingly sudden shifts of emphasis: "Exulting is he, a smasher of foreheads, so that none can stand near him. . . . . He fights without end, he spares not, and there is nothing left over (from his destruction). He is a master of graciousness, rich in sweetness, and he conquers by love. His city loves him more than its own self and takes more joy in him than in its (own local) god."[13] Here, in two adjacent statements, it is claimed that the king conquers by lustful destruction and that he conquers by kindly love. We are again dealing with a personality of more than one side, a spectrum in which one color or another may be emphasized. But here speculative thought has its reasons in producing a balance of forces. Government must be gracious but terrible, just as the sun and the Nile are gracious but terrible in their effective power.

The starting-point of our consideration is the fact that the king of Egypt was a god and that he was a god for the purposes of the Egyptian state. This was not stated in a nice compact formulation which made the pharaoh the personification of the land of Egypt or even embodied rule as a personified principle. But the supreme god, Rē, intrusted the land to his son, the king. From the Old Kingdom on, an effective title for the Egyptian pharaoh was the "Son of Rē." In mythology the only son of Rē was the air-god Shū, but the pharaoh was made Son of Rē for the specific purpose of ruling Rē's chief concern, the land of Egypt. "As for Egypt, men say since (the time of) the gods, she is the only daughter of Rē, and it is his son that is upon the throne of Shū."[14] Implicit in this statement there was a pairing of god and goddess, Egypt as the only daughter of Rē and pharaoh as the Son of Rē, in those brother-sister terms which made up the couples of Egyptian deities. Just as the husband was urged by the books of wisdom to take kindly care of the wife, because "she is a field advantageous to her lord,"[15] so the king had ownership, authority, and responsibility over his land. It was his to control with power, but if he were wise, he would also nurture with care.

The Egyptian stated repeatedly that the king was the physical son who issued from the body of the sun-god Rē. To be sure, it was recognized that he had been born of a woman in this world. But the father who had begotten him was definitely a god. Rē himself had to insure the proper divine rule of the land of Egypt. Looking toward the future, he made earthly visits to produce rulers. A story about the origin of the Fifth Dynasty tells of the humble mother of the coming rulers. "She is the wife of an (ordinary) priest of Rē, Lord of Sakhebu, who is pregnant with three children of Rē, Lord of Sakhebu, and he (Rē) has said of them that they shall exercise this beneficent office (of king) in this entire land."[16]

Even the problem of the earthly father, in view of the fact that kings did exist and apparently did produce sons who became kings, was not insurmountable. For purposes of procreation the supreme god assumed the form of the living king and gave that seed which was to become the "Son of Rē." Hatshepsūt was clearly the daughter of Thutmōse I, but the account of that divine birth which permitted her to become pharaoh of Egypt makes it clear that there was a substitution here, and that the supreme god, Amon-Rē, was her effective father. The queen-mother was selected by the gods, and it was recommended that Amon visit her while the pharaoh was still in his youthful vigor. "[Amon took] his form [as] the majesty [of] this her husband, the King (Thutmōse I). . . . . Then he went to her immediately; then he had intercourse with her. . . . . The majesty of this god did all that he desired with her. The words which Amon, Lord of the Thrones of the Two Lands, spoke in her presence: 'Now Khenemet-Amon-Hatshepsūt is the name of this my daughter whom I have placed in thy body. . . . . She is to exercise this benefi[cent king]ship in this entire land.' "[17] No words could more explicitly state the divine purposes and divine methods. The pharaoh was produced by the supreme deity, masquerading as the ruling king, to be a god in order to rule the land.

In this solar theology the king of Egypt issued out of the body of the sun-god and, on death, returned to the body of his progenitor. Here is the statement of the death of a pharaoh: "Year 30, third month of the first season, day 9: the god entered his horizon. The King of Upper and Lower Egypt, Sehetepibrē, went up to heaven and was united with the sun-disk, so that the divine body was merged with him who made him."[18] This is the necessary completion of filial attachment to the supreme god: from conception through life to the final triumph over death, the king was the "Son of Rē." As we shall see, an alternative system of thought made the dead king Osiris, ruler of the realm of the dead.

The formal list of titles which denominated the king of Egypt breaks into three groups. We have already seen that he was called the son and successor of the sun-god; we shall shortly discuss his identification with the god Horus; we shall now consider him as incorporating the responsibilities for the two parts of Egypt.

Physically and culturally the land of Egypt breaks into the narrow trough of the Nile Valley and the spreading Delta. Upper Egypt has ties to the desert and to Africa; Lower Egypt faces out to the Mediterranean Sea and to Asia. From time immemorial these two regions have had a self-conscious separation. Lying so close together and yet apart from neighbors, they are aware of their differences. The old texts bring out this feeling of contrast. One who had impulsively left his office expressed his bewilderment over the forces that had led him to such unaccountable action: "I do not know what sundered me from my place; it was like a dream, as if a man of the Delta were (suddenly) to see himself in Elephantine."[19] Just as today, the dialects of these two regions varied enough to cause misunderstanding. An inept writer was chided with these words: "Thy narratives . . . . are confused when heard, and there is no interpreter who can unravel them; they are like the speech of a man of the Delta with a man of Elephantine."[20] These two regions were then disparate, and they were traditionally and continuingly competitive. Yet they were a unity in their isolation from the rest of the world, and they were a unity in their dependence upon the Nile. It was a function of government to make

Upper and Lower Egypt an effective single nation. This was done by incorporating authority and responsibility for both regions in a single figure, the god-king.

By his formal titles he was Lord of the Two Lands, that is, owner and master; he was King of Upper Egypt and King of Lower Egypt, the wearer of the double crown which symbolized the union of the two regions; and he was the "Two Ladies," that is, the incorporation of the two tutelary goddesses who represented the north and the south. A parallel title, the "Two Lords," expressed the dogma that the two competing gods of Lower and Upper Egypt, Horus and Seth, were also physically resident and reconciled within the person of the king. An important ritual activity of the king's coronation was the "Uniting of the Two Lands," a ceremony somehow in relation to the throne of a dual kingship.

Now this self-consciousness about two different parts of the land was expressed administratively in a duality of office and officers. There were two viziers, two treasurers, and often two capitals. There had to be a recognition of the separate needs of the two areas, a sort of states' rights in administration. But the two lands had no final rule except in the single person of the pharaoh, who partook of the divinity of each area in exactly balanced measure. This worked. In all stable periods of Egyptian history there was only one king of the united Two Lands. The god-king was a successful expression of national unity.

The third group of formal titles for the pharaoh makes him the incorporation of the god Horus, a falcon whose divine province was the heavens. As in the case of the other two types of titles, the "Son of Rē," and the embodiment of the deities of the Two Lands, the identification with Horus seems to have made the pharaoh the king of all Egypt. We are not precisely sure how this came to be. It is true that the myths indicate that Horus contested for and won the rule of his dead father, the god Osiris. Thus Horus came to be the living king who had succeeded the dead king, Osiris. Every living king was Horus, and every dead king Osiris. But we moderns would like to reconcile the idea of the kingly Horus as son and successor of Osiris and the idea of the "Son of Rē," as kingly successor of the sun-god. In consecutive lines of a single text the pharaoh is called the son of Osiris, who issued from the body of Isis, and it is stated that Rē begot his majesty.[21]

Perhaps again we should not seek to sunder ideas which were complementary and thus gave added strength to the throne. Probably we have concentration on two different aspects of the divinity of the pharaoh. The title "Son of Rē" emphasized the story of his physical birth as a god, whereas the title "Horus" emphasized his divine credentials to rule in the palace, as the god who had been awarded the kingship by the divine tribunal. At any rate, Horus ruled the entire land and not simply a part. All the titles taught that there was but one being who could hold sway over all Egypt by divine right.

The divine person of the pharaoh was too holy for direct approach. An ordinary mortal did not speak "to" the king; he spoke "in the presence of" the king. Various circumlocutions were employed to avoid direct reference to the king: "May thy majesty hear," instead of "mayest thou hear," and "one gave command," instead of "he gave command." One of these circumlocutions, *per-aa*, "the Great House," gave rise to our word "pharaoh," in somewhat the same way as we modernly say: "The White House today announced. . . . ."

It is not clear that this avoidance of verbal contact with awful majesty was paralleled by an avoidance of physical contact with the royal person. To be sure, there is a somewhat obscure tale about a courtier who was touched by the king's ceremonial staff, after which the king gave him firm assurances that he was to suffer no hurt thereby. The mere bumping with a stick is not enough to justify the magnification of the tale into something worth carving on a tomb wall. Arguably the blight of majesty was so terrible that it had to be exorcised by royal words.[22] Possibly we personally overvalue this text, as it has been pointed out to us that the king's assurances may be rather an apology than the exorcising of a blight. A royal apology might be a sufficient mark of attention to warrant recording in a tomb.

A similar uncertainty clouds the next example. A late story has a rather puzzling joke. The shadow of the sunshade of a foreign prince fell upon an Egyptian, and there was an ironic warning to the Egyptian to beware, for the shadow of the pharaoh of Egypt had touched him. This sounds as though an intimate part of the royal person like the shadow was too fraught with holiness for human approach.[23] If so, the body of the king will also have been dangerous for the ordinary mortal. But the pharaoh certainly had his personal attendants and body servants, and there must have been means of delivering them from the blight of majesty. The first principle is surely that of Diodorus (i. 70), that the royal servants were selected from the highest classes, close to the king in blood. The second principle will have been that the other gods had their personal attendants, who cared for their most intimate needs, and so the divine king could also have his priestly servants, authorized to act for his person and thus not to be blasted by contact with a god. It is significant that the same epithet, "pure of hands," was used for the priests who served the gods and for the personal attendants on the king.

As our evidence on the physical unapproachability of the pharaoh is weak, we wish to adduce a few additional points, none of which clinches the case. Certain individuals were granted close access to the king and exempt from any blight of holiness. This was probably implicit in such titles as "Sole Companion," "Privy Councilor of the House of the Morning," "He Who Is Beside the King" (literally, "under the head of the King"). Some favored individuals were graciously permitted to kiss the royal foot, instead of kissing the ground before the pharaoh (Urk. I, 41; 53; BAR, I, 260). The uraeus-serpent on the brow of the king was a fire-spitting sorceress, who protected the royal person from any approach of unauthorized persons. Whether these instances fall short of a dogma of unapproachability or not is an open question to us.

Just as the person of the king arguably had a dangerously high voltage, so also his lofty responsibilities involved knowledge and abilities beyond the ken of ordinary man. As one of his chief ministers said: "Now his majesty knows what takes place. There is nothing at all which he does not know. He is (the god of wisdom) Thoth in everything: there is no subject which he has not comprehended."[24] Or his groveling courtiers told him: "Thou art like Rē in all that thou doest. What thy heart desires flows forth. If thou desirest a plan in the night, at dawn it comes into being quickly.

We have seen a multitude of thy marvels since thou didst appear as King of the Two Lands. We cannot hear, nor can our eyes see (how it happens); yet (things) come into being everywhere."[25] This was superhuman; it was the closely guarded secret of kingship. At a time when the state was overthrown and rule crumbled into anarchy, it was thought to be the release of this "secret" that permitted the impious fragmentation of divine rule: "Behold, it has come to (a point where) the land is stripped of the kingship by a few irresponsible people. . . . . Behold, the secret of the land, whose limits are unknown, is divulged, so that the (royal) residence is overthrown in an hour. . . . . The secrets of the kings of Upper and Lower Egypt have been divulged."[26]

We cold modern analysts view the doctrines of the divinity, the blighting majesty, and the mystery of the Egyptian king as mere propaganda devices to bolster the person of a man who was solely responsible for the state. But they cannot be brushed aside for that reason. They had the reality of long-continuing success. They were as real in ancient Egypt as in Solomon's Temple at Jerusalem —or as in modern Japan.

He was a lonely being, this god-king of Egypt. All by himself he stood between humans and gods. Texts and scenes emphasize his solitary responsibility. The temple scenes show him as the only priest in ceremonies before the gods. A hymn to a god states: "There is no one else that knows thee except thy son, (the king), whom thou causest to understand thy plans and thy power."[27] It was the king who built temples and cities, who won battles, who made laws, who collected taxes, or who provided the bounty for the tombs of his nobles. The fact that the pharaoh might not have heard about a battle until it was reported to the royal court was immaterial; the literary and pictorial myth of Egypt's might demanded that he be shown as defeating the enemy single-handed. An Egyptian in a provincial town might make contractual provision for the delivery of goods to his tomb after death; the reigning pharaoh need have nothing to do with this transaction; in the age-long framework of mortuary activity the goods would come as an "offering which the king gives," a mark of royal favor.

Only the national gods might intervene in the affairs of the state: the sun-god might ask the king to clear away the sand from the Sphinx, or Amon might commission the king to undertake a campaign against the Libyans. Otherwise pharaoh was the state, because he was himself a national god, specifically charged to carry out the functions of the state.

Because we can penetrate the trappings of divinity and discern the human heart of the pharaoh, we can sympathize with the loneliness of his administration. The other gods might temporarily escape to realms outside this world. He alone was a god who had to live out his solitary life surrounded by humans. Those humans through daily intimacy might dare to encroach upon his omniscience and omnipotence. One aged king has left a weary warning to his son and successor: "Thou that hast appeared as a god, listen to what I have to say to thee, so that thou mayest be king over the land and ruler over the river banks, so that thou mayest achieve an overabundance of good. Hold thyself together against those subordinate (to thee), lest that should happen to whose terrors no thought has been given. Do not approach them in thy loneliness. Fill not thy heart with a brother, know not a friend, nor create for thyself intimates—that has no (happy) outcome. . . . . I gave to the poor and brought up the orphan . . . . (but) it was he who ate my food that raised up troops (against me) . . . . and they who were clothed in my fine linen looked upon me as (mere) dried weeds."[28] The penalty of being a god was the removal of divinity from the world of humanity. The gods had sent him forth to tend mankind, but he was not of mankind.

This is perhaps the most fitting picture of the good Egyptian ruler, that he was the herdsman for his people. The functions of the state were to own, control, drive, discipline, and defend; they were also to cherish, nurture, shelter, and enlarge the population. The god-sent controller of the Egyptian people was the herdsman who kept them in green pastures, fought to secure fresh pastures for them, drove off the voracious beasts who attacked them, belabored the cattle who strayed out of line, and helped along the weaklings.

The Egyptian texts use the same picture. One of the pharaohs stated why the god had made him ruler: "He made me the herdsman of this land, for he discerned that I would keep it in order for him; he intrusted to me that which he protected."[29] In a time of distress, men looked toward the ideal king of the future: "He is the herdsman of every one, without evil in his heart. His herd may be cut down (in numbers), but he will spend the day in caring for them."[30] Elsewhere the king is called "the goodly herdsman, watchful for all mankind whom their maker has placed under his supervision."[31] The sun-god "appointed him to be shepherd of this land, to keep alive the people and the folk, not sleeping by night as well as by day in seeking out every beneficial act, in looking for possibilities of usefulness."[32] The antiquity of this concept of the king is visible in the fact that a shepherd's crook is one of the earliest insignia of the pharaoh and is the origin of one of the words meaning "to rule."

The concept of the herdsman has its negative pole in the implication that men are simply cattle, property on a lower stage of existence. This attitude is never given in a single statement, because the view that the pharaoh was the Lord, or Possessor, of the Two Lands was taken for granted, and the texts naturally concentrated attention on the proper care of property rather than on the fact of property itself. For example, one long story deals with an injustice done to a peasant and his protests that those who administer justice have a responsibility to take a constructive rather than a passive attitude toward their clients. It was necessary to reject certain customary expressions of indifference to the fortunes of ordinary men. For example, a proverb, "The poor man's name is pronounced (only) for his master's sake," is cited as an expression of nonjustice against which the peasant is struggling.[33] A magistrate was urged by other officials not to intervene on behalf of the peasant, because the latter had gone over the head of his immediate master. Do not disturb the ordinary disciplinary rights of a master; "behold, it is what they (normally) do to peasants of theirs who go to others instead of to them"; the operation of justice should not interfere with the control of property.[34] Characteristically this text has an ultimate triumph of justice, because the Egyptians always rejected the narrow belief that the owner has no responsibility to maintain his property. At the positive pole, the herdsman's duty was to nurture and build up his herds.

The herdsman is primarily the pastor, the "feeder," and a first responsibility of the state was to see that the people were fed. Thus the king of Egypt was the god who brought fertility to

Egypt, produced the life-giving waters, and presented the gods with the sheaf of grain which symbolized abundant food. Indeed, an essential function of his kingship was that of a medicine man, whose magic insured good crops. In one of the ceremonials of kingship, the pharaoh encircled a field four times as a rite of conferring fertility upon the land.[35] He controlled the water which made Egypt and made her fertile. "The Nile is at his service, and he opens its cavern to give life to Egypt."[36] As his courtiers told him: "If thou thyself shouldst say to thy father, the Nile, the father of the gods: 'Let water flow forth upon the mountains!' he will act according to all that thou hast said."[37]

As the pharaoh controlled the water of Egypt, the Nile, so also he was a rainmaker for the foreign countries. One text makes the king of the Hittites say that his land must make overtures to pharaoh, for "if the god accepts not its offering, it sees not the waters of heaven, since it is in the power of" the king of Egypt.[38] Pharaoh himself was a little more modest; he did not pose as the rainmaker for lands abroad but as the intermediary to the gods for water. Thinking of a diplomatic deputation which he had sent to Syria and Anatolia, "his majesty took counsel with his own heart: 'How will it go with those whom I have sent out, who are going on a mission to Djahi in these days of rain and snow which come in winter?' Then he made an offering to his father, (the god) Seth; then he came praying and said: 'Heaven is in thy hands, and earth is under thy feet. . . . . [Mayest] thou [delay] to make the rain and the north wind and the snow until the marvels reach me which thou hast assigned to me!' . . . . Then his father Seth heard every word, and the heavens were peaceful, and summer days came for [him]."[39]

All nature that had reference to the prosperity of Egypt was under the sway of the pharaoh. He was the "lord of the sweet breeze," the cooling wind from the Mediterranean which made Egypt habitable.[40] Nay, even more, as the master-magician he controlled the moon and the stars, so that the months, days, and hours came with regular cadence. A hymn of joy at the accession of one of the kings runs: "Be gay of heart, the entire land, for the goodly times have come! A lord has been given to all lands! . . . . The waters stand and are not dried up, and the Nile carries a high (flood). (Now) the days are long, the nights have hours, and the moons come normally. The gods are at rest and happy of heart, and people live (in) laughter and wonder!"[41] By doctrine and by continuing ritual, pharaoh was the god who gave to Egypt its normal times and seasons, who brought the abundant waters, and who gave the fertile crops.

In actual practice there was administrative justification for the dogma of treating pharaoh as a water- and field-god. It seems that the central government also maintained the national astronomical and calendrical offices, although we lack full proof here. As one document in the case we cite a black ebony bar in the collections of the Oriental Institute museum at the University of Chicago. This is part of an astronomical apparatus for charting the movements of the stars, and it was inscribed with the name of Tūtankhamon. Whether this was his royal hobby, or whether the observation of the heavenly bodies was a function of kingship, we cannot be sure. We can say that the dogma that the pharaoh was responsible for food, water, and seasons was carried out by the function of bureaus of the royal government.

Diodorus paints a dreadful picture of the king of Egypt as the slave of regulations which controlled his every hour and every act. "The hours of both the day and night were laid out according to a plan, and at the specified hours it was absolutely required of the king that he should do what the laws stipulated and not what he thought best" (i. 70–71). Diodorus goes on to state that these regulations covered not only the king's administrative actions but also his own freedom to take a walk, bathe, or even sleep with his wife. He was allowed no personal initiative in his governmental functions but was required to act only in conformance with the established laws. Diodorus insists that the last of the pharaohs were quite happy in this tightly laced straitjacket of prescription because they believed that men who followed their natural emotions fell into error, whereas the kings, in depending rigidly on the law, were personally freed from responsibility for wrongdoing.

Diodorus' hollow shell of a king is paralleled by the empty picture which Herodotus (ii. 37) gives of Egyptian religion at his time, when he says that the Egyptians were more religious than any other nation—the word used is *theosebēs*, "god-fearing." It turns out that Herodotus means that they were slavishly devoted to ritual, most scrupulous about ceremonial cleanliness and the prescribed forms, but without the slightest indication of spirituality or of a working ethics.

In the next chapter we wish to draw a distinction between an earlier and a later period of ancient Egyptian history. In the earlier period the spirit was broadly one of conformance to precept, but the proof was laid upon the individual to show himself worthy by his own actions and his own freedom of decision within general law. In the later period the spirit was solely one of conformance to precept, with the individual charged to exhibit patience and humility in following that which the gods had laid down. It is our belief that Diodorus and Herodotus were both relating a practice and a spirit which were not normal to the Egypt discussed in these chapters. The atmosphere of their times was one of withdrawal into long-hallowed practice; the earlier atmosphere was one of free play of individual initiative within the general framework of human law and what we have called the "divine order."

The earlier kings of Egypt, of the period when that culture was developing as a native growth, were encouraged to express individuality as a part of the divine and worldly order to which they belonged. This earlier scene emphasized personal justice rather than impersonal law. We shall take up the concept of justice in the next chapter, which is devoted to an examination of "The Values of Life"; for the present the reader must accept our word that Egyptian *maʿat* means "justice," one of the essential attributes of the Egyptian state, and that this justice does not appear to have been codified in statutes and precedents but was expressed in right-dealing in relation to persons and situations. The ruler who dispensed justice was urged to dispense it in relation to need, indeed, to give more than was due. The state thus did have a responsibility to act with initiative to meet the needs of the nation.

We shall not defend this thesis that rule was personal and flexible—paternalistic, if you please—except to throw out one or two examples of protest against impersonal nonjustice. That peasant whom we have mentioned as struggling against injustice did not humbly submit to discipline from a magistrate. Instead he cried out bitterly: "So then the son of Meru goes on erring!" and went on with a series of bitter charges against the lack of ruling principle in the high official: that he was like a town without a mayor or a ship without a skipper.[42] Similarly, Ramses II, when abandoned in battle, turned angrily against the imperial god Amon and cried out: "What is the matter with thee, my father Amon! Has a father ever forgotten his son? Have I ever done anything apart from thee?" and continued to recite his benefits to the god as deserving of better return.[43] There is here no resignation to destiny or to the inscrutable plans of the gods; there is here an indignant sense that personal worth must be rewarded. It would be easy to multiply examples from the earlier period of Egyptian history to show that rulers did not operate in an impersonal mechanism of law and custom but were free-acting individuals.

To be sure, there was a prescribed pattern for the ideal king and there were hallowed precedents; let us examine some of the prescriptions laid down for the good ruler. He turns out to be a composition of love and terror, which the Egyptians took to be complementary colors in the same spectrum. Good rule was paternalistic, and there was a devotion to the principle of disciplinary control. That is not as fantastic as it may seem to a generation given over to a progressive education. The Egyptian word "to teach" is also the word "to punish," like our word "discipline," and it was apparently felt that "whom the Lord loveth he chasteneth." The components of good rule were god-given authority and godlike magnanimity.

In the preceding chapter we examined the text of the Memphite Theology, in which the continuing creative principles were the heart which conceived thought and the tongue which produced command. In that connection we mentioned a pair of related attributes of the sun-god, which were themselves personified as deities, Hū, "authoritative utterance," or the commanding speech which brings a situation into being, and Sia, "perception," the cognitive reception of an object, idea, or situation. These are godlike qualities, the perception of something in integrated and constructive terms and the consequent authoritative utterance which creates something new.

These two qualities were not confined to the sun-god; they were also attributes of the king. To the pharaoh it was said: "Authoritative utterance is indeed that which is in thy mouth, and perception [is that which] is in [thy heart]."[44] Two other texts may be cited as combining these two qualities of discernment and command as essential kingly characteristics,[45] but we are more interested in the fact that some texts added a third member to the combination which a ruler needed. In the two passages, "authoritative utterance, perception, and justice are with thee"[46] and "authoritative utterance is in thy mouth, perception is in thy heart, and thy tongue is the shrine of justice,"[47] the word *ma͑at*, "justice" or "rightdealing" or "truth," is added as the moral control which must accompany intelligence and authority.

Justice was the quality which accompanied a good ruler to the throne. In a time of national disorder, it was prophesied that a king would arise to unite the Two Lands, "and justice will come into its place, and unrighteousness will be driven out."[48] A poet rejoicing at the accession of a new king cried out: "Justice has banished deceit!"[49] a consummation of proper times, as is indicated by the accompanying words: "and normalcy has come down (again) into its place."[50] Daily the king offered up justice to the god, symbolically presenting the little hieroglyph of the goddess Ma͑at, "Truth" or "Justice." By this fact of daily ritual offering, justice did tend to become a mere form, which might be delivered through literal conformance to law or ritual.

But there was also a constant insistence that justice is something more positive than mere neutral conformance, that it lies in doing more than is required. The longest discourse on justice referred to divine law in equating justice and goodness: "But justice (lasts) forever and goes down into the necropolis with him who renders it. When he is buried and joined to the earth, his name is not wiped out on earth, but he is remembered for goodness. That is a principle of the divine order."[51] The writer related justice to a golden rule of doing unto others what might be expected from them. "Do to the doer in order to cause him to do (for thee). That is thanking him for what he may do; that is parrying something before it is shot."[52] Carrying the thought even further, the writer rejected injustice as lying in mere minimal performance of duty, like the ferryman who insisted upon payment before conveying passengers across the stream. Addressing the indifferent magistrate, he said: "Behold, thou art a ferryman who carries over (only) the one who has a fare, a straight-dealer whose straight-dealing is clipped short."[53] Such impersonal rule, lacking in paternal benevolence, was really the absence of rule: "Behold, thou art a town without its mayor, ... like a ship which has no captain, a company without its leader."[54] Insistently through the texts ran the obligation of the ruler to render on the basis of need and not on the basis of a *quid pro quo* trade. Intelligent perception of situations, the ability to command with authority, and straightforward justice were three main attributes of rule, and proper justice involved the quality of mercy.

Perhaps we may use a single text to summarize the combination of benevolence and force which characterized good rule as personified in the king. It is the instruction which a high official left for his children.[55] "Adore ye within your bodies King Nemaatrē, living forever, and associate his majesty with your hearts. He is perception which is in your hearts, for his eyes search out every body. He is Rē, by whose beams one sees; he is one who makes the Two Lands brighter than (does) the sun-disk. He is one who makes the land greener than (does) a high Nile. (Thus) he has filled the Two Lands with strength and life. Nostrils are chilled if he inclines toward rage, so that he is peaceful in order that the air may be breathed. He gives food to those who follow him and supplies provisions to him who treads his path. The king is the *ka*, and his mouth is abundance. That means that he brings into being him who is to be."

The equation of the king with the *ka* as a constructing and provisioning force deserves a brief comment. The *ka* was that detached part of the personality which planned and acted for the rest of the person. Pictorially the *ka* was shown in the arms extended for support and protection. It was born with the individual as an identical twin, accompanied him through life as the sustaining, constructing force, and preceded him in death to effect his successful existence in the next world. It is hard to supply a succinct translation for this concept, although we like the term "vital force," which has been used by some. Elsewhere the king is again called: "The goodly *ka* that makes the Two Lands festive and meets the needs of the entire land."[56] The ruler was thus seen as the constructive vital force of Egypt, creating and sustaining.

Resuming our text: "He is (the fashioning god) Khnum for all bodies, the begetter who brings people into being. He is (the kindly goddess) Bastet, who protects the Two Lands; (but) he who adores him will escape his arm. He is (the punishing goddess) Sekhmet against him who transgresses his command; (but) he is mild toward him who has troubles." In those last two equations we find the characteristic balance of protection and force, punishment and magnanimity. The text then concludes with the injunction that loyalty to the king means life and success, disloyalty means obliteration. "Fight for his name; be pure for his life; and ye shall be free from (any) trace of sin. He whom the king has loved will be a revered (spirit), but there is no tomb for him who rebels against his majesty: his corpse shall be cast into the water. If ye do these things, your bodies shall be sound. (So) shall ye find it forever."

As there was a constant urging of the ruler toward the positive pole of justice, so there was always an urging him away from the negative pole of the arbitrary use of authority. The punishment of infractions of rule was certainly necessary, but it was also necessary to temper the exercise of force against excess. "Beware lest thou punish wrongfully. Do not slaughter: that is not to thy advantage; but thou shouldst punish with beatings and with arrests. Thereby this land shall be (well) founded." The one crime deserving death is treason against the state. "The exception is the rebel, when his schemes are discovered, for the god knows the treacherous of heart, and the god strikes down his sins in blood."[57]

THE KING'S OFFICIALS

This statement has been devoted to the ideals of good rule as personified in the king. Only through protest has it appeared that there was a practical situation in which the king had to delegate authority and government to others, and in which the growth of the state led to a venal and job-holding bureaucracy. In part, we could ignore that, as this chapter is devoted to the functions of the state as formulated in the speculation of men, and those functions were summed up in the ideals laid down for the good ruler. But it would be unfair to leave the impression that the Egyptians were so devoted to principle that they carried it successfully into practice. There was a constant fragmentation of rule, breaking it down into the subordinate functions and functionaries, until the minor bureaucrats were far removed from the god-king in whom were embodied the good principles of government.

In a country where offices multiply beyond the limit of personal accountability, the goal becomes office-holding as a sinecure with potentially high rewards. We possess many documents from ancient Egypt urging the young man to become a scribe or government clerk because it is a respectable, clean, and easy job. "Put writing in thy heart, so that thou mayest protect thine own person from any (kind of) labor and be a respected official."[58] Other lines of activity were burdensome; "the scribe, however, he is the one who directs the work of everybody (else). He pays out taxes by writing, so that he has no (real) obligations."[59]

This implicit contempt for responsibility went along with the feeling that the job should provide left-handed resources. We are given a moving description of the poor man thrust into the law courts without a sponsor; the court squeezes him, and he hears the cry: "Silver and gold for the clerks of the court! Clothes for the attendants!"[60] In that situation he might well burst out: "Seizers! robbers! plunderers! officials!—and yet appointed to punish evil! Officialdom is the refuge of the arrogant—and yet appointed to punish falsehood!"[61] Under this weight of cynical and corrupt officials, the ordinary citizen groaned: "The land is diminished, but its rulers are increased. (The land is) bare, but its taxes are heavy. The grain is little, but the grain measure is large and measured (by the tax officials) to overflowing."[62]

Of course, there are exaggerations on both sides, the picture of the ideal rule of justice was never one of attainment, and the corruption of the ruling class differed from age to age and from individual to individual. Egypt was never wholly noble or wholly corrupt. The definition of justice and the conflict between a moral justice and the arbitrary exercise of authority were perennial issues in the land.

It is often difficult for us to be sure whether protests against corruption were based on high moral grounds or arose out of politics, the attack of the outs against the ins. For example, an Egyptian official denounced the Twentieth Dynasty tomb robberies, in which high administrators surely played a lucrative part. Was the protesting official activated by sincere indignation against the desecration of holy property and the cynical participation of his colleagues? Or was he one who had not got his "cut" and was trying "to put the squeeze on the gang"?[63] Was the lofty revolution of Akhnaton against the all-embracing control of the old imperial gods—a revolution which used the slogan of *ma^cat*, "justice"—a moral protest against the abuse of power or simply a political move to secure power for a new party? We cannot give final answers to these questions; the situation will never permit a simple arbitrary analysis; and our answers may arise out of personal prejudices. I, for example, am incurably romantic and charitable; whether politics played a part or not, I believe that men were swayed by rightful wrath against abuses. The divine order, which made man one with the gods, demanded that humans have something of the divine in them. And justice was the food upon which the gods lived.

Since the king was the state by official doctrine, and since he had to delegate his authority and responsibility to others, it will be instructive to examine the words in which he deputized rule to his chief officer, the vizier. These words were a formulation of the principles of rule, with one minor qualification. Delegated authority lays a greater emphasis on the how of rule rather than the why. It will operate more in an atmosphere of law and precedent than in an atmosphere of unconstrained and topical justice. To the magistrate law and justice may be the same.

Nevertheless, the vizier was sufficiently high placed to use his own discretion at times, and there is evidence that the best of viziers would play by ear rather than note. At least, that is our interpretation of ruling the land "with his fingers." The text in question is a hymn to the god Amon-Rē as the magistrate to whom the poor and helpless may turn. "Amon-Rē . . . . thou vizier of the poor man! He does not accept an unrighteous reward; he does not speak (only) to him who can bring witnesses; he does not give attention (only) to him who makes promises. (No), Amon judges the land with his fingers; his words belong to the heart. He separates the unjust and consigns him to the fiery place, but the righteous to the west."[64] The divine pattern for the official operated in terms of justice and need rather than law and property.

When the king was installing the vizier in office, he had certain general charges to make about the spirit of rule, as distinct from the practices of administration.

"Look thou to this office of vizier; be vigilant concerning [all] that is done in it. Behold, it is the supporting (post) of the entire land. Now, with regard to the vizierate, behold, it is by no means sweet—nay, it is bitter. . . . . Behold, it does not mean giving his attention (only) to officials and councilors, nor (yet) making [dependents] of everybody. . . . . Therefore, see to it for thyself that all [things] are done according to that which conforms to the law and that all things are done according to the precedent therefor in [setting every man in] his just deserts." The reason given for conformance to law and precedent is that a public official cannot escape public knowledge of his actions. "Behold, as for the official who is in public view, the (very) waters and winds make report of all that he does; so, behold, his deeds cannot be unknown. . . . . Now the officials' place of refuge lies in acting in conformance with the regulations, that is, in doing that [concerning] which a commitment has been made [to] the petitioner. . . . ."[65]

Thus far there has been little moral motivation in the instructions. The vizier is in public view, and the "bitterness" of his office lies in the rigid application of law. What follows shows the same austerity, although the emphasis shifts to unmoved equity in administering law. "The abomination of the god is an exhibition of partiality. This is the instruction, and thus shalt thou act: 'Thou shalt look upon him whom thou knowest like him whom thou knowest not, upon him who has access to [thy person] like him who is far [from thy household].' . . . . Do not be severe with a man wrongfully; thou shouldst be severe (only) over that which merits severity. Inspire fear of thyself, so that men fear thee, (for) the official who is feared is a (real) official." That sounds harsh, and it therefore must be mitigated by words of caution. "Behold [the respect for an official (comes from the fact) that he dispenses] justice. Behold, if a man inspires the fear of himself a million times, there is something wrong with him in the opinion of the people, and they do not say of him: '[There is] a man!' . . . . Behold, (thus) thou shouldst attach to thy carrying-out of this office thy carrying-out of justice."[66]

These are the terms of good government as expressed by the king to his first official. They are somewhat formal; justice lies in the impartial administration of law rather than the redress of human injustice. The words of the vizier himself in commenting on his activities mitigate this impression only slightly: "When I judged a petitioner, I showed no partiality, I did not incline my brow because of a reward, ... but I rescued the timid man from the arrogant."[67] A trace of mercy does appear here, but there is no insistence on anything except probity and evenhandedness. Perhaps the answer is that justice outside the law could not be delegated by one man to another, but each man must discover for himself where he might make exceptions to law in order to achieve justice. Perhaps the answer is that perception, authoritative utterance, and justice were godly characteristics, which were retained by the godly pharaoh. At any rate, it was safer for a human deputy to find his "place of refuge" in "conformance with the regulations." On the other hand, full discretion to operate within or without the legal statutes could be conceded to the divine pharaoh, who was himself "the lord of destiny and he who creates fortune."[68] Such a one, in the unimpeded exercise of intelligence, command, and justice, could inspire those twin products of good government: love and fear.

In this chapter we have seen that the universe was of a single substance and that the king was the point of contact between men and gods as the divine ruler vested with concern for the state. We have seen that his responsibility as herdsman for his people implied a balance of force and tender care. We have seen that the king was supposed to exercise a creative intelligence, an ability to issue proper commands, and a justice which was something more than law. His officials were more constrained to law and precedent, but the king's divine qualities permitted him a discretion in the effecting of proper rule.

Involved in all this discussion there are unanswered questions dealing with the moral purposes of the state, outside of the mere aspect of the state as property. Such problems involve the purposes of individual or group life and moral distinctions between right and wrong. Now we shall wrestle with some of those questions.

NOTES

1. Urk. IV, 614–18.
2. Memphite Theology, 60–61.
3. Sehetepibrē.
4. Leyden Amon Hymn, 4:21–26.
5. Beatty IV, Recto.
6. Beatty I, 9:7–10.
7. Destruction, 1–24.
8. Beatty I, 3:10—4:3.
9. Pyr. 393–404.
10. Mutter und Kind, 1:9—2:6.
11. Smith, 19:6.
12. Sinuhe, B44–45.
13. Ibid., 55–67.
14. Israel, 12–13.
15. Ptahhotep 330.
16. Westcar, 9:9–11.
17. Urk. IV, 219–21.
18. Sinuhe, R5; cf. Urk. IV, 896.
19. Sinuhe, B224–26.
20. Anast. I, 28:5–6.
21. Nauri, 3–4.
22. Urk. I, 232.
23. Wenamon, 2:45–47.
24. Urk. IV, 1074.
25. Kubban, 13–14.
26. Admon., 7:2–6.
27. Aton Hymn, 12.
28. Amenemhet, 1:2–6.
29. Berlin Leather Roll, 1:6.
30. Admon., 12:1.
31. Dümichen, Hist. Inschr., II, 39:25.
32. Cairo 34501.
33. Peasant, B18–20.
34. Peasant, B42–46.
35. Analecta orientalia, 17:4 ff.
36. Egyptian Religion, 1933, p. 39.
37. Kubban, 21–22.
38. Anast. II, 2:4.
39. Marriage, 36–38.

40. *Egyptian Religion*, 1933, p. 41.
41. Sall. I, 8:7—9:1.
42. Peasant, B1, 188 ff.
43. Kadesh Poem, 26.
44. Petrie, *Koptos*, xii, 3:4.
45. Pyr. 300, 307.
46. Admon., 12:12.
47. Kubban, 18.
48. Neferrohu, 68–69.
49. Sall. I, 8:9–10.
50. *Ibid.*, 8:8.
51. Peasant, B307–11.
52. *Ibid.*, B109–11.
53. *Ibid.*, B171–73.
54. *Ibid.*, B189–92.
55. Sehetepibrē.
56. *Amarna*, III, 29.
57. Merikarē, 48–50.
58. Lansing, 9:3.
59. Sall. I, 6:8–9.
60. Anast. II, 8:5–7.
61. Peasant, B296–98.
62. Neferrohu, 50–51.
63. Cf. *JEA*, 22:186.
64. Bologna 1094, 2:3–7.
65. Urk. IV, 1087–89.
66. *Ibid.*, 1090–92.
67. *Ibid.*, 1082.
68. Inscr. dédic., 36.

CHAPTER IV
EGYPT: THE VALUES OF LIFE

THE NATURE OF THIS ANALYSIS

IN THE two preceding chapters few would quarrel with the generalizations that the ancient Egyptian saw his wider universe in terms of his own immediate environment and experience and that the state had been intrusted to the divine pharaoh so that he might control and nurture it as a herdsman tends his cattle. Now, however, we are to search for the values which the ancient Egyptian attached to life. If our thesis so far is valid, that man was an essential part of a consubstantial universe and that man therefore applied the norm of the human to the nonhuman, we shall need to know what norm he applied to himself. Here we come to the real problem of speculative thought: What am I here for? Here it is not possible to compound out one nice generalization to cover two thousand years of history. And such generalizations as may be made will not find as wide an acceptance among other scholars, because we inevitably use our own personal philosophies to evaluate the philosophies of others. Our conclusions may be fairly accurate on the nature of the evidence, but on the value of the evidence we shall hang our personal estimates.

What were the purposes of life? In order to secure a visible picture of the possible answers, we might make a visit to Egypt and go down into two structures which should be comparable.[1] Each is the tomb of an Egyptian vizier, that highest official of the land, the first deputy under the king. Near the Step Pyramid at Saqqara we enter the tomb of a vizier of the Old Kingdom, a man who lived about 2400 B.C. The rooms are crammed and packed with vigorous scenes of life and the lust for more life. The vizier is shown spearing fish, while his servants bring a bellowing hippopotamus to bay. The vizier supervises the roping and butchering of cattle, the plowing and harvesting of the fields, the carpenters and metal-workers in their shops, and the building of boats for his funeral services.

93

He presides over the vigorous punishment of tax delinquents, and he watches the games of children. Even when he is in repose, as when he listens to his wife playing the harp, he gives the impression of high potential, of being ready to spring into action. Nonspiritual and active life is the full account of this tomb. This is his monument for eternity; this is how he wants to be remembered; this is the good life which he wishes to extend into eternity.

We leave this tomb and walk a few hundred yards to the tomb of a vizier of the Late Period, a man who lived about 600 B.C. Eighteen hundred years have brought a quietude, a pious calm. Here we see no exuberant noble, no bellowing hippopotamus, no tumbling children. The walls are covered with ritual and magical texts. There are a few posed and dull pictures of the vizier frozen in hieratic attitude before the god of the dead. There are a few vignettes to illustrate the texts with scenes of the underworld and the genii who live there. The life of this world is completely lacking; the funeral services and the world of the dead are the only concerns of this man. His monument for eternity concentrates on the next world instead of this life. His good consists in magic, ritual, and the favor of his god.

That is our problem. At one pole there is an emphasis on life, on action, and on the material world; at the other pole, an emphasis on death, on repose, and on religion. Clearly our discussion must bridge the gap and must be historical in order to give the change from one stage to the other. We shall see two major periods of Egyptian thought, the aggressive and optimistic earlier times and the submissive and hopeful later times, with a long period of transition between. It was like a hurricane, with strong winds blowing to the east, then a dead center of uncertain balance, and then the winds blowing just as strongly to the west. The earlier winds to the east were radical and individualistic; the later winds to the west were conservative and communal. But, as we said before, it depends upon who analyzes the trends; another man has seen the earlier trend as a compliance to group forms and the later as an interest in personal well-being. Inevitably the discussion involves the religious, political, and social prejudices of the analyst.

THE OLD AND MIDDLE KINGDOMS

The emergence of Egypt into the light of history seems to be a very sudden phenomenon, symbolized in the abrupt appearance of stone architecture of highest technical perfection. Dr. Breasted once dramatized this brilliant flowering in these words:

> In the Cairo Museum you may stand in the presence of the massive granite sarcophagus which once contained the body of Khufu-onekh, the architect who built the Great Pyramid of Gizeh. . . . . Let us in imagination follow this early architect to the desert plateau behind the village of Gizeh. It was then bare desert surface, dotted only with the ruins of a few small tombs of remote ancestors. The oldest stone masonry construction at that time had been erected by Khufu-onekh's great-grandfather. Only three generations of architects in stone preceded him. . . . . There probably were not many stone masons, nor many men who understood the technique of building in stone as Khufu-onekh took his first walk on the bare Gizeh Plateau, and staked out the ground plan of the Great Pyramid. Conceive, then, the dauntless courage of the man who told his surveyors to lay out the square base 755 feet on each side! . . . . [He knew that it would] take nearly two and a half million blocks each weighing two and one-half tons to cover this square of thirteen acres with a mountain of masonry 481 feet high. . . . . The Great Pyramid of Gizeh is thus a document in the history of the human mind. It clearly discloses man's sense of sovereign power in his triumph over material forces. For himself and for his sovereign the pharaoh's engineer was achieving the conquest of immortality by sheer command of material forces.[2]

This vivid picture illustrates the sudden surge of vigor and the zest for action and accomplishment which characterized the Old Kingdom of Egypt. From the same general period come some of Egypt's highest intellectual achievements, such as that philosophy of the Memphite Theology which we discussed previously and the scientific attitude expressed in the Edwin Smith Surgical Papyrus. This raises questions about the antecedents of these daring and forceful people. They hardly seem visible in the modest products of predynastic Egypt. And yet we cannot see that this is a reason for assuming that these achievements must therefore have been introduced by conquering invaders. That simply takes an unknown and thrusts it out into unknown realms. Sometimes the spirit of man soars in dizzy flight beyond the plodding pace which cultural evolution would see as normal, and there is good reason to believe that this whole surge of power was quite local, enjoying only the stimulus of similar wonderful developments known from Mesopotamia. The reasons for this sudden spurt of power are not clear.

It was a revolution, the abrupt flowering of a slow development under the influence of some stimulation which remains obscure. One may argue that the stability of state and society which permitted the beginnings of the Egyptian dynasties laid new demands on individual men. They were organized more effectively through the specification of function. One man was charged to be an architect, another to be a seal-cutter, another to be a record clerk. These functions had previously been avocations in a more simple society. Now they were important enough to be vocations and called forth the accumulation of abilities which had been latent but growing in the earlier periods. For centuries the Egyptians had been gathering slow strength within the Nile Valley until their day arrived, and they sprang upward with a suddenness which is miraculous to us. The Egyptians also had a sense of something very wonderful. They found themselves capable of great accomplishment. Material success was their first goal of the good life.

We can feel the relish with which a noble of the Old Kingdom relates his advances in station: "(The King) made me Count and Overseer of Upper Egypt. . . . . Never before had this office been conferred upon any servant, but I acted for him as Overseer of Upper Egypt to satisfaction. . . . . I filled an office which made my reputation in this Upper Egypt. Never before had the like been done in this Upper Egypt."[3] The attitude was a frontier spirit of visible accomplishments, of the first success in a new line. This was a youthful and self-reliant arrogance, because there had been no setbacks. Man was enough in himself. The gods? Yes, they were off there somewhere, and they had made this good world, to be sure; but the world was good because man was himself master, without need for the constant support of the gods.

Man's world was not completely devoid of god, because the rules under which the world operated had been laid down by god, or the gods, and any man who transgressed those rules was accountable to god. Even in this early time, the word "god" is used in the singular in referring to his system, his desires for man, or his judging violations of the system. It is not quite clear in the Old Kingdom what god is involved in this singular use. Sometimes it is certainly the king, sometimes it is certainly the creator or supreme god, who had laid down the broad, general rules for the game of life. But sometimes there appear to be unification and personification of correct and efficient behavior summed up in the will of "the god" who is not as august or as distant as the king or the creator-god. If the hypothesis of consubstantiality is valid, this unification and universality of deity is a problem which we have already faced. It was not monotheism; it was monophysitism applied to deity.

Where the principles of proper behavior concern table etiquette or administrative procedure, it is likely to be "the *ka*" that has a governing interest as "the god."[4] As we explained in the previous chapter, the *ka* was the detached part of the human personality which protected and sustained the individual. As such it could well be the divine force within man which governed his proper and successful activity. The frequency of Old Kingdom names like "Rē-is-my-*ka*" and "Ptah-is-my-*ka*" suggests that, through the principles of consubstantiality and free substitution, the *ka* was thought to be a man's god, sometimes godship in general, and sometimes a specific god, like a name saint or a patron saint.

We are here referring to the Old Kingdom, when the gods of the pantheon were more remote from common man, although not necessarily from his intermediating *ka*. That situation changed later. In the latter part of the Empire an Egyptian expressed a close personal relation to a specifically named god, who was his protector and controller. That direct relation to a personal god may be visible before the Empire in the "town god," the equivalent of the local saint. In the early Eighteenth Dynasty, for example, a wish for a noble runs: "Mayest thou spend eternity in gladness of heart and in the favor of the god who is in thee,"[5] for which a variant runs: "in the favor of thy town god."[6] However, (*a*) these concepts are rarely clear cut or firmly identifiable; and (*b*) in certain contexts "the god" is the king or a specific god of universal control, like the creator-god.

The independent self-reliance of the Egyptian of the Pyramid Age is indicated by the physical decentralization of the tombs of the nobles of the period. At first the high officials were buried in close juxtaposition to the god-king whom they had served; through his certainty of eternity their hopes for continued existence would be realized. Very soon, however, they exhibited sufficient self-confidence to move away from the king and seek their own eternity in their own home districts. Within the general framework of divine rule they were independently successful in this life; they had assurance that this success was applicable to the future. Under their own momentum they could carry on into future life, join their *ka*'s over there, and become *akh*'s, "effective beings," for a vigorous eternal life. Their own accumulation of worldly success guaranteed, by legal contract and by precedent, a conquest over death. In that sense there was a decided democratic—or, more precisely, individualistic—trend throughout the Old Kingdom.

"Individualism" is a better term than "democracy" for this spirit, because it applied chiefly to personal rule of conduct and not to political government. A sense of personal adequacy may lead to decentralization of government and thus bring a limited sense of democratic ambition. But we do not see in ancient Egypt that political democracy which chapter v will indicate for Mesopotamia. The dogma of the divinity of the Egyptian pharaoh was a cohesive force too strong to be fractured by individualistic forces.

No servile dependency upon a god was necessary in this early period for the greatest goods of life: success in this world and continued life in the next. Man was generally accountable to the king, to the creator-god, and to his own *ka*, but he was not humbly suppliant to a named god of the pantheon, and he was not formally responsible to Osiris, the later ruler of the dead. His wealth and position in this life gave him confidence that he was fully effective now and later, and—as the lively tomb scenes show—he wanted a next world just as gay and exciting and successful as this world.

We want to emphasize just as strongly as we can that the Egyptians of these times were a gay and lusty people. They relished life to the full, and they loved life too fully to surrender its hearty savor. That is why they denied the fact of death and carried over into the next world the same vigorous and merry life which they enjoyed here.

We possess for this early period a book of etiquette for an official, "the utterances of beautiful speech . . . . as the instruction of the ignorant in knowledge and in the rules of good speech, which are of advantage to him who will listen and of disadvantage to him who may abuse them."⁷ This contains the gospel of the "go-get-

ter," the bald rules for a young man who is on the make. It has
been summarized as follows:

> The ideal picture is that of a correct man, who wisely avoids impulse and fits
> himself by word and deed into the administrative and social systems. An assured
> career as an official awaits him. No moral concepts like good and bad come into
> discussion here; rather the standard lies in the characteristics of the knowing man
> and the ignorant man, perhaps best given in the words "smart" and "stupid."
> Smartness can be learned. . . . . So rules are provided for a man's career. If he
> pays attention, he will be smart; he will find the right way in all life's situations
> through this smartness; and through this correct attitude he will bring his career
> to success.[8]

This book contains precepts for getting on with superiors,
equals, and inferiors. Thus one who comes into competition with
a speaker who is better at argument is advised to "cut down on bad
talk by not opposing him"; one who meets an equal is to show his
superiority by silence so that the attending officials may be impressed; and an inferior opponent is to be treated with indulgent
disregard, for thus "thou shalt smite him with the punishment of
the (truly) great."[9] He who sits at the table of a superior is urged
to maintain a sedate countenance, to take only what he is offered,
and to laugh only when his host laughs; thus the great one will be
pleased and will accept whatever one may do.[10] An official who
must listen to the pleas of clients should listen patiently and without rancor, because "a petitioner wants attention to what he says
(even) more than the accomplishing of that for which he came."[11]
It is seemly to found a household, to love and cherish a wife, because "she is a field of advantage to her master"; and one must be
careful to hold her from gaining mastery in the household.[12] There
is a practical, materialistic wisdom in the injunction: "The wise
man rises early in the morning to establish himself,"[13] or in the
advice to be generous to one's hangers-on, because no one can
foresee the exigencies of the future, and it is wise to build up the
insurance of a body of grateful supporters.[14]

It would be unfair to leave the impression that the entire text is
opportunistic and materialistic. There is one passage which urges
on the official that honesty is the best policy, but even this arises
out of experience rather than principle. "If thou art a leader who
directs the affairs of a multitude, seek for thyself every benevolent
opportunity until thy conduct shall be without fault. Justice is of

advantage, and its utility lasts. It has not been disturbed since the time of its maker, whereas there is punishment for him who passes by its laws. . . . . It is (true that) evil may gain wealth, but the (real) strength of justice is that it lasts, for a man can say: 'It was the property of my father (before me).' "[15] Here lay the values of that age: a transmittable property and the experience that a man "got on" in the world if he was smart enough to follow certain common-sense principles. A success visible to all men was the great good. These were the supreme values of the Old Kingdom, and they continued in value throughout Egyptian history.

It was easy to worship success as long as success conferred its benefits on all men, as long as well-tended pyramids and tombs were the visible symbols of the lasting power of worldly success. But that happy state did not last. The Old Kingdom of Egypt collapsed into turmoil heels over head. The old values in position and property were swept away in an anarchy of force and seizure. The Egyptians ascribed their woes in part to a dissolution of their own character, but also to the violent presence of Asiatics in the Egyptian Delta. However, it is doubtful whether the Asiatics came in as an invading and suppressing horde; it is much more likely that an inner breakdown of rule in Egypt permitted small groups of Asiatics to come in and settle but that these insignificant penetrations were result rather than cause of the breakdown.

The real source of the collapse was a progressive decentralization. Rulers other than the dynastic pharaohs felt their individual capacity for independence and set up competitive government until the strain fractured Egypt into a lot of warring factions. This was part of the individualistic, self-seeking trend which had been gaining momentum throughout the Old Kingdom. Now, with the single, central control dissipated, there was anarchy in the competing grabs for power, which went right down to the lowest strata of society. Egypt had been moving away from autarchy in the direction of separatism based on individual capacity to act, but the nation was unprepared to take advantage of the breakdown of autarchy by the immediate institution of a system of rule on a broader basis. In the confusion there was no rule.

We have many expressions of the bewilderment of the Egyptian at the overturn of his old world. Instead of the prized stability and security, the land whirled around dizzily like a potter's wheel. The former rich and powerful were now in rags and hunger, whereas the former poor had property and power. We of the present day read with a wry amusement the protests that there was a thoroughgoing cheapening of the high court of justice and a disregard for the statutes of the law, that poor men were now able to wear fine linen, that servant girls were insolent to their mistresses, and that the laundryman arbitrarily refused to carry his bundle. The visible continuity of life through the care and preservation of the tombs of the great was abruptly fractured; tombs were plundered, including the pyramids of the pharaohs, and the treasured dead lay exposed upon the desert plateau. The crisp frontier lines which had given geometric order to Egypt were erased; the red desert had pushed its way into the fertile black soil, the provincial states were "hacked to pieces," and foreigners from abroad had entered Egypt. When the provinces refused to pay taxes, the central control of agriculture broke down, and no one would plow even when the Nile was in beneficial flood. The old profitable commerce with Phoenicia and Nubia had disappeared, so that the appearance of a few miserable traders from the desert offering herbs and birds was now a remarkable phenomenon.[16]

Egypt may have been moving steadily toward individualism and decentralized power, but it had still had the single keystone of the kingship. When this had been removed, the whole arch had fallen. "Behold, it has come to a point where the land is robbed of the kingship by a few irresponsible men. . . . . Behold, the secret of the land, unknowable in its extent, has been exposed, and the (royal) residence has been overthrown within an hour."[17] We have seen in the earlier wisdom literature that the norm for the good life had been the successful official. Now the officials were in hunger and want. "Behold, no office at all is in its (proper) place, like a stampeded herd without its herdsman."[18] "Changes have taken place, so that it is no (longer) like last year, but one year is more burdensome than another."[19] The old values of a successful individual career, which showed to the world property, administrative position, and a tomb provisioned unto eternity had been swept away. What values could be found to replace them?

In the upset, some found only the negative answers of despair or

skepticism. Some turned to suicide, and we read that the croco-
diles of the river were sated because men went to them of their
own accord.[20] One of the finest documents of Egyptian literature
records the debate of a would-be suicide with his own *ba*, or soul.
Life was too much for him, and he proposed to seek his death by
fire. It was symptomatic of the times that the soul, which should
have exhibited the consistent and directing attitude toward death,
was the wavering member to the debate and could find no satisfactory answer to the man's melancholy. It first was inclined to
accompany him no matter what his end might be; then it shifted
and tried to hold him back from violence. Still it had no constructive arguments for realizing a good life on this earth and could only
urge the man to forget his cares and seek sensual enjoyment.
Finally, after the man had contrasted the miseries of this life with
the sober pleasures of the next world, the soul agreed to make a
home with him no matter what his fate might be. There was no
answer except that this world was so bad that the next must be a
release.

This document carries a philosophy of pessimism worth our
study. The man presented his argument to his soul in four poems of
uniform tristichs contrasting life with the release of death. The
first poem urged that the man's name would be in bad odor if he
followed the advice of his soul to give himself up to pleasure. He
had his own standards still, and he would not permit his good name
to be damaged.

> Behold, my name will reek through thee
> More than the stench of fishermen,
> More than the stagnant swamps where they have fished.

> Behold, my name will reek through thee
> More than the stench of bird-droppings,
> On summer days when the sky is hot.[21]

In six more stanzas the man presented the evil odor of his reputation if he followed the cowardly advice of his soul. Then in a
second poem he turned to a lament over the breakdown of standards
in the society of his day. Three of the stanzas in this poem run as
follows:

> To whom can I speak today?
> (One's) fellows are evil;
> The friends of today do not love.

(To whom can I speak today?)
>The gentle man has perished,
>But the violent man has access to everybody.

To whom can I speak today?
>No one remembers (the lessons of) the past;
>No one at this time does (good in return) for doing
>(good).[22]

From these evils of life the man turned to contemplate death as a blessed release.

Death (stands) before me today
>(Like) the recovery of a sick man,
>Like going out-doors (again) after being confined.

Death (stands) before me today
>Like the fragrance of myrrh,
>Like sitting under a shade on a breezy day.

Death (stands) before me today
>As a man longs to see his house,
>After he has spent many years held in captivity.[23]

Finally, the man urged the high privileges of the dead, who had the power to oppose evil and who had free access to the gods.

Nay, but he who is yonder
>Shall be a living god,
>Inflicting punishment upon the doer of evil.

Nay, but he who is yonder
>Shall be a man of wisdom,
>Not stopped from appealing to Rē when he speaks.[24]

This man was ahead of his day in rejecting the active values of this life in favor of the passive values of future blessedness. As we shall see, such submissiveness characterized a period a thousand years later. This was a tentative move in the pessimism of the period—that one should seek death as a release instead of emphasizing the continuance of the life as known here.

In this debate the man's soul at one point urged upon him the futility of taking life seriously and cried out: "Pursue a holiday (mood) and forget care!"[25] This theme of nonmoral hedonism occurs again in another text of the period, where the argument is: The old standards of property and position have broken down; we have no certainty about future happiness, so let us grasp what happiness we can in this world. The past shows only that this life is brief and transitory—but transitory to an unknowable future.

"Generations pass away and others go on since the time of the ancestors. . . . . They that build buildings, their places are no more. What has been done with them?

"I have heard the words of (the past sages) Imhotep and Hardedef, with whose sayings men speak so much—(but) what are their places (now)? Their walls are crumbled, their places are non-existent, as if they had never been.

"No one returns from (over) there, so that he might tell us their disposition, that he might tell us how they are, that he might still our hearts until we (too) shall go to the place where they have gone."[26]

Since that wisdom which was so highly prized in the earlier age had not guaranteed for the wise a visible survival in well-kept tombs, and since it was impossible to tell how the dead fared in the other world, what was left for us here? Nothing, except to snatch at the sensual pleasures of the day.

"Make holiday and weary not therein! Behold, it is not given to a man to take his property with him. Behold, no one who goes (over there) can come back again!"[27]

Thus the first two reactions to the defeat of a successful and optimistic world were despair and cynicism. But they were not the only reactions. Egypt had still a spiritual and mental vigor which refused to deny the essential worth of individual man. He was still an object of value to himself. If his old standards of value in physical and social success had proved to be of ephemeral nature, he began to grope for other standards which might have a more lasting nature. Dimly and uncertainly he became aware of the great truth that the things which are seen are temporal but that the things which are unseen may be of the very stuff of eternity. And eternal life was still his great goal.

Now the words which we have just used and the words which we are going to use prejudice the discussion in terms of modern ethical judgments. That is deliberate. We consider the Egyptian Middle Kingdom to have reached moral heights in its search for the good life. This is a personal prejudice, in which we follow Professor Breasted, although our own analysis of the factors differs slightly from his. A counterview has been urged by others. They point out that the Egyptians of the earliest fully visible period, the Old Kingdom, reached heights which were never surpassed later—in technical ability (as in the Great Pyramid and in sculpture), in science (as in a remarkable surgical papyrus and in the institution of a calendar), and in philosophy (as in the Memphite Theology). This view would deny any assumption of progress beyond those points. Indeed, it would protest the claim of progress at all and would insist that we see change only and that this change is within the limits of a culture very largely static from the beginnings. The more it changes, the more it exhibits itself to be the same. There is undoubted truth to this. The materialism which we stressed as characterizing the Old Kingdom was still an important factor in this new period. The social-moral advances which we shall claim for this new period were already indicated in the Old Kingdom (increasing democratization, concept of justice, etc.). This view would also protest the imposing of our consciously self-righteous standards of moral judgment upon the ancient Egyptians. Have we the right to translate *ma^cat* as "justice," "truth," or "righteousness," instead of "order," "regularity," or "conformity"? Have we the right to hail increasing democracy of viewpoint in ancient Egypt as "an advance," which was "good"?

We insist that one has the right to make moral judgments and to talk in terms of progress or decline. These are subjective matters, not strictly scientific. But any generation has the right—nay, even the duty—of presenting the evidence objectively and then of giving a subjective valuation to the evidence. We know that objectivity cannot be completely divorced from subjectivity, but a scholar can attempt to show just what the evidence is and just where his personal criticism comes in. In the period which we are going to examine now, we would agree that a hard practical materialism still continued strong, that the anti-ethical force of magic played a large role, and that the moral impulses which we shall stress had been present earlier and continued later. But we are satisfied that there were changes of emphasis in this period and that these shifts of emphasis look like advances to a modern American.

The two great changes which we can see are a decline in the emphasis on position and material property as being the good of this life, with a corresponding shift of emphasis to proper social action as being the good, and a continuation of the individualistic trend of the Old Kingdom to the point where all good things were potentially open to all men. These two trends are ultimately the same: if the good in life is within the quest of any man, rich or poor, then power and wealth are not ultimates, but right relations to other men are strongly recommended.

Three quotations will give us the new emphases. A struggle of the previous period had been to build and maintain a tomb, an imposing funerary monument lasting to eternity. The Middle Kingdom continued the physical establishment but introduced a new note: "Do not be evil, (for) kindliness is good. Make thy monument to be lasting through the love of thee. . . . . (Then) the god will be praised by way of rewarding (thee)."[28] Here the monument which lasted came through other men's grateful reaction to benevolence. A second passage gives clearly the statement that the god delighted more in good character than in elaborate offerings; the poor man could thus have as good a title to god's interest as the rich. "More acceptable is the character of a man just of heart than the ox of the evildoer."[29]

The most remarkable passage of the period is one which occurs only here and—as far as we know—was not repeated later. It stands isolated, and yet it was not foreign to the highest aspiration of the times; it is a reason for prizing the spirit of this age beyond those which preceded or followed. It stated simply that all men were created equal in opportunity. In these words the supreme god gave the purposes of creation.

> I relate to you the four good deeds which my own heart did for me . . . . in order to silence evil. I did four good deeds within the portal of the horizon.
>
> I made the four winds that every man might breathe thereof like his fellow in his time. That is (the first) of the deeds.
>
> I made the great floodwaters that the poor man might have rights in them like the great man. That is (the second) of the deeds.

> I made every man like his fellow. I did not command
> that they might do evil, (but) it was their hearts that
> violated what I had said. That is (the third) of the
> deeds.

> I made that their hearts should cease from forgetting the
> west, in order that divine offerings might be made to
> the gods of the provinces. That is (the fourth) of the
> deeds.[30]

The first two passages of this text state that wind and water are equally available to all men of any degree. In a land where prosperity depended upon securing a proper share in the inundation waters and where water control must have been a powerful factor in setting one man in domination over another, an assurance of equal access to water meant basic equality of opportunity. The statement, "I made every man like his fellow," that is, "all men are created equal," was coupled with the god's insistence that he had not intended that they do evil, but that their own hearts had devised wrong. This juxtaposition of equality and wrongdoing says that social inequality is no part of god's plan, but man must bear that responsibility alone. This is a clear assertion that the ideal society would be fully equalitarian. Certainly, ancient Egypt never came near that ideal, except as we moderns do in the pious postponement of full equality to the future life. But it was still a valid sublimation of the highest aspirations of the time. Wistfully it says: All men should be equal; the creator-god did not make them different.

The final good deed of the supreme god was to call men's attention to the west, the region of eternal life, and to urge upon them pious service of their local gods in order to attain the west. These were important changes of this period, the democratization of the next world and closer attachment to the gods. All men might now enjoy eternity in the same terms as had the king alone in the previous period. We do not know just what kind of continued existence the ordinary man of the Old Kingdom had been conceded. He was to continue with his *ka*, and he was to become an *akh*, an "effective" personality. The pharaoh of the Old Kingdom, however, was to become a god in the realm of the gods. Now that future of the pharaoh was open also to commoners. They were to become gods as he had become a god. Whereas only the dead king had become Osiris in the earlier period, now every deceased Egyptian became the god Osiris. Further, his becoming an Osiris and attaining eternal blessedness was put in relation to an afterlife judgment in which his character was assessed by a tribunal of gods.

Pictorially, this judgment of character was already a weighing of justice. In the future this was to become a judgment before Osiris as the god of the dead, with the man's heart placed in the scales against the symbol for justice. Those elements were already present in the Middle Kingdom, Osiris as god of the dead and a judgment of the deceased in terms of justice, but they were not yet put together into a single consistent scene. Instead there was still a carry-over of the older order in which the supreme god, the sun-god, was the judge. There was democratization of the next world and Osirianization, but the entry to the eternal life was not wholly within the control of Osiris. We have reference to "that balance of Rē, in which he weighs justice";[31] and the deceased was assured that "thy fault will be expelled and thy guilt will be wiped out by the weighings of the scales on the day of reckoning characters, and it will be permitted that thou join with those who are in the (sun)-barque,"[32] and that "there is not a god who will contest a case with thee, and there is not a goddess who will contest a case with thee, on the day of reckoning characters."[33] It was a tribunal of the gods, presumably under the presidency of the supreme god, to whom the deceased must make his report. "He shall reach the council of the gods, the place where the gods are, his *ka* being with him and his offerings being in front of him, and his voice shall be justified in the reckoning up of the surplus: though he may tell his faults, they will be expelled for him by all that he may say."[34] All this shows that there was a judging of the dead in terms of weighing the excess or deficiency of his good against his bad and that a favorable outcome of the weighing was a prerequisite to eternal blessedness. This weighing was a calculation of *maᶜat*, justice.

We have met *maᶜat* before. Basically, it is probably a physical term, "levelness, evenness, straightness, correctness," in a sense of regularity or order. From that it can be used in the metaphorical senses of "uprightness, righteousness, truth, justice." There was a real emphasis on this *ma^{c}at* in the Middle Kingdom in the sense of social justice, righteous dealing with one's fellow-men. That was the main theme of the story of the eloquent peasant, which comes from this period. Throughout his pleadings the peasant demanded from the high official simple justice as a moral right. Just dealing had its minimum in the conscientious carrying-out of responsibilities. "Cheating diminishes justice, (but) filling (to) good (measure)—neither too low nor overflowing—is justice."[35] But, as we saw in the preceding chapter, justice was not simply legal commerce but was the seeking-out of good in relation to need: ferrying across the river the poor man who could not pay and doing good in advance of any known return. And a theme of the Middle Kingdom was social responsibility: the king was a herdsman who cherished his herds; the official had a positive duty toward the widow and the orphan; in short, every man had rights which imposed responsibilities upon other men. Even the sculptures of the time sought to bring out this emphasis on conscientious character and moved from a delineation of majesty and force to a portrayal of concern for obligations. Such careworn portraits of the pharaohs of the Middle Kingdom are well known.

All this has been eloquently urged by Breasted, and we need not document it in further detail. If one seeks to state his argument differently, it would simply be in a difference of definition of "conscience" or of "character" and a failure to give the story the simple and straightforward emphasis which he achieves. In the previous period there had been a demand for justice in this world and for the next,[36] and there had certainly been character in the forceful personalities who had built a great state. But here in the Middle Kingdom greater emphasis in some lines and lesser emphasis in others permitted an age of real social conscientiousness, in which the psychological and moral basis was the belief that every man is the careworthy creation of the god.

Up to this time, the Middle Kingdom, the trend in ancient Egypt had been centrifugal and atomistic: individual man had been the valued unit. First his individual abilities had been marked out for value, then his individual rights had been recognized. Egypt had been moving somewhat blindly along the road from theocratic autarchy toward democracy of a kind. The spirit was still an encouragement to fill this life with activity, and each man was given an opportunity to realize the bustling, practical, important life here. Consequently, they continued to love this life and defy death. The definition of success may have shifted slightly, but it was still true that a successful life carried over and repeated itself happily in the next world. Consequently, the tombs, which were the bridges between two existences, continued to stress the abundance of life. The scenes of hunting, shipbuilding, and merrymaking were as vigorous as ever. Only an increased attention to scenes of the burial and a few representations of religious feasts suggest to us a new sobriety. It was still the case that the greatest good lay in the good life here and not an escape from this life to a different future life or a resigned submission to the gods. Individual man still enjoyed himself.

THE EMPIRE AND LATER

We come now to the cause of the great transition in the Egyptian ethos. We come to the second political revolution, the Second Intermediate Period, lying between the Middle Kingdom and the Empire, between the eighteenth and sixteenth centuries B.C. Again the central government broke down; again there was competition for the rule by a number of small princelings. Probably a weakening of personal force and character in the central government unleashed the self-seeking individualism of local princes. But the great difference this time was the forceful and conquering incursion of foreigners. Asiatic princes, whom we call the Hyksos, established themselves in armed camps within Egypt and dominated the land with a firmness which was repressive to the still flowering Egyptian spirit. For the first time Egypt as a whole suffered a setback in that philosophy which said: We are the center and summit of the world; we are free to permit expansion of spirit to the individuals of our community. Now, for the first time, that community was aware of a serious threat from the outside world. Now, for the first time, that community had to draw together into a unity in order to meet and avert that threat.

Egypt did unite and throw out the "vagabonds," who had dared to rule the land "in ignorance of Rē."[37] But the threat was not met by driving them out of Egypt; it was necessary to pursue them into Asia and to keep on pounding them so that they might never again threaten the land of the Nile. There was built up a psychosis for security, a neuropathic awareness of danger similar to that which has characterized Europe in modern times. That common sentiment for security welded the Egyptians into a self-conscious nation. It has been pointed out that only in this period of liberation do the Egyptians speak of their troops as "our army," instead of crediting the forces to the king.[38] There was a patriotic fervor which put the country's interests before the interests of the individual.

Such a unified spirit was born of the sense of common peril. The common desire for security need not have survived after the Egyptian Empire extended the military frontier of Egypt well into Asia and thus removed the peril from the immediate frontier. That should have given the external security which would relieve the need for communal solidarity. However, it was a restless age, and there were perils on the distant horizon which could be invoked to hold the community together, since unity was to the advantage of certain central powers. When the threat of the Hyksos had subsided, the threat of the Hittites appeared and endangered the Asiatic Empire of Egypt. Thereafter came the Sea Peoples, the Libyans, and the Assyrians. A fear psychosis, once engendered, remained present. And there were forces in Egypt which kept alive this fear psychosis in order to maintain the unified purpose of Egypt.

The course of empire is justified in terms of a crusade, the acceptance of a "manifest destiny" to extend one culture in domination over another. Whether empire is basically economic or political, it must have a religious, spiritual, and intellectual vindication. In Egypt that sanction came through the god-king who stood for the state, and it came through the other national gods who participated in the removal of a threat to Egypt by supporting the extension of the frontiers of the land. The national gods commissioned the pharaoh to march forth and widen the land; indeed, they marched with him at the head of the divisions of his army. The extension of the nation was their own extension.

In how far the gods invested in Egyptian victory in a strictly economic sense is uncertain. We do not know whether the temples acted as bankers to finance foreign conquest and empire. They probably did so when they became wealthy and had extensive assets, because empire constantly increased their wealth. At any rate, they did invest in Egyptian victory in a spiritual-propagandistic sense, in giving a divine blessing and a divine guaranty to empire. For this they received an economic return. This is rather explicitly stated in the monuments; the pharaoh erected buildings, established and endowed feasts, and presented land and serfs to the god who had given the victory. The previously modest temples in Egypt grew in physical size, in personnel, in land, and in total property, until they became the dominating factor in Egyptian political, social, and economic life. It has been estimated that, after the Empire had had three hundred years of active life, the Egyptian temples owned one out of every five inhabitants of the nation and owned almost one-third of the cultivable land.[39] Naturally the temples were interested in perpetuating and tightening a system which was so greatly to their advantage. In order to secure their advantage, they had to insist on the group solidarity of the people for the national interest which had made the temples rich and strong. Ultimately they swallowed up not only the people but also the pharaoh.

Now look at the implications of this history in terms of the individual human. The previous tendency from the Old Kingdom up to the Empire had been centrifugal, atomistic, individualistic: the good life was to be found in the fullest expression of each person. Now the tendency was centripetal, nationalistic, communal: the good life was to be found in the group interest, and the individual was called upon to conform to the asserted needs of the group. Any wavering and tentative approach to an individualistic expression was canceled out; any sense that the Egyptian community was a thing of value in itself was a cardinal doctrine.

A revolution of this spiritual and intellectual kind is not established by a congress which draws up a manifesto of change; it takes place so gradually as to be perceptible only over the centuries. Even a rebellion against the change, such as characterized the Amarna Revolution, was perhaps as much an unsystematized protest against the power mechanics of the change as a protest against the principles of the change. For centuries the Egyptian texts went on reiterating the older formulas, while the Egyptian tombs repeated the older lusty enjoyment of the manifold opportunities of this life. It is just as if we Americans should turn gradually to a socialistic government and a rationalistic ethics while repeating our slogans of democracy and Calvinistic Protestantism; we should be unaware of the change for a long time after it had been effective.

Thus there were centuries of empire before the force of the change became visible in Egyptian literature and art. Only gradually were the old stereotypes replaced by new formulas. When the revolution was complete, we find that the goals of life had shifted from a vigorous, individualistic existence in this world, which would be rewarded by repetition in the next world, to a conforming and formalistic life in this world. As far as the individual Egyptian was concerned, his horizon of opportunity had become circumscribed; he was advised to submit because he was presented with an escape from this world's limitations by a promise of better things in the next world. Those better things were now less of his own agency and more the gift of the gods. There was thus not only a shift from the individual to the group but also a shift from an enjoyment of this world to the promise of the next world. That will explain the contrast between those two tombs which we outlined previously in this chapter, where the earlier monument presented gay and vigorous depictions of field, shop, and market place, whereas the later monument concentrated on the ritual approach to afterlife.

Let us try to document this thesis from the literature and particularly from the wisdom literature. One's first impression is that the late instructions in correct behavior are just like the earlier instructions; in much the same Polonius language they tell the young official how to get on in his profession. Effective practical etiquette— at table, in the street, or in the law court—is the continuing theme. But gradually one is aware of differences. The reasons given for the injunctions have changed. Back in the older days a man had been advised to take good care of his wife, because "she is a field of advantage to her master." Now the man was told to remember the patience and devotion of his own mother and to treat his wife in accordance with his loving gratitude to his mother.[40] Whereas the older texts had enjoined patience and impartiality upon the official when dealing with poor clients, now he was to take positive action on behalf of the poor. "If thou findest a large debt against a poor man, make it into three parts, throw out two, and let one remain." Why should one take such an uneconomical action? The answer is that he cannot live with his own conscience unless he does. "Thou wilt find it like the ways of life. Thou wilt lie down and sleep (soundly). In the morning thou wilt find it (again) like good news. It is better to be praised as one whom people love than (to have) riches in the storehouse. Better is bread when the heart is happy than riches under (the weight of) troubles."[41] This was a change from the older texts; position and property were not so important now as the sense of right relations with other men. A man belonged to society, not to himself alone.

The key word for the developed spirit of this period was "silence," which we may render also with "calm, passivity, tranquillity, submission, humility, meekness." This "silence" is linked with weakness or poverty in such contexts as "Thou art Amon, the lord of the silent, who comes at the voice of the poor,"[42] and "Amon, the protector of the silent, the rescuer of the poor."[43] Because of that equation these characteristic expressions of humility have been designated as a religion of the poor.[44] It is true that meekness has always been a virtue recommended to the dispossessed, but our essential point is that every Egyptian of this period was dispossessed in terms of a right to self-expression; he had been cut off from the encouragement to voluntary self-development and was now constrained to a deterministic submission to the needs of the group. In proof of this assertion that the spirit of humility was not confined to the poverty-stricken, we would point out that a very high-placed official was at pains to describe himself as "truly silent"[45] and that even the high priest of Amon might insist that he was "properly and truly silent."[46] In the spirit of the times the active and successful official found it necessary to emphasize his conformance to the national pattern of obedience.

As the objectionable contrast to the silent man, the texts offered the "heated" or "passionate" man, who was "loud of voice." In terms reminiscent of the First Psalm, the contrast is drawn (also Jer. 17:5-8):

As for the passionate man in the temple, he is like a tree growing in the open. Suddenly (comes) its loss of foliage, and its end is reached in the ship-yards; (or) it is floated far from its place, and a flame is its burial-shroud.

(But) the truly silent man holds himself apart. He is like a tree growing in a garden. It flourishes; it doubles its fruit; it (stands) before its lord. Its fruit is sweet; its shade is pleasant; and its end is reached in the garden.[47]

Now silence had often been enjoined in the earlier period, but it had been a topical silence: do not speak or resist unless you are smart enough.[48] Indeed, it had been emphasized that eloquence might be found in the lowest grades of society and that it should be encouraged there when found.[49] Now, in this changed spirit, the continuing injunction was silence alone. In dealings with superiors or in the government offices, it was submissive silence which would give you ultimate success.[50] This was related to the designs of the god, "who loves the silent man more than him who is loud of voice,"[51] and whose protection would confound one's opponents.[52] "The dwelling of god, its abomination is clamor. Pray thou with a loving heart, all words of which are hidden. Then he will supply all thy needs; he will hear what thou sayest and will accept thy offering."[53] The well of wisdom is not free for all who wish to drink therefrom; "it is sealed to him who can discover his mouth, (but) it is open to him who is silent."[54]

The new deterministic philosophy was rather definitely stated in terms of the will of god, placed over against man's helplessness. "The god is (always) in his success, (whereas) man is (always) in his failure." This statement of man's essential need of god was continued in an early expression of *Homo proposuit sed Deus disponit:* "One thing are the words which men say, (but) another thing is what the god does."[55] Gone was the earlier reliance upon man himself within the general pattern of the world order; now he specifically and always failed unless he conformed to that which the god directed.

Thus this period came to have a strong sense of fate or external determining force. One may say that this had not been entirely absent in earlier times in some magical force or other. The *ka* had been a semidetached part of personality which had affected a man's career. But now the god Fate and the goddess Fortune stood outside the personality in remote but firm control. One could not pursue one's own interest without regard to these regulators on behalf of the gods. "Cast not thy heart in pursuit of riches, (for) there is no ignoring Fate and Fortune. Place not thy heart upon externals, (for) every man belongs to his (appointed) hour."[56] Man was charged not to search too deeply into the affairs of the gods, because the deities of destiny were his controlling limitation. "Do not (try to) find for thyself the powers of the god himself, (as if) there were no Fate and Fortune."[57]

It is possible to emphasize the role of fate exclusively in this period. There was still some voluntarism within the determined scheme of things. The young man was warned against a fatalism which prevents his searching for wisdom: "Beware lest thou say: 'Every man is according to his (own) nature. Ignorant and wise are of one piece (only). Fate and Fortune are carved on the nature (of a man) in the writings of the god himself. Every man passes his lifetime in an hour.' (Nay), teaching is good, and there is no wearying in it, and a son should answer with the utterances of his father. I cause thee to know what is right in thy (own) heart, so that thou do what is correct in thy sight."[58]

If success lay only with god and man was doomed to failure, we should expect to find expressions of the sense of personal shortcoming, ultimately stated as a consciousness of sin. Such expressions do appear at this time. To be sure, the nature of sin is not always clear, and it may involve only ritual irregularity rather than ethical wrongdoing. But we can insist upon an acknowledgment of error when a man says: "Though the servant is normally (disposed) to do evil, yet the Lord is normally (disposed) to be merciful."[59] In another case it was the specific crime of perjury that led a man to say of his god: "He caused men and gods to look on me as if I were a man that does abominations against his Lord. Righteous was Ptah, Lord of Truth, toward me, when he disciplined me."[60]

What is left for men when they are denied voluntary self-expression and are put into a rigid framework of conformance? Well, there was an escape from the limitations of this world in the promise of the next world, and it is possible to see an intensification of the desire for escape in Egypt, leading ultimately to monasticism and apocalyptic promise. But the promise of something distant is an uncertain thing in the day-by-day activity of a person; he wants something warmer right now. Thus the sense of personal wrongdoing called forth its antidote in a sense of divine nearness and mercy. The individual was swallowed up in a great impersonal system and felt lost. Very well, there was a god who was interested in him, who punished his transgressions, and who then healed him with mercy. Again and again the texts call upon a god or goddess to come in compassion to suffering man. "I cried out to my Mistress; (then) I found that she came to me with sweet airs. She showed mercy to me, (after) she had made me behold her hand. She turned about again to me in mercy; she caused me to forget the sickness that had been [upon] me. Yea, the Peak of the West is merciful if one cries out to her."[61]

Thus, in compensation for the loss of individual voluntarism and the imposition of group determinism, there emerged a warmer personal relation between an Egyptian and his own god, and the period of the late Empire has been characterized by Breasted as the "age of personal piety." There was love and trust on the part of the worshiper; there was justice and mercy on the part of the god. In the revolution of Egyptian feeling, the good life lay no longer in cultivation of personality but in the surrender of personality to some greater force, with the recompense for surrender a security offered by that greater force.

It would take too long to argue the full development of this changed psychology of a people. The substitution of god's mercy for the encouragement of the individual spirit did not prove satisfactory. The joy went out of life. The Egyptian was called upon to rest content in humility and faith. Humility he did show. But faith is "assurance of things hoped for, a conviction of things not seen." He might and did still hope for better things in the world to come, but his conviction of things not seen was limited by the experience of things seen. He saw that his own personal god, who showed him mercy in his weakness, was also little and weak like himself. He saw that the great gods of Egypt, the national gods, were rich, distant, powerful, and demanding. The priesthood of Egypt was still growing in power and control and demanded blind conformance to the system that gave the temples power and control. Individual man was caught in a strait jacket of rites and obligations, and his only comfort lay in soothing words and distant promises.

He turned from a lusty appreciation of this life to means of escape from this life.

In the desire for escape from the present, the Egyptian turned not only to the afterworld future but also to the happy past. As we saw in chapter i, the Egyptians had always had a strong sense of the achievement, power, and dignity of earlier times. Constantly they invoked the good models of their past, whether the mythological times of the rule of the gods or the hazily historical times of the earliest kings.

Earlier in this chapter we quoted an old bit of agnosticism, in which the writer said in effect: The former sages Imhotep and Hardedef are much quoted, but they were unable to protect their tombs or their physical property; what did their wisdom avail them, after all? In later times the expression about these ancestors was different: Their wisdom did avail them, for they had left a memorial worthy of reverence. "As for those learned scribes since the times which came after the gods . . . . their names have come to be lasting forever, although they (themselves) have gone. . . . . They did not make for themselves pyramids of metal, with tombstones of iron. They were not able to leave heirs in children. . . . . But they made heirs for themselves in writings and in the wisdom literature which they left. . . . . Books of wisdom were their pyramids, and the pen was their child. . . . . Is there (anyone) here like Hardedef? Is there another like Imhotep? . . . . They are gone and forgotten, but their names through (their)writings cause them to be remembered!"[62]

This strong sense of a rich and proud past comforted an age which felt uncertainty in its present. Ultimately this nostalgia for earlier times grew into archaism, with a rather blind and ignorant copying of the forms of a distant past. Personal piety was not able to make the concept of a single fatherly god adequate. The search for the spiritual support of religion went instead over to a recourse to oracles and over to strict ritualistic observance, until religion became as empty as Herodotus saw it. Within the confinement of a system of national conformance even the god-king became a mere puppet of the laws, as Diodorus saw him. Egypt had not had the opportunity or the capacity to work out the interrelation of man and god in terms satisfactory to both. To put it in a different context, Egypt had not had the opportunity or the capacity to work out the interrelation of the individual and the community in terms of benefit to both. There the Hebrews went farther, but there we are still struggling at the present day.

THE INTELLECTUAL ROLE OF EGYPT

Did ancient Egypt contribute any significant element to the continuing philosophy, ethics, or world-consciousness of later times? No, not directly in fields which one may specify, as in the case of Babylonian science, Hebrew theology, or Greek or Chinese rationalism. One might critically say that the weight of ancient Egypt was not consonant with her size, that her intellectual and spiritual contributions were not up to her length of years and her physical memorial, and that she herself was unable to realize on her promising beginnings in many fields.

But the very size of Egypt left its mark on her neighbors. The Hebrews and the Greeks were deeply conscious of a past power and a past stability of this colossal neighbor and had a vague and uncritical appreciation of "all the wisdom of the Egyptians." This high appreciation gave them two factors for the stimulation of their own thinking: a sense of high value outside their own times and places, so that their philosophies had the benefit of some historical setting, and a curiosity about the more obvious Egyptian achievements: accomplishments in art and architecture, governmental organization, and a sense of geometric order. If in gratifying that curiosity about Egypt they came across intellectual or ethical advances made by Egypt, these could only be valid to them in terms of their own experiences, because they were already ancient history in Egypt. The Hebrews or Greeks had to rediscover for themselves any elements which had already lost persuasive force in Egypt. That culture had reached her intellectual and spiritual heights too early to develop any philosophy which could be transmitted in cultural heritage to the ages. Like Moses, she had had a distant glimpse of the Promised Land, but it was left to others to cross the Jordan and begin the Conquest.

NOTES

1. The two tombs are those of Mereruka, a vizier of the Sixth Dynasty, and of Bekenrenef, a vizier of the Twenty-sixth Dynasty. References in Porter and Moss, *Topographical Bibliography*, Vol. III: *Memphis*, pp. 140 ff., 171 ff.

2. "Dedication Address," December 5, 1931.

3. Urk. I, 105–6.

4. Ptahhotep, *passim.*

5. Urk. IV, 117.

6. *Ibid.*, 499.

7. Ptahhotep, 42–50.

8. Anthes, *Lebensregeln und Lebensweisheit der alten Aegypter*, pp. 12–13.

9. Ptahhotep, 60–83.

10. *Ibid.*, 119–33.

11. *Ibid.*, 264–69.

12. *Ibid.*, 325–32.

13. *Ibid.*, 573.

14. *Ibid.*, 339–49.

15. *Ibid.*, 84–98.

16. Admon., *passim.*

17. *Ibid.*, 7:2–4.

18. *Ibid.*, 9:2.

19. Khekheperresonbu, 10.

20. Admon., 2:12.

21. Leb., 93–95; 86–88.

22. *Ibid.*, 103–16.

23. *Ibid.*, 130–42.

24. *Ibid.*, 142–47.

25. *Ibid.*, 68.

26. Harris 500, 6:2–9.

27. *Ibid.*, 7:2–3.

28. Merikarē, 36–37.

29. *Ibid.*, 128–29.

30. Coffin Texts, B3C, ll. 570–76; B6C, ll. 503–11; B1Bo, ll. 618–22; see Breasted, *Dawn of Conscience*, p. 221.

31. TR 37; Rec., 30:189.

32. Coffin Texts, I, 181.

33. Bersheh, II, xix, 8:8–9.

34. BIFAO, 30:425 ff.; "thou" changed to "he" in last clause.

35. Peasant, B, 250–52.

36. E.g., Pyr. Spr. 260; cf. Sethe, *Kommentar*, I, 394: "Der rote Faden in dem Texte ist: Gerechtigkeit, in dem was dem Toten im Leben zuteil wurde und in dem, was er selbst nach seinem Tode thut."

37. Urk. IV, 390.

38. Breasted, *Ancient Records*, Vol. II, §39, n. *d.*

39. Schaedel, *Die Listen des grossen Papyrus Harris*, p. 67.

40. Anii, 7:17—8:3.

41. Amenemope, 16:5–14.

42. Berlin 20377; Erman, *Denksteine*, pp. 1086 ff.

43. Berlin 6910, Aeg. Inschr., II, 70.

44. JEA, 3:83 ff.

45. Urk. IV, 993; cf. *ibid.*, 66; BIFAO, 30:504—all Eighteenth Dynasty.

46. *Bibl. Eg.*, IV, 279, 281; Cairo 42155; both Bekenkhonsu of Nineteenth Dynasty.

47. Amenemope, 6:1–12.

48. Prisse, 1:1–3; 8:11–12; 11:8–11; Peasant, B, 298–99; B, 313–16; Khekheper-resonbu, Verso, 4; Sall. II, 9:9—10:1.

49. Ptahhotep, 58–59; Peasant, B, 74–80.

50. Anii, 3:17—4:1; 9:10; Amenemope, 22:1–18; 22:20—23:11.

51. Beatty IV, Recto, 5:8; cf. Beatty IV, Verso, 5:1–2.

52. Amenemope, 23:10–11.

53. Anii, 4:1–4.

54. Sall. I, 8:5–6.

55. Amenemope, 19:14–17.

56. *Ibid.*, 9:10–13.

57. *Ibid.*, 21:15–16.

58. Beatty IV, Verso, 6:5–9.

59. Berlin 20377.

60. British Museum 589.

61. Turin 102.

62. Beatty IV, Verso, 2:5—3:11.

SUGGESTED READINGS

The references given in the notes to chapters ii–iv are of an abbreviated character known to Egyptologists who may wish to check our translations. Such references normally refer to the source documents. For more general reading there is no work on ancient Egypt covering the same ground as that given in these chapters. However, certain titles may be listed as providing valuable discussions along similar lines. James H. Breasted, *Development of Religion and Thought in Ancient Egypt* (New York: Scribner's, 1912), was a brilliant pioneer work, which is still unsurpassed, even by the same author's *The Dawn of Conscience* (New York: Scribner's, 1933). There are useful chapters in George Steindorff and Keith C. Seele, *When Egypt Ruled the East* (Chicago, 1942), and in *The Legacy of Egypt*, edited by S. R. K. Glanville (Oxford, 1942). Readers wishing translations of Egyptian texts within a single volume are referred to Adolf Erman, *The Literature of the Ancient Egyptians*, translated from German into English by Aylward M. Blackman (London, 1927). In addition to Breasted's two books, an authoritative work on Egyptian religion is Erman's *Die Religion der Aegypter* (Berlin and Leipzig, 1934). Two recommended brief discussions are to be found in brochures: Alan H. Gardiner, *The Attitude of the Ancient Egyptians to Death and the Dead* (Cambridge, 1935), and Rudolf Anthes, *Lebensregeln und Lebensweisheit der alten Aegypter* (Leipzig, 1933).

MESOPOTAMIA
THORKILD JACOBSEN

CHAPTER V

MESOPOTAMIA: THE COSMOS AS A STATE

INFLUENCE OF ENVIRONMENT IN EGYPT AND MESOPOTAMIA

I N PASSING from ancient Egypt to ancient Mesopotamia, we are leaving a civilization whose enduring monuments still stand, "proud pyramids of stone proclaiming man's sense of sovereign power in his triumph over material forces." We are moving on to a civilization whose monuments perished, whose cities—in the words of the prophet—"have become heaps." There is scant reminder of ancient grandeur in the low gray mounds which represent Mesopotamia's past.

It is altogether fitting that this should be so. It suits the basic moods of the two civilizations. Were the Egyptian to come back today, he would undoubtedly take heart from the endurance of his pyramids, for he accorded to man and to man's tangible achievements more basic significance than most civilizations have been willing to do. Were the Mesopotamian to return, he could hardly feel deeply disturbed that *his* works have crumbled, for he always knew, and knew deeply, that as for "mere man—his days are numbered; whatever he may do, he is but wind."[1] To him the center and meaning of existence always lay beyond man and his achievements, beyond tangible things, in intangible powers ruling the universe.

How the Egyptian and the Mesopotamian civilizations came to acquire these very different moods—one trusting, the other distrusting, man's power and ultimate significance—is not an easy question. The "mood" of a civilization is the outcome of processes so intricate and so complex as to defy precise analysis. We shall therefore merely point to a single factor which would seem to have played a considerable role—the factor of environment. Chapters ii–iv have already stressed the active role of the environment in shaping the outlook of early Egypt. Egyptian civilization arose in a compact country where village lay reassuringly close to village,

125

the whole ringed around and isolated by protecting mountain barriers. Over this sheltered world passed every day a dependable,
never failing sun, calling Egypt back to life and activity after the
darkness of night; here rose every year the trusty Nile to fertilize
and revivify the Egyptian soil. It is almost as though Nature had
deliberately restrained herself, as though she had set this secure
valley apart so that man could disport himself unhindered.

It is small wonder that a great civilization arising on such a
scene should be filled with a sense of its own power, should be
deeply impressed with its own—with human—accomplishments.
Chapter iv defined the attitude of early Egypt as "a frontier spirit
of visible accomplishments, of the first success in a new line. There
was a youthful and self-reliant arrogance, because there had been
no setbacks. Man was enough in himself. The gods? Yes, they
were off there somewhere, and they had made this good world, to
be sure; but the world was good because man was himself master,
without need for the constant support of the gods."

The experience of Nature which gave rise to this mood found
direct expression in the Egyptian notion of the cosmos. The Egyptian cosmos was eminently reliable and comforting. It had—to
quote chapter ii—"reassuring periodicity; its structural framework and mechanics permitted the reiteration of life through the
rebirth of life-giving elements."

Mesopotamian civilization grew up in an environment which
was signally different. We find there, of course, the same great
cosmic rhythms—the change of the seasons, the unwavering sweep
of sun, moon, and stars—but we also find an element of force and
violence which was lacking in Egypt. The Tigris and the Euphrates
are not like the Nile; they may rise unpredictably and fitfully,
breaking man's dikes and submerging his crops. There are scorch-
ing winds which smother man in dust, threaten to suffocate him;
there are torrential rains which turn all firm ground into a sea of
mud and rob man of his freedom of movement: all travel bogs
down. Here, in Mesopotamia, Nature stays not her hand; in her
full might she cuts across and overrides man's will, makes him
feel to the full how slightly he matters.

The mood of Mesopotamian civilization reflects this. Man is

not tempted to overrate himself when he contemplates powers in nature such as the thunderstorm and the yearly flood. Of the thunderstorm the Mesopotamian said that its "dreadful flares of light cover the land like a cloth."[2] The impression which the flood made on him may be gathered from the following description:

> The rampant flood which no man can oppose,
> Which shakes the heavens and causes earth to tremble,
> In an appalling blanket folds mother and child,
> Beats down the canebrake's full luxuriant greenery,
> And drowns the harvest in its time of ripeness.
>
> Rising waters, grievous to eyes of man,
> All-powerful flood, which forces the embankments
> And mows mighty *mesu*-trees,
> (Frenzied) storm, tearing all things in massed confusion
> With it (in hurtling speed).[3]

Standing amidst such powers, man sees how weak he is, realizes with dread that he is caught in an interplay of giant forces. His mood becomes tense; his own lack of power makes him acutely aware of tragic potentialities.

The experience of Nature which produced this mood found direct expression in the Mesopotamian's notion of the cosmos in which he lived. He was in no way blind to the great rhythms of the cosmos; he saw the cosmos as order, not as anarchy. But to him that order was not nearly so safe and reassuring as it was to the Egyptian. Through and under it he sensed a multitude of powerful individual wills, potentially divergent, potentially conflicting, fraught with a possibility of anarchy. He confronted in Nature gigantic and wilful individual powers.

To the Mesopotamian, accordingly, cosmic *order* did not appear as something given; rather it became something achieved—achieved through a continual integration of the many individual cosmic wills, each so powerful, so frightening. His understanding of the cosmos tended therefore to express itself in terms of integration of wills, that is, in terms of social orders such as the family, the community, and, most particularly, the state. To put it succinctly, he saw the cosmic order as an order of wills—as a state.

In presenting this view here, we shall discuss first the period in which it may be assumed to have originated. We shall then take up the question of what the Mesopotamian saw in the phenomena of the world around him, in order to show how it could be possible for him to apply an order from the social sphere, the state, to the basically different world of Nature. Lastly, we shall discuss that order in detail and comment on those forces which played the most prominent part in it.

DATE OF THE MESOPOTAMIAN VIEW OF THE WORLD

The Mesopotamian's understanding of the universe in which he lived seems to have found its characteristic form at about the time when Mesopotamian civilization as a whole took shape, that is, in the Proto-literate period, around the middle of the fourth millennium B.C.

Thousands of years had already passed since man first entered the valley of the Two Rivers, and one prehistoric culture had followed another—all basically alike, none signally different from what one might have found elsewhere in the world. During those millenniums agriculture was the chief means of support. Tools were fashioned from stone, rarely from copper. Villages, made up of patriarchal families, seem to have been the typical form of settlement. The most conspicuous change from one such culture to another, surely not a very profound one, seems to have been in the way pottery was made and decorated.

But with the advent of the Proto-literate period the picture changes. Overnight, as it were, Mesopotamian civilization crystallizes. The fundamental pattern, the controlling framework within which Mesopotamia is to live its life, formulate its deepest questions, evaluate itself and evaluate the universe, for ages to come, flashes into being, complete in all its main features.

In the economic sphere appeared *planned large-scale irrigation by means of canals*, a form which forever after was to be characteristic of Mesopotamian agriculture. Concurrent with this and closely interrelated with it was a spectacular increase in population. The old villages expanded into cities; new settlements were founded throughout the country. And, as village grew into city, the political pattern of the new civilization emerged—*Primitive Democracy*. In the new city-state ultimate political power rested with a general assembly of all adult freemen. Normally the everyday affairs of the community were guided by a council of elders; but in times of crisis, for instance, when war threatened, the general assembly could confer absolute powers on one of its members and proclaim him king. Such kingship was an office held for a limited term; and, as the assembly could confer it, so it could also revoke it when a crisis was past.

The centralization of authority which this new political pattern made possible may have been responsible, along with other factors, for the emergence of a truly *monumental architecture* in Mesopotamia. Imposing temples now began to rise in the plain, often built on gigantic artificial mountains of sun-dried bricks, the famous *ziqqurats*. Works of such imposing proportions clearly presuppose a high degree of organization and direction in the community which achieved them.

As these things were happening in the economic and social fields, new peaks of achievement were attained in the more spiritual fields of endeavor. *Writing* was invented, at first serving to facilitate the ever more complicated accounting which had become necessary with the expansion of city and temple economy. Eventually it was to become the vehicle of a most significant literature. Moreover, Mesopotamia produced *art* worthy of the name; and the works of these early artists compare very well with the best of later periods.

In economics, in politics, and in the arts Mesopotamia thus found at this early stage its guiding forms, created set ways in which to deal with the universe in its various aspects as they confronted man. It would not be surprising, therefore, to find that the view taken of the universe as a whole should likewise have clarified and taken form at that time. That this actually happened is indicated by the world view itself. As we have already mentioned, Mesopotamian civilization interpreted the universe as a state. However, the basis of interpretation was not the state that existed in historic times but the state as it had been before history—a Primitive Democracy. We have therefore the right to assume that the idea of a cosmic state crystallized very early, when Primitive Democracy was the prevalent type of state—indeed, with Mesopotamian civilization itself.

Assuming, then, that the Mesopotamian view of the universe was as old as Mesopotamian civilization itself, we must next ask how it could be at all possible to take such a view. Certainly for us it has no meaning whatever to speak of the universe as a state—of stones and stars, winds and waters, as citizens and as members of legislative assemblies. Our universe is made up largely of things, of dead matter with neither life nor will. This leads us to the question of what the Mesopotamian saw in the phenomena which surrounded him, the world in which he lived.

The reader will remember from the first chapter that "the world appears to primitive man neither inanimate nor empty but redundant with life." It was said of primitive man that "any phenomenon may at any time face him not as 'It' but as 'Thou.' In this confrontation 'Thou' reveals individuality, qualities, will." Out of the repeated experience of the "I-Thou" relationship a fairly consistent personalistic view may develop. Objects and phenomena in man's environment become personified in varying degrees. They are somehow alive; they have wills of their own; each is a definite personality. We then have what the late Andrew Lang disapprovingly described as "that inextricable confusion in which men, beasts, plants, stones, stars are all on one level of personality and animated existence."[4]

A few examples may show that Lang's words well describe the Mesopotamian's approach to the phenomena around him. Ordinary kitchen salt is to us an inanimate substance, a mineral. To the Mesopotamian it was a fellow-being whose help might be sought if one had fallen victim to sorcery and witchcraft. The sufferer would then address it as follows:

> O Salt, created in a clean place,
> For food of gods did Enlil destine thee.
> Without thee no meal is set out in Ekur,
> Without thee god, king, lord, and prince do not smell incense.
> I am so-and-so, the son of so-and-so,
> Held captive by enchantment,
> Held in fever by bewitchment.
> O Salt, break my enchantment! Loose my spell!
> Take from me the bewitchment!—And as my Creator
> I shall extol thee.[5]

As Salt, a fellow-creature with special powers, can be approached directly, so can Grain. When a man offered up flour to conciliate an angry deity, he might say to it:

> I will send thee to my angry god, my angry goddess,
> Whose heart is filled with furious rage against me.
> Do thou reconcile my angry god, my angry goddess.

Both Salt and Grain are thus not the inanimate substances for which we know them. They are alive, have personality and a will of their own. So had any phenomenon in the Mesopotamian world whenever it was approached in a spirit other than that of humdrum, practical, everyday pursuits: in magic, in religion, in speculative thought. In such a world it obviously gives better sense than it does in our world to speak of the relations between phenomena of nature as social relations, of the order in which they function as an order of wills, as a state.

By saying that the phenomena of the world were alive for the Mesopotamian, that they were personified, we have made things simpler than they actually are. We have glossed over a potential distinction which was felt by the Mesopotamian. It is not correct to say that each phenomenon was a person; we must say that there was a will and a personality in each phenomenon—in it and yet somehow behind it, for the single concrete phenomenon did not completely circumscribe and exhaust the will and personality associated with it. For instance, a particular lump of flint had a clearly recognizable personality and will. Dark, heavy, and hard, it would show a curious willingness to flake under the craftsman's tool though that tool was only of horn softer than the stone against which it was pressed. Now, this characteristic personality which confronts one here, in this particular lump of flint, may meet one also over there, in another lump of flint, which seems to say: "Here I am again—dark, heavy, hard, willing to flake, I, Flint!" Wherever one met it, its name was "Flint," and it would suffer itself to flake easily. That was because it had once fought the god Ninurta, and Ninurta had imposed flaking on it as a punishment.[6]

We may consider another example—the reeds which grew in the Mesopotamian marshes. It is quite clear from our texts that, in themselves, they were never divine. Any individual reed counted merely as a plant, a thing, and so did all reeds. The concrete individual reed, however, had wonderful qualities which inspired awe. There was a mysterious power to grow luxuriantly in the marshes. A reed was capable of amazing things, such as the music which would come out of a shepherd's pipe, or the meaningful signs which would take form under the scribe's reed stylus and make a story or a poem. These powers, which were to be found in every reed and were always the same, combined for the Mesopotamian into a divine personality—that of the goddess Nidaba. It was Nidaba who made the reeds thrive in the marshes; if she were not near, the shepherd could not soothe the heart with music from his reed pipe. To her would the scribe give praise when a difficult piece of writing had come out from under his stylus and he saw it to be good. The goddess was thus the power in all reeds; she made them what they were, lent them her mysterious qualities. She was one with every reed in the sense that she permeated it as an animating and characterizing agent; but she did not lose her identity in that of the concrete phenomenon and was not limited by any or even all existing reeds.[7] In a crude but quite effective manner the Mesopotamian artists suggested this relationship when they depicted the reed-goddess. She is shown in human form as a venerable matron. But the reeds also are there: they sprout from her shoulders—are bodily one with her and seem to derive directly from her.

In a great many individual phenomena, such as individual lumps of flint or individual reeds, the Mesopotamian thus felt that he was confronted by a single self. He sensed, as it were, a common power-center which was charged with a particular personality and was itself personal. This personal power-center pervaded the individual phenomena and gave them the character which they are seen to have: "Flint" all lumps of flint, Nidaba all reeds, etc.

Even more curious than this, however, is the fact that one such self might infuse itself into other different selves and, in a relation of partial identity, lend them of its character. We may illustrate by quoting a Mesopotamian incantation by which a man sought to become identical with Heaven and Earth:

> I am Heaven, you cannot touch me,
> I am Earth, you cannot bewitch me![8]

The man is trying to ward off sorcery from his body, and his attention is centered on a single quality of Heaven and Earth, their sacred inviolability. When he has made himself identical with them, this quality will flow into him and merge with his being, so that he will be secure from attacks by witchcraft.

Very similar is another incantation in which a man endeavors to drench every part of his body in immunity by such identification with gods and sacred emblems. It reads:

> Enlil is my head, my face is the day;
> Urash, the peerless god, is the protecting spirit leading my way.
> My neck is the necklace of the goddess Ninlil,
> My two arms are the sickle of the western moon,
> My fingers tamarisk, bone of the gods of heaven;
> They ward off the embrace of sorcery from my body;
> The gods Lugal-edinna and Latarak are my breast and knees;
> Muhra my ever-wandering feet.[9]

Here again the identity sought is only partial. Qualities of these gods and sacred emblems are to infuse the man's members and make him inviolable.

As it was thought possible for a man to achieve partial identity with various gods, so could one god enjoy partial identity with other gods and thus share in their natures and abilities. We are told, for instance, that the face of the god Ninurta is Shamash, the sun-god; that one of Ninurta's ears is the god of wisdom, Ea—and so on through all of Ninurta's members.[10] These curious statements may be taken to mean that Ninurta's face derived its dazzling radiance from, and thus shared in, that brilliance which is characteristically the sun-god's and concentrates itself in him. In similar manner, his ear—for the Mesopotamians believed the ear, not the brain, to be the seat of intelligence—shares in that supreme intelligence which is the outstanding characteristic of the god Ea.

Sometimes such statements of partial identity take a slightly different form. We are told, for instance, that the god Marduk is the god Enlil when there is question of ruling and taking counsel, but that he is Sîn, the moon-god, when he acts as illuminer of the night, etc.[11] This apparently means that the god Marduk, when he rules and makes decisions, partakes of the personality, qualities, and abilities of the divine executive par excellence, the god Enlil. When, on the other hand, Marduk, as the planet Jupiter, shines in the nightly skies, he shares in those special powers which characterize the moon-god and have their center in him.

Any phenomenon which the Mesopotamian met in the world around him was thus alive, had its own personality and will, its distinct self. But the self which revealed itself, for example, in a particular lump of flint, was not limited by that particular lump; it was in it and yet behind it; it permeated it and gave it character as it did all lumps of flint. And as one such "self" could permeate many individual phenomena, so it might also permeate other selves and thereby give to them of its specific character to add to the qualities which they had in their own right.

To understand nature, the many and varied phenomena around man, was thus to understand the personalities in these phenomena, to know their characters, the direction of their wills, and also the range of their powers. It was a task not different from that of understanding other men, knowing their characters, their wills, the extent of their power and influence. And intuitively the Mesopotamian applied to nature the experience he had of his own human society, interpreting it in social terms. A particularly suggestive example will illustrate this. Under our eyes, as it were, objective reality assumes the form of a social type.

According to Mesopotamian beliefs, a man who had been bewitched could destroy the enemies who had bewitched him by burning images of them. The characteristic self of the enemy stared up at him from the image. He could get at it and harm it there, as well as in the person. And so he consigned the images to the fire while addressing it as follows:

> Scorching Fire, warlike son of Heaven,
> Thou, the fiercest of thy brethren,
> Who like Moon and Sun decidest lawsuits—
> Judge thou my case, hand down the verdict.
> Burn the man and woman who bewitched me;
> Burn, O Fire, the man and woman who bewitched me;
> Scorch, O Fire, the man and woman who bewitched me;
> Burn them, O Fire;
> Scorch them, O Fire;
> Take hold of them, O Fire;
> Consume them, O Fire;
> Destroy them, O Fire.[12]

It is quite clear that the man approaches the fire for the destructive power he knows to be in it. But the fire has a will of its own; it will burn the images—and in them his enemies—only if it so chooses. And in deciding whether to burn the images or not, the fire becomes a judge between the man and his enemies: the situation becomes a lawsuit in which the man pleads his cause and asks the fire to vindicate him. The power which is in fire has taken definite form, has been interpreted in social terms; it is a judge.

As the fire here becomes a judge, other powers take form in similar pregnant situations. The thunderstorm was a warrior; he flung deadly lightning, and one could hear the roar emitted by the wheels of his war chariot. The earth was a woman, a mother; she gave birth each year to the new vegetation. In such cases the Mesopotamians did only what other people have done throughout the ages. "Men," as Aristotle says, "imagine not only the forms of the gods but their ways of life to be like their own."[13]

If we were to try to single out a typically Mesopotamian feature, we should perhaps point to the degree to which this people found and emphasized organized relationships of the powers they recognized. While all people tend to humanize nonhuman powers and frequently visualize them as social types, Mesopotamian speculative thought seems to have brought out and systematized to an unusual degree the implications of social and political function latent in such typifying and to have elaborated them into clear-cut institutions. This particular emphasis would seem to be closely bound up with the nature of the society in which the Mesopotamian lived and from which he derived his terms and his evaluation.

When the universe was taking form for the Mesopotamian, he lived, we have argued, in a Primitive Democracy. All great undertakings, all important decisions, originated in a general assembly of all the citizens; they were not the affair of any single individual. It is accordingly natural that, in trying to understand how the great cosmic events were brought about, he should be especially intent upon the ways in which the individual forces of the cosmos co-operated to run the universe. Cosmic institutions would naturally come to loom important in his view of the universe, and the structure of the universe would stand out clearly as the structure of a state.

THE STRUCTURE OF THE COSMIC STATE

The commonwealth of the Mesopotamian cosmos encompassed the whole existing world—in fact, anything that could be thought of as an entity: humans, animals, inanimate objects, natural phenomena, as well as notions such as justice, righteousness, the form of a circle, etc. How such entities could all be seen as members of a state we have just shown; they had in them will, character, and power. But though all things that could be imagined were members of the cosmic state, they were not all members on the same political level. The criterion of differentiation was power.

In the state on earth there were large groups of people who had no share in the government. Slaves, children, and perhaps women had no voice in the assembly. Only the adult freemen met there to decide on public affairs; they alone were citizens in the true sense. Quite similarly in the state which the universe constituted. Only those natural forces whose power inspired the Mesopotamian with awe, and whom he therefore ranked as gods, were considered full citizens of the universe, were thought to have political rights and to exercise political influence. The general assembly in the cosmic state was therefore an assembly of gods.

We hear about this assembly often in Mesopotamian literature, and we know in general how it functioned. It was the highest authority in the universe. Here the momentous decisions regarding the course of all things and the fates of all beings were made and were confirmed by the members of the assembly. Before that stage was reached, however, proposals were discussed, perhaps even heatedly, by gods who were for or against them. The leader of the assembly was the god of heaven, Anu. At his side stood his son Enlil, god of the storm. One of these usually broached the matters to be considered, and the gods would then discuss them. Through such discussions (the Mesopotamians called it "asking one another") the issues were clarified, and the consensus would begin to stand out. Of special weight in the discussion were the voices of a small group of the most prominent gods, "the seven gods who determine destinies." In this way, full agreement was finally reached, all the gods assented with a firm "Let it be," and the decision was announced by Anu and Enlil. It was now "the verdict, the word of the assembly of the gods, the command of Anu and Enlil." The executive duties (the task of carrying out the decisions) seem to have rested with Enlil.

LEADERS OF THE COSMIC STATE

We have seen that the gods who constituted the divine assembly were powers which the Mesopotamians recognized in and behind the various phenomena of nature. Which of these powers, then, played the most prominent roles in the assembly, influenced most the course of the universe? In a sense we may answer: "The powers in those elements of the cosmos which were seen to be the greatest and most prominent."

Anu, the highest of the gods, was god of the sky, and his name was the everyday word for "sky." The dominant role which the sky plays—even in a merely spatial sense—in the composition of the visible universe, and the eminent position which it occupies, high above all other things, may well explain why Anu should rank as the most important force in the cosmos.

Enlil, the second highest of the gods, was god of the storm. His name means "Lord Storm," and he personifies the essence of the storm. No one who has experienced a storm in flat, open Mesopotamia can possibly doubt the might of this cosmic force. The storm, master of all free space under the sky, ranked naturally as the second great component of the cosmos.

As third basic component of the visible universe comes the earth. Earth, so near to man, so vitally important to him in so many of its aspects, was difficult to view and hold fast within the scope of a single concept. We meet it as "Mother Earth," the fertile giver of blessings to man, and as the "queen of the gods" and "lady of the mountains." But the earth is also the source of the life-giving waters in rivers, canals, and wells; waters which stream from a vast sea within. And as the source of these waters the earth was viewed as male, as *En-ki*, "lord of the earth," more originally perhaps "Lord Earth." The third and fourth in rank of the Mesopotamian gods were these two aspects of the earth, Ninhursaga and Enki. They round off the list of the most important cosmic elements that must rank highest and exercise the greatest influence on all that is.

A. The Power in the Sky: Authority

But considerations of size and position alone could hardly have suggested the specific character and the function which these powers were assumed to have in the universe. The Mesopotamian conceived both character and function in direct confrontation with the phenomena when they "revealed" themselves and deeply affected him.

The sky can, at moments when man is in a singularly receptive mood, reveal itself in an almost terrifying experience. The vast sky encircling one on all sides may be felt as a presence at once overwhelming and awesome, forcing one to his knees merely by its sheer being. And this feeling which the sky inspires is definite and can be named: it is that inspired by majesty. There is in it the experience of greatness or even of the tremendous. There comes a keen realization of one's own insignificance, of unbridgeable remoteness. The Mesopotamians express this well when they say, "Godhead awesome as the faraway heavens, as the broad sea." But, though a feeling of distance, this feeling is not one of absolute separation; it has a strong element of sympathy and of the most unqualified acceptance.

Beyond all, however, the experience of majesty is the experience of power, of power bordering on the tremendous, but power at rest, not consciously imposing its will. The power behind majesty is so great that it need not exert itself. Without any effort on its part it commands allegiance by its very presence; the onlooker obeys freely, through a categorical imperative rising from the depths of his own soul.

This majesty and absolute authority which can be experienced in the sky the Mesopotamians called Anu. Anu was the overpowering personality of the sky, the "Thou" which permeated it and could be felt through it. If the sky was considered apart from him, as it could be, it receded into the category of things and became a mere abode for the god.

The "Thou" which met the Mesopotamian when he confronted the sky was so powerfully experienced that it was felt to be the very center and source of all majesty. Wherever else he found majesty and authority he knew it to be that power in the sky, to be Anu. And he did find it elsewhere; indeed, authority, the power

which produces automatic acceptance and obedience, is a basic
constituent in all organized human society. Were it not for unques-
tioning obedience to customs, to laws, and to those "in authority,"
society would dissolve in anarchy and chaos. So in those persons in
whom authority resided—the father in the family, the ruler in the
state—the Mesopotamian recognized something of Anu and Anu's
essence. As the father of the gods, Anu was the prototype of all
fathers; as the "pristine king and ruler," he was the prototype of
all rulers. To him belong the insignia in which the essence of royalty was embodied—the scepter, the crown, the headband, and
the shepherd's staff—and from him did they derive. Before any
king had yet been appointed among men these insignia already
were, and they rested in heaven before Anu. From there they descended to earth. Anu also calls to kingship; and when the king
commands and the command is unquestioningly and immediately
obeyed, when it "comes true," it is again the essence of Anu
which manifests itself. It is Anu's command that issues through the
king's mouth; it is Anu's power that makes it immediately effica-
cious.

But human society was to the Mesopotamian merely a part of
the larger society of the universe. The Mesopotamian universe—
because it did not consist of dead matter, because every stone, every
tree, every conceivable thing in it was a being with a will and character of its own—was likewise founded on authority; its members,
too, willingly and automatically obeyed orders which made them
act as they should act. These orders *we* call laws of nature. So the
whole universe showed the influence of the essence peculiar to
Anu.

When in the Babylonian creation story the god Marduk is given
absolute authority, and all things and forces in the universe automatically conform themselves to his will so that whatever he orders
immediately comes to pass, then his command has become identical
in essence with Anu and the gods exclaim: "Thy word is Anu."

We see thus that Anu is the source of and active principle in all
authority, both in human society and in the larger society which is
the universe. He is the force which lifts it out of chaos and anarchy and makes it into a structure, an organized whole; he is the
force which insures the necessary voluntary obedience to orders,

laws, and customs in society and to the natural laws in the physical world, in short, to world order. As a building is supported by, and reveals in its structure the lines of, its foundation, so the Mesopotamian universe is upheld by, and reflects in *its* structure, a divine will. Anu's command is the foundation of heaven and earth.

What we have said here at some length about the function of Anu is said briefly and concisely by the Mesopotamians themselves. When the great gods address Anu in the "Myth of the Elevation of Inanna," they exclaim:

> What thou hast ordered (comes) true!
> The utterance of prince and lord is (but)
> what thou hast ordered, (that with which) thou art in agreement.
> O Anu! thy great command takes precedence,
> who could say no (to it)?
> O father of the gods, thy command,
> the very foundation of heaven and earth,
> what god could spurn (it)?[14]

As the absolute sovereign of the world, the highest power in the universe, Anu is described in such words as these:

> Wielder of the scepter, the ring, and the *palu*
> who callest to kingship,
> Sovereign of the gods, whose word prevails
> in the ordained assembly of the great gods,
> Lord of the glorious crown, astounding
> through thine enchantment,
> Rider of great storms, who occupies the dais of sovereignty,
> wondrously regal—
> To the pronouncements of thy holy mouth
> are the Igigi attentive;
> In fear before thee move the Anunnaki,
> Like storm-swept reeds bow to thy orders
> all the gods.[15]

B. The Power in the Storm: Force

Turning from Anu, god of the sky, to Enlil, god of the storm, we meet a power of a somewhat different cast. As his name *En-lil*, "Lord Storm," suggests, he was in a sense the storm itself. As the storm, the undisputed master of all space between heaven and earth, Enlil was palpably the second greatest power of the visible universe, second only to the sky above him.

In the storm he "reveals" himself. The violence, the force, which fills it and is experienced in it was the god, was Enlil. It is thus through the storm, through its violence and force, that we must seek to understand the god and his function in the universe.

The city of Ur had long held sway over Babylonia. Then it fell before a merciless attack by Elamitic hordes which swept down upon it from the eastern mountains. The utter destruction of the city was wrought, in our terms, by the barbaric hordes which attacked it. Not so in terms of the Mesopotamian's own understanding of his universe: the wild destructive essence manifest in this attack was Enlil's. The enemy hordes were but a cloak, an outward form under which that essence realized itself. In a deeper, truer sense the barbaric hordes were a storm, Enlil's storm, wherewith the god himself was executing a verdict passed on Ur and its people by the assembly of the gods; and as that storm the enemy attack is seen and described:

> Enlil called the storm.
>   The people mourn.
> Exhilarating winds he took from the land.
>   The people mourn.
> Good winds he took away from Shumer.
>   The people mourn.
> He summoned evil winds.
>   The people mourn.
> Entrusted them to Kingaluda, tender of storms.
>
> He called the storm that will annihilate the land.
>   The people mourn.
> He called disastrous winds.
>   The people mourn.
> Enlil—choosing Gibil as his helper—
> Called the (great) hurricane of heaven.
>   The people mourn.
>
> The (blinding) hurricane howling across the skies,
>   —The people mourn—
> The shattering storm roaring across the land,
>   —The people mourn—
> The tempest which, relentless as a floodwave,
> Beats down upon, devours the city's ships,
> All these he gathered at the base of heaven.
>   The people mourn.

> (Great) fires he lit that heralded the storm.
> The people mourn.
> And lit on either flank of furious winds
> The searing heat of desert.
> Like flaming heat of noon this fire scorched.[16]

This storm is the true cause of the city's downfall:

> The storm ordered by Enlil in hate, the storm
> which wears away the country,
> covered Ur like a cloth, enveloped it like a linen sheet.[17]

It is the cause of the destruction wrought:

> On that day did the storm leave the city;
> that city was a ruin.
> O father Nanna, that town was left a ruin.
> The people mourn.
> On that day did the storm leave the country.
> The people mourn.
>
> (Dead) men, not potsherds,
> Covered the approaches.
> The walls were gaping,
> The high gates, the roads,
> Were piled with dead.
> In the wide streets, where feasting crowds would gather,
> Scattered they lay.
> In all the streets and roadways bodies lay.
> In open fields that used to fill with dancers,
> They lay in heaps.
>
> The country's blood now filled its holes,
> like metal in a mold;
> Bodies dissolved—like fat left in the sun.[18]

In the great catastrophes of history, in the crushing blows voted by the assembly of the gods, there is Enlil, essence of the storm. He is force, executor of the verdicts of the gods.

But not only as divine sheriff, as executor of all punitive decrees in the cosmic state, is Enlil active. He participates in all legitimate exercise of force, and thus it is he who leads the gods in war. The great Mesopotamian myth of creation, *Enuma elish*, has had a somewhat turbulent career; as its hero we find sometimes one, sometimes another, god. There can be little doubt, however, that the myth, in its original form, centered around Enlil. As such, it describes the dangers which once beset the gods when they were threatened with attack from the powers of chaos: how neither the command of Enki nor that of Anu, reinforced by the authority of the assembly of gods, could stay them; how the gods assembled and chose young Enlil to be their king and champion; and how Enlil vanquished the enemy, Ti'amat, by means of the storms, those forces which express the essence of his being.

Thus, in the society which the Mesopotamian universe constitutes, Anu represents authority, Enlil force. The subjective experience of the sky, of Anu, is, as we have seen, one of majesty, of absolute authority which commands allegiance by its very presence. The onlooker obeys it not through any outward pressure but through a categorical imperative which rises within his own soul. Not so with Enlil, the storm. Here, too, is power; but it is the power of force, of compulsion. Opposing wills are crushed and beaten into submission. In the assembly of the gods, the ruling body of the universe, Anu presides and directs the proceedings. His will and authority, freely and voluntarily accepted, guide the assembly much as a constitution guides the actions of a lawmaking body. Indeed, his will is the unwritten, living constitution of the Mesopotamian world state. But whenever force enters the picture, when the cosmic state is enforcing its will against opposition, then Enlil takes the center of the stage. He executes the sentences imposed by the assembly; he leads the gods in war. Thus Anu and Enlil embody, on a cosmic level, the two powers which are the fundamental constituents of any state: authority and legitimate force; for, while authority alone may suffice to hold a community together, such a community becomes a state only when it develops organs to back up its authority with force, when its staff, to quote Max Weber, "successfully displays the monopoly of a legitimate physical compulsion." For this reason we can say that, while it is the powers of Anu that make the Mesopotamian universe an organized society, it is the complementary powers of Enlil that define this society as a state.

Because Enlil is force, his character is one of peculiar duality: he is at one and the same time the trust and the fear of man. He is force as legitimate force, upholder of the state, a rock of strength even to the gods. Man greets him in words like these:

> O Thou who dost encompass all heaven and earth, fleet god,
> Wise instructor of the people,
> Who dost survey the regions of the world;
> Prince, counselor, whose word is heeded,
> Whose spoken word . . . . gods cannot alter,
> The utterance of whose lips no god may spurn;
> Great Lord, ruler of gods in heaven,
> Counselor of gods on earth, judicious prince.[19]

Yet, because Enlil is force, there lie hidden in the dark depths of his soul both violence and wildness. The normal Enlil upholds the cosmos, guarantees order against chaos; but suddenly and unpredictably the hidden wildness in him may break forth. This side of Enlil is truly and terribly the abnormal, a scattering of all life and of life's meaning. Therefore, man can never be fully at ease with Enlil but feels a lurking fear which finds expression frequently in the hymns which have come down to us:

> What has he planned . . . . ?
> What is in my father's heart?
> What is in Enlil's holy mind?
> What has he planned against me in his holy mind?
> A net he spread: that is the net of an enemy.
> A snare he set: that is the snare of an enemy.
> He has stirred up the waters, and will catch the fishes.
> He cast his net, and will (bring) down the birds.[20]

This same fear shows in other descriptions of Enlil, who may let his people perish in the merciless storm. The god's rage is almost pathological, an inner turmoil of the soul which renders him insensate, inaccessible to all appeals:

> O father Enlil, whose eyes are glaring (wildly),
> How long—till they will be at peace again?
> O thou who covered up thy head with a cloth—how long?
> O thou who laid thy head upon thy knees—how long?
> O thou who closed thy heart like an earthen box—how long?
> O mighty one who with thy fingers sealed thine ears—how long?
> O father Enlil, even now they perish![21]

C. The Power in the Earth: Fertility

The third great component of the visible cosmos is the Earth, and the Mesopotamians acknowledged it as the third most important power in the universe. Their understanding of this power and its ways was gained, as with sky and storm, in direct experience of it as inner will and direction. Correspondingly, the ancient name of this deity, *Ki*, "Earth," had difficulty in maintaining itself and tended ever more to give way to other names based on significant characteristics. The earth revealed itself to the Mesopotamians before all as "Mother Earth," the great inexhaustible mysterious source of new life, of fertility in all its forms. Every year she gives birth anew to grass and plants. The arid desert becomes green overnight. The shepherds drive out their flocks. Ewes and goats give birth to lambs and kids. Everything thrives and increases. On the good fields of Shumer "grain, the green maiden, lifts her head in the furrow"; soon a rich harvest will fill granaries and storehouses to overflowing. Well-fed humanity, full of beer, bread, and milk, will feel abundant life surge through their bodies in a wave of profound well-being.

The force active in all this—the power manifesting itself in fertility, in birth, in new life—is the essence of the earth. The earth, as a divine power, is *Nin-tu*, "the lady who gives birth"; she is *Níg-zi-gál-dím-me*, "the fashioner of everything wherein is the breath of life." Reliefs show her as a woman suckling a child; other children are tucked away under her dress and peep out wherever they can; embryos surround her. As the incarnation of all reproductive forces in the universe, she is the "mother of the gods" and also the mother and creator of mankind; indeed, she is—as an inscription states—the "mother of all children." If she so wills, she may deny an evildoer offspring or even stop all birth in the land.

As the active principle in birth and fertility, in the continual renewal of vegetation, the growth of crops, the increase of flocks, the perpetuation of the human race, she holds with right her position as a dominant power, takes her seat with Anu and Enlil in the assembly of the gods, the ruling body of the universe. She is *Nin-mah*, "the exalted queen"; she is "queen of the gods," "queen of kings and lords," the "lady who determines fates," and the "lady who makes decisions concerning (all) heaven and earth."

D. The Power in the Water: Creativity

But the earth, so near to man, so varied and manifold in characteristics, is—as we have mentioned—not easily comprehended as an entity by the mind. It is too rich and diverse for any single concept to express fully. We have just described one of its basic aspects, the fertile soil, the active principle in birth and procreation, Mother Earth. But from the earth also come the life-giving sweet waters, the water in wells, in springs, in rivers; and in very early times these "waters which wander in the earth" seem to have been considered as part of its being, an aspect among many aspects under which it might be viewed. If so viewed, however, the power manifest in it was male, *En-ki*, "lord of the earth." In historical times only Enki's name and the role he plays in certain myths give any indication that he and the sweet water for which he stands were once merely an aspect of the earth as such. The waters and the power in them have emancipated themselves, have their own independent individuality and peculiar essence. The power which revealed itself to the Mesopotamian in his subjective experience of water was a creative power, a divine will to produce new life, new beings, new things. In this respect it was akin to the powers in the earth, in the fertile soil. And yet there was a difference—that between passive and active. The Earth, Ki, Ninhursaga, or whatever else we may choose to call her, was immobile; hers is the passive productivity, fertility. Water, on the other hand, comes and goes. It flows out over the field, irrigating it; then it trickles away and is gone. It is as though it were possessed of will and purpose. It typifies active productivity, conscious thought, creativity.

Moreover, the ways of water are devious. It avoids rather than surmounts obstacles, goes around and yet gets to its goal. The farmer, who works with it in irrigation, easing it along from canal to canal, knows how tricky it can be, how easily it slips away, takes unforeseen turns. And so, we may assume, the idea of cunning, of superior intelligence, came to be imparted to Enki. This aspect of his being would be further developed by contemplation of the dark, brooding, impenetrable waters of wells and lagoons, which suggested perhaps the more profound intellectual qualities, wisdom and knowledge. In the functioning of the universe the powers which are peculiarly Enki's manifest themselves often and in many places. They are directly active in the roles played by water everywhere: when it falls from heaven as rain, when it comes flowing down in the rivers, when it is led through canals out over fields and orchards where it produces the crops of the country and the prosperity of the people. But Enki's essence is also manifest in all knowledge. It is the creative element in thought, whether it produces new effective patterns of action, such as wise counsel (Enki is the one who gives to rulers their broad intelligence and "opens the door of understanding") or produces new things, as in the skill of the craftsman (Enki is the god of the craftsmen par excellence). Beyond all, however, his essence, his powers, show themselves in the powerful spells of the incantation priests. It is he who gives the powerful orders which constitute the priest's spells, orders which will assuage angry forces or drive away evil demons that have attacked man.

The range of the forces which are Enki's, the place which they occupy in the organized universe, is expressed with great precision in the office which Enki holds in the world state. He is a *nun*, that is, a great nobleman of the realm outstanding by experience and wisdom—a councilor, not unlike the Anglo-Saxon *witan*. But he is not a king, not a ruler in his own right. The position he holds in the world state he holds by appointment. His authority derives from Anu and Enlil; he is their minister. In modern terms one might perhaps call him Secretary of Agriculture in the universe. He is charged with overseeing rivers, canals, and irrigation and of organizing the productive forces of the country. He smooths out such difficulties as may arise by wise counsel, by arbitration, and by reconciliation. We may quote from a Sumerian hymn which describes him and his office clearly and well:

> O Lord, who with thy wizard's eyes, even when wrapped in thought,
>   immobile, yet dost penetrate all things,
> O Enki, with thy limitless awareness, exalted counsel
>   of the Anunnaki,
> Very knowing one, who dost exact obedience when turning his wit
>   to conciliation and decision,

Settling of legal strife; counselor
    from sunrise until sunset,
O Enki, master over prudent words, to thee
    I will give praise.
Anu thy father, pristine king and ruler
    over an inchoate world,
Empowered thee, in heaven and on earth, to guide and form,
    exalted thee to lordship over them.
To clear the pure mouths of the Tigris and Euphrates,
    to make verdure plentiful,
Make dense the clouds, grant water in abundance
    to all plowlands,
To make corn lift its head in furrows and to make
    pasture abundant in the desert,
To make young saplings in plantations and in orchards
    sprout, where planted like a forest—
These acts did Anu, king of gods, entrust to thee;
    while Enlil granted thee his potent awesome name. . . . .
As ruler over all that has been born
    thou art a younger Enlil,
Younger brother of him, thou art, who is sole god
    in heaven and on earth.
To fix, like him, the fates of North and South
    he truly has empowered thee.
When thy righteous decision and pronouncement cause
    deserted cities to be reinhabited,
When, O Sabara, countless people have been settled
    throughout the country far and wide,
Thou dost concern thee with their sustenance,
    a father, in truth, thou art to them.
They praise the greatness of their Lord and God.[22]

SUMMARY: THE COSMIC STATE AND ITS STRUCTURE

With Enki we may halt the detailed presentation of entities and powers in the Mesopotamian's universe. The list is long; some are powers within things and phenomena in nature, others—at least to our way of thinking—represent abstract concepts. Each of them influenced the course of the world in one particular way, within one well-defined sphere of action. All derived their authority from some power higher up in that hierarchy of powers which constituted the universe. In some cases, as in that of Enki, it was the highest authority, Anu, or Enlil, who had conferred the office in question. Frequently, however, it was somebody lower down in the scale;

for just as a human state embodies many different subsidiary power-structures at various levels—families, great estates, etc.—each with its own organization but all integrated with the larger structure of the state, so did the cosmic state. It, too, had such minor power-groups: divine families, divine households, divine estates with stewards, overseers, servants, and other attendants.

But the basic lines of the view which the Mesopotamians took of their universe have, we hope, become clear. We may summarize as follows: The Mesopotamian universe did not, like ours, show a fundamental bipartition into animate and inanimate, living and dead, matter. Nor had it different levels of reality: anything that could be felt, experienced, or thought had thereby established its existence, was part of the cosmos. In the Mesopotamian universe, therefore, everything, whether living being, thing, or abstract concept—every stone, every tree, every notion—had a will and character of its own.

World order, the regularity and system observable in the universe, could accordingly—in a universe made up exclusively of individuals—be conceived of in only one fashion: as an order of wills. The universe as an organized whole was a society, a state.

The form of state under which the Mesopotamians viewed the universe, furthermore, was that of Primitive Democracy, which seems to have been the form of state prevalent in the age when Mesopotamian civilization itself came into being

In the Primitive Democracy of early Mesopotamia—as in the fully developed democracies of the classical world—participation in government belonged to a large part of, but by no means to all, the members of the state. Slaves, children, and women, for instance, had no share in government in democratic Athens; neither had similar groups in the Mesopotamian city-states any voice in the popular assembly. Correspondingly, in the universal state there were many members who had no political influence, no share in its government. To these groups belonged, to mention one example, man. Man's position in the state of the universe precisely paralleled that of the slave in the human city-state.

Political influence was wielded in the universe only by those members who, by virtue of the power inherent in them, could be classed as gods. They alone were truly citizens in the political sense. We have mentioned a few of the most important: sky, storm, earth, water. Each god, furthermore, was seen as the expression or manifestation of a will and power to be thus and act thus. Enlil, for instance, is the will and power to rage in a storm and also the will and power to destroy a populous city in an attack by barbaric mountaineers; both storm and destruction were seen as manifestations of one and the same essence. But the realization of these many wills does not produce anarchy or chaos. Each power has limits within which it functions, task and office which it performs. Its will is integrated with those of other powers in the total pattern of conduct which makes the universe a structure, an organized whole.

The basic integration is traceable to Anu. The other powers voluntarily adapt themselves to his authority. He gives to each its task and office in the world state; and so his will is the "foundation" of the universe, reflected throughout its structure.

But, as any state *must* be, the Mesopotamian universe is dynamic, not static. Mere assignment of tasks and offices does not make a state. The state is, and functions through, the co-operation of the wills that hold the offices, in their readjustment to one another, in their alignment for concerted action in a given situation, in questions of general concern. For such alignment of wills the Mesopotamian universe has a general assembly of all citizens. In this assembly Anu presides and directs proceedings. Questions are discussed by the members pro and con until a consensus begins to stand out; the scales are weighted for it by assent from the seven most prominent gods, among them Anu and Enlil; and thus destinies, the great coming events, are shaped, are agreed to, are backed by the united wills of all the great powers of the universe, and are carried into effect by Enlil. Thus functions the universe.

REFLECTIONS OF THE WORLD VIEW IN EARLY MYTHS

The philosophy which we have outlined, the apprehension of reality as a whole under the aspect of a state, originated, we have argued, with Mesopotamian civilization itself around the middle of the fourth millennium before our era.

As a philosophy of existence as a whole, as the fundamental view of a civilization, this view must have had in large measure the character of an axiom. And just as the science of mathematics is very little concerned with its axioms because they are not problems but the patent, the immediately obvious verities from which it starts out, so Mesopotamian thought of the third millennium takes no particular interest in its philosophic basis. We have—and that is undoubtedly more than an accident—no early Sumerian myth which sets as its theme the basic questions: Why is the universe a state? How did it come to be one? Instead, we find the world state taken for granted. It forms the generally known and generally accepted background against which other stories are set and to which they have reference, but it is never the main theme. The main theme is some detail: some question about fitting one or a group of individual features into the over-all pattern is asked and answered by the myth. We are dealing with the products of an age which has solved the big questions, an age of interest in details. Only much later, when the "cosmic state" was perhaps not quite so self-evident, were the fundamental issues in that view of the world taken up for consideration.

The questions which the prolific and varied mythological literature of the third millennium posed and answered may be summed up, for the greater part, under three heads. There are, first, *myths of origin* which ask about the origin of some particular entity within the cosmos or some group of such entities: gods, plants, men. The answer given is usually in terms of birth, more rarely in terms of creation or craftsmanship. The second group consists of *myths of organization*. The myths of this group ask how some feature within, or some area of, the existing world order was brought about: how some god or other obtained his function and offices, how agriculture became organized, how certain freak classes of human beings came to be and were assigned their status. The myths answer: "By divine decree." Lastly, in a sense a subgroup under the myths of organization, there are *myths of evaluation*. The myths of this group ask by what right something or other holds its position in the world order. Such myths will weigh the farmer against the shepherd or, in a different approach to the same question, grain against wool; they will inquire into the relative merits of the costly gold and the lowly, but more useful, copper; etc. The evaluations implicit in the existing order are affirmed and traced to divine decision. We turn first to myths which deal with details of origins.

A. DETAILS OF ORIGINS

We can comment upon only a few typical examples of stories dealing with origins and shall choose mostly such stories as we have already referred to while summing up the current types.

"THE MYTH OF ENLIL AND NINLIL": THE MOON AND HIS BROTHERS

"The Myth of Enlil and Ninlil" answers the question: How did the moon originate, and how did this bright celestial deity come to have three brothers, all connected with the nether world? The myth takes us to the city of Nippur in central Babylonia, at the beginning of time, names the city by its time-honored names, Duranki and Durgishimmar, and identifies the river flowing by it, its quay, harbor, well, and canal, as the Idsalla, Kargeshtinna, Karusar, Pulal, and Nunbirdu, respectively, all localities in historical Nippur and well known to the listeners. Then the myth identifies the inhabitants of the city. They are the deities Enlil, Ninlil, and Ninshebargunu.

> We are living in that very city, (in) Duranki,
> We are living in that very city, (in) Durgishimmar.
> This very river, the Idsalla, was its pure river,
> This very quay, the Kargeshtinna, was its quay,
> This very harbor, the Karusar, was its harbor,
> This very well, the Pulal, was its well of sweet water,
> This very canal, the Nunbirdu, was its sparkling canal.
> No less than ten *iku* each—if measured—were its tilled fields.
> And the young man therein was Enlil;
> And the young maiden therein was Ninlil;
> And the mother therein was Ninshebargunu.[23]

Ninshebargunu warns her young daughter about going to bathe alone in the canal; prying eyes might see her; a young man might violate her.

> In those days did the mother who had borne her instruct the young maiden, did Ninshebargunu instruct Ninlil:
> > "In the pure stream, O woman, in the pure stream do not bathe!
> > In the pure stream, O Ninlil, in the pure stream, O woman,
> >   do not bathe!

> O Ninlil, do not climb onto the bank of the canal Nunbirdu.
> With his shining eyes will the lord, with his shining eyes
>   will he espy thee;
> With his shining eyes will he espy thee, the great mountain,
>   father Enlil;
> With his shining eyes will espy thee, the . . . . shepherd, the
>   determiner of fates.
> Forthwith he will embrace thee, he will kiss thee!"

But Ninlil is young and headstrong.

> Did she listen to the instructions which she gave her?
> In that very stream, the pure one, in that very stream, the pure one,
>   does the (young) woman bathe.
> Onto the bank of the canal, the bank of Nunbirdu, does Ninlil climb.

Everything goes as Ninshebargunu had feared. Enlil sees Ninlil, tries to seduce her, and, when she refuses, takes her by force. He leaves her pregnant with Sîn, the moon-god.

But Enlil's crime has not gone unnoticed. On his return to town, while he is walking across the square—thus we must visualize Kiur, the large open court in the temple—he is arrested and taken before the authorities. The assembly of the gods, the fifty great gods and the seven whose opinion carries special, decisive weight, condemns him to banishment from the city as guilty of rape. (The meaning of the word which we translate "ravisher" is somewhat more general: "one who is under a taboo relating to matters of sex.")

> Enlil came walking into Kiur,
> And while Enlil was passing through Kiur
> The fifty great gods
> And the seven gods whose word is decisive
>   caused Enlil to be arrested in Kiur:
> "Enlil, the ravisher, must leave the town;
> This ravisher Nunamnir, must leave town."

In compliance with the penalty which has been imposed upon him, Enlil then leaves Nippur and makes his way out of the land of the living toward the sinister realm of Hades. But Ninlil follows him.

> Enlil, (in obedience) to the verdict which was given,
> Nunamnir, (in obedience) to the verdict which was given, went.
> And Ninlil followed.

Then Enlil, who is not willing to take her with him outright, begins to fear that other men on the road may misuse the unprotected girl as he himself has done. The first man he meets is the gatekeeper at the town gate. So Enlil stops, takes the place and assumes the likeness of the gatekeeper, and orders him not to say anything if Ninlil should ask.

> Enlil calls unto the gatekeeper:
> "O man of the gate, O man of the bolt,
> O man of the lock, O man of the sacred bolt,
> Thy queen Ninlil is coming.
> If she asks thee about me,
> Do thou not tell her where I am."
> Enlil called unto the gatekeeper:
> "O man of the gate, O man of the bolt,
> O man of the lock, O man of the sacred bolt,
> Thy queen Ninlil is coming.
> The maiden so sweet, so beautiful,
> Thou shalt, O man, not embrace, thou shalt,
>   O man, not kiss!
> To Ninlil, so sweet, so beautiful,
> Has Enlil shown favor; he has looked upon her
>   with shining eyes."

Accordingly, when Ninlil arrives, she finds Enlil in his disguise. She does not recognize him but thinks he is the gatekeeper. He says that his king Enlil has recommended her to him, and she in turn declares that, since Enlil is his king, she is his queen and that she carries Enlil's child, Sîn, the moon-god, under her heart. Enlil as the gatekeeper then pretends—this seems to be understood—to be profoundly perturbed at the thought that she is taking with her to Hades the bright scion of his lord, and he proposes union with her to beget a son who may belong to Hades and take the place of his king's son, the bright moon.

> Let the precious scion of (my) king go to heaven;
>   let my (own) son go to the nether world.
> Let my (own) son go to the nether world as (changeling for)
>   the precious scion of (my) king.

He then embraces Ninlil and again leaves her with child, the god Meslamtaea (who we know was considered a brother of Sîn, the moon). Enlil then continues his way toward Hades, and Ninlil takes up her pursuit. Two more times he stops, the first time when he comes to "the man of the river of Hades," whom he similarly impersonates, engendering the god Ninazu, also a god of the underworld, and the second time when he comes to the ferryman at the river of Hades. In the ferryman's guise he engenders a third god of the nether world, but, as the name of this god is damaged in the text, he cannot yet be identified. Here—very abruptly to our way of thinking—the story comes to a close with a short hymn of praise to Enlil and Ninlil, ending:

> Enlil is lord, Enlil is king.
> Enlil's word cannot be altered;
> Enlil's impetuous word cannot be changed.
> Praise be to mother Ninlil,
> Praise! (to) father Enlil.

The story here told cannot, we think, be considered a pleasant one. Even though it is always extremely dangerous to apply one's own moral standards to cultures and peoples so remote in time and in space, there seems to be a particularly unwholesome air around this tale and the way it is told. Yet, we must not forget two things. First, this story comes from a society in which woman's honor was an unknown concept. Violation of an unmarried woman was an offense against her guardian; violation of a married woman was an offense against her husband; and both were offenses against society and its laws. In no case, however, were they offenses against the woman. She and her feelings simply did not count. For that reason there is a moral conflict involved when Enlil breaks the laws of society in raping Ninlil. In what happens to her after that, only Enlil's honor could be injured; and he avoids that by his handling of the men she meets. Second, and far more important, we must make clear to ourselves that Ninlil, whose plight cannot help appealing to us, and who seems a central character, holds almost no interest to the storyteller. His sole concern is with the children she is to bear—with the origin of the moon-god and his three divine brothers. Ninlil exists for him merely as the potential mother of these children, not as a human being interesting in herself. For that reason the story ends in a manner which seems to us abrupt. But for the storyteller there was nothing of interest to relate after the last divine child was in existence. It is only we who wonder about what further happened between Ninlil and Enlil and should like to be told that Ninlil was finally accepted by Enlil as his wife.

It is from the point of view of the children, then, that the myth is to be understood and interpreted. Why does the bright celestial moon-god come to have three brothers, all powers of the lower, infernal regions? Why does Enlil, the storm, a cosmic force which belongs to the world above, have children who belong to the nether world? The myth answers in psychological terms. It seeks the cause in Enlil's own nature with its curiously dark and violent strains. It is this element of wildness and violence which makes him break the laws and taboos of society, of the world above, when he takes Ninlil by force and Sîn is engendered. The consequences are banishment, imposed by the forces which uphold that world and its fundamental order, by the assembly of the gods.

Enlil's later children are engendered after he has been put beyond the pale of the world of light, when he is on his way to Hades and under its sinister shadow. Therefore, the children he now engenders belong in Hades, and their infernal affinities are confirmed by the words Enlil speaks to induce Ninlil to unite with him. For such is the power of Enlil's word that it is binding, that it comes true however and whenever it is spoken. Therefore, and very aptly, the myth ends in a paean to Enlil's word which cannot be altered, cannot be changed.

The immediate answer to the question of the myth: "Why are Enlil's children so different?" is thus, "Because Enlil so decreed!" But the myth, in giving that answer, is not yet satisfied. It probes behind the immediate answer: tells of the events and of the situation which caused Enlil to speak as he did. And it shows that these events were in no sense accidental but were precipitated by a fundamental contrast in Enlil's own nature. Background for the myth is the view of the universe as a state. Enlil, Ninlil, Sîn, and all the other characters in the story are forces in nature. But, since the mythmaker sees these forces as "Thou's," as members of a society, his endeavor is to understand them through psychological analysis of their character and through their corresponding reaction to the laws which govern the state of the universe.

An origin myth of a different character, and in a sense far less so-phisticated, is the Tilmun myth.[24]

The myth of Enlil and Ninlil was concerned with a single, seem-ingly anomalous fact: the difference in character of the sons of Enlil. It traced their origin to find that difference ultimately grounded in contrasts within Enlil's own nature. The Tilmun myth is not in that sense wrestling with a problem. It endeavors to trace a causal unity between a great many disparate phenomena and shows their common origin in a conflict of two natures, male and female. It tells the story of a battle of wills in their mutual at-traction and mutual antagonism, of constant Mother Earth, Nin-hursaga, and Enki, god of the fickle waters.

The story opens in the island of Tilmun—modern Bahrein in the Persian Gulf. This island was allotted to Enki and Ninhursaga when the world was divided among the gods. After Enki, at Nin-hursaga's suggestion, has provided the island with fresh water, he proposes to her, and, though she at first refuses, she finally ac-cepts him. Their daughter is the goddess Ninsar, the plants, born of the marriage of soil, Ninhursaga, and water, Enki. But, as the waters of the yearly inundation in Mesopotamia recede and return to the river bed before vegetation comes up, so Enki does not stay to live with Ninhursaga as her husband but has already left her be-fore the goddess of the plants is born. And, as vegetation in the late spring clusters around the rivers, so Ninsar comes to the river's edge where Enki is. But Enki sees in the goddess of the plants just another young girl. He unites with her, but he does not go to live with her. The goddess of the plants gives birth to a daughter representing—we would guess—the plant fibers used in the weaving of linen. Such fibers are obtained by soaking plants in water until the soft matter rots away and only the tough fibers remain. They are, therefore, in a sense the child of plants and water. Then the story repeats itself; the goddess of the dyestuff, with which cloth is dyed, is born, and she in turn gives birth to the goddess of cloth and weaving, Uttu. By now, however, Ninhur-saga has realized how fickle Enki is and puts Uttu on her guard.

Forewarned, Uttu insists on marriage: Enki must bring gifts of cucumbers, apples, and grapes—apparently to serve as the customary marriage-gift—and only then will she be his. Enki complies and when, as a regular suitor, he presents himself at the house with the gifts, Uttu joyfully lets him in. The wine which he gives her makes Uttu intoxicated, and he takes his pleasure of her. A lacuna interrupts the story at this point and obscures the course of events. Eight plants have sprouted forth, and Ninhursaga has not yet announced what their names, nature, and qualities shall be. Then she suddenly discovers that Enki has already determined all this on his own and has eaten the plants. At this final slight, Ninhursaga is seized with a burning hatred, and she curses the god of the waters. At her terrible curse—which apparently typifies the banning of the fresh waters to darkness underground and to slow death when wells and rivers dry up in the summer season—all the gods are thoroughly disturbed. But the fox appears and promises to bring Ninhursaga to them. It makes good its promise. Ninhursaga comes, relents, and finally heals the sick Enki by helping to give birth to eight deities, one for each ailing part of his body. It has been suggested that these deities are the plants which Enki had swallowed and which had thus become lodged in his body. The myth ends with the assigning of stations in life to these deities.

As we have stated, this myth endeavors to trace a causal unity among many disparate phenomena; but it is a unity causal in the mythopoeic sense only. When plants are seen as born of soil and water, we can still follow, although with reservations. Toward the end of the myth, however, the deities born that Enki may be healed have no intrinsic connection either with soil, who bears them, or with water. Their names, however, happen to contain elements which recall the words for certain parts of the body, those parts of Enki's body which are healed. For instance, the deity $\acute{A}$-zi-mu_4-a, whose name can be understood as "the growing straight of the arm," was born to heal Enki's arm. And here is the connection. We must remember that in mythopoeic thought a name is a force within the person propelling him in a certain direction. Since the name $\acute{A}$-zi-mu_4-a can be understood as meaning "the growing straight of the arm," though this deity—as far as we know—had nothing to do with arms, the question could not but present itself: "Whose arm did this deity cause to grow straight?" The myth is ready with an answer: "Enki's." It is here satisfied with establishing a connection; it does not probe for a deeper relationship of nature between the two forces, the two gods, involved.

Seen on its own terms, however, and viewed with mythopoeic logic, the myth greatly deepens our understanding of two great forces in the universe, earth and water; for in the Mesopotamian universe understanding means psychological insight. In the myth we get to know the deep antithesis which underlies the fruitful interplay of these forces in nature; we follow it as it rises to its climax in an open break threatening to destroy water forever; and we end on a note of relief with reconciliation, with restoration of harmony in the universe. We also learn, in following the interaction of these forces, their importance as sources of life: From them come plants, from them come weaving and clothing, to them are due numerous potent and beneficial forces in life—numerous minor gods. An area of the universe has become intelligible.

Before we leave this myth, we should call attention to an interesting bit of speculation which it contains, to the picture it gives of the world when it was young. The definite and identifiable character of things in the world came late. In the dawn of time the world was as yet only a world of promise, a world in the bud, not settled in definite form. Neither animals nor men had yet acquired their habits and characteristics; they had not yet their defining traits. They were only potentially what they now are. The raven did not yet croak; the lion did not kill; the wolf did not snatch lambs. Disease and old age had as yet no existence as such, had not acquired their recognizable symptoms and characteristics, and could therefore not identify themselves as "disease" and "old age," definite forms which they were only later to assume.

The first lines of the opening section of the myth are addressed directly to Enki and Ninhursaga; these deities are the "you" of the text. Then the story lapses into ordinary narrative style:

> When you were dividing the virgin earth (with your fellow-gods)
>   —you—the land of Tilmun was a region pure;
> When you were dividing the pure earth (with your fellow-gods)—
>   you—the land of Tilmun was a region pure.

The land of Tilmun was pure, the land of Tilmun was fresh,
The land of Tilmun was fresh, the land of Tilmun was bright.
When they lay down on the ground all alone in Tilmun—
   Since the place where Enki lay down with his spouse
     was a fresh place, a bright place. . . . .
When they lay down on the ground all alone in Tilmun—
   Since the place where Enki lay down with his spouse
     was a fresh place, a bright place—
The raven in Tilmun did not croak (as the raven does nowadays),
The cock(?) did not utter the crow of a cock (as the cock does
   nowadays),
The lion did not kill,
The wolf did not seize lambs,
The dog knew not (how) to make the kids crouch down,
The donkey foal knew not (how) to eat grain,

. . . .
Eye disease did not say, "I, eye disease,"
Headache did not say, "I, headache,"
The old woman there did not say, "I, old woman,"
The old man there did not say, "I, old man," . . . .

B. DETAILS OF WORLD ORDER

Of the next group of myths, those which deal with the establishment of some facet of world order rather than with the origins of
things and forces as such, we shall give only two examples. The
first of these is a myth, unfortunately in a rather damaged condition, which tells how the natural economy of Mesopotamia became
organized.

ENKI ORGANIZES THE WORLD MANOR[25]

The beginning of this myth, now lost, probably related how Anu
and Enlil appointed Enki. Where the text becomes readable, Enki is
making a tour of inspection in his territory, which includes most of
the world as then known, and visiting the larger administrative
units in it.

Enki stops in each country, blesses it, and by his blessing en-
dows it with prosperity and affirms its special functions. Next he
organizes all the bodies of water and what has to do with water.
He fills the rivers Euphrates and Tigris with clear water and appoints a god to oversee them. Then he fills them with fish and
sets out canebrakes. To care for these, he appoints another divine
overseer. Then he regulates the sea and appoints a divine

overseer who is to run it. From the sea Enki turns to the winds which bring the rains and then to agricultural pursuits. He looks after the plow, opens up the furrows, and lets grain grow on the field. He also ranges granaries side by side. From the fields he moves on to town and village, appoints the brick-god to take care of brickmaking; he lays foundations, builds walls, and appoints the divine master-builder, Mushdama, as overseer of such works. Finally, he organizes the wild life of the desert under the god Sumukan, while he builds pens and sheepfolds for the tame animals, placing the latter in charge of the shepherd-god Dumuzi or Tammuz. Enki has instituted every important function in the economic life of Mesopotamia; he has set it going; and he has appointed a divine overseer to keep it going. Order in nature is seen and interpreted exactly as if the universe were a large, smoothly running estate organized by a capable manager.

ENKI AND NINMAH: INTEGRATION OF ODDITIES[26]

The order of the universe, patent and obvious to the human mind and generally admirable as well, is, nevertheless, not always and in every detail the order man would have preferred. Even the optimistic Alexander Pope, as the reader will recall, thought he could go no further in his praise than to call this "the best possible world," which is obviously a far cry from calling it "the ideal world." The ancient Mesopotamians likewise found things in the world which they considered unfortunate, or at least queer; and it puzzled them that the gods had arranged it that way. Problems of this kind are dealt with in the myth which we shall now consider. It offers an answer well in keeping with the Mesopotamians' social and psychological approach to forces in the universe: the gods, for all their power, have their human sides. Their emotions, especially after too much beer, are likely to get the better of their judgment; and, when that happens, they are in danger of being tripped up by their own power, by the binding force of their own commands.

The myth deals—as do so many Sumerian tales—with Enki, the god of the sweet waters, and Ninhursaga, the goddess of the earth. In this myth she is called by her epithet Ninmah, "the exalted lady," and we shall keep this name in recounting the story. We begin once more in the days when the world was young:

> In the days of yore, the days when sky had been
> separated from earth,
> In the nights of yore, the nights when sky had been
> separated from earth.

In those remote times the gods themselves had to work for a living. All the gods had to use the sickle, the pickax, and the other agricultural implements; to dig canals; and generally to earn their bread by the sweat of their brows. And they hated it. The very wise one, he of broad understanding, Enki, lay in deep slumber upon his couch without ever rising from it. To him the gods turned in their misery; and his mother Nammu, the goddess of the watery deep, took their complaints before her sleeping son. Nor did she go in vain. Enki ordered Nammu to get all in readiness to give birth to "the clay that is above the *apsu*." ("Above the *apsu*" means below the earth but above the watery deep which lies under the earth and is more or less identical with the goddess Nammu herself.) This clay was to be severed from Nammu as one severs a human infant from its mother. The goddess Ninmah, the earth, was to stand above her—the earth is, of course, above the subterranean waters —and help her when she gave birth, and eight other goddesses were to assist.

In this fashion, we must assume, the clay above the *apsu* was born, and from it man was fashioned. However, a serious gap in the text interrupts the story at this point and prevents us from knowing with certainty how mankind came into being. When the text again becomes readable, Enki is preparing a feast for Ninmah and for his mother, presumably to celebrate her delivery. All the great gods are invited, and all praise Enki highly for his cleverness; but, as the party gets under way, Ninmah strikes a sour note:

> As Enki and Ninmah drink much beer, their hearts become elated,
> and Ninmah calls over to Enki:
> "How good or how bad is man's body (really)?
> As my heart prompts me, I can make its lot good or (make it) bad."

Enki is not slow to accept the challenge: "The lot thou hast in mind, be it good or bad, verily I will balance(?) it."

So Ninmah takes of the clay above the *apsu* and models it into a freak human being, one with some bodily defect: a man who cannot hold back his urine, a woman who is unable to bear children, a being who has neither male nor female organs. All in all, six such beings take form under her fingers; but for every one of them Enki is ready with a special lot or fate. He finds a place in society for all of them, a way in which they can gain a living. The being with neither male nor female organs, presumably a eunuch, Enki destines to wait on the king, the barren woman is placed among the ladies-in-waiting to the queen, etc. There can be little doubt that these six freaks formed by Ninmah correspond to definite classes of persons in Sumerian society who, for one reason or another, differed bodily from normal human beings and therefore posed a problem.

But now the contest is on in earnest. Enki has shown that his perspicuity is a match for even the worst Ninmah can think up. Now he proposes that they change sides. He will make freaks, and she shall figure out what to do with them. And so Enki sets to work. We do not know about his first effort, for the text of the myth is damaged at this place; but we hear about the second, a being by the name of *U₄-mu-ul*, "my day is remote"—that is, a very old man whose birthday lies far back in the past. The eyes of this unfortunate are diseased, his life is ebbing, his liver and heart give him pain, his hands tremble—to mention just a few of the things wrong with him. This creature Enki presents to Ninmah. Enki calls over to Ninmah:

> I determined the lot for the men thou didst fashion,
>   whereby they might subsist.
> Do thou now determine a lot for the man I have fashioned,
>   whereby he may subsist.

This, however, is entirely beyond Ninmah. She approaches the creature and puts a question to him, but he cannot answer; she proffers him a piece of bread she has been eating, but he is too feeble to stretch out his arm to take it; etc. Angrily she upbraids Enki: the creature he has fashioned is not a live man. But Enki only tauntingly reminds her how he was able to cope with anything she could think up and find ways for her creatures to make a living.

Another break in the text prevents us from following the details of their quarrel. When the text again is preserved, the quarrel has reached its climax. Through the second of the two creatures which Enki created, he brought into the world sickness and all the other miseries attendant upon old age. Undoubtedly his first creature, whose description is lost in a lacuna, carried a similar load of human evils. With neither of them could Ninmah cope. She was unable to integrate them with the world order, unable to find a useful place for them in society. But they are here to stay, an unmitigated evil. It is possible that it was the effect of these creatures alone (of old age and of the earlier, as yet unknown, evils) on Ninmah's land and city that drove her to desperation; it is also possible that she suffered still further humiliations at Enki's hand. She complains:

> My city is destroyed, my house is wrecked, my children
>   have been taken captive.
> I have been forced to leave Ekur, a fugitive(?); even
>   I escape not from thy hand.

So she curses him: "Henceforth thou shalt not dwell in heaven, thou shalt not dwell on earth." This confines the god of the sweet waters to the dark regions below the earth. The curse is reminiscent of another which she pronounced upon Enki in the Tilmun myth and is seemingly intended to explain the same puzzling feature of the universe: Why are the beneficent sweet waters banned to live in eternal darkness below the earth? For that is where one finds them if one digs deep enough. Enki can do nothing once the curse has been uttered, for it has behind it all the decisive force inherent in a command of one of the great gods. He answers Ninmah: "A command issuing from thy mouth, who could change it?"

Nevertheless, it seems possible that this frightening sentence was somehow alleviated and that, as in the Tilmun myth, a reconciliation was brought about. The text of the myth becomes extremely fragmentary and difficult at this point, so we cannot tell for certain. However, the very fact that the myth does go on at some length shows that Ninmah's curse was not the final and decisive result of the conflict.

The myth which we have here retold undertakes to explain a number of puzzling features in the world order: the curious abnormal groups—eunuchs, hierodules, etc.—which formed part of Mesopotamian society; the unpleasant, seemingly unnecessary evils which accompany old age; etc. In rendering its account, however, the myth not only explains; it passes judgment. These features do not really belong in the world order; they were not part of the plan. They came in in a moment of irresponsibility, when the gods were in their cups and succumbed momentarily to envy and a desire to show off. Moreover, the myth analyzes and evaluates the various features differently. While the freaks which Ninmah made were comparatively harmless and could still be integrated with the social order by the clever Enki, there was no hope whatever when Enki turned his nimble brain to mischief.

In this implicit evaluation of the features whose origin it describes, our myth forms a connecting link, as it were, with the third large group of myths: that which takes as its main theme the evaluation of features in the world order.

C. DETAILS OF EVALUATION

Some of the myths within this group take almost the same form as hymns of praise. They are concerned with a single element in the universe—a deity, an object, or whatever it may be—and extol its qualities in a minute analysis of all its features. Such a myth, for instance, is the "Myth of the Pickax," which tells how Enlil made that indispensable implement and explains its qualities and uses. Other myths within the group, however, are concerned with two entities of the universe, balancing one against the other in a reasoned effort to understand and justify their relative positions in the existing order. These myths frequently take the form of a dispute between the two elements involved, each extolling its own virtues until the dispute is adjudicated by some god. A single passage may serve as illustration. It comes from a myth in which copper, useful but less highly valued, disputes with silver the latter's right to stand in a place of honor as courtier in the royal palace. The copper argues the "uselessness" of silver:

> When the cold weather has set in, you cannot provide an adz
> which can cut firewood(?);
> When harvest time has come, you cannot provide a sickle which
> can cut the grain.
> Therefore man will take no interest in thee, ...[27]

In a country like Mesopotamia, in which the chief industries were sheepherding and farming, it is only natural that these two modes of life should form favorite subjects of comparison and evaluation. Which is the better, the more important, the more useful? We possess no less than three myths which take up this theme. One tells the origin of "sheep" and "grain" from the very beginning, when the gods alone enjoyed them, and goes on to recount a long dispute which they had as to which should take precedence over the other. Another myth relates the dispute between two divine brothers, Enten and Emesh, sons of Enlil, one seemingly typifying the farmer, the other the shepherd. Their quarrel is settled by Enlil in favor of the farmer. The liveliest treatment of the theme, however, is given in a myth entitled "The Wooing of Inanna."

"THE WOOING OF INANNA": RELATIVE MERITS OF SHEPHERD AND FARMER[28]

This myth tells how both the divine farmer Enkimdu and the divine shepherd Dumuzi sued for the hand of the goddess Inanna, who is here seen not as the spouse of Anu and queen of heaven but merely as a young marriageable girl. Her brother and guardian, the sun-god Utu, is in favor of the shepherd and tries to influence his sister.

> Her brother, the warrior, the hero, Utu,
>   says to holy Inanna:
> "The shepherd ought to marry thee, my sister.
> Why, O maiden Inanna, art thou not willing?
> His butter is good, his milk is good;
> All the shepherd's products are splendid.
> Dumuzi ought to marry thee, Inanna."

But the brother's words fall on deaf ears. Inanna has made up her mind; she wants a farmer:

> Never shall the shepherd marry me;
> Never shall he drape me in his tufted cloth;
> Never shall his finest wool touch me.
> Me, the maiden, shall the farmer,
> And he only, take in marriage—
> The farmer who can grow beans,
> The farmer who can grow grain.

So the farmer it is, and the poor shepherd feels despondent. He has not only lost his suit; he has been rejected in favor of a farmer, and that wounds his pride deeply. So he begins to compare himself

THE COSMOS AS A STATE

with the farmer. For everything the farmer makes, the shepherd finds some of his own products which will match the farmer's in value:

> In what does the farmer surpass me? A farmer me! A farmer me!
> In what does the farmer, does Enkimdu, the man of dike and canal
> . . . . surpass me?
> If he should give me his black cloth, I would give the farmer
> my black wool for it;
> If he should give me his white cloth, I would give the farmer
> my white wool for it.
> If he should pour out for me his prime beer, I would pour out for the
> farmer my yellow milk in return.

The myth continues through all the products of grassland and farm, milk as a match for beer, small cheeses as a match for beans, cottage cheese with honey as a match for bread. And then, the shepherd feels, he would even have a surplus of butter and milk.

The situation which the shepherd here imagines is a typically oriental contest of gifts. He who gives most is the better man; he owes the other nothing, the other is in his debt. And so, as the shepherd proceeds with his soliloquy, he feels better and better and gets in really high spirits. Brazenly, he drives his sheep to the very bank of the river into the heart of the cultivation. There suddenly he sees the farmer and Inanna and, abashed at what he has been doing, immediately takes to his heels to escape into the desert. Both Enkimdu and Inanna run after him, and—if we interpret the text rightly—Inanna calls out to him:

> Why must I race with thee, O shepherd, I with thee,
> shepherd, with thee?
> Thy sheep are free to eat grass on the bank;
> Thy sheep are free to pasture(?) in my stubble(?) field.
> They may eat grain in the fields of Uruk;
> Thy lambs and kids may drink water in my Adab canal.

Though she prefers a farmer for a husband, she harbors no ill feelings toward the shepherd:

> While thou, a shepherd, canst not—just to become my husband—
> be turned into a farmer, (the kind of man) I befriend,
> Canst not be turned into my friend, the farmer Enkimdu, into my
> friend the farmer,
> I will bring thee wheat, I will bring thee beans. . . . .

And so the story ends with a reconciliation. It has compared farmer and shepherd; it has by implication given preference to the farmer, for it is he whom the goddess marries. However, it is at pains to show that putting the farmer ahead of the shepherd is really a matter of personal preference only, the whim of a young girl. Actually one is as good as the other, both are equally useful and necessary members of society; the produce of one balances that of the other. Though there is rivalry between them, there should not be enmity. The farmer must know that Inanna liked the shepherd well enough to throw open the stubble fields to his flocks and permit him to water his sheep at the farmer's canals. Farmer and shepherd must try to get along well together.

With this we may conclude our survey of the older mythological material from Mesopotamia. The bulk of this material is known to us from copies written at the end of the third and the early part of the second millenniums B.C. But the myths themselves are undoubtedly much older. They show clearly for what they are: answers to questions of detail. They treat such varied problems as the origin, the place, and the relative value of all kinds of specific entities or groups of entities within the cosmos. They are one, however, in the underlying view which they take of the world. Their cosmos is a state, an organization of individuals. And the myths are one also in the approach which they take to the problems. It is a psychological approach: the key to understanding the forces which one meets in nature is felt to lie in the understanding of their characters, exactly as the key to understanding men lies in understanding their characters.

REFLECTION OF THE WORLD VIEW IN LATER MYTHS: "ENUMA ELISH"

But though the view of the universe as a state thus underlies all these tales—or precisely because it underlies them, is the very soil from which they grow—there is little effort to present that view as a whole. A proper cosmogony treating of the fundamental problems of the cosmos as it appeared to the Mesopotamians—its origin and the origin of the order which it exhibits—does not appear until the earlier half of the second millennium B.C. Then it is given in a grandiose composition named *Enuma elish*, "When Above."[29] *Enuma elish* has a long and complicated history. It is written in Akkadian,[30] seemingly Akkadian of approximately the middle of the second millennium B.C. At that period, then, the composition presumably received the form in which we now have it. Its central figure is Marduk, the god of Babylon, in keeping with the fact that Babylon was at that time the political and cultural center of the Mesopotamian world. When later on, in the first millennium B.C., Assyria rose to become the dominant power in the Near East, Assyrian scribes apparently replaced Marduk with their own god Assur and made a few changes to make the story fit its new hero. This later version is known to us from copies of the myth found in Assyria.

The substitution of Assur for Marduk as the hero and central figure of the story seems to have been neither the only nor the first such substitution made. Behind our present version with Marduk as the hero undoubtedly lies a still earlier version wherein, not Marduk, but Enlil of Nippur played the central role. This more original form can be deduced from many indications in the myth itself. The most important of these is the fact that Enlil, although he was always at least the second most important Mesopotamian deity, seems to play no part whatever in the myth as we have it, while all the other important gods have appropriate roles. Again, the role which Marduk plays is not in keeping with the character of that god. Marduk was originally an agricultural or perhaps a solar deity, whereas the central role in *Enuma elish* is that of a god of the storm such as Enlil was. Indeed, a central feat ascribed to Marduk in the story—the separating of heaven and earth—is the very feat which other mythological material assigns to Enlil, and with right, for it is the wind which, placed between the sky and the earth, holds them apart like the two sides of an inflated leather bag. It seems, therefore, that Enlil was the original hero of the story and was replaced by Marduk when our earliest known version was composed around the middle of the second millennium B.C. How far the myth itself goes back, we cannot say with certainty. It contains material and reflects ideas which point backward through the third millennium B.C.

A. Fundamentals of Origin

We may now turn to the content of the myth. It falls roughly into two sections, one dealing with the origin of the basic features of the universe, the other telling how the present world order was established. There is, however, no rigid separation of these two themes. The actions of the second part of the myth are foreshadowed in, and interlock with, the events told in the first.

The poem begins with a description of the universe as it was in the beginning:

> When a sky above had not (yet even) been mentioned
> (And) the name of firm ground below had not (yet even) been
>   thought of;
> (When) only primeval Apsu, their begetter,
> And Mummu and Ti'amat—she who gave birth to them all—
> Were mingling their waters in one;
> When no bog had formed (and) no island could be found;
> When no god whosoever had appeared,
> Had been named by name, had been determined as to (his) lot,
> Then were gods formed within them.[31]

This description presents the earliest stage of the universe as one of watery chaos. The chaos consisted of three intermingled elements: Apsu, who represents the sweet waters; Ti'amat, who represents the sea; and Mummu, who cannot as yet be identified with certainty but may represent cloud banks and mist. These three types of water were mingled in a large undefined mass. There was not yet even the idea of a sky above or firm ground beneath; all was water; not even a swampy bog had been formed, still less an island; and there were yet no gods.

Then, in the midst of this watery chaos, two gods come into existence: Lahmu and Lahamu. The text clearly intends us to understand that they were begotten by Apsu, the sweet waters, and born of Ti'amat, the sea. They represent, it would seem, silt which had formed in the waters. From Lahmu and Lahamu derive the next divine pair: Anshar and Kishar, two aspects of "the horizon." The mythmaker apparently viewed the horizon as both male and female, as a circle (male) which circumscribed the sky and as a circle (female) which circumscribed the earth.

Anshar and Kishar give birth to Anu, the god of the sky; and

Anu engenders Nudimmut. Nudimmut is another name for Ea or Enki, the god of the sweet waters. Here, however, he is apparently to be viewed in his oldest aspect as representing the earth itself; he is *En-ki*, "lord of the earth." Anshar is said to have made Anu like himself, for the sky resembles the horizon in so far as it, too, is round. And Anu is said to have made Nudimmut, the earth, in his likeness; for the earth was, in the opinion of the Mesopotamians, shaped like a disk or even like a round bowl:

> Lahmu and Lahamu appeared and they were named;
> Increasing through the ages they grew tall.
> Anshar and Kishar (then) were formed, surpassing them;
> They lived for many days, adding year unto year.
> Their son was Anu, equal to his fathers.
> Anshar made his firstborn, Anu, to his own likeness,
> Anu, to his own likeness also, Nudimmut.
> Nudimmut excelled among the gods, his fathers;
> With ears wide open, wise, mighty in strength,
> Mightier than his father's father Anshar,
> He had no equal among his fellow-gods.

The speculations which here meet us, speculations by which the ancient Mesopotamians thought to penetrate the mystery concealing the origin of the universe, are obviously based upon observation of the way in which new land is actually formed in Mesopotamia. Mesopotamia is an alluvial country. It has been built through thousands of years by silt which has been brought down by the two great rivers, the Euphrates and the Tigris, and has been deposited at their mouths. This process still goes on; and day by day, year by year, the country slowly grows, extending farther out into the Persian Gulf. It is this scene—where the sweet waters of the rivers meet and blend with the salt waters of the sea, while cloud banks hang low over the waters—which has been projected back into the beginning of time. Here still is the primeval watery chaos in which Apsu, the sweet waters, mingles with Ti'amat, the salt waters of the sea; and here the silt —represented by the first of the gods, Lahmu and Lahamu—separates from the water, becomes noticeable, is deposited.

Lahmu and Lahamu gave birth to Anshar and Kishar; that is, the primeval silt, born of the salt and the sweet waters in the original watery chaos, was deposited along its circumference in a gigantic ring: the horizon. From Anshar, the upper side of this ring, and from Kishar, its lower side, grew up through days and years of deposits Anu, heaven, and Nudimmut-Enki, earth. As *Enuma elish* describes this, Anu, the sky, was formed first; and he engendered Nudimmut, the earth.

This presentation breaks the progression by pairs—Lahmu-Lahamu, Anshar-Kishar—after which we expect a third pair An-Ki, "heaven and earth"; instead, we get Anu followed by Nudimmut. This irregularity suggests that we are here dealing with an alteration of the original story perhaps made by the redactor who introduced Marduk of Babylon as hero of the myth. He may have wanted to stress the male aspect of the earth, Ea/Enki, since the latter figured as father of Marduk in Babylonian theology. Originally, therefore, Anshar-Kishar may have been followed by An-Ki, "heaven and earth." This conjecture is supported by a variant of our story preserved in the great ancient Mesopotamian list of gods known as the An-Anum list. Here we find an earlier, more intact version of the speculation: from the horizon, from Anshar and Kishar as a united pair, grew the sky and the earth. Sky and earth are apparently to be viewed as two enormous disks formed from the silt which continued to be deposited along the inside of the ring of the horizon as the latter "lived many days, added year unto year." Later on, these disks were forced apart by the wind, who puffed them up into the great bag within which we live, its under side being the earth, its upper side the sky.

In speculating about the origin of the world, the Mesopotamians thus took as their point of departure things they knew and could observe in the geology of their own country. Their earth, Mesopotamia, is formed by silt deposited where fresh water meets salt water; the sky, seemingly formed of solid matter like the earth, must have been deposited in the same manner and must have been raised later to its present lofty position.

B. FUNDAMENTALS OF WORLD ORDER

Just as observed facts about the physical origin of his own country form the basis for the Mesopotamian's speculations about the origin of the basic features in the universe, so, it would seem, does a certain amount of knowledge about the origin of his own political organization govern his speculations as to the origin of the organization of the universe. The origin of the world order is seen in a prolonged conflict between two principles, the forces making for activity and the forces making for inactivity. In this conflict the first victory over inactivity is gained by authority alone; the second, the decisive victory, by authority combined with force. The transition mirrors, on the one hand, a historical development from primitive social organization, in which only custom and authority unbacked by force are available to insure concerted action by the community, to the organization of a real state, in which the ruler commands both authority and force to insure necessary concerted action. On the other hand, it reflects the normal procedure within the organized state, for here also authority alone is the means brought to bear first, while force, physical compulsion, is only resorted to if authority is not sufficient to produce the conduct desired.

To return to *Enuma elish:* With the birth of the gods from chaos, a new principle—movement, activity—has come into the world. The new beings contrast sharply with the forces of chaos that stand for rest and inactivity. In a typically mythopoeic manner this ideal conflict of activity and inactivity is given concrete form in a pregnant situation: the gods come together to dance.

> The divine companions thronged together
> and, restlessly surging back and forth, they dis-
>   turbed Tiʾamat,
> disturbed Tiʾamat's belly,
> dancing within (her depth) where heaven is founded.
> Apsu could not subdue their clamor,
> and Tiʾamat was silent . . . .
> but their actions were abhorrent to her
> and their ways not good. . . . .

The conflict is now manifest. The first power of chaos to come out openly against the gods and their new ways is Apsu.

> Then Apsu, the begetter of the great gods,
> called his servant Mummu, saying to him:
> "Mummu, my servant, who dost gladden my heart,
> come let us go to Tiʾamat."
> They went; and seated before Tiʾamat,
> about the gods their firstborn they took counsel.

> Apsu began to speak,
> saying to pure Ti'amat:
> "Abhorrent have become their ways to me,
> I am allowed no rest by day, by night no sleep.
> I will abolish, yea, I will destroy their ways,
> that peace may reign (again) and we may sleep."

This news causes consternation among the gods. They run around aimlessly; then they quiet down and sit in the silence of despair. Only one, the wise Ea/Enki, is equal to the situation.

> He of supreme intelligence, skilful, ingenious,
> Ea, who knows all things, saw through their scheme.
> He formed, yea, he set up against it
> the configuration of the universe,
> and skilfully made his overpowering sacred spell.
> Reciting it he cast it on the water (—on Apsu—),
> poured slumber over him, so that he soundly slept.

The waters to which Ea here recites his spell, his "configuration of the universe," are Apsu. Apsu succumbs to the magic command and falls into a deep slumber. Then Ea takes from him his crown and drapes himself in Apsu's cloak of fiery rays. He kills Apsu and establishes his abode above him. Then he locks up Mummu, passes a string through his nose, and sits holding him by the end of this nose-rope.

What all this signifies is perhaps not immediately evident; yet it can be understood. The means which Ea employs to subdue Apsu is a spell, that is, a word of power, an authoritative command. For the Mesopotamians viewed authority as a power inherent in commands, a power which caused a command to be obeyed, caused it to realize itself, to come true. The authority, the power in Ea's command, was great enough to force into being the situation expressed in the command. And the nature of this situation is hinted at when it is called "the configuration of the universe"; it is the design which now obtains. Ea commanded that things should be as they are, and so they became thus. Apsu, the sweet waters, sank into the sleep of death which now holds the sweet waters immobile underground. Directly above them was established the abode of Ea— earth resting upon Apsu. Ea holds in his hands the nose-rope of captive Mummu, perhaps—if our interpretation of this difficult figure is correct—the cloud banks which float low over the earth.

But, whatever the details of interpretation may be, it is significant that this first great victory of the gods over the powers of chaos, of the forces of activity over the forces opposing activity, was won through authority and not through physical force. It was gained through the authority implicit in a command, the magic in a spell. It is significant also that it was gained through the power of a single god acting on his own initiative, not by the concerted efforts of the whole community of the gods. The myth moves on a primitive level of social organization where dangers to the community are met by the separate action of one or more powerful individuals, not by co-operation of the community as a whole.

To return to the story: In the dwelling which Ea has thus established on Apsu is born Marduk, the real hero of the myth as we have it; but in more original versions it was undoubtedly Enlil's birth that was told at this juncture. The text describes him:

> Superb of stature, with lightning glance,
> and virile gait, he was a leader born.
> Ea his father, seeing him, rejoiced,
> and brightened and his heart filled with delight.
> He added, yea, he fastened on to him twofold divinity.
> Exceeding tall he was, surpassing in all things.
> Subtle beyond conceit his measure was,
> incomprehensible, terrible to behold.
> Four were his eyes and four his ears;
> fire blazed whenever he moved his lips.

But while Marduk grows up among the gods, new dangers threaten from the forces of chaos. They maliciously chide Ti'amat:

> When they killed Apsu, thy husband,
> thou didst not march at his side but sat quietly.

Finally they succeed in rousing her. Soon the gods hear that all the forces of chaos are making ready to do battle with them:

> Angry, scheming, restless day and night,
> they are bent on fighting, rage and prowl like lions.
> Gathered in council, they plan the attack.
> Mother Hubur—creator of all forms—
> adds irresistible weapons, has borne monster serpents,
> sharp toothed, with fang unsparing;
> has filled their bodies with poison for blood.

> Fierce dragons she has draped with terror,
> crowned with flame and made like gods,
> so that whoever looks upon them shall perish with fear,
> and they, with bodies raised, will not turn back their breast.

At the head of her formidable army Tiᵓamat has placed her second husband, Kingu. She has given him full authority and intrusted to him the "tablets of destinies," which symbolize supreme power over the universe. Her forces are ranged in battle order ready to attack the gods.

The first intelligence of what is afoot reaches the always well-informed Ea. At first, a typical primitive reaction, he is completely stunned, and it takes some time before he can pull himself together and begin to act.

> Ea heard of these matters,
> lapsed into dark silence, wordlessly sat.
> Then, having deeply pondered and his inner turmoil quieted,
> arose and went to his father Anshar,
> went before Anshar, his father who begot him.
> All Tiᵓamat had plotted he recounted.

Anshar also is deeply disturbed and smites his thigh and bites his lip in his mental anguish. He can think of no better way out than to send Ea against Tiᵓamat. He reminds Ea of his victory over Apsu and Mummu and seems to advise him to use the same means he used then. But this time Ea's mission is unsuccessful. The word of an individual, even the powerful word of Ea, is no match for Tiᵓamat and her host.

Anshar then turns to Anu and bids him go. Anu is armed with authority even greater than that of Ea, for he is told:

> If she obey not thy command,
> speak unto her our command, that she may subside.

If Tiᵓamat cannot be overpowered by the authority of any one god, the command of all gods, having behind it their combined authority, must be used against her. But that, too, fails; Anu is unable to face Tiᵓamat, returns to Anshar, and asks to be relieved of the task. Unaided authority, even the highest which the gods command, is not enough. Now the gods face their hour of gravest peril. Anshar, who has thus far directed the proceedings, falls silent.

> Anshar grew silent, staring at the ground,
> he shook his head, nodded toward Ea.
> Ranged in assembly, all the Anunnaki,
> lips covered, speechless sat.

Then, finally, rising in all his majesty, Anshar proposes that Ea's son, young Marduk, "whose strength is mighty," champion his fathers, the gods. Ea is willing to put the proposal to Marduk, who accepts readily enough but not without a condition:

> If I am to be your champion,
> vanquish Ti?amat, and save you,
> then assemble and proclaim my lot supreme.
> Sit down together joyfully in Ubshuukkinna;
> let me, like you, by word of mouth determine destiny,
> so that whatever I decide shall not be altered,
> and my spoken command shall not (come) back (to me),
>   shall not be changed.

Marduk is a young god. He has abundant strength, the full prowess of youth, and he looks ahead to the physical contest with complete confidence. But, as a young man, he lacks influence. It is for authority on a par with that of the powerful senior members of the community that he asks. A new and unheard-of union of powers is here envisaged: his demand foreshadows the coming state with its combination of force and authority in the person of the king.

And so the call goes out, and the gods foregather in Ubshuukkinna, the court of assembly in Nippur. As they arrive, they meet friends and relatives who have similarly come to participate in the assembly, and there is general embracing. In the sheltered court the gods sit down to a sumptuous meal; wine and strong drink soon put them in a happy and carefree mood, fears and worries vanish, and the meeting is ready to settle down to more serious affairs.

> They smacked their tongues and sat down to the feast;
> They ate and drank,
> Sweet drink dispelled their fears.
> They sang for joy, drinking strong wine.
> Carefree they grew, exceedingly, their hearts elated.
> Of Marduk, (of) their champion, they decreed the destiny.

The "destiny" mentioned is full authority on a par with that of the highest gods. The assembly first gives Marduk a seat of honor and then proceeds to confer the new powers on him:

> They made a princely dais for him.
> And he sat down, facing his fathers, as a councilor.
> "Thou art of consequence among the elder gods.
> Thy rank is unsurpassed and thy command is Anu('s).
> Marduk, thou art of consequence among the elder gods;
> Thy rank is unequaled and thy command is Anu('s).
> From this day onward shall thy orders not be altered;
> To elevate and to abase—this be within thy power.
> What thou hast spoken shall come true, thy word shall
>   not prove vain.
> Among the gods none shall encroach upon thy rights."

What the assembly of the gods here confers upon Marduk is kingship: the combination of authority with powers of compulsion; a leading voice in the counsels of peace; leadership of the army in times of war; police powers to penalize evildoers.

> We gave thee kingship, power over all things.
> Take thy seat in the council, may thy word prevail.
> May thy weapon not yield, may it smite thy foes.
> Grant breath of life to lord(s) who put (their) trust
>   in thee.
> But if a god embraces evil, shed his life.

Having conferred authority upon Marduk, the gods want to know that he really has it, that his command now possesses that magic quality which makes it come true. So they make a test:

> They placed a garment in their midst
> And said to Marduk their firstborn:
> "O Lord, thy lot is truly highest among gods.
> Command annihilation and existence, and may both
>   come true.
> May thy spoken word destroy the garment,
> Then speak again and may it be intact."
> He spoke—and at his word the garment was destroyed.
> He spoke again, the garment reappeared.
> The gods, his fathers, seeing (the power of) his word,
> Rejoiced, paid homage: "Marduk is king."

Then they give him the insignia of kingship—scepter, throne, and royal robe(?)—and arm him for the coming conflict. Marduk's weapons are the weapons of a god of storm and thunder—a circumstance understandable when we remember that the story was originally the story of the storm-god Enlil. He carries the rainbow, the arrows of lightning, and a net held by four winds.

He made a bow, designed it as his weapon,
let the arrow ride firmly on the bowstring.
Grasping his mace in his right hand, he lifted it;
and fastened bow and quiver at his side.
He bade lightning precede him,
and made his body burn with searing flame.
He made a net to encircle Tiᵓamat,
bade the four winds hold on, that none of her escape.
The south wind, north wind, east wind, west wind,
Gifts from his father Anu, did he place along the edges
   of the net.

In addition, he fashions seven terrible storms, lifts up his mace, which is the flood, mounts his war chariot, "the irresistible tempest," and rides to battle against Tiᵓamat with his army, the gods, milling around him.

At the approach of Marduk, Kingu and the enemy army lose heart and are plunged into utter confusion; only Tiᵓamat stands her ground and challenges the young god to battle. Marduk returns the challenge, and the fight is on. Spreading his mighty net, Marduk envelops Tiᵓamat in its meshes. As she opens her jaws to swallow him, he sends in the winds to hold them open. The winds swell her body, and through her open mouth Marduk shoots an arrow which pierces her heart and kills her. When her followers see Marduk treading on their dead champion, they turn and try to flee; but they are caught in the meshes of his net, and he breaks their weapons and takes them captive. Kingu also is bound, and Marduk takes from him the "tablets of destinies."

When complete victory has thus been achieved, Marduk returns to Tiᵓamat's body, crushes her skull with his mace, and cuts her arteries; and the winds carry her blood away. Then he proceeds to cut her body in two and to lift up half of it to form the sky. To make sure that the waters in it will not escape, he sets up locks and appoints guards. He carefully measures the sky which he has thus made; and, as Ea after his victory over Apsu had built his abode on the body of his dead opponent, so now Marduk builds his abode on that part of Tiᵓamat's body which he has made into the sky. By measuring he makes certain that it comes directly opposite Ea's dwelling to form a counterpart of it.

Here we may pause again for a moment to ask what all this

means. At the root of the battle between Marduk or Enlil and Tiʾ-amat, between wind and water, there probably lies an age-old interpretation of the spring floods. Every spring the waters flood the Mesopotamian plain and the world reverts to a—or rather to "the"—primeval watery chaos until the winds fight the waters, dry them up, and bring back the dry land. Remnants of this concept may be seen in the detail that the winds carry away Tiʾamat's blood. But such age-old concepts had early become vehicles for cosmological speculation. We have already mentioned the existence of a view that heaven and earth were two great disks deposited by silt in the watery chaos and forced apart by the wind, so that the present universe is a sort of inflated sack surrounded by waters above and below. This speculation has left clear traces in Sumerian myths and in the An-Anum list, and here in *Enuma elish* we have a variant of it: it is the primeval sea, Tiʾamat, that is blown up and killed by the winds. Half of her—the present sea—is left down here; the other half is formed into the sky, and locks are affixed so that the water does not escape except once in a while when some of it falls down as rain.

Thus, through the use which it makes of its mythological material, *Enuma elish* accounts in two ways for the creation of the sky. First, the sky comes into being in the person of the god Anu, whose name means sky and who is the god of the sky; then, again, the sky is fashioned by the wind-god out of half of the body of the sea.

In a period, however, when emphasis had already shifted from the visual aspects of the great components of the universe to the powers felt as active in and through them, Anu, as the power behind the sky, would already be felt as sufficiently different from the sky itself to make this inherent contradiction less acute.

Quite as significant as the direct cosmological identification of the actors in these events, however, is the bearing which the events have on the establishing of the cosmic order. Under pressure of an acute crisis, a threatening war, a more or less primitively organized society has developed into a state.

Evaluating this achievement in modern, and admittedly subjective, terms, we might say that the powers of movement and activity, the gods, have won their final and decisive victory over the powers of rest and inertia. To accomplish this, they have had to exert themselves to the utmost, and they have found a method, a form of organization, which permits them to pull their full weight. As the active forces in a society become integrated in the form of the state and thus can overcome the ever threatening tendencies to chaos and inertia, so the active forces in the Mesopotamian universe through that same form, the state, overcome and defeat the powers of chaos, of inactivity and inertia. But, however that may be, this much is certain—that the crisis has imposed upon the gods a state of the type of a Primitive Democracy. All major issues are dealt with in a general assembly, where decrees are confirmed, designs are formulated, and judgments are pronounced. To each god is assigned a station, the most important going to the fifty senior gods, among whom are the seven whose opinion is decisive. In addition to this legislative and judiciary assembly, however, there is now an executive, the young king, who is equal in authority to the most influential members of the assembly, is the leader of the army in war, the punisher of evildoers in peacetime, and generally active, with the assent of the assembly, in matters of internal organization.

It is to tasks of internal organization that Marduk turns after his victory. The first was organizing the calendar—ever a matter for the ruler of Mesopotamia. On the sky which he had fashioned he set up constellations of stars to determine, by their rising and setting, the year, the months, and the days. The "station" of the planet Jupiter was established to make known the "duties" of the days, when each had to appear:

> To make known their obligations,
> that none might do wrong or be remiss.

He also set on heaven two bands known as "the ways" of Enlil and Ea. On both sides of the sky, where the sun comes out in the morning and leaves in the evening, Marduk made gates and secured them with strong locks. In the midst of the sky he fixed the zenith, and he made the moon shine forth and gave it its orders.

> He bade the moon come forth; intrusted night to her;
> Made her a creature of the dark, to measure time;
> And every month, unfailingly, adorned her with a crown.

> "At the beginning of the month, when rising over the land,
> Thy shining horns six days shall measure;
> On the seventh day let half (thy) crown (appear).
> At full moon thou shalt face the sun.
>
> . . . .
>
> (But) when the sun starts gaining on thee in the depth
> of heaven,
> Decrease thy radiance, reverse its growth."

The text goes on with still more detailed orders.

Many further innovations introduced by the energetic young ruler are lost in a large lacuna which breaks the text at this point. When the text becomes readable again, Marduk—seemingly in response to a plea from them—is occupied with plans for relieving the gods of all toilsome menial tasks and for organizing them into two great groups:

> Arteries I will knot and bring bones into being.
> I will create Lullu, "man" be his name,
> I will form Lullu, man.
> Let him be burdened with the toil of the gods,
>   that they may freely breathe.
> Next, I will dispose of the ways of gods;
> Verily—they are clustered like a ball,
>   I shall make them distinct.

Distinct, that is, in two groups. Following a suggestion of his father, Ea, Marduk then calls the gods to assembly; and in the assembly he asks them, now functioning as a court, to state who it was who was responsible for the attack, who stirred up Ti'amat. And the assembly indicts Kingu. So Kingu is bound and executed, and from his blood mankind is created under Ea's direction.

> They bound him, held him before Ea,
> Condemned him, severed his arteries.
> And from his blood they formed mankind.
> Ea then toil imposed on man, and set gods free.

The exceeding skill which went to fashion man commands the admiration of our poet.

> That work was not meet for (human) understanding.
> (Acting) on Marduk's ingenious suggestions Ea created.

Thereupon Marduk divided the gods and assigned them to Anu, to abide by Anu's instructions. Three hundred he stationed in heaven to do guard duty, and another three hundred were given tasks on earth. Thus the divine forces were organized and assigned to their appropriate tasks throughout the universe.

The gods are truly grateful for Marduk's efforts. To express their gratitude, they take pick in hand for the last time and build him a city and temple with throne daises for each of the gods to use when they meet there for assembly. The first assembly is held on the occasion of the dedication of the temple. As usual, the gods first sit down to a banquet. Thereupon matters of state are discussed and decided, and then, when the current business has been disposed of, Anu rises to confirm Marduk's position as king. He determines the eternal status of Marduk's weapon, the bow; he determines the status of his throne; and, finally, he calls upon the assembled gods to confirm and determine Marduk's own status, his functions in the universe, by recounting his fifty names, each expressing one aspect of his being, each defining one of his functions. With the catalogue of these names the poem comes to an end. The names summarize what Marduk is and what he signifies: the final victory over chaos and the establishing of the ordered, organized universe, the cosmic state of the Mesopotamians.

With *Enuma elish* we have reached a phase of Mesopotamian civilization in which the ancient world view which had formed the subconscious, intuitively accepted framework for all individual speculations begins itself to become a theme of conscious inquiry. Whereas the older myths answered questions concerning origins, order, and evaluation of details, *Enuma elish* answers questions concerning fundamentals. It deals with the origin and the order of the universe as a whole. It deals, however, only with origin and order, not with evaluation. The fundamental question of evaluation concerns the justice of the world order. This question *was* taken up, but not mythologically. The answers given will form the subject of chapter vii, which deals with "the good life." Before that, however, we should consider the reflection of the Mesopotamian view of world order in social and political life. We turn to the function of the state.

NOTES

1. Gilgamesh Epic, Old Babylonian version, Yale Tablet IV, 7–8.
2. *CT* XV, 15. 12.

3. Reissner, *SBH* VII, rev. 17–24. The flood serves in this passage as metaphor for the divine verdict.

The English form of the quotations from ancient poetry in these chapters is the work of Mrs. Frankfort, who has been extraordinarily successful in conveying the beauty of the original with a minimum of poetic license.

4. "Mythology," *Encyclopaedia Britannica* (11th ed.), Vol. 19, p. 134.

5. *Maqlû*, Tablet VI, 111–19.

6. Verdict on Flint in *Lugal-e*.

7. Cf. the Nidaba hymn, *OECT* I, 36–39.

8. *Maqlû*, Tablet III, 151–52.

9. *Ibid.* VI, 1–8.

10. *KAR* 102.

11. *CT* XXIV, 50, No. 47406 obv. 6 and 8.

12. *Maqlû*, Tablet II, 104–15.

13. *Politics* 1252[b].

14. *RA* XI, 144 obv. 3–5.

15. Thureau-Dangin, *Rit. acc.*, 70 obv. 1–14.

16. Kramer, *AS* XII, 34 and 36, ll. 173–89.

17. *Ibid.*, p. 38, ll. 203–4.

18. *Ibid.*, pp. 38 and 40, ll. 208–18.

19. *KAR* 25. iii. 21–29, and 68 obv. 1–11.

20. *KAR* 375. ii. 1–8.

21. Reissner, *SBH*, pp. 130 ff., ll. 48–55.

22. *CT* XXXVI, Pl. 31, 1–20.

23. Kramer, *Mythology*, nn. 47 and 48.

24. *Ibid.*, nn. 54 and 55.

25. *Ibid.*, n. 59.

26. *Ibid.*, n. 73.

27. Chiera, *SRT*, 4 obv. 17–22.

28. *Ibid.*, 3.

29. Latest translation: Heidel, *The Babylonian Genesis*. See literature there quoted.

30. A Semitic language which had long been spoken side by side with Sumerian in Mesopotamia and which by the end of the third millennium B.C. completely superseded its rival and became the only language spoken in the country.

31. I.e., within Apsu, Mummu, and Ti'amat.

CHAPTER VI

MESOPOTAMIA: THE FUNCTION
OF THE STATE

THE first subject with which we are to deal is "the function of the state," that is, the particular function which the human state in Mesopotamia was thought to fulfil in the functioning of the universe as a whole. Before we go any further, however, it will be well to consider our modern term "state," lest it trip us up when we apply it to ancient Mesopotamian concepts. When we speak of a state, we usually imply inner sovereignty and independence of all external control. Moreover, we think of a state as dominating a specific territory, and we see as its chief aim the protection of its members and the furthering of their well-being.

Now in the Mesopotamian view of the world, these attributes do not—indeed, cannot—belong to any human organization. The only truly sovereign state, independent of all external control, is the state which the universe itself constitutes, the state governed by the assembly of the gods. This state, moreover, is the state which dominates the territory of Mesopotamia; the gods own the land, the big estates, in the country. Lastly, since man was created especially for the benefit of the gods, his purpose is to serve the gods. Therefore no human institution can have its primary aim in the welfare of its own human members; it must seek primarily the welfare of the gods.

But if our term "state" thus rightly applies only to the state which the Mesopotamian universe constituted, what, then, we may ask, are the political units on the human level which we find throughout Mesopotamian history and which historians call city-states and nations? The answer would seem to be that they are secondary power-structures within the true state. The so-called "city-state" is a private organization and has a primarily economic purpose; it is the manor, the estate, of some great god. The national state also is a secondary power structure, but it has a political

185

function; it may be considered an extension of the executive organs of the world state, a police force.

Having thus defined in general the entities with which we are dealing, we may consider in more detail the function they fulfil in the universe, in the cosmic state.

THE MESOPOTAMIAN CITY-STATE

Throughout the third millennium B.C. Mesopotamia was made up of small political units, the so-called "city-states." Each such state consisted of a city with its surrounding territory, cultivated by the people of the city. Sometimes a city-state included more than one city. There might be two or three towns and a number of villages which were dependent on and administered by the chief city. From time to time conquerors arose who succeeded in uniting most of the city-states into a single large national state under their rule; but these national states usually lasted for a relatively short time, after which the country would divide into city-states again.

Central in the city-state was the city, and central in the city was the temple of the city god. The temple of the city god was usually the greatest landowner in the state, and it cultivated its extensive holdings by means of serfs and sharecroppers. Other temples belonging to the city god's spouse, to their divine children, and to deities associated with the chief god similarly had large land holdings, so that it has been estimated that around the middle of the third millennium B.C. most of the lands of a Mesopotamian city-state were temple lands. The larger part of the inhabitants were accordingly earning their livelihood as sharecroppers, serfs, or servants of the gods.

In this situation lie the economic and political realities expressed in the Mesopotamian myths which state that man was created to relieve the gods of toil, to work on the gods' estates. For the Mesopotamian city-state *was* an estate, or rather—like the medieval manor with which we have compared it—it had an estate as basis. That basic estate, the main temple with its lands, was owned and run by the city god, who himself gave all important orders.

To carry out these orders the city god had at his disposal a large staff of divine and human servants. The human servants worked in the house and in the fields and were organized accordingly. The divine servants, minor gods, served as overseers of the work. Each such minor god had his own special province in the running of the estate; and here he infused his divine powers into the labor of his human underlings, so that it prospered and bore fruit.

We are particularly well informed[1] about the organization of the main temple in the city-state of Lagash, which belonged to a god by the name of Ningirsu. This temple may therefore serve as an example.

There are, first, the divine servants of Ningirsu, minor gods who belong to his family and entourage. They fall into two groups: some have their tasks in the manor house, the temple itself; others work on the temple lands, in the fields.

Among the gods who are busy in the manor house we find the son of the owner, the god Igalimma, who is doorkeeper at the Holy of Holies and admits visitors who seek audience with Ningirsu. Another son of Ningirsu, Dunshagana, is the chief butler. He supervises the preparation and serving of food and drink, keeps an eye on the temple breweries, and sees to it that the shepherds deliver lambs and milk products for the god's table. Next come two armorers, who take care of Ningirsu's weapons and follow him as armor-bearers in battle. In more peaceful pursuits Ningirsu has the support of a divine counselor, who discusses the needs of his city with him. His personal needs are cared for by a body-servant, the god Shakanshabar, who runs errands for Ningirsu, and by his divine chamberlain Urizi, who has charge of the god's dwelling-quarters, sees to it that the god's bed is well and properly made every night, etc. In the stables of the manor we find the coachman, Ensignun, Ningirsu's charioteer, who cares for the god's donkeys and his chariot. Here is also Enlulim, the divine goatherd, who cares for the flocks of the temple and sees to it that there is plenty of milk and butter.

Returning to the dwelling-quarters, we note Ningirsu's musician, who is in charge of the musical instruments and whose task it is to fill the court with joy when he plays. There is also a drummer. He performs chiefly when Ningirsu is disturbed or upset; then the deep beat of the drum will help to soothe the god's heart and to still his tears. Ningirsu has seven daughters by his wife Baba. They act as ladies-in-waiting at his court.

Outside the manor house, in the fields, lie the duties of the god Gishbare, the bailiff of Ningirsu, who is charged with making the fields yield, causing the water to rise in the canals, and filling the temple granaries. Here also is the divine inspector of fisheries, who stocks the ponds with fish, looks after the reed thickets, and sends in his reports to Ningirsu. The wild life on the estate is in the care of a divine gamekeeper or forester, who is to see that the birds lay their eggs in peace and that the young of birds and beasts grow up unmolested.

A divine sheriff, finally, enforces the ordinances in the town, keeping watch on its walls and patrolling it, club in hand.

While these divine overseers bless the tasks performed on Ningirsu's estate, the actual menial labor is done by humans. These human toilers, whether sharecroppers, serfs, or temple servants, shepherds, brewers, or cooks, were organized in groups under human overseers in a hierarchy which culminated in the highest human servant of the god, the *ensi*, manager of the god's estate and manager of his city-state.

We call the *ensi* "manager" of the god's estate; and his position vis-à-vis the god was actually closely parallel to that of an estate manager, a steward, vis-à-vis the owner. A steward appointed to manage an estate is expected, first of all, to uphold and carry on the established order of that estate; secondly, he is to execute such specific commands as the owner may see fit to give with respect to changes, innovations, or ways to deal with unexpected situations. Quite similarly, the *ensi* was expected to uphold the established order of the god's temple and city in general, and he was expected to consult the god and carry out any specific orders which the god might wish to give.

To the first part of the *ensi*'s task belonged the administration of the temple and its estate. He was in complete charge of all the agricultural tasks, of temple forests, and temple fisheries, of the spinneries, looms, mills, breweries, bakeries, kitchens, etc., which formed part of the temple manor. Minute accounts were kept of all these activities by a corps of scribes, and these accounts were submitted to and approved by him. As he managed the temple of the city god, so his wife managed the temple and estate of the divine spouse of the city god, and his children managed the temples of the children of the city god.

In addition to these tasks, the *ensi* was responsible for law and order in the state and was to see to it that everybody was justly treated. Thus we hear about one *ensi* that he "contracted with the god Ningirsu that he would not deliver up the orphan and the widow to the powerful man."[2] The *ensi*, therefore, was the highest judicial authority. But he had other duties also: he was commander-in-chief of the army of the city-state, he negotiated for his lord the god with *ensi*'s representing the gods of other city-states, and he made war and peace.

With these last functions we touch on the other aspect of the *ensi*'s task, that of executing the specific commands of the god; for war and peace involved decisions which went beyond the normal order, decisions which could be made only by the god himself. Among other questions which the city-god himself must decide was whether to rebuild the main temple.

To ascertain the will of his master, the *ensi* commanded several approaches. He might receive an order through the occurrence of something unusual and portentous in nature, an omen whose significance the priests could interpret from long catalogues in which such omens and their meanings were listed. He might, however, also seek answer to a definite question by sacrificing an animal to the god and reading the god's message in the shape of the liver of the sacrificial animal. If the answer was not clear at first, he could repeat the process. Still another way of communicating with the god, the most direct one, was through dreams. The *ensi* would go to the temple at night, sacrifice, pray, and lie down to sleep. In dreams the god might then appear to him and give him his orders.

We possess several detailed accounts of how such orders were transmitted from the god to his human steward. An example is an order from the god Ningirsu to his steward Gudea, *ensi* of Lagash.[3] This order concerned the rebuilding of Ningirsu's temple, Eninnu. Gudea first noticed that something was amiss when the river Tigris, which Ningirsu controlled, failed to rise as usual and flood the fields. Gudea immediately betook himself to the temple, and there he had a dream. In the dream he saw a gigantic man with a divine crown, with wings like a great bird, and with a body which ended below in a floodwave. To the right and left of this man lions were lying. The man commanded Gudea to build his temple. Then day broke on the horizon. Next, a woman emerged and proceeded to raze a building plot. In her hand was a stylus of gold and a clay tablet on which constellations of stars were set down; these she studied. Then came a warrior who held a tablet of lapis lazuli upon which he sketched the plan of a house. Before Gudea stood a brick mold and a basket; bird-men unceasingly poured water into a trough; and a male donkey to the right of the god was impatiently pawing the ground.

Though Gudea realized the general purport of this dream, that he was to rebuild Ningirsu's temple, the meanings of the details were not clear to him at all. He therefore decided to consult the goddess Nanshe, who lived in a smaller town in his realm and was especially apt at interpreting dreams. The journey took time, for he stopped at every temple on the way to pray for help and support. Finally he arrived, however, and went straight to the goddess to place his problem before her. She was ready with an answer (how it was conveyed we are not told; all we have is the answer itself): the man with the crown and the wings was Ningirsu commanding Gudea to rebuild his temple Eninnu. The daylight was Gudea's personal god, who would be active all over the world, bringing success to the trade expeditions which Gudea would send out to get building materials for the temple. The goddess who studied the tablet with the stars was determining the particular star under which it would be propitious to rebuild the temple. The plan the god was drawing was that of the temple. Brick mold and basket were the brick mold and basket for the sacred bricks of the temple; the bird-men working incessantly signified that Gudea would permit himself no sleep before he carried out his task; and the impatient donkey pawing the ground symbolized the *ensi* himself, impatient to begin the work.

But the command had not yet been made specific. What kind of temple did Ningirsu want? What should it contain? Nanshe advised Gudea to seek further information from the god. He was to build a new war chariot for Ningirsu, furnish it lavishly, and bring it in to the god to the sound of drums. Then Ningirsu, "who delights in gifts," would heed Gudea's prayers and tell him exactly how the temple should be built. Gudea followed this advice, and, after spending several nights in the temple without result, he finally saw Ningirsu, who told in detail what units the new temple must contain.

> Gudea awoke, he had been sleeping; he shook himself, it was a dream.
> In acceptance, he bowed his head to the commands of Ningirsu.

Now Gudea could go ahead. He called his people together, told them of the divine command, assigned levies to the building operations, sent out trade expeditions, etc. Now he had his orders, knew what he was to do.

We have here described a divine order to undertake the building of a temple. But in similar manner, by direct divine command, originated all significant undertakings. The god commanded the undertaking of a war, the conclusion of a peace, the introduction of new laws and customs to regulate the community.

The role of the city-state within that larger state which the universe constitutes is thus reasonably clear. It is a private institution with a function which is mainly economic. It belongs to and is headed by a private citizen of the cosmic state, one of the great gods; it is his manor. As a manor, it provides the god with the essentials of life: food, clothing, and shelter. It provides these in such abundance that the god can live the life which befits him, the life of a nobleman surrounded by servants, attendants, and material wealth. Thus he is allowed free and unhindered self-expression.

Now each great god is, as we have seen, the power in and behind some great force of nature—the sky, the storm, or whatever it may be. By upholding a great god, by providing the economic basis which permits that god to enjoy full and free self-expression, the city-state is upholding some great power of the universe and assuring its freedom to function as it should. And this is the function of the human city-state within the cosmos. In this manner it contributes to maintaining and perpetuating the ordered cosmos and its powers.

THE MESOPOTAMIAN NATIONAL STATE

Different in function from the city-state, active on the political rather than on the economic plane, was the national state in Mesopotamia. Both city-state and national state were power-structures which rose ultimately above the purely human level; each had its apex in a great god. But, whereas the lines of the city-state focused on a great god in his capacity as a private citizen of the cosmic state, the lines of the national state focused on a gread god in his capacity as an official of the cosmic state. The national state thus became an extension of a governmental organ of the only true and sovereign state.

The ruling body in the cosmic state is, as will be remembered, the assembly of the gods. Here Anu acts as leader of the debate, while Enlil represents the executive powers as sheriff and commander of the armed forces. However, though Enlil typifies the element of force in the world government, he is not its only representative. The assembly may choose any one of its members to maintain internal order and to lead the armed forces, proclaiming him king. The god chosen king then exercises these functions among the gods, while he acts on earth through his human steward, the ruler of his city-state. That human steward accordingly dominates the other rulers in Mesopotamia and through them their city-states. For example, the period around the middle of the second millennium B.C., when the city-states of Inanna, namely, Kish and Agade, successively held sway in Mesopotamia, was the "period of reign" of Inanna. Later on, when Ur dominated, its god Nanna held office as king among the gods.

So strong, however, were the ties linking Enlil to these executive functions that the kingship was often referred to directly as "the Enlil functions," and the god who held this office was thought of as acting under Enlil's guidance.

The functions of kingship were twofold: to punish evildoers and uphold law and order internally and to conduct foreign wars and protect Mesopotamia externally. Two examples may serve to clarify the theory.

When Hammurabi, after thirty years as ruler of the small city-state of Babylon, succeeded in subjugating all of southern Mesopotamia, his success meant—in cosmic terms—that Marduk, the city-god of Babylon, had been chosen by the divine assembly, acting through its leaders Anu and Enlil, to administer the Enlil functions. Correspondingly, Marduk's human steward, Hammurabi, had been intrusted with the administration of these functions on earth. Hammurabi tells about it as follows:

> When lofty Anu, king of the Anunnaki, and Enlil, lord of heaven
>   and earth,
> who determine the destinies of the country, appointed Marduk,
>   the firstborn
> son of Enki, to execute the Enlil functions over the totality of the
>   people, made him great among the Igigi, called Babylon by its
>   exalted name, made it
> surpassing(ly great) in the world, and firmly established for him
>   in its
> midst an enduring kingship whose foundations are (as) firmly
>   grounded as
> (those of) heaven and earth—then did Anu and Enlil call me to
>   afford well-being to the people,
> me, Hammurabi, the obedient, godfearing prince, to cause right-
>   eousness to appear in the land,
> to destroy the evil and the wicked, that the strong harm not the
>   weak
> and that I rise like the sun over the black-headed people, lighting
>   up the land.[4]

Marduk, as we see from this passage, is to act as executive for Enlil, Hammurabi for Marduk. Since the passage is taken from the introduction to Hammurabi's law code, it is only natural that those of the Enlil functions which have reference to the maintaining of law and order are especially stressed.

Before the Enlil functions passed to Marduk and Babylon, they were held by the city of Isin and by its goddess Nininsina. We may quote from a text in which the goddess herself tells about her duties; she stresses her function as leader of foreign wars:

> When the heart of the great mountain Enlil has become turbulent,
> when he has knit his brows against a foreign land and determined
>   the fate of a rebellious country,
> then my father Enlil sends me to the rebellious country against
>   which he has knit his brows,
> and I, woman and hero, I, the mighty warrior, I go against it![5]

She continues with a description of the punishment which her armed might inflicts upon the foreign land and tells how she reports back to Enlil in Nippur.

Since the human steward acts for the city-god, even when the city-god has been chosen king and exercises the Enlil functions, the appointment of the human steward also is in such a case no longer a private affair of the city-god's; it needs confirmation from the divine assembly. Accordingly, we hear how, when Nanna, the god of Ur, became king of the gods, he had to travel to Nippur to seek office for his steward, Shulgi. In Nippur, Nanna is received in audience before Enlil, and his proposal is accepted. Says Enlil:

> Let my shepherd, Shulgi, cause pain to rebellious countries;
> let commands of righteousness be in his mouth(?).[6]

He mentions the two outstanding aspects of the office: leadership in war and the upholding of justice. Then Nanna brings back to his human protégé the glad tidings that his candidacy has been accepted.

A more complete and detailed description of such confirmation of an appointment is contained in a petition of the ruler Ishme-Dagan of Isin. He asks first that Enlil give him lordship in north and south and that Anu, at Enlil's suggestion, give him "all shepherd staves." Then each of the other great gods is besought to add some feature, to help in a particular way. When thus the appointment and its powers have been fully outlined, the king asks:

> May Enki, Ninki, Enul, Ninul, and those of the Anunnaki who
>   are fate-determining lords,
> (as also) the spirits of Nippur, (and) the genii of Ekur, among
>   the great gods
> speak concerning the destiny which they have determined, their
>   immutable "Let it be."[7]

That is, may the assembly of the gods confirm the appointment by their assenting votes.

The fact that the Mesopotamian universe was conceived of as a state—that the gods who owned and ruled the various city-states were bound together in a higher unity, the assembly of the gods, which possessed executive organs for exerting outward pressure as well as for enforcing law and order internally—had far-reaching consequences for Mesopotamian history and for the ways in which historical events were viewed and interpreted. It vastly strengthened tendencies toward political unification of the country by sanctioning even the most violent of means used toward that end. For any conqueror, if he was successful, was recognized as the agent of Enlil. It also provided—even at times when national unity was at a low ebb and the many city-states were, for all practical purposes, independent units—a background on which international law could work. We see, already at the dawn of history, that a boundary dispute between the neighboring city-states Lagash and Umma was viewed as a dispute between two divine landowners, Ningirsu, the god of Lagash, and Shara, the god of Umma. As such it could be taken to court and adjudicated by Enlil in Nippur. Enlil implemented his decision through the ruler who was then his human representative, Mesilim, king of Kish. Mesilim measured the disputed territory and marked the boundary line which Enlil had designated.[8]

In a similar manner other "kings" throughout Mesopotamian history acted as mediators and judges in disputes between city-states, fulfilling their tasks as Enlil's representatives. Thus Utuhegal of Uruk, after he had freed and united Shumer, settled boundary disputes between Lagash and Ur.[9] Again, Urnammu, the first king of the Third Dynasty of Ur, brought a similar dispute before the judge of the gods, the sun-god Utu, and "in accordance with the righteous verdict of Utu he had the underlying facts cleared up and confirmed (by witnesses)."[10]

This tendency to view what was, in purely human terms, a naked conflict of force as a legal procedure in the state of the gods, as an execution of a divine verdict, appears in full light in an inscription in which Utuhegal tells how he liberated Shumer from its Gutian oppressors.[11] After an introduction stating the misrule which the Gutians had instituted, Utuhegal tells how Enlil gave a verdict deposing them. Then follows Enlil's commission to Utuhegal, a divine deputy is assigned to him to accompany him and authorize his action as that of a legally empowered agent. And, finally, we hear about his campaign and victory.

The function which the national state performed as extension of the executive organs of the cosmic state was important but not indispensable. There had been a time when the kingship rested in heaven before Anu and had not yet descended to earth, and there were times in history when the gods appointed no human king on earth. Still the universe continued in its course. And, just as the national kingship itself was not indispensable, so was any particular incumbent of this office still less indispensable. From time to time the god and city that exercised the kingship were judged unfit for the function, if only for the reason that the divine assembly desired a change. Then the city "was smitten with weapons," and the kingship was either conferred on another god and city or held in abeyance.

When such momentous events were shaping, the royal city began to feel its grip slipping, its functioning becoming inefficient. All omens and signs became confused, the gods gave no clear answers to man's questions, no orders were transmitted, sinister portents appeared, and with fear and foreboding man awaited the catastrophe.

The gods of the doomed city suffered with it. We know, for instance, the feeling which gripped Ningal, goddess of Ur, in the days when the fall of that city was approaching, when a coming assembly of the gods would decide that the kingship which Ur had held should pass away from it and the city should perish in Enlil's terrible storm. The goddess herself tells about those days:

> When I was grieving for that day of storm,
> that day of storm, destined for me, laid upon me, heavy with tears,
> that day of storm, destined for me, laid upon me, heavy with tears,
> on me, a woman—
> though I was trembling for that day of storm,
> that day of storm, destined for me, laid upon me, heavy with tears,
> that cruel day of storm destined for me—
> I could not flee before that day's fatality.
> And of a sudden I espied no happy days within my reign.
> no happy days within my reign.
> Though I would tremble for that night,
> that night of cruel weeping destined for me,
> I could not flee before that night's fatality.
> Dread of the storm's floodlike destruction weighed on me,
> and of a sudden on my couch at night,
> upon my couch at night no dreams were granted me.
> And of a sudden on my couch oblivion,
> upon my couch oblivion was not granted.
> Because (this) bitter weeping had been destined for my land,
> and I could not, even if I scoured the earth—a cow seeking her calf—
> have brought my people back,
> because (this) bitter sorrow had been destined for my city,
> even if I, birdlike, had stretched my wings,

and, like a bird, flown to my city,
yet my city would have been destroyed on its foundation,
yet Ur would have perished where it lay.
Because that day of storm had raised its hand,
and even had I screamed out loud and cried:
"Turn back, O day of storm, (turn) to (thy) desert,"
the breast of that storm would not have been lifted from me.[12]

Though Ningal knows that it is hopeless, that the minds of the gods
are made up, she does her utmost to sway the assembly when the
fateful verdict is given, first imploring the leaders Anu and Enlil,
then, when that has failed, even making a last attempt in the assembly itself—all to no avail.

Then verily, to the assembly, where the crowd had not yet risen,
while the Anunnaki, binding themselves (to uphold the decision),
were still seated,
I dragged my feet and I stretched out my arms.
In truth, I shed my tears in front of Anu.
In truth, myself I mourned in front of Enlil:
"May not my city be destroyed!" I said indeed to them.
"May Ur not be destroyed!" I said indeed to them.
"And may its people not be killed!" I said indeed to them.
But Anu never bent toward those words,
and Enlil never with an, "It is pleasing, let it be,"
did soothe my heart.
(Behold,) they gave instruction that the city be destroyed,
(behold,) they gave instruction that Ur be destroyed,
and as its destiny decreed that its inhabitants be killed.[13]

And so Ur goes down before the onslaught of barbarians. The gods
have decided—as another hymn says of this event:

To bring on other days, annihilate the plan
and—while the storms foamed like a flood—
subvert the ways of Shumer.[14]

We quote these lines because they sum up what was involved in
the national kingship. The national kingship was the guaranty of
"the ways of Shumer" (that is, the ways of civilized Mesopotamia), the orderly, lawful pattern of life. Its function in the world
was to give protection against enemies external and internal, to insure the reign of justice and righteousness in human affairs.

THE STATE AND NATURE

With this discussion of the city-state and the national state we have outlined the function of the human state in general in the Mesopotamian universe. The city-state had an economic function. It provided a great god and his entourage with the economic basis which would enable him to live a full life, to realize his nature unhindered. The national state had a political function. It was an extension of the executive organs of the state of the universe and enforced on the human level the gods' decisions, insuring armed protection of their estates, upholding justice and righteousness as a basis for the intercourse of their servants, men.

Yet we should not leave our subject, the function of the state, without calling attention to a curious and interesting aspect which somehow fails to stand out when the human state is seen from the viewpoint of the universal state. That aspect is the relation of the human state to nature.

We have mentioned that the city-state furnishes the economic background which permitted the gods to live a full life in unhindered self-expression. This self-expression differed for the different gods; each had his own particular mode of life, his own characteristic observances and rites. This is apparent in the great cult festivals, which sometimes center in a marriage rite, sometimes in a battle drama, and sometimes in a death and revival drama. These cult festivals were matters of state; frequently the king or the ruler of the city-state performed the chief role in the cult drama. But why should they be matters of state?

We may consider one of these cult festivals in some detail. Around the end of the third millennium the city of Isin, which was then the ruling city in southern Mesopotamia, celebrated yearly the marriage of the goddess Inanna to the god Dumuzi or Tammuz. It is understandable that a marriage should be a typical form of self-expression for the youthful goddess, and—in the view of the universe as a state—it is only logical that her human servants and retainers should officiate at the wedding and take part in the celebration as guests and spectators. Since the goddess is an incarnation of the fertility of nature, and her husband, the shepherd-god Dumuzi, incarnates the creative powers of spring, it is understandable that this annual union of god and goddess signifies and *is* the reawakening of nature in spring. In the marriage of these deities the fertility and the creative powers of nature themselves becomes manifest. But why, we may ask, should human servants of the gods, the human ruler and—so it seems—a priestess, transcend their human status, take on the identity of the deities Dumuzi and Inanna, and go through their marriage? For this is what took place in the rites. The answer to that question lies back beyond the times when the view of the world as a state took form, back in a remote prehistoric age when the gods were not yet anthropomorphic rulers of states and cities but were still directly the phenomena of nature. In those days man's attitude was not merely one of passive obedience; it called for active intervention, as it does among many primitives today. It is one of the tenets of mythopoeic logic that similarity and identity merge; "to be like" is as good as "to be." Therefore, by being like, by enacting the role of, a force in nature, a god, man could in the cult enter into and clothe himself with the identity of these powers, with the identity of the gods, and through his own actions, when thus identified, cause the powers involved to act as he would have them act. By identifying himself with Dumuzi, the king is Dumuzi; and similarly the priestess is Inanna—our texts clearly state this. Their marriage is the marriage of the creative powers of spring. Thus through a willed act of man is achieved a divine union wherein is the all-pervading, life-giving re-creative potency upon which depends, as our texts tell us, "the life of all lands" and also the steady flow of days, the renewal of the new moon throughout the new year.[15]

As in this marriage rite, so also with the other types of cult festivals. In the death and revival drama man becomes the god of vegetation, the god of the grass and plants which have disappeared over the dry summer and the cold winter. Having become the god, man lets himself be found and thus causes the return of the god, of the new vegetation that springs up everywhere when spring comes. These rites usually comprise wailing processions lamenting the god who has been lost, a search for the god, finding him, and the triumphant return with him.[16]

This same approach underlies the battle drama. Each new year, when floods threatened to bring back the primeval watery chaos, it was of the essence that the gods should fight again that primeval battle in which the world was first won. And so man took on the identity of a god: in the cult rite the king became Enlil or Marduk or Assur, and as the god he fought the powers of chaos. To the very end of Mesopotamian civilization, a few centuries before our era, the king, every new year in Babylon, took on the identity of Marduk and vanquished Kingu, leader of Ti'amat's host, by burning a lamb in which that deity was incarnate.[17]

In these festivals, which were state festivals, the human state contributed to the control of nature, to the upholding of the orderly cosmos. In the rites man secured the revival of nature in spring, won the cosmic battle against chaos, and created the orderly world each year anew out of chaos.

Though these functions of the human state have been integrated to some degree with the view of the universe as a state, though the festivals are seen as the activities, the self-expression, of a divine nobility—the marriages of the gods, their battles, their death and revival—in which humans take part as servants will in the great events of their masters' lives, yet the deeper significance, the inner sense of these festivals, lies outside of and is not truly founded in the view of the universe as a state. It should therefore not cause wonder that they cannot stand out in true perspective in a presentation of that view; they represent an older layer of "speculative thought."

According to the view of the world as a state, man is the slave of the great cosmic forces; he serves them and obeys them; and his only means of influencing them is by prayer and sacrifice, that is, by persuasion and gifts. According to the older view which created the festivals, man could himself become god, could enter into the identity of the great cosmic forces in the universe which surrounded him, and could thus sway it by action, not merely by supplication.

NOTES

1. Largely through the account in Gudea's Cyl. B.
2. Urukagina Cones B and C XII, 23–28.
3. Gudea, Cyl. A.
4. CḤ I, 1–44. Line-division not that of original.
5. Chiera, SRT 6, iii, 32–37.

6. *TSR* II. 86 and *BE* XXXI, 24, i, 22–23.

7. *PBS* X₂, 9, rev. i, 16–20.

8. Entemena, Cone A.

9. *YOS* IX, Nos. 18–20.

10. Urnammu Clay-nail B.

11. Utuhegal inscription, *RA* IX, 111 ff., and X, 99 ff.

12. Kramer, *AS* XII, pp. 26 and 28, ll. 88–112.

13. *Ibid.*, p. 32, ll. 152–64.

14. *BE* XXXI, 3, 1–3.

15. Cf. Chiera, *SRT* 1, V, 14 ff.

16. Cf., e.g., De Genouillac, *TRS* I, No. 8.

17. *CT* XV, Pl. 44, ll. 8′ ff.

CHAPTER VII

MESOPOTAMIA: THE GOOD LIFE

THE PRIME VIRTUE: OBEDIENCE

IN A civilization which sees the whole universe as a state, obedience must necessarily stand out as a prime virtue. For a state is built on obedience, on the unquestioned acceptance of authority. It can cause no wonder, therefore, to find that in Mesopotamia the "good life" was the "obedient life." The individual stood at the center of ever wider circles of authority which delimited his freedom of action. The nearest and smallest of these circles was constituted by authorities in his own family: father and mother, older brother and older sister. We possess a hymn which describes a coming golden age, and we find that age characterized as one of obedience, as

> Days when one man is not insolent to another, when a son reveres his father,
> days when respect is shown in the land, when the lowly honor the great,
> when the younger brother . . . . respects(?) his older brother,
> when the older child instructs the younger child and he (i.e., the younger) abides by his decisions.[1]

The Mesopotamian is constantly admonished: "Pay heed to the word of thy mother as to the word of thy god;" "Revere thy older brother"; "Pay heed to the word of thy older brother as to the word of thy father"; "Anger not the heart of thy older sister."

But obedience to the older members of one's family is merely a beginning. Beyond the family lie other circles, other authorities: the state and society. There is the foreman where one works; there is the bailiff who oversees agricultural works in which one takes part; there is the king. All these can and must claim absolute obedience. The Mesopotamian looked with disapproval and pity, but also with fear, on the crowd which had no leader: "Soldiers without a king are sheep without their shepherd."[2]

A crowd with no leader to organize and direct it is lost and bewildered, like a flock of sheep without a shepherd. It is also dangerous, however; it can be destructive, like waters which break the dams that hold them and submerge fields and gardens if the canal inspector is not there to keep the dams in repair: "Workmen without a foreman are waters without a canal inspector."[3]

Finally, a leaderless, unorganized crowd is useless and unproductive, like a field which brings forth nothing if it is not plowed: "Peasants without a bailiff are a field without a plowman."[4]

Hence an orderly world is unthinkable without a superior authority to impose his will. The Mesopotamian feels convinced that authorities are always right: "The command of the palace, like the command of Anu, cannot be altered. The king's word is right; his utterance, like that of a god, cannot be changed!"[5] And, as there are circles of human authority in family, society, and state, to circumscribe the freedom of the individual, so there are circles of divine authority which may not be trespassed upon. Here again we find more immediate and more remote ties of allegiance. For the ties of the individual to the great gods were—at least in the third millennium—of a somewhat remote character. He served them as a member of his community rather than as an individual; he worked their estates for them, with his neighbors and compatriots he obeyed their laws and decrees, and he took part in their yearly festivals as a spectator. But, just as the serf rarely has intimate personal relations with the lord of the manor, so the individual in Mesopotamia looked upon the great gods as remote forces to whom he could appeal only in some great crisis and then only through intermediaries. Close and personal relations—relations such as he had to the authorities in his family: father, mother, older brother and sister—the individual had only to one deity, to his personal god.

The personal god was usually some minor deity in the pantheon who took a special interest in a man's family or had taken a fancy to the man himself. In a sense, and probably this is the original aspect, the personal god appears as the personification of a man's luck and success. Success is interpreted as an outside power which infuses itself into a man's doings and makes them produce results. It is not man's own ability which brings results, for man is weak and has no power to influence the course of the universe to any appreciable degree. Only a god can do that; therefore, if things come out as man has hoped, or even better, it must needs be that some god has taken an interest in him and his doings and brought him success. He has, to use the Mesopotamian expression for success, "acquired a god." This original aspect of the personal god as the power behind a man's success stands out quite clearly in such sayings as

> Without a (personal) god man cannot make his living,
> the young man cannot move his arm heroically in battle,[6]

and in the way the personal god is linked with forethought and planning:

> When thou dost plan ahead, thy god is thine;
> when thou dost not plan ahead, thy god is not thine.[7]

That is to say, only when you plan ahead do you have a chance to succeed; only then is your god with you.

Since the personal god is the power which makes a man's actions succeed, it is quite natural that he or she should also carry the moral responsibility for those actions. When Lugalzaggisi, the ruler of Umma, had attacked and partly destroyed the city of Lagash, the men of Lagash placed the blame unhesitantly on Lugalzaggisi's deity: "May his personal deity, the goddess Nidaba, bear this crime on her neck!"[8] That is, may the proper divine authorities who rule the universe hold her responsible for what she has aided and abetted.

To this personal god, then, before any other, a man owed worship and obedience. In every house there was a small chapel for the personal god where the owner of the house worshiped and brought his daily offerings.

> A man must truly proclaim the greatness of his god;
> A young man must wholeheartedly obey the command of his god.[9]

REWARDS OF OBEDIENCE

Now, if this monotonous theme of obedience—to family, to rulers, to gods—was the essence of the good, that is, the correct, life in ancient Mesopotamia, what, we may ask, did man stand to gain by leading the good life? The answer is best given in terms of the Mesopotamian world view, in terms of man's position in the cosmic state. Man, you will remember, was created to be the slave of the gods. He is their servant. Now, a diligent and obedient servant can call on his master for protection. A diligent and obedient servant, moreover, can expect to be promoted, to receive favors and rewards from his master. A slothful, disobedient servant, on the other hand, can hope for none of these things. Thus the way of obedience, of service and worship, is the way to achieve protection; and it is also the way to earthly success, to the highest values in Mesopotamian life: health and long life, honored standing in the community, many sons, wealth.

When we view the Mesopotamian universe from the aspect of what the individual can gain for himself, the personal god becomes a pivotal figure. He is the individual's link with the universe and its forces; he is the Archimedean point from which it may be moved. For the personal god is not remote and awesome like the great gods; he is near and familiar; and he cares. One can talk to him, plead with him, work on his pity—in short, use all the means which a child uses to get his way with his parents. The character of the relationship may be exemplified by a letter from a man to his god, for the Mesopotamians frequently wrote letters to their gods. Perhaps they thought that one could not always be certain to find the god at home when one called, whereas the god would be sure to look at his correspondence. Again, it may often have been because the writer was too ill to come in person and therefore had recourse to a letter. In the case of the letter which we shall quote, it would appear that the writer refrains from coming in person because he is sulking. His feelings are hurt because he thinks his god neglects him. He hints that such neglect is very unwise on the part of the god, for faithful worshipers are hard to get and difficult to replace. But if the god will only comply with his wishes, then he will be there right away and adore him. Finally, he works on the god's pity: the god must consider that there is not only himself but that he has a family and poor little children who also suffer with him. The letter reads:

> To the god my father speak; thus says Apiladad, thy servant:
> "Why have you neglected me (so)?
> Who is going to give you one who can take my place?

Write to the god Marduk, who is fond of you,
that he may break my bondage;
then I shall see your face and kiss your feet!
Consider also my family, grownups and little ones;
have mercy on me for their sake, and let your help reach me!"[10]

The bondage of which the letter speaks is some illness. Illness of any kind was seen as an evil demon who had seized the victim and held him captive. Such a case actually goes beyond the powers of the personal god. The personal god can help a man in his undertakings, can give him standing and respect in his community; but he is not strong enough to tear him from the clutches of an evil, lawless demon. However—and this is the most wonderful thing about having connections with those in high places—the personal god has influential friends. He moves in the circles of the great gods, knows them well. So now, when his ward has been seized by an evil demon, it is time to use whatever influence he has to set the cumbersome machinery of divine justice in motion: "Write to the god Marduk, who is fond of you," says our letter.

Now we who live in a modern state take for granted that the machinery of justice—courts, judges, police—is at the disposal of any man who considers himself wronged. But that is a very modern notion. We need go back only to medieval England to find a state in which it could be very difficult to get the king's court to take up one's case. And the early Mesopotamian state, upon which the cosmic state was patterned, was of far more primitive cast than medieval England. In this primitive state there was as yet no developed executive machinery to carry out the verdict of the court. Execution was left to the winning party; and for that reason a court would not touch a case unless it was certain that the plaintiff had power behind him, a powerful protector who would guarantee that the judgment would be executed. Accordingly, the first step for the personal god was to find such a protector among the great gods. Usually Ea, the god of the sweet waters, was willing to undertake the protectorship. But Ea was so august and remote that the personal god would not approach him directly. He would go to Ea's son, Marduk, and Marduk would then urge his father to act. If Ea agreed to act, he would send his messenger—a human incantation priest—to go with the personal god to the court of the gods, where the messenger would appeal on Ea's behalf that the sun-god (the divine judge) accept this particular case for judgment. This appeal was directed to the rising sun in an impressive ceremony in the temple. After praising the sun as judge, as able to give legal relief against all kinds of demons and to heal the afflicted, the priest continued:

> Sun-god, to relieve them is in thy power;
> thou dost set straight conflicting testimonies as (were they but) one statement.
> I am the messenger of Ea;
> for the relief of the plagued man he has sent me hither,
> (and) the message which Ea gave I have repeated to thee.
> (As for) the man, the son of his god, judge his case, pronounce sentence for him,
> drive off the evil illness from his body.[11]

Through the decision of the sun-god, guaranteed by the mighty Ea, the evil demon was thus constrained to release its hold.

The cases in which the personal god was asked to use his influence to procure divine justice are among those most typical of his usefulness, but naturally he was asked to use it for general well-being and advancement also. He is to say a good word for his ward whenever he can; the ruler Entemena, for example, prays that his personal god be allowed to stand forever before the great god Ningirsu, petitioning for health and long life for Entemena.[12]

If we sum up, then, what our texts tell us about the rewards for the "good life," we find life to be a pretty arbitrary affair. Through obedience and service man may win the good will of his personal god. The personal god may use his influence with the higher gods to obtain favors for his protégé from them. But even justice is such a favor; it cannot be claimed, but it is obtained through personal connections, personal pressure, through favoritism. Even the most perfect "good life" held out but a promise, not a certainty, of tangible rewards.

EVALUATION OF FUNDAMENTALS: THE DEMAND FOR A JUST WORLD

While the conception of the cosmic state remained relatively stable throughout the third millennium, the actual human state developed considerably. The central power grew stronger, the machinery of justice became more efficient, punishment followed crime with ever greater regularity. The idea that justice was something to which man had a right began slowly to take form, and in the second millennium—appropriately the millennium of the famous Code of Hammurabi—justice as right rather than justice as favor seems to have become the general conception.

This idea, however, could not but conflict violently with the established view of the world. There emerged fundamental problems, such as the justification of death and the problem of the righteous sufferer. These two problems do not arise with equal clarity, but both have behind them an equally passionate urgency.

A. The Revolt against Death: The Epic of Gilgamesh

The less articulate, less rationalized, of the two was probably the revolt against death. We meet it as a smoldering resentment, a deep-seated feeling of wrong; it is more a feeling than a thought. Yet it can hardly be doubted that this feeling has its basis in the new concept of human rights, in the claim for justice in the universe. Death is an evil—it is as harsh as any punishment, is, indeed, the *supreme* punishment. Why must a man suffer death if he has committed no wrong? In the old, arbitrary world this question had no sting, for both good and evil were arbitrary matters. In the new world of justice as a right it became terribly urgent. We find it treated in the Epic of Gilgamesh, which must have been composed around the beginning of the second millennium. This epic is based on older material, but the older stories have been woven into a new whole, grouped around a new theme, that of death.

In his youthful energy, Gilgamesh, ruler of Uruk in southern Babylonia, drives his people too hard. The people appeal to the gods to create a counterpart to him, that they may compete with each other and the people may find rest. The gods comply and create Enkidu, who becomes Gilgamesh's companion and friend. Together the friends set out on dangerous adventures. They penetrate to "the cedar forest" in the west, where they slay the terrible monster Huwawa who guards the forest for Enlil. On their return the goddess Inanna falls in love with Gilgamesh, and, when he will have none of her, she sends the awesome "bull of heaven" against him to kill him. Here again, however, the two heroes conquer. They battle with, and kill, the bull. There seem to be no limits to their strength and power. Even the most terrible opponents go down before their weapons. They can afford to treat a mighty goddess in the most arrogant fashion. Then Enlil decides that Enkidu must die as punishment for slaying Huwawa. So the unconquerable Enkidu falls ill and dies. Until now death has meant little to Gilgamesh. He has accepted the normal standards of a fearless hero and the normal standards of his civilization: death is unavoidable, and it is of no avail to worry about it; if one has to die, let his death be a glorious one, met in combat with a worthy opponent, so that his fame may live. Before the campaign against Huwawa, when Enkidu's courage had failed him momentarily, Gilgamesh upbraided him sternly:

> Who, my friend, was ever so exalted (that he could)
> rise up to heaven and lastingly dwell with Shamash?
> Mere man—his days are numbered,
> whatever he may do, he is but wind.
> You are—already now—afraid of death.
> Where is the fine strength of your courage?
> Let me lead,
> and you (tarrying) can call out to me: "Close in, fear not!"
> And if I fall, I shall have founded fame.
> "Gilgamesh fell (they will say) in combat with terrible Huwawa."

He goes on to relate how in that case Enkidu will be telling Gilgamesh's son about his father's prowess. Here death holds no terror; it is part of the game, and it is mitigated to some extent by fame, for one's name will live in future generations.

But Gilgamesh then knew death only in the abstract. It had never touched him directly in all its stark reality. It does so when Enkidu dies.

> "My friend, my younger brother—who with me in the
>   foothills
> hunted wild ass, and panther in the plains;
> Enkidu, my friend, my younger brother—who with me
>   in the foothills

hunted wild ass, and panther in the plains;
who with me could do all, who climbed the crags,
seized, killed the bull of heaven;
flung down Huwawa, dwelling in the cedar forest.
Now—what sleep is this that seized you?
You have grown dark and cannot hear me."
He did not raise his eyes.
(Gilgamesh) touched his heart, it was not beating.
Then he covered his friend, as if he were a bride. . . . .
His voice roared out—a lion . . . . ,
a lioness chased from her whelps.
Again and then again he turned toward his friend,
tearing his hair and scattering the tufts,
stripping and flinging down the finery off his body.

The loss which has been visited upon him is too great to bear. He refuses with all his soul to accept it as reality.

He who with me has shared all hazards—
the fate of man has overtaken him.
All day and night have I wept over him
and would not have him buried—
my friend might yet rise up at my (loud) cries,
for seven days and nights—
until a maggot dropped from his nose.
Since he is gone, I can no comfort find,
keep roaming like a hunter in the plains.

The thought of death continues to haunt Gilgamesh. He has but one thought, one aim, to find everlasting life; and so he sets out upon his quest. At the end of the world, beyond the waters of death, lives an ancestor of his who obtained eternal life. He must know the secret. To him will Gilgamesh go. Alone he wanders the long way to the mountains where the sun sets, follows the dark passage through which the sun travels at night, almost despairing of ever seeing the light again, and finally comes out at the shore of a wide sea. Whomsoever he meets on his travels he questions about the way to Utnapishtim and about eternal life. All tell him the quest is hopeless.

Gilgamesh, whither are you wandering?
Life, which you look for, you will never find.
For when the gods created man, they let

death be his share, and life
withheld in their own hands.
Gilgamesh, fill your belly—
day and night make merry,
let days be full of joy,
dance and make music day and night.
And wear fresh clothes,
and wash your head and bathe.
Look at the child that is holding your hand,
and let your wife delight in your embrace.
These things alone are the concern of men.

But Gilgamesh cannot give up, cannot resign himself to the common lot. The yearning for everlasting life consumes him and drives him on. On the shore of the sea he meets Utnapishtim's boatman and gains passage over the waters of death. Thus he finally finds Utnapishtim and can ask him how one achieves eternal life; but Utnapishtim cannot help him. The fact that he himself lives forever is due to unique circumstances that will never be repeated. When the gods in days of old had decided to destroy mankind and, led by Enlil, sent the flood, Utnapishtim and his wife alone were rescued. Utnapishtim had been forewarned; he had built a big boat, and in that he had saved himself, his wife, and pairs of all living things. Later on, Enlil repented the sending of the flood as a rash act and gave Utnapishtim eternal life as a reward for saving life on earth. But such circumstances obviously will not recur.

Yet Gilgamesh may try to fight death. Utnapishtim bids him contend with sleep, a magic sleep which is but another form of death. And Gilgamesh succumbs almost at once. He is about to perish when Utnapishtim's wife, out of pity on him, wakes him just in time. But the quest has failed. Dejected, Gilgamesh takes his departure to return to Uruk. At that moment, Utnapishtim's wife urges her husband to give him a parting gift, and Utnapishtim tells Gilgamesh about a plant which grows on the bottom of the sea and which rejuvenates him who partakes of it. Once more the sagging spirits of Gilgamesh revive. Accompanied by Utnapishtim's boatman, Urshanabi, he finds the right place, dives down, and comes up with the precious plant in his hands. Back they sail toward Uruk, reach the shore of the Persian Gulf, and continue inland on foot. But the day is warm and the journey tiring. When Gilgamesh sees an invitingly cool pool, he flings off his clothes and goes in for a swim. The plant he leaves on the bank. And while it is lying there a snake smells it, comes out of its hole, and snatches it away.

Therefore—because they ate of that plant—snakes do not die. When they become old, they slough off their old bodies and are reborn in youthful vigor. Mankind, cheated of Gilgamesh's plant, cannot thus return eternally to youth; and Gilgamesh, full of bitterness, contemplates the ironic end of his quest.

> Then Gilgamesh sat down and wept,
> tears streaming down his cheeks.
>
> . . . .
>
> "For whose sake, Urshanabi, have I strained my muscles?
> For whose sake has my heart's blood been spent?
> I brought no blessing on myself—
> I did the serpent underground good service."

The Epic of Gilgamesh does not come to a harmonious end; the emotions which rage in it are not assuaged; nor is there, as in tragedy, any sense of catharsis, any fundamental acceptance of the inevitable. It is a jeering, unhappy, unsatisfying ending. An inner turmoil is left to rage on, a vital question finds no answer.

B. THE RIGHTEOUS SUFFERER: "LUDLUL BEL NEMEQI"[13]

More articulate, more reasoned, and therefore less forceful in its expression is the rebellion against the general unjustness of the world. But—as we have already mentioned (p. 208)—it, too, has its basis in the swing from "justice as favor" to "justice as right" which precipitated the protest against death.

As the human state grew more centralized and tightly organized, its policing grew more effective. Robbers and bandits, who had been an ever present threat, now became less of a menace, a less powerful element in daily life. This decrease of the power of human robbers and bandits seems to have influenced the evaluation of the cosmic robbers and bandits, the evil demons. They loomed less large in the cosmic state. It has been pointed out by Von Soden that there was a subtle change in the concept of the personal god around the beginning of the second millennium. Before that time he had been thought to be powerless against demons who attacked his ward and had had to appeal to some great god for help. With the advent of the second millennium, however, the demons had lost power, so that the personal god was fully capable of protecting his human ward against them. If now they succeeded in an attack, it was because the personal god had turned away in anger and had left his ward to shift for himself. Offenses which would anger a personal god came to include, moreover, almost all serious lapses from ethical and moral standards.

With this change, minute as it may seem, the whole outlook on the world actually shifted. Man no longer permitted his world to be essentially arbitrary; he demanded that it have a firm moral basis. Evil and illness, attacks by demons, are no longer considered mere happenings, accidents: the gods, by allowing them to happen, are ultimately responsible, for only when an offense has been committed should the personal god be angered and turn away. Thus in human moral and ethical values man had found a yardstick with which he presumptuously proceeded to measure the gods and their deeds. A conflict was immediately apparent. Divine will and human ethics proved incommensurable. The stinging problem of the righteous sufferer emerged.

We have several Mesopotamian treatments of this problem. Here, however, we shall deal only with the one best known, the composition called *Ludlul bel nemeqi*, "I will praise the lord of wisdom." It is a counterpart of, though much inferior to, the Book of Job. The hero of the poem knows himself to have been righteous, to have lived the good life, but doubts about the value of living assail him:

> I only heeded prayer and supplication,
> my very thought was supplication, sacrifice habitual to me.
> The days when gods were worshiped were my heart's delight,
> those when I followed (the procession) of the goddess were
>   my gain and profit.
> Adoration of the king was joy to me,
> music for him a source of pleasure.
> And I instructed my estate to observe the ritual of the gods,
> I taught my people to revere the names of the goddess.

> Illustrious royal deeds I likened to (the deeds) of gods,
> and I taught soldiers to revere the palace.
> Would that I knew these things are pleasing to a god.

For, in spite of his righteousness, evils of the most serious kind have befallen him:

> *Alu*-disease covers my body like a garment;
> sleep in a net enmeshes me;
> my eyes stare but see not,
> my ears are open, but hear not,
> weakness has seized my body.

He laments that

> The lash laid upon me holds terror;
> I have been goaded, piercing is the sting.
> All day a persecutor chases me,
> at night he gives me no respite at all.

His god has abandoned him:

> No god came to my aid, or grasped my hand,
> my goddess did not pity me or succor me.

Everyone has already given him up for dead and acts accordingly:

> The grave was open still when they rifled my treasures,
> while I was not yet dead, already they stopped mourning.

All his enemies are jubilant:

> My evil-wisher heard of it and his face brightened,
> to her who wished me evil they brought happy tidings
> and her liver felt good.

And there the problem is, neatly posed: a man who has been righteous throughout may yet be dealt with by the powers who govern existence as though he were the blackest offender. For his pious deeds he has received the wages of the ungodly; he has been treated like one

> Who has not bowed his face, is not seen to prostrate himself,
> from whose mouth prayers and supplication are barred.

The reality of the problem cannot be disputed. The case of the righteous sufferer may be rare in such extreme form, yet none could be blind to its general validity. Righteousness, the good life,

is no guaranty of health and happiness. Often, indeed, the unrighteous life seems a better way to success.

Is there an answer? Our text gives two: one to the mind, which
struggles with an intellectual problem; one to the heart, whose
emotions have been stirred by contemplation of the wrongs done
to this particular righteous sufferer. The answer to the mind is a
denial that human standards of values can be applied to the gods.
Man is too small, too limited in outlook, to pass judgment on things
that are divine. He has no right to set up his human values against
the values which the gods hold.

> What seems praiseworthy to one's self, is but contemptible be-
>   fore the god(s),
> What to one's heart seems bad, is good before one's god.
> Who may comprehend the mind of gods in heaven's depth?
> The thoughts of a god are like deep waters, who could fathom
>   them?
> How could mankind, beclouded, comprehend the ways of gods?

Human judgment cannot be true judgment, for man is a creature of
the moment; he can take no long-range view, his mood changes
from moment to moment, he cannot attain to the deeper understanding which motivates the timeless and eternal gods.

> Who came to life yesterday, died today.
> In but a moment man is cast into gloom, suddenly crushed.
> One moment he will sing for joy,
> and in an instant he will wail—a mourner.
> Between morning and nightfall men's mood may change:
> when they are hungry they become like corpses,
> when they are full they will rival their god,
> when things go well they will prate of rising up to heaven
> and when in trouble, rant about descending into Hades.

What, therefore, is man's judgment that he should presume to set it
up against that of a god?

But, though this stern *non licet* may satisfy the mind, may show
that its question is not permissible, it will hardly satisfy the heart.
Deep emotions have been stirred, a sense of bitter wrong has been
evoked. And so to the heart our poem holds out as answer the duty
to hope and to trust. The righteous sufferer did not remain in his
sufferings. When all hope seemingly had fled, then came his deliv-

erance; in his darkest hour the gods had mercy on him and turned to him full of goodness and light. Marduk restored him to health and dignity, purified him, and all was happiness again. Thus our poem is an encouragement to trust and hope. The ways of the gods may seem inexplicable to man, but that is because man lacks the deeper understanding which actuates the gods. And though man may be plunged in the deepest despair, the gods do not abandon him; he shall and must trust to their mercy and goodness.

C. The Negation of All Values: A Dialogue of Pessimism[14]

It is a well-known fact that, as a civilization grows old, its basic values are in danger of losing their hold upon the individuals who participate in it. Skepticism, doubt, and indifference begin to undermine the spiritual structure which comprises the civilization. Such skepticism toward all values, utter negation of the possibility of a "good life," begins to make its appearance in Mesopotamian civilization in the first millennium B.C. This skepticism has found expression in a long dialogue between a master and his slave; it is known as the "Dialogue of Pessimism."

The pattern of the dialogue is extremely simple. The master announces to the slave that he intends to do a particular thing, and the slave encourages him by enumerating all the pleasant aspects of what the master proposes. But by then the master has already tired of his idea and states that he will not do the thing in question. This, too, is praised by the slave, who enumerates all the darker sides of the proposed activity. In this manner all the typical activities of a Mesopotamian nobleman are weighed and found wanting. Nothing is inherently good, nothing is worth while, whether it be seeking favors at court, the pleasures of the table, razzias against nomads in the desert, the excitement of a rebel's life, the beginning of a lawsuit, or what not. We shall quote a few of the stanzas, first about love:

> "Servant, agree with me!" "Yes, my lord, yes!"
> "I will love a woman!" "So love, my lord, so love!
> The man who loves a woman forgets want and misery!"
> "No, slave, I will not love a woman!"
> "Love not, my lord, love not!

Woman is a snare, a trap, a pitfall;
woman is a sharpened iron sword
which will cut a young man's neck!"

About piety:

"Slave, agree with me!" "Yes, my lord, yes!"
"Straightway order me water for my hands,
and bring it hither. I will make a libation to my god!"
"Do, my lord, do! (As for) the man who makes a libation
to his god, his heart is at ease;
he makes loan upon loan!"
"No, slave, I will not make a libation to my god!"
"Make it not, my lord, make it not!
Teach the god to run after thee like a dog
when he demands, be it 'my service,' be it 'thou hast
not asked,' be it anything else, from thee."

In other words, "be uppish with the god"; let him feel that he depends upon you for service, for prayer, and for many other things, so that he will run after you, begging you to worship him.

No better than piety fares charity:

"Slave, agree with me!" "Yes, my lord, yes!"
"I say, I will give alms to my land!"
"So do, my lord, so do!
(As for) he man who gives alms to his land,
his alms have been put on the palms of the god
Marduk himself."

That is, it is as though Marduk himself received them and will reciprocate to the giver.

"No, slave, I will not give alms to my land!"
"Do it not, my lord, do it not!
Mount thou upon the ruined mounds of ancient
cities and walk around;
behold the skulls of those of earlier and later times.
Who is the evildoer, who is the benefactor?"

It is all one whether man does good or evil; none will remember it in times to come. We know not who was good, who evil, among the ancients; they lie forgotten in their forgotten cities.

And so the argument sums up: there is nothing which is truly good; all is vanity.

"Slave, agree with me!" "Yes, my lord, yes!"
"Now then, what is good?
To break my neck and thy neck,
to fall into the river—that is good!"

With the world all vanity, only death seems attractive. The slave answers stoically with an ancient saying which expresses resignation:

"Who is tall enough to reach up to heaven;
who is broad enough that he might encompass the earth?"

If it is vain to seek for an absolute good, we might as well resign and give up; we cannot do the impossible. But once more the master changes his mind:

"No, slave, I will kill only thee and let thee precede me!"
"And would my lord want to live (even) three days after me?"

asks the slave. If there is no profit in life, if nothing is good, if all is vanity, what benefit can the master possibly see in prolonging life? How can he suffer it for even three more days?

And with this denial of all values, denial that a "good life" existed, we end our survey of Mesopotamian speculative thought. Mesopotamian civilization with the values it embodied was about to lose its hold on man. It had run its course and was ready to give way before new and different, more vigorous, patterns of thought.

NOTES

1. *STVC*, 66 and 67; *TRS*, 15, 11th KI-RU-GÚ.
2. *RA* XVII, p. 123, rev. ii., 14′–15′.
3. *Ibid.*, 16′–17′.
4. *Ibid.*, 18′–19′.
5. *Ibid.*, p. 132; K4160, 1–3.
6. *STVC* I, i, 15–18.
7. *RA* XVII, p. 122, iii and iv, 5–8.
8. Urukagina, Clay Tablet.
9. *STVC* I, i, 1–4.
10. *YOS*, 2, 141.
11. *Bīt Rimki* Tablet III.
12. Entemena, Brick B.
13. Langdon, *Babylonian Wisdom*, pp. 35–66.
14. *Ibid.*, pp. 67–81.

SUGGESTED READINGS

DHORME, ÉDOUARD. *Les Religions de Babylonie et d'Assyrie.* Paris, 1945.

HEHN, JOHANNES. *Die biblische und die babylonische Gottesidee.* Leipzig, 1913.

HEIDEL, ALEXANDER. *The Babylonian Genesis.* Chicago, 1942.

————. *The Gilgamesh Epic and Old Testament Parallels.* Chicago, 1946.

JACOBSEN, THORKILD. "Sumerian Mythology: A Review Article," *Journal of Near Eastern Studies*, V (1946), 128–52.

KRAMER, SAMUEL N. *Sumerian Mythology: A Study of Spiritual and Literary Achievement in the Third Millennium B.C.* Philadelphia, 1944.

LANGDON, STEPHEN. *Babylonian Wisdom.* . . . . London, 1923.

PALLIS, SVEND AA. *The Babylonian Akîtu Festival.* Copenhagen, 1926.

VON SODEN, WOLFRAM. "Religion und Sittlichkeit nach den Anschauungen der Babylonier," *Zeitschrift der Deutschen Morgenländischen Gesellschaft*, Vol. LXXXIX (1935).

SPEISER, E. A. "Some Sources of Intellectual and Social Progress in the Ancient Near East," *Studies in the History of Culture.* Philadelphia, 1942.

THE HEBREWS

WILLIAM A. IRWIN

CHAPTER VIII

GOD

ISRAEL came late into the course of oriental history. When the Hebrew tribes broke into Palestine in the fourteenth century B.C. in the invasion that was to prove the beginning of their career as a nation, the glory of Egypt was already waning. Her imperial greatness and her intellectual creativeness had become matters of the past. Shumer was but an echo of half-forgotten history, though its remarkable achievements had passed into the rich treasure of Semitic Babylonia. But of this, too, the great age was gone, save only as the glories of Hammurabi were later to be revived for a brief period by Nebuchadrezzar. By the time of Israel's first great era of constructive thinking in the age of the prophets, Assyria had reached almost its zenith, soon to totter to its eternal doom. The fruitful period of Israel's maturity, too often lightly dismissed as "late," paralleled in time the greatness of the Achemenids in one direction and in the other the supremacy of Athenian leadership in the age of Pericles, later the career of Alexander, and then the dominance of Hellenism throughout the East.

It is no surprise, then, to find that, heir as she consciously and obviously was of the achievements of the Orient and continuing her vigor into what we commonly speak of as the classical age, Israel's intellectual life bridges two worlds. Her primitivism is apparent, perhaps the most striking feature brought into relief by the critical studies of the last hundred years. It would serve no good end to delay over it here; suffice it that a large portion of the concepts surveyed in the preceding chapters find their parallels, if not direct survivals, in Israel's outlook on the world. It is clear that the founders of the Hebrew nation and their heirs and successors for many generations brought with them and continued to live in the pervasive thought-life of the world of their times.

But if this were all or even the significant aspect of Hebrew thinking, there would be no occasion for discussing it in this book. Israel was a small nation, relatively unimportant among the powers of the ancient East; in so far as she conformed to the pattern of her contemporaries she has now no better claim on our attention than have Edom, Moab, and Damascus. We do scant justice to historic reality—indeed, we fail completely to understand the genius of Israel—if we do not recognize wherein, and the extent to which, she differed from her neighbors and contemporaries, great and small alike. For rooted and molded in the cultures of the ancient East, Israel yet far transcended them and attained a world of thinking and of concepts much like our own. The differences of kind that separate us are much less than those that set Israel off from the peoples with whom she was in close contact, both in space and in time. Or, to put it in other terms, the boundary between the ancient world and the modern is to be traced, not in the Aegean or the middle Mediterranean, but in the pages of the Old Testament, where we find revealed Israel's attainments in the realms of thought, her facility in literary expression, her profound religious insights, and her standards of individual and social ethics.

Israel's great achievement, so apparent that mention of it is almost trite, was monotheism. It was an achievement that transformed subsequent history. Our indebtedness at this day is evident on a moment's thought. With some entail of that danger always implicit in superlatives one may raise the question whether any other single contribution from whatever source since human culture emerged from the stone ages has had the far-reaching effect upon history that Israel in this regard has exerted both through the mediums of Christianity and Islam and directly through the world of Jewish thinkers themselves. In the other direction Israel's uniqueness in this regard in the ancient world has been richly implied by the previous chapters in this book. Over against the polytheistic naturalism of Babylonia and the confused "consubstantial" ideas of the Egyptian pantheon, Israel affirmed, "The Lord our God, the Lord is one"; "All the gods of the nations are vanities, but the Lord made the world." Traditional dogmas have robbed the Hebrew thinkers of their proper due through a doctrine of divine revelation which has lifted the achievement out of human categories of thought. But our function here, while not calling in question the former, is to show the reality of the latter and to appraise the achievement of Israel's speculative thinkers.

The story of this achievement is one of the contentious issues of Hebrew history. Was Abraham a monotheist? Or did this concept come into Hebrew history with Moses? What was the faith of Samuel, of David, of Amos? On all such questions students of the Old Testament fall into diverse camps. And certainly this is not the place to undertake adjudication of issues that have occupied whole monographs. A few general comments, and then an apparently dogmatic decision, will serve our present needs. That the ancient East showed trends toward a monotheistic faith is a familiar idea. Further, it conforms to all that we know of Israel's genius and her historic relations to believe that from the first her thinkers were more or less aware of these movements of thought. It is neither shocking nor novel to admit that Israel's monotheism was evidently in some way built on these older attempts. But, on the other hand, even the best of them fell far short of what Israel came to believe. I have the assurance of Professor Wilson that, whatever one is to say of the still unsolved problem of Akhnaton's alleged monotheism, it was at the best quite different from and inferior to Israel's. Even if we should accept the middle course, however dubious, of assuming that Moses was the father of Israel's monotheism and that he worked in full consciousness of this great Egyptian heresy, yet the differences between the two are such as to compel the conclusion that he thus brought into being a new thing in human history. And certainly this view is not weakened if we prefer the view more commonly held among critical scholars that monotheism was the crowning achievement of the prophetic age, wrought out in the very time when the brute might of Assyria was overrunning the world and threatening the extinction of Hebrew nationality.

However all this may be, even if we were obliged to qualify the belief that in the opening oracles of the Book of Amos we actually see Israel's monotheism taking its nascent form right under our eyes, yet at least the passage reveals the sort of thinking that certainly at some time led to Israel's great discovery. The words are familiar:

Thus saith the Lord,
>   For three transgressions of Damascus
>   and for four I will not turn back its punishment,
>   because they have threshed Gilead
>   with threshing sleds of iron;
>   but I will send fire into the house of Hazael
>   and it shall devour the palaces of Ben-Hadad [Amos 1:3–4].

And thus in reiterated phraseology the prophet moves round, as in the swing of a scythe of destiny, from Damascus to Gaza, to Tyre, to Edom and Ammon and Moab, before coming at length to his own people. It is the accepted critical view that the list has been somewhat expanded since Amos' day; but the reduction so demanded does not affect the basic significance of the passage. Two things stand out for present consideration. Note how the accepted limitations of the thought of the prophet's time have been ignored or transcended. Here is no little national god minding his own business strictly behind the borders or at most the military outreach of his own people. Indeed, one may speculate on the absurdity of Amos' position, as it must have seemed to his contemporaries, and most of all to the foreign lands here so boldly castigated by this peasant spokesman of a petty deity. What had the God of Israel to do with Damascus, the power that for a hundred years had wasted and ravaged his land, had enslaved and despoiled and brutally maltreated his people, while he looked on impotent? How well the "practical" men of the time might scoff! But indifferent to all alleged lack of realism and logic, Amos swept on round Israel's land with words of rebuke for all these neighbor and enemy countries. Here, then, is our first observation: the "national god" concept is for Israel broken and discarded. The God of Israel is a being who has powers and responsibilities and authority over all the lands of Israel's neighbors. We must admit notable exceptions from the list. There is nothing here about Egypt, not a word of Assyria or of Urartu, whichever seemed to Amos' day the dominant power. The list concerns only the principalities round about Israel. But the prophet has gone too far to stop here; he has set out on a line of thought that has no proper boundaries short of attributing to Yahweh universal rule. And, indeed, in further oracles of his book Amos introduces some nameless nation

of his age in a role of divine judgment that implies the Lord's
dominion far out also into the midst of the great powers of the
time.

But this in itself could be of little more significance than the oriental trends toward monotheism already mentioned. Monotheism
in itself may be no more than despotism in religion. The great
achievement of Israel was not primarily that she asserted the one-
ness of the world and of God, but rather the character of the God so
affirmed. Amos' thought goes beyond a mere implication of the
supremacy of his God. The Lord's coming punishment of Israel's
neighbors is for moral reasons. Damascus and Ammon have practiced barbarities in war; Tyre and Gaza have inhumanly sold
whole peoples into slavery; and so the indictment runs on. Now, all
these practices were standard, accepted conduct in the eighth century B.C. Once more the scoffer might have found occasion to
jeer: this common peasant getting himself excited over what
everyone was doing! The independence of Amos' thinking here evidenced is of less importance for us, however, than his moral judgment. The nations are condemned for the depravity of their morals. And here is the point: they are so condemned in the name of the
God of Israel! It is his righteousness, be it observed, not his might
or his glory or any other of the divine qualities prized in the time,
which provides the ground of his supremacy. Here we see the
meaning of that phrase so commonly employed in the study of Hebrew history: Israel's monotheism was an ethical monotheism.

Those who sat in the history classes of the late James H. Breasted will recall his treatment of the alleged solar monotheism of
Egypt of the fourteenth century B.C. He pointed out that it came
as the culmination of a century of Egyptian imperialism. In his
phrase, this "monotheism was imperialism in religion." The
Egyptian sun-worshiper leaving his narrow valley found the same
sun shining not only in the hills of Palestine and Syria but also
in the upper valley of the Nile beyond the traditional limits of
Egypt; and so he was impelled to conclude that there was but one
sun, hence, sun-god. It appears to be a comparable process that we
see working itself out, first in the mind of Amos, and then becoming the accepted faith of all the prophets and later of the nation.
The standards of decency and honor and human compassion which

were valid and prized among individuals in the little communities of Palestine did not cease their high demands when one stepped over the boundary into Syria or Philistia; but there alike men were human, with human needs and, consequently, with human standards. Amos would have denied emphatically the light assertion of certain folk of easy morals in our day that "east of Suez" there "ain't no Ten Commandments." Indeed, in one famous passage which again witnesses the incredible vigor of thought of this simple peasant, Amos does more than imply, he asserts in unmistakable language the common human bond among diverse and remote races.

> Are you not as the Ethiopians to me,
>   O children of Israel, says the Lord;
> Did I not bring up Israel
>   from the land of Egypt;
> and the Philistines from Caphtor,
>   and the Syrians from Kir? [Amos 9:7.]

The Negroes of central Africa, and Israel's two traditional enemies, the Philistines on one side and the Syrians on the other, as human beings stood on the same footing as the "chosen people" themselves. The passage is a valuable commentary on the judgments found in chapters 1 and 2 of the Book of Amos, for it might be claimed that some at least of these are partisan in their motivation —that Amos thunders his denunciations because his own people were the sufferers. But even in that list of divine judgments there are some that cannot be disposed of so lightly; and this utterance about God's care of the Philistines and Syrians serves to corroborate what one may deduce there. The basis of Amos' moral thinking is a sense of common humanity.

And this, it will be observed, is carried over into the concept of the nature of God: God utters his judgments upon cruelty and inhumanity. Now this is a line of thought that was to receive notable development in the course of time and to provide one of the distinctive aspects of the Hebrew outlook on the world. Notwithstanding the notable passages we have mentioned and others not less worthy of remark, Amos appears in the record we have of him somewhat as a stern moralist. He is a prophet of impending doom; he utters the judgments of God upon a careless and selfish people.

Only at one or two points do his pronouncements leave room for argument that at heart he cherished a deep hope for the reformation and salvation of his people. But when we move on to his immediate successor, if not younger contemporary, all is changed. Though Hosea was not less concerned with the ruin that social selfishness was bringing upon the nation, yet his mood is emotional rather than judicial. He is a man of deep affection and tender motivation. It is he who has left for us that striking and charming picture of God as a loving father leading his people as though holding the hand of a toddling infant in its first uncertain steps:

> I taught Ephraim to walk;
>   I took them in my arms . . . .
> with human bonds I drew them,
>   with cords of love. . . . .
> How shall I give you up, Ephraim;
>   how shall I let you go, Israel?
> My heart turns within me;
>   all my tenderness is kindled.
> I will not perform my fierce anger,
>   I will not turn about to destroy Ephraim;
> For I am God and not man [Hos. 11:3–4, 8–9].

Also we recall the famous passage with which the Book of Jonah closes. The ill-tempered prophet wanted the great city destroyed just to "save his face" as a predictor; but the Lord rebuked him. "Should I not have compassion on Nineveh, that great city, in which are more than a hundred and twenty thousand people who know not their right hands from their left; and also many cattle?" (Jon. 4:11.) One thinks, too, of the words:

> Like as a father pitieth his children
>   so the Lord pitieth them that fear him.
> For he knoweth our frame;
>   he remembereth that we are dust [Ps. 103:13–14].

And the corollary and complement of all is represented by an equally famous passage, "Thou shalt love the Lord thy God with all thy heart and with all thy soul and with all thy might" (Deut. 6:5). Here we see what may well be adjudged the culmination of Israel's monotheistic achievement: the one God of the universe is a God of righteousness, but still more he is a God of love: "His tender mercies are over all his works" (Ps. 145:9). The significance of this in the long sequel of history a moment's thought will suffice to show. And the revolutionary nature of Israel's discovery is sufficiently evident by reference to the chapters by Professors Wilson and Jacobsen; in their surveys of Egypt and Babylonia, to the question of the attitude of the gods toward humankind, they pointed out that, while these could on occasion be most beneficent, on the whole their relation with man was little better than one of indifference. They had their own concerns, and only by special effort could they be induced to turn aside to the troublesome interruptions of mundane affairs. And this is a problem that has tormented human thought throughout the centuries. It is said that a religious thinker of the past generation, when asked what inquiry he would make of the Sphinx if assured that it would answer truly just a single question, replied, "Is the Universe friendly to me?" It was a profound insight; for man's most poignant question throughout all ages has been "What is my place in a world of great and seemingly callous might?" And Israel's great attainment was the vision that we may walk this earth with the confident tread of a son in his father's house.

Implicit in monotheism is a movement toward transcendence. And in Israel's monotheism it was inevitable. A God such as envisaged by Israel must be exalted in divine quality far above puny man, above this earth, and above all that is of the earth and earthy. A pregnant symbol of the many expressions of this throughout the Old Testament is the great vision of Isaiah; he "saw the Lord seated upon a throne high and lifted up, and his train filled the temple. Above him were the seraphim . . . . and one cried unto another and said, Holy, Holy, Holy is the Lord of Hosts, the whole earth is full of his glory. And the foundations of the threshold shook at the voice of him who cried and the house was filled with smoke" (Isa. 6:1–5). Israel's characteristic thought of God was that he was awful in holiness, terrible in righteousnes. And on this side of the vast gulf in quality that separated him from the divine stood man, frail mortal and sinful, whose best righteousnesses were in the light of that pure countenance "but as filthy rags." This will make clear one reason why Israel abhorred apotheosis, whether of the king or of any other; for the Hebrew thinkers

God was in heaven, and man below. This provides also the basis
of their concept of sin, on both of which topics more must be said
presently.

Such, then, was the Hebrew view of the nature of the world.
At its center there sat enthroned a Being of unutterable greatness
and holiness, who was at once its creator and sustainer. But Israel
never went the distance of abstracting this One into a cold and remote absolute. It is of the very essence of Hebrew thought that
God is a person. The I-Thou relation in which primitive man saw
his natural environment was maintained, no, rather, was sublimated, in Israel's faith: the world was to be understood in terms of
personality. Its center and essence was not blind force or some
sort of cold, inert reality but a personal God. And for them personality meant the sort of concept that they, and we, in turn, apply to human nature.

Now a person, so understood, can be in only one place at any
one given time. Yet our uncertain ideas of extrasensory perception
provide an analogy to Israel's thought at this point; for God had, as
it were, extensions of his personality so that he could reach out
into many places. His proper abode was, for later thought at least,
in the heavens, where he sat on a throne of majesty, surrounded by
the host of his ministrants. But from him went out powers comparable with the somewhat later notion of emanations. By his spirit
or by his word, he accomplished his purposes. And in the course of
time still other mediums of his activity were conceived.

Yet, even so, the religious demand for the omnipresence of God
was not met. In earlier times, it would appear, there was a belief
in a sort of differentiation of localized manifestations of God.
Thus Absalom, while in Geshur, vowed a vow to the Yahweh in
Hebron (or so he claimed as part of his scheme of revolt) and, in
course of time, went away from the official shrine in Jerusalem in
order to pay this vow in Hebron. Such appears to be the implication also of the assurance that "in every place where I record my
name will I come unto thee and bless thee" (Exod. 20:24). It is
difficult to see how in that time such local manifestations of the
deity could fail to be credited with diverse qualities dependent on
the nature of such manifestations and so to assume almost the
status of separate personalities. It would seem, too, that we are to

recognize a handling of the problem in the famous vision in chapter i of the Book of Ezekiel. It describes a remarkable structure on which the God of Israel came down out of the north along the road which his people had taken in their mournful journey into captivity; and there he, too, came seeking his lonely, heartsick exiles.

So far as this goes, then, it indicates that Israel's answer was in freeing God of the limitations of fixed abode: He could leave his house and go where necessity of whatever sort called him. Yet it is apparent that such explanation will not take account of all Israel's thought. For while to the devout even of the later time God was in his holy temple, yet he could and would hear the prayer of his people afar in Palestine or in the lands of the dispersion. Apparently this was in large measure accomplished by an extension of the divine personality or of the divine powers so that God could hear, see, and act at a distance which for man was quite out of consideration. For practical purposes of religious faith the result was not unlike the later concept of the immanence of God.

The substance and features ascribed to this cosmic Person are not clearly grasped; indeed, it is probable that Hebrew thought recoiled from the question. This at least seems certain, however, that the Person was conceived of as possessing a quasi-human form. There can be no doubt that such is the meaning of the account in the creation stories where man was made in the image of God; and a large number of other passages corroborate the view. Many of these are poetic and in their details must be discounted as mere symbolism; still so much is an irreducible minimum. But the divine substance is far from certain. It was a later teacher who declared that "God is a spirit"; yet the belief is not diverse from that of the Old Testament. But what was a spirit? It could flit about here and yonder, could suddenly appear or disappear, could exercise superhuman powers; but none of this is determinative, for we find that certain human beings could do the same. One thinks, for example, of the stories of Elijah and Elisha. For popular thought of our day, a spirit presumably is a personality without a material body. But it is far from clear that such was an ancient concept. We recall Paul's discussion of spiritual bodies, apparently composed of some nonearthly substance (I Cor. 15:35–58). Whether, then, the Hebrews conceived of spirit as a finer kind of matter, as in certain

strands of Greek thought, is not apparent. We find considerable use
of the imagery of fire relevant to the person and appearances of
God. But it would be bold to claim then that Israel thought of
God as possessing a body made up of some sort of celestial fire.
And with that we must dismiss the problem.

However, another question comes into consideration at this
point. In proportion as God is exalted in transcendent holiness and
power, he is removed from human approach. A comparison with
concepts of the manlike God of earlier time will make this clear.
God came down and walked in the garden and talked with the
guilty pair; he accepted Abraham's hospitality one afternoon as
he journeyed across the Judean hills; he informed Noah of the
coming flood, and, when the latter had obeyed the divine warning
and gone into the ark, he shut the door. Hosts of similar incidents
will suggest themselves. Briefly, such a God was so close and ap-
proachable that one never knew at what casual moment, coming
suddenly round a corner, he might meet him face to face. The significance of this for religious faith is obvious. But the transcendent
God is remote. Furthermore, he is preoccupied with his mighty
concerns. How can frail man hope that such a one will be interested
in the needs and hopes and fears of a tiny spark of animated dust?
It is a problem that higher religion carries implicit in its advance.
As man exalts God in transcendent quality, at the same time he
pushes him steadily farther off from human need. It will serve the
purpose of orientation for us to realize that to serve just this problem is one of the functions of the Christian doctrine of the Trinity.
Obviously this was not the formulated solution of ancient Israel.
To some extent, however, Israel employed the device of intermediaries between God and the world; the angels which became
highly characteristic of later thought are one manifestation of
this.

But much more important in its historic significance is the use
made by the sages of the concept of the divine wisdom through
which God made the world and by which he deals with men. It is
a matter that will call for more extended treatment presently; for
the present we must be content merely to mention it as of relevance at this point. Clearly, however, the characteristic Hebrew
treatment of this problem was just the affirmation that the God

who is transcendent in holiness, enthroned afar, is yet very near to each devout soul and attentive to the need of his people. It is thus that the psalmists individually cry to the Lord for help and celebrate the answer to their prayers. No need for them to invoke intermediaries—whether priest or angel or divine being: the Lord was a God of loving-kindness and tender mercy. He kept eternal watch above his own: "The Lord is thy keeper. . . . . He will not suffer thy foot to be moved. . . . . Thou shalt not fear for the terror by night nor for the arrow that flieth by day" (Ps. 121:3, 5; 91:5).

Revolutionary as much of this was in the history of human thinking, yet, in surveying it, one is conscious of a certain impatience to get on to the basic problem that confronts us in this discussion: What were the processes of thought by which Israel came to such views? Rooted in the past as she was, intimately a part of the culture of the ancient world and heir of its thought, it is apparent at once that such wide divergence unavoidably implies bold and vigorous thinking, not by a few individuals, by but a long succession of them through the nation's history. Our inherited doctrine of divine inspiration has functioned to obscure this inescapable conclusion. We must later take note of the understanding of this mystery that Israel's own thinkers held, and we shall see that it effectively spans the gulf between the seemingly irreconcilable opposites of the dilemma. Israel could be the medium of divine revelation and yet could in the same act preserve her intellectual independence; indeed, only because of the latter could the former be realized. For the moment, however, the important concern is the searching criticism which Israel applied to the thought that she inherited from and shared with her world. Creative skepticism was at home in this profoundly religious people. Here is the seeming paradox that a people, freely recognized as supremely *the* religious people of the ancient world, at the same time were without a peer in the power and scope of their critical intellectualism. But indeed it is not paradoxical, for religion that is not criticized quickly deteriorates into mere superstition. It was only by virtue of their skeptical mood that the Hebrew thinkers were able to attain a view of the world that still shapes our outlook.

This critical mood is well manifested in Israel's attitude to the pagan gods and their symbols. While deeply dependent on the mythology of their contemporaries, the Hebrew thinkers yet came to repudiate the reality of the symbols in which these clothed the physical reality of the world. We know very little of the story, doubtless of protracted question and debate, that lies back of Israel's attainment of this uniqueness in the ancient world. There is some reason to believe that it rests ultimately in a deep moral conviction. The religions of Canaan, ornate as they were with divine symbols in public worship and private shrines, were in large measure characterized by the features of so-called nature worship. And everyone knows what this has inevitably entailed. Canaanite worship of the forces of life meant public immorality as a sacred rite and commonly of a disgusting depravity.

It is true that Israel in considerable measure gave herself for a time to this as the accepted means of securing the increase of the fields and of flocks and herds; we recall the reiterated complaint that they "forgot the Lord their God and went after the Baals and Ashtoreth." Yet there were, even in early times, and increasingly with the passing of the centuries, men who stood aloof and condemned the thing for the depravity that it was. It is such moral revulsion that speaks in the prophetic warnings and denunciations where we commonly meet the scathing summary of this whole system of religion: "Upon every high hill and under every green tree thou didst bow thyself playing the harlot" (Jer. 2:20). It was apparently, then, a deep ethical motivation that at length found expression in the dogma now familiar but in its cultural environment of astonishing radicalism: "Thou shalt not make unto thee any graven image nor any likeness of anything that is in the heavens above or in the earth beneath or in the waters that are under the earth: thou shalt not bow down thyself to them nor serve them" (Exod. 20:4–5). And, be it observed, the passage runs on, "For the Lord thy God is a jealous God." All was gathered up in Israel's theological uniqueness and in her consciousness of that uniqueness. The righteousness and holiness of God imposed upon the Israelite an exacting standard of action and thought and, in turn, revealed the depravity of pagan religion, however pompous or ancient.

Such is the mood that finds notable expression in a term employed especially by Isaiah. For him the gods of the nations were "nothingnesses"—so we render his contemptuous word. But in its original form it appears to have a much deeper force. He called them ʾelilim, which, it has been suggested, is nothing else than a Hebrew corruption of the name of the great god of ancient Shumer, whose might and attributes were carried over into Semitic Babylonia; Enlil is held up to contempt by this bold thinker of little Israel as a thing nonexistent, no, rather as the very symbol and essence of insignificance and nonexistence. But what was on this view only implicit in Isaiah's choice of a term was developed fully by the great prophet of the Exile, whom, for lack of better information, we call Second Isaiah. With biting wit that might do credit to Lucian, he laughs the great gods of Babylon out of countenance. He had watched the sacred New Year procession; he had seen, for the pious but benighted Babylonian, a profound mystery taking place under the eyes of the beholder as Marduk and Nabu went out in solemn pilgrimage to the Akitu house, there to settle the fates of the incoming year; he had witnessed the annual festival in which Marduk triumphed over all his foes, cosmic and terrestrial, and himself died that life might once more return to the world. But this critical Jew saw, not the mystery of an ancient Mass, but a solemn farce: two great hulks of dead matter nearly breaking the backs of suffering brutes condemned to carry the weight of alleged gods!

> Bel stoops; Nabu leans!
> Their idols are on beasts, on cattle;
> what you revere is loaded up,
> a burden to the weary [Isa. 46:1].

Again, with like sarcasm, he ridicules the entire faith and vogue of idols: one cuts a tree for firewood, using it for heating and for cooking; but still a sizeable piece remains, until as an afterthought it is given to a craftsman who, with a deal of labor, shapes it into a pretense of human form—and then men bow down to it and say, "Deliver me, for thou art my god!" (Isa. 44:9–17.) What useful material is a stick of wood, he seems to say, You can cook your meals with it, you can heat your house, and, if any is left, you can make a god to which you may pour out the deepest aspirations of your soul! All alike wood!

Yet all such thought might well seem no more than a sort of sublimated national bigotry. The crucial question is whether Israel's thinkers could apply the same rigid standards of criticism to their own inherited dogmas, in particular to those of the nature, attributes, and activity of Yahweh himself. Their intellectual attainment will be realized only when we admit fully, as the evidence demands, that Hebrew religion achieved freedom from an idolatry (to use a common term) similar to that of the rest of the ancient East—Yahweh was, through the earlier period of the nation's life in Palestine, worshiped in physical form, just as Marduk or Amon or any of the rest of them in their lands. It argues much, then, of the intellectual vigor and independence of generations of unknown Hebrew thinkers that still far back in the nation's history the invisibility of Yahweh had become a dogma of the orthodox religion. In full repudiation of the power and mystic realism of symbols a writer in Deuteronomy argues that even in the personal presence of their God, manifest in the great theophany on Sinai, no physical form was apparent but only an invisible presence felt in power and in religious perception:

> The Lord spoke to you out of the midst of the fire: ye heard the voice of words, but ye saw no form; only ye heard a voice. And he declared unto you his covenant, which he commanded you to perform. . . . . . Take ye therefore good heed unto yourselves; for ye saw no manner of form on the day that the Lord spoke unto you in Horeb out of the midst of the fire; lest ye corrupt yourselves, and make you a graven image in the form of any figure, the likeness of male or female . . . . and lest thou lift up thine eyes unto heaven and when thou seest the sun and the moon and the stars, even the whole host of heaven, thou be drawn away and worship them and serve them, which the Lord thy God hath allotted unto all the peoples under the whole heaven" [Deut. 4:12–19].

How characteristic of Israel's religion this feature became is so well known to us that its force is in danger of being blunted. But for the contemporary world it was heresy of the first order, such, in fact, as to set the Hebrews off as a *peculiar* people in a sense quite different from what their own thinkers boasted. An aspect of this is portrayed by a dramatic incident of a later time. When Pompey in 63 B.C. stormed Jerusalem, he forced his way into the

Holy of Holies, much to the horror of the Jews, in order to see for himself what was the inmost secret of this unusual religion. And there he found—we all know what: nothing but an empty room! The perplexity of this leader from the image-ridden West, standing in the presence of a mystery that still evaded him, is a true symbol of Israel's place in the ancient world: a place that might well be equally unique in the modern, save for our debt to Israel herself.

But Israel's heterodoxy did not stop here. The very existence of her God came in for critical examination. Only so, it would seem, was the certitude of orthodoxy attained; when questions of his reality and his nature had been honestly met, then, and then only, could the best thinkers affirm: "All the gods of the nations are vanities; but the Lord made the heavens" (Ps. 96:5). The full story of this intellectual quest is not preserved; we are dependent in considerable part on casual allusions, but fortunately also we possess some more formal discussions of the problem. One familiar expression of the skeptical mood reveals a group of thinkers who had gone far to the left in their conclusions. The orthodox, as always, despised the skeptical as "fools"; and so we read, "The fool has said in his heart, There is no God" (Pss. 14:1, 53:1). Our accepted exegesis of this bold denial is that it means only a repudiation of divine activity in human affairs, since, so it is said, the Hebrews never doubted the existence of God. But surely such reasoning does little credit to our intellectual integrity; could there be a worse case of prejudging an issue? The words, both in English and in Hebrew, say as clearly as can be, "God does not exist."

It is quite possible that these bold heretics arrived at their conclusion through a failure to see any evidence of divine participation in current affairs; but certainly they reached a denial of the reality of God. It may be that they anticipated modern atheists who see no need of a God, since the world is getting along tolerably well without one. Indeed, this is the implication of the criticism turned against them by the pious author of the psalm: when God looks down to see if there are any wise, he finds godless oppressors who "know nothing" and consequently "eat up [his] people as they eat bread." Still, the writer proceeds, though these folk are subject

to great terror, they lack wisdom—they cannot read meaning in
their disturbing experiences. Then, as though thinking of unmistakable evidence of the reality of God, he concludes with a pious
wish that the salvation of God would come out of Zion.

Comparable to this heresy are the musings of a thinker who relates his search for evidence on which to base the grandiose claims
of orthodoxy, but all he found was emptiness and his own frustration. To understand the fine flavor of his barbed cynicism, we must
attend even to his introduction in which, with assumed pomposity,
he mocks the very words of prophetic announcements:

The words of Agur the son of Jakeh, the prophetic utterance, the oracle of a
mere man, Le'ithiel (i.e., "I have struggled with God and have prevailed"):

> Indeed I am a sub-human brute;
>   I have not the intelligence of a man.
> I have not learned wisdom
>   nor attained knowledge of holy things.
> Who was it that went up to heaven and came down
>   again?
> Who gathered the wind in his fist?
> Who bound the waters in his garment?
> Who set firm the limits of the earth?
> What is his name, and what his son's name?
> For you know [Prov. 30:1–4].

Little need be said in exposition of the passage. It will be apparent how the writer scoffs, not alone at the prophets with their bold
claim of direct knowledge of the unseen, but at the priests, who
proclaimed proficiency in holy things, and at the wise men, also,
with their confidence in intelligence and "wisdom." By contrast
all he will assert is his humanity; indeed, worse, he must be a
brute, for he knows nothing of all these boasted attainments. But
where, he asks, is empirical evidence for such claims? Who went
up to heaven and saw all this with his own eyes? Then, listing the
cosmic ascriptions with which orthodoxy loved to embellish the
might of God, he poses the troublesome query: "Where is the objective evidence on which this imposing structure of faith (or credulity) is reared?" With biting irony he turns to his pious contemporaries, and, leaving them in full possession of the field of dispute
as with a bow of mock humility, we can imagine, he asks simply:
"You know the answer; won't you tell me?"

Once more it is claimed that the writer does not question the reality of God. But, however that may be, he certainly denies any real knowledge of him. He demands reputable evidence for the claims of current belief. As D. B. MacDonald comments, he "has his place in the purest rationalistic tradition." It may be that his thinking is too materialistic; like the Apostle Thomas, he seems to say that only the evidence of the senses is valid. But, whatever uncertainty we may retain on details of his outlook, it is important to recognize his demand that religious thinking must be honest and subject to the same rigorous standards as any other reliable processes of thought.

But in all this we must not minimize the importance for our purpose of the besetting tendency in Israel to what is sometimes described as practical atheism, the denial that God concerns himself with human affairs, however real he may actually be. Everyone is familiar with such pervasive mood against which the prophet known as Malachi uttered his reproofs. In this case the public attitude expressed itself in habitual carelessness in the practice of the public rites of worship. Since God had not fulfilled the promises of the prophets to re-establish the Judean state, so the interpretation runs, the Jews in Jerusalem were swept along from disappointment to despair to infidelity. But it is important to realize that this was no new thing; the pre-Exilic prophets were obliged to take account of the same cynical mood. A brief but arresting passage occurs in connection with the work of Jeremiah. The people are quoted as saying: "It is not he, neither will evil come upon us, neither shall we see sword and famine" (Jer. 5:12). The situation is apparent. Jeremiah had warned them of impending disaster, at the same time arguing divine displeasure as the cause of present troubles. But they denied this facile interpretation. The course of events was following natural laws; the trouble was the might of Babylon and its aggressiveness—what need to bring the Lord into consideration at all? To such reasoning the prophet was compelled to find an answer. Similar is the implication of the violent disagreement through the eighth and seventh centuries within the ranks of the prophets themselves, the canonical prophets denouncing their popular colleagues for false leadership, and the latter retorting in kind. A typical example is the public dispute of Jeremiah

with Hananiah (Jeremiah, chap. 28) which entailed the problem
of the ultimate authority and sanction of the prophetic utterance.
The so-called true prophets seem to us commanding figures, and
their pronouncements appear to have been turned off easily under
divine inspiration, however we conceive that process; but it is important that we recognize the course of serious thinking entailed
before they dared appear in public and announce themselves religious leaders. The attitudes and objections here sketched insured
that intellectually, as truly as in other regards, it was no light matter to be a prophet of the Lord.

But the most famous skeptic of the Old Testament is the writer
who, for lack of further information, we call by the title we have
attached to his book. There is no denying that Ecclesiastes admitted the existence of a God. But what did this profit? For such a
God—remote, selfish, indifferent, jealously watching the pre-
sumptions of troublesome man, and at the most conceding certain
meager favors that served to redeem human life from stark intol-
erability! This is incidental, however. What we note is the free
and frank doubt of orthodoxy which reveals itself in every chapter
of his book. Over against this he sets up a philosophical system of
cosmic determinism, a sort of universal wheel of time on which
life and nature and history are forever wearily repeating themselves as often as the cycle of time brings round once more the
things that have receded into the past.

Now it is clear, however we may regard such conclusions, that
they are the outcome of vigorous, independent thinking. And the
book shows unmistakably the nature of that thinking. Ecclesiastes
tells us that he undertook certain experiments. He tried wisdom
and folly; he investigated the seeming solace of wine; he gave
himself to the pursuit of pleasure—but in all, he is at pains to as-
sure us, his heart guided him in wisdom. Or, rendered in intelligible modern terms, he was prompted, not by the frivolity of the
voluptuary, but by a serious philosophic purpose. He was conduct-
ing a scientific experiment upon himself, observing his own reactions and earnestly seeking through these experiences to find the
abiding value, if any, that life possesses. And further studies were
based on observation of the steady flow of events past his place of
quiet reflection. It is because of what he saw in the widest survey

of life that he concluded, "Vanity of vanities; all is vanity." Actually this phrase that every unthinking person today bandies about glibly contains a deeper implication not fully suggested by this common translation. The Hebrew word "all" here has the definite article. What Ecclesiastes says is that "the all"—that is, the totality of things, the entire purport of the universe—lacks meaning or value. Whatever may be thought of this conclusion, at least here is philosophy in the full sense of the term, though certainly not in its full scope as we have come to know it. But for the moment our interest is more in the philosopher's methods than in either his results or the extent of his research. And what has been said leaves it abundantly clear that, admitting some unevenness in his application of the method, his thinking was of the sort that we have come to call empirical. He reasoned from observed facts.

The Book of Ecclesiastes is regarded as quite late. As a matter of fact, definite criteria of its date are meager. Nonetheless it is well to concede its late origin, in a time when the Jews were in touch with Greek life and when some of them had grown familiar with Greek thinking. How far, then, are we to discount the book as an example of Hebrew methods of thought? The answer would seem to be that we have for long put this sort of question on a false basis. We are steadily learning the debt of Greece to the Orient; and while no serious person could deny the opposite influence so long affirmed, still the greatness and the long course of oriental thought in the full tradition of which Ecclesiastes stood renders it wiser to recognize that in his mental furnishing he was a thorough Jew, though possibly at some points he had been stimulated by the speculation of the West. His conclusions are not in the tradition of Jewish orthodoxy, but his type of mind and his methods are intimately a part of the questioning mood that had been at home in Israel for many centuries.

This will perhaps suffice to show the remarkably modern character of Israel's mental equipment, though indeed, as our discussion proceeds, much more that has relevance here will come before us. However, we turn to the question that has been forcing itself on our consideration. What evidence could suffice for a people of such pronounced critical disposition to support their unique and astonishing religious beliefs which we sketched a little ago!

Unfortunately for this purpose, the Hebrew thinkers, unlike the Greek, commonly left not so much a record of their processes of thought as of their conclusions. In particular this is true of those whom we may call the orthodox theologians. What information is provided, for example, of the basis of Abraham's faith? Or of that of the author of the pentateuchal narratives in general? And the prophets were characteristically concerned to hurl their denunciations and promises in telling phrase such as might bring conviction rather than to carry their audiences along by reasoned processes to a desired conclusion. The apologetic for Israel's faith thus does not lie on the surface. Still, if one will dig a little deeper, the facts will in some part presently reveal themselves.

Israel, we must keep in mind, was an oriental nation among the great nations of the ancient Orient. Their culture was the matrix in which hers was shaped. And we recall how the chapters both on Egypt and on Babylonia found a ground of explanation of the religions of the two regions in the physical conditions in which the peoples lived. The sun-drenched valley of the Nile and the flooded plains of ancient Shumer both exerted profound influence in the molding of the outlook of ancient men for whom Egypt or Babylonia were the world and their forces the realities by which man must direct his life. A similar approach to the religion of Israel could prove fruitful. The rugged terrain of northwest Arabia, of which Syria and Palestine, it has sometimes been remarked, may be regarded as merely the largest and richest oasis, the numerous mountain peaks, the volcanoes apparently active at some period in ancient history, the desert with its speaking silences, the uncertainties of the weather in a land where all is dependent on the annual rainfall—all these and much more of the same sort are reflected in Israel's religion. Of her earliest faith we cannot safely say more than that it was inherited and uncritically accepted from ancestors who had come, by the ways that have shaped the mind of primitive man, to the position surveyed in chapter 1. And it is against this background that all her later speculation must be examined, just as we, too, however secular and objective we seek to make our investigation of the nature of the world and of man, have come to it through a long heritage of the past that accepted fully the personal explanation of the world. The problem, then, for

Israel, just as for us, is not how she came to believe in the existence of the divine but rather how her experiences shaped that belief and how her people supported it when they had arrived at some sort of intellectual self-consciousness.

The basic fact for Israel's faith was the physical world. But here we encounter one of the prime distinctions between this nation and her neighbors. For Israel's God rose out of and transcended the status of a nature-god. God and nature were intimately related, as the Babylonians and Egyptians also believed, yet for Israel they were nonetheless distinct and diverse. This may be described as a debasing of nature, since it remained no longer divine. Yet the actuality of Israel's thought was rather the reverse. Nowhere in the ancient East do we find such sublime concepts and descriptions of nature as in Israel. It is more accurate, then, to speak rather of the sublimation of God and the elevation of nature as an expression of the divine power and activity. In reality the highest concepts of her neighbors are so fully carried over that one could easily confuse the situation and regard Yahweh as a God of mountain and earthquake and storm and fertility in just the same sense as for the others. His voice was heard in the thunder; he shook the world in earthquakes; his rain fell on the thirsty ground; he flashed abroad in the lightning; he was present in birth and increase. But the essential distinction is supplied by a Hebrew writer, who, though speaking of a single incident, employs language that is a symbol of all:

> Behold the Lord passed by, and a great and strong wind rent the mountains and broke in pieces the rocks before the Lord; but the Lord was not in the wind; and after the wind an earthquake, but the Lord was not in the earthquake; and after the earthquake a fire; but the Lord was not in the fire [I Kings 19:11–12].

These were but "the whisper of his word, but the thunder of his power who might understand?" (Job 26:14.) The point is obvious. God, for Israel, was supreme above nature and employed it for his purposes. However intimately related to natural phenomena, God was more than, and distinct from, them. For "after the fire" came "a still, small voice."

Yet the intimate relation of God and the forces and phenomena of nature give the latter a quality that one searches far to find, short of the English romanticists of the eighteenth century, and

imparts to their descriptions a beauty and elevation and withal a
majesty such as, one may venture the judgment, to rank them with
the best poetry of any age. The Hebrew, too,

> . . . . felt
> A presence that disturbs . . . . with the joy
> Of elevated thoughts; a sense sublime
> Of something far more deeply interfused,
> Whose dwelling is the light of setting suns,
> And the round ocean and the living air,
> And the blue sky and the heart of man.

Indeed, it was only by virtue of his profound debt to the long Hebrew tradition in our Western culture that Wordsworth was able
to rise to such concepts. Israel's sense of the wonder of nature as
interfused with a presence is well illustrated in a passage that por-
trays the might and majesty of the sea, that enemy on which the
Hebrew characteristically looked with suspicion and fear but
which is here sublimated into an expression of the power of God:

> They that go down to the sea in ships,
>   that do business in great waters:
> these see the works of the Lord
>   and his wonders in the deep.
> For he commandeth and raiseth the stormy wind
>   which lifteth up the waves thereof.
> They mount up to the heavens; they go down again to the depths;
>   their soul melteth away because of trouble.
> They reel to and fro and stagger like a drunken man
>   and are at their wits' end.
> Then they cry unto the Lord in their trouble
>   and he bringeth them out of their distresses.
> He maketh the storm a calm
>   so that the waves thereof are still.
> Then they are glad because they are quiet.
> So he bringeth them unto their desired haven [Ps. 107:23-30].

Similar is the mood of the striking description in Psalm 65,
which, if we may illustrate the greater by the less, has been the inspiration of our fine hymn "For Those in Peril on the Sea":

> By terrible things thou wilt answer us in righteousness
>   O God of our salvation,
> Thou that art the confidence of all the ends of
>   the earth
>   and of them that are afar off upon the sea:

> who by his strength setteth fast the mountains,
>> being girded about with might;
> who stilleth the roaring of the seas,
>> the roaring of their waves
>> and the tumult of the peoples.
> They also that dwell in the uttermost parts are
>> afraid at thy tokens
> thou makest the outgoings of the morning and the
>> evening to rejoice [Ps. 65:5–8].

Can one find more effective expression of the awesome majesty of the mountains than in the simple couplet of some unknown Hebrew poet:

> In his hand are the deep places of the earth;
> The strength of the hills is his also [Ps. 95:4].

For quieter mood, for the charm of the peaceful landscape beneath the favor of a bounteous heaven, drinking in rest and refreshment from the quiet autumn rain, we turn once more to Psalm 65; it runs on:

> Thou visitest the earth and waterest it
>> thou greatly enrichest it . . . .
> thou waterest its furrows abundantly,
>> thou settlest the ridges thereof
> thou makest it soft with showers
>> thou blessest the springing thereof
> thou crownest the year with thy goodness
>> and thy paths drop fatness [Ps. 65:9–11].

A comparable theme is presented in prose, which, however, in its rhythms (preserved even after the hazards of translation), in its balanced expression, and in its mood of lingering affection rises to pure lyric:

> For the Lord thy God bringeth thee into a good land, a land of brooks of water, of fountains and springs flowing forth in the valleys and hills, a land of wheat and barley and vines and pomegranates, a land of olive trees and honey, a land wherein thou shalt eat bread without scarceness: thou shalt not lack anything in it; a land whose stones are iron and out of whose hills thou canst dig copper [Deut. 8:7–9].

Even that topic which for us is the commonest of the commonplace, employed to fill awkward gaps in conversation, was for the

Hebrew transfused with a sense of the sublime. Here is an Old Testament account of the weather:

> The land whither ye go over to possess it, is a land of hills and valleys, and drinketh water of the rain of heaven, a land which the Lord thy God careth for: the eyes of the Lord thy God are always upon it from the beginning of the year even unto the end of the year [Deut. 11:11–12].

One might occupy all the space allotted for these chapters in citation of striking passages of Israel's feeling for nature. Perhaps, though, we may delay over just a few more. The Hebrew's personalizing of nature and his transfusion of it with his highest religious experiences is well shown in this passage from the Book of Isaiah. The very fact that in essence this attitude is close to the I-Thou relationship with which chapter 1 has familiarized us demonstrates vividly the distance the Hebrew traveled beyond his contemporaries:

> Ye shall go out with joy
> and be led forth with peace.
> The mountains and the hills
> shall break forth before you into singing
> and all the trees of the field
> shall clap their hands [Isa. 55:12].

It is reminiscent of that justly famous couplet in the speech of the Lord in the Book of Job:

> When the morning stars sang together
> and all the sons of God shouted for joy [Job 38:7].

But one may not dismiss the subject without a comment on the Hebrew's love of animate nature, no less striking than his sense of the majesty of the inanimate. Obviously the great expression of this is in the so-called Song of Songs. Who can forget the following, that even yet richly expresses the charm of "the springtime, the only pretty ring-time"?

> Rise up my love, my fair one,
> and come away.
> For lo the winter is past;
> the rain is over and gone;

> the flowers appear on the earth;
> the time of the singing of birds is come
> and the voice of the turtle dove is heard in our
> land. . . . .
> O my love, that art in the clefts of the rock,
> in the covert of the steep place,
> Let me see thy countenance
> Let me hear thy voice [Cant. 2:10–14].

It seems a far leap from this idyllic beauty to the grace and power of the war horse described in words of which Carlyle wrote that "there is nothing more sublime in any literature":

> The glory of his snorting is terrible!
> He paweth in the valley and rejoiceth in his strength.
>   He goeth out to meet the armed men.
> He mocketh at fear and is not dismayed,
>   neither turneth he back from the sword.
> The quiver rattleth against him
>   the flashing spear and the javelin.
> He swalloweth the ground with fierceness and rage.
>   He will not turn aside at the blast of the trumpet
> but as often as he heareth the trumpet he says, Aha!
> He smelleth the battle afar off,
>   the thunder of the captains and the shouting [Job 39:20–25].

How much, too, we learn of the Hebrew zest of life and delight in physical power, such as we have sometimes associated with the Greek temper, from the obvious converse of this brief denial: the Lord "taketh not pleasure in the strength of a horse, nor in the legs of a man."

But we must proceed with the more prosaic, though admittedly more important, matters of Israel's theological apologetics. All nature was the work of the Lord and visible evidence of his reality, of his power, and of his immediate participation in affairs of the world. Yet the notable skeptical mood of Israel insures that, though we cannot trace the process as fully as we would, still the argument was certainly subjected to steady re-examination and maintained its supremacy only after debate. Some of this we have already sketched.

A significant contribution to this line of thought came about through the experience of the deported Jews in the Babylonian cap-

tivity. Carried off from Jerusalem, which they had in their provincialism supposed to be one of the great cities of the world, and
planted in the plain of Babylonia not far from the great imperial city
itself, the exiles, when the first pangs of homesickness had passed,
began to realize wonders and achievements of Babylonian civilization such as shamed their poor rustic culture. And, as time went
on, the more open-minded learned of the pomp and magnificence
of the religion of their captors and the might of supreme Marduk
before whom, by the accepted test of arms, Yahweh's puny strength
had but mocked his people's need. A mood of disillusionment, it
would seem, set in and carried many of the Jews far along the road
of assimilation and denial of their religious heritage. It was a larger
world into which they had come.

From imperial Babylon lines of close communication led out
eastward into Iran, of which the captives had scarce ever heard,
and westward through Asia Minor to the Greek world. In the city
itself merchants and governmental officials from the far ends of the
known world might be met day by day. How petty and remote
Judah and all for which it stood must have seemed to the ostensibly
liberal minded. And as a climax of all this impact of foreign culture that was slowly eating the vitals out of the Jewish faith was
the fact that at just this time the Babylonian study of the heavens
was attaining the status of a real science. Before the astonished
Jews there was unfolded a world of immensity, of wonder, and of
regularity such as to render ludicrous the traditional claim that Yahweh, god of the tiny land of Palestine, had made not alone the sun
and moon but the host of the stars also.

Here we meet, certainly not the first interrelation of science and
religion (for that reaches back into the very beginnings of man's
thought about the world), but one of the earliest clashes of the two,
in a form much like what has been familiar right to our own day.
Indeed, these very considerations arose within our own times relevant to recent disclosures of astronomy. But how could they be
met in the sixth century B.C.? Did the Jews abandon their faith for
the new-found false Messiah, science? Certainly not the best of
them! Did they retire into intellectual isolation and refuse to admit the findings of science? Did they satisfy themselves with reaffirmation of ancient dogmas? Not at all. It is again an index of

their intellectual vitality that instead they met the problem with high courage, recognized the validity of the new knowledge and its destructive implications, and then, embracing the facts, rebuilt their faith on a new and better basis into a greater religion than it was before.

Fortunately there lived among these perplexed people the great poet-thinker whom we call Second Isaiah. He realized that the difficulty was inherent, not in the character of Yahweh, but in the unworthy thought of him which his people held. Seizing boldly on the very findings of science which were sweeping more tender-minded Jews off their feet, he claimed that, far from nullifying faith in Israel's God, these were but evidences of his greatness and of his reality. For God was maker and master of the physical universe. "Lift up your eyes on high and see who hath created these things, that bringeth out their host by number; he calleth them all by name; great in might and strong in power, not one is lacking" (Isa. 40:26).

However, already familiar elements of the cosmological argument also received fresh and vigorous handling by Second Isaiah. It is not merely the enlarged world of his time that impinged on his consciousness with fresh conviction, but in a mood very much like that of the philosophic scientists of today he adduced the consideration that the ordered world declares its origin in a universal mind.

> Who hath measured the waters in the hollow of his
> hand,
>   and hath meted out the heaven with the span,
> and comprehended the dust of the earth in a measure,
>   and weighed the mountains in scales
>   and the hills in a balance?
> Who directed the spirit of the Lord? . . . .
> With whom took he counsel? . . . .
> Who . . . . taught him knowledge
>   and showed him the way of understanding? [Vss. 12–14.]

This was evidently a real contribution to Israel's thinking, for in a later age the wisdom writers turn frequently to it as a favorite theme, and in particular it serves as the basis of the lengthy dissertation upon the transcendent intelligence of the divine that is

put into the mouth of the Lord in the latter part of the Book of
Job.

> Where wast thou when I laid the foundations of the earth?
>   Declare if thou hast intelligence.
> Who determined its measures?—if you possess knowledge.
>   Whereupon were its foundations fastened?
> Or who laid its cornerstone? . .... .
> Hast thou commanded the morning since thy days began,
>   and caused the dayspring to know its place?
> Where is the way to the dwelling of light?
>   And as for darkness, where is its place? . . . .
> Canst thou bind the cluster of the Pleiades
>   or loose the bands of Orion? . . . .
> Knowest thou the time when the wild goats of the rock
>   bring forth?
> Or canst thou number the months that they fulfil? [38:4—39:2.]

And so this lengthy survey of the complex interaction of animate
and inanimate creation runs on. It will be noted that, in part, this
is a mere disparagement of human knowledge: that the world contains much more than mortal mind can compass. But basic to the
discussion is that it treats of the wonders of the infinite intelligence
which not alone established these wonders but holds them in their
proper relations.

It is important to realize that Second Isaiah wrote with conscious
realization of the problem of apologetics; he took up the issue specifically and of set purpose. It is a sort of undertone running
through his poems. He treats it relevant to the claims of the great
contemporary pagan gods; but this does not alter the point of prime
interest that he was answering the question "How can man know
rationally that God exists and that he is the sort of being which
Jewish tradition claims him to be?" To this end his favorite device
is to picture a cosmic assize in which Yahweh is at once plaintiff
and judge; he advances his arguments and introduces his witnesses
and then challenges the defendants to make out their case. But at
this point only silence ensues; and the decision goes to Yahweh,
not by default, but by the demonstration of the complete powerless-
ness and inanity of the others. And Yahweh's argument, in addition to what we have already noted, is that he has been operative
in history and still is the vital force in the affairs of men. Notwith-

standing certain new features which were introduced into this consideration, it is important to recognize that Second Isaiah is here but applying an opinion that was very old among Israelite thinkers. It had received notable expression by Isaiah a hundred and fifty years before in his bold claim that the God of Israel was using the Assyrians for his great purposes. But it was not uniquely his; for it is the theme running throughout the Old Testament. The Hebrew thinkers, with a penetration that might have spared some later thought its worst blunders, recognized that the meaning of the world can be understood, if at all, only in the light of and by inclusion of human life, which is its highest expression. For them, then, "the proper study of mankind was man."

This is peculiarly the field of investigation of the wise men. They were primarily students of human life from the ethical and metaphysical point of view. In their age-long investigation, carried on by successive generations of scholars, history and society provided facilities in a sense comparable with those offered in modern scientific experimentation. It is scarcely an exaggeration to claim that they were empirical, though admittedly the method had not yet come to self-consciousness and hence could easily fall below scientific strictness or give way to traditional dogma. Nonetheless, their activity is in itself demonstration of the keen intellectualism of ancient Israel and the distance this people had gone in methods of sound thinking. The wise men sought to evolve codes of conduct that might conduce to the accepted ideal of the good life, but as well they saw everything taking its place in a continuing stream of action and history which was leading on to determined results in the divine purpose. This very alluring topic we abandon with cursory comment, to take it up at more length a little later. However, a related aspect of the topic has already been mentioned and calls for some orientation at this point. We took occasion to note that Amos' thought of the universality of God was in some way dependent on his sense of a common human standard of right and wrong. At the appropriate place we shall advance further evidence that such was actually Amos' thinking. It is clear, then, that in this was one of the fruitful sources of Israel's convictions as to the being and nature of God. The universality of the human regard for those higher qualities which the Hebrew gathered up in the concept of righteousness found rational explanation best in a cosmic origin which some modern thinkers describe as a Process; but for the Hebrew mind that Process was personal. In the unceasing human striving from the good to the better, in the contempt of the base and mean, in the universal homage to the true and noble and unselfish, there was for Israel's thought, just as for ours, a profound mystery that compelled speculation to venture beyond the immediate and tangible, out into the region of cause and nature and being. Israel's thinkers concluded that here is the ultimate revelation of the character of God: He is righteousness and truth.

In addition to the argument from the wonders and the apparent intelligence of the world, and from the course of human history, past and future, as he believed it might be calculated, Second Isaiah had one other consideration which is presented with such brevity that there is danger of reading into it perhaps more than he meant. In his favorite figure of a great court scene, he has the Lord in several passages say of Israel, "You are my witnesses" (Isa. 43:10, 12; 44:8). The context in some measure may suggest that he is thinking of Israel as the recipient of God's bounty and mighty deliverances, of which now she could testify. Yet though this may be uppermost in the passages, the further concept cannot be absent that Israel can testify out of her whole knowledge of God. However that may be in these passages, it is certain that such consideration came to have force in Jewish thought. A psalmist exclaims, "O taste and see that the Lord is good"; again:

> The judgments of the Lord are true
>   and righteous altogether
> More to be desired are they than gold,
>   yea than much fine gold
> Sweeter also than honey
>   and the droppings of the honeycomb [Ps. 19:9–10].

> O how I love thy law; it is my meditation all the day [Ps. 119:97].

And this is but the merest sample of the immense bulk of such utterances that one might excerpt from the Psalms and other poetry of the Old Testament. The devout Israelite felt and knew that in his personal experience of his God he had a treasure of the rarest quality. And in this, finally, it would appear, he found the proof of the reality and the goodness of the Person whom his traditional faith postulated as the center and meaning of the physical universe. It is apparent that the question of the validity of such thinking comes into consideration. Did the Hebrew ever go behind his processes of observation and thought to question their finality? But this question we can take up more effectively as part of Israel's whole understanding of human life.

CHAPTER IX

MAN

IT IS said that for the ancient Hebrew there were three realities: God, man, and the world. The remark is, however, less profound than it may appear; for what more is there? And how could he have taken account of less, being the person that he was? But, in any case, it is now time to turn to the second of these entities.

Israel was fully aware of that most critical question of all man's thought—the problem that man is to himself. The Hebrew thinkers meditated upon this strange two-legged creature that struts about in such pompous mood, arrogantly rivaling the gods yet knowing full well that he is much less than divine, conscious of his close relation with the beasts but refusing to be a brute, and always —even in his proudest moments—haunted with a sense of insufficiency and with the knowledge that the nemesis which dogs his every footstep will ultimately overtake him. And what, then, of all he has hoped and done? In itself such thinking is not remarkable, for even primitive man had early learned to ask questions about his origin and nature. But the uniqueness of Israel's thought is in the elevation of its conclusions, an answer to the problem of man that even in this modern day some regard as superior to much of recent thought as well as to the aberration which Greek speculation fastened upon Western culture.

The consciousness of the problem was widely diffused among Hebrew thinkers, if we may judge from frequent allusion and formal discussion. One of the notable passages of more extensive treatment is Psalm 90, which in majestic wording sketches the agelessness of the world, and the eternity of the divine, by contrast with which man is transient, frail, and fallible:

> Before the mountains were brought forth
> or ever thou hadst formed the earth and the world,
> even from everlasting to everlasting thou art, O God. . . . .
> A thousand years in thy sight
> are but as yesterday when it is past,
> and as a watch in the night.

But as for man:

> Thou carriest them away as with a flood; they are as
>   a sleep;
>   in the morning they are like grass that groweth up:
> in the morning it groweth up and flourisheth,
>   in the evening it is cut down and withereth. . . . .
> Thou hast set our iniquities before thee,
>   our secret sins in the light of thy countenance. . . . .
> We spend our years as a sigh [Ps. 90:2–9].

Scarcely less deserving of mention is the explicit formulation of the question in Psalm 8:

> O Lord our Lord, how excellent is thy name
>   in all the earth!
>   who hath set thy glory upon the heavens.
> When I survey thy heavens
>   the work of thy fingers,
> the moon and the stars
>   which thou hast ordained,
> what is man . . . . ?

In the immensity and might of the physical universe, man is so fleeting and so little; yet, as we shall see, man, so this thinker maintains, holds a place of unique significance.

One influence that stimulated Israel's interest in the problem was the obvious similarity that exists between man and the beasts. We are told that in his three thousand proverbs Solomon "spoke of birds and of beasts and of creeping things" (I Kings 4:32–33). But this had been a very old interest in the Orient, where fables of plants and animals of the sort familiar to the modern world under the title *Aesop's Fables* had been long employed in teaching and speculation about the nature of man. The well-known fable of Jotham in chapter 9 of Judges is the clearest illustration of this that we possess from Israel, but certain passages in the Book of Proverbs, some prophetic figures, and, most of all, this clear statement in the account of Solomon's career demonstrate that the Hebrew thinkers recognized our kinship with the lower animals. But then what? Is man nothing but a more intelligent brute? In view of the freedom of Israel's skeptical thought, it is not surprising that the

question found answer in the affirmative. Nor shall we think it remarkable that our familiar acquaintance, Ecclesiastes, is the one to
voice this with frankness. He states his conclusion:

> I said in my heart in regard to the sons of men that, since God has created
> them and he sees that they are in their nature but beasts, the fate of the sons of
> men and the fate of beasts is one: as this dies, so dies that; they have all the same
> spirit, and man has no superiority above the beasts, for all is futile. . . . . Who
> knows whether the spirit of man goes upward, and the spirit of the beast goes
> down into the earth? [Eccles. 3:18–21].

There we have frank and complete repudiation of man's higher
claims. Our life, just like that of the animals, is told in purely biological terms. And when death overtakes us, nothing has happened
but biological and then chemical dissolution. But the very terms of
Ecclesiastes' pessimism reveal that the consensus of Hebrew
thought was against him. He is clearly at pains to criticize and
repudiate an accepted belief.

Similar is the mood of the "friends" in the Book of Job. It is apparent that they assign man a lowly place. Bildad, indeed, alludes
to "man that is a maggot, and the son of man that is a worm"
(Job 25:8). And Eliphaz, in a comparable utterance, stresses the
frailty and transcience of human life:

> . . . . them that dwell in houses of clay,
>   whose foundation is in the dust,
>   who are crushed before the moth!
> Betwixt morning and evening they are destroyed;
>   they perish forever without any regarding it.
> Is not their tent-cord plucked up within them?
>   They die, and that without wisdom [Job 4:19–21].

But we must beware of deducing a similar inference from the contrite confession of a psalmist:

> But I am a worm and no man
>   a reproach of men and despised of the people [Ps. 22:6].

It means, indeed, just the opposite of the view of Job's friends. For
it is clear that it is the writer himself who, as a worm, is less than
human—so he claims. The characteristic belief of Israel, indeed,
finds nowhere more challenging formulation than in the Psalter,
and most notably in that Eighth Psalm, from which we quoted a

moment ago. The relevant passage is rendered in the King James translation:

> What is man that thou art mindful of him,
>   and the son of man that thou visitest him?
> For thou hast made him a little lower than the angels,
>   and hast crowned him with glory and honor [Ps. 8:4–6].

But the word here rendered "angels" is ʾelohim, the familiar and regular term for God. And nowhere does it certainly mean angels. There is no evidence whatever that would support the action of the seventeenth-century translators at this point; it rests only on dogmatic presuppositions which precluded their rising to the boldness of the Hebrew concept. The passage says as clearly as may be: "Thou hast made him a little lower than God"!

In few regards is the uniqueness of Hebrew thought more evident than in this concept of the basic character of human life. Indeed to this day (not merely until the time of King James' translators), we have but inadequately approached the majesty of the conception that man is in his nature "but little lower than God." And such a view was propounded by a people who had no less painful cause than our own generation to know the depraved possibilities of the human heart, and who, on the other hand, maintained an unrivaled faith in a transcendent God. But yet the paradox—for them, man is "but a little lower" and "crowned with glory and honor." Here is none of the contamination of flesh, of the essential badness of matter, of the evil of the world and all that it signifies: ideas which we have erroneously fathered on the Orient, and which in turn have distorted our religious thinking for two millenniums. But they are Greek and not Hebrew, traceable not to Moses but to Plato! True the Hebrew would grant the terms of our familiar hymn, "Frail children of dust, and feeble as frail"; but in that feebleness there was no taint of original sin. On the contrary, man is of exalted origin; and his destiny, by implication, is likewise one of majesty. Echoing the words of the creation story, our psalmist goes on: "Thou madest him to have dominion over the works of thy hands; thou hast put all things under his feet" (Ps. 8:6).

It is, indeed, in the accounts of the Creation that we find the basic and almost complete statement of the Hebrew answer to the problem of man. God made him in his own image. Or, in another narrative, he was shaped by divine hands from dust of the earth, and then God blew into his nostrils the breath of life, and man became a living being. There is at once both man's earthy and his divine nature. But the important thing to emphasize is that our mention of such antithesis is un-Hebraic. For Israel it was a single and consistent idea. God had made the world also; and on all that he made, step by step, he pronounced the judgment that it was good. The world, like man, came fresh from the hands of the Creator, trailing clouds of glory. Such was Hebrew and Jewish thought throughout. However bad the troubles that might fall, however thick the gloom, yet Israel's basic conviction was that the world was permeated with its divine origin and high purpose.

There exists an unsolved problem as to the ultimate nature of matter. Our theology has postulated a dogma of *creatio ex nihilo*. But certainly this is not asserted in the Old Testament. On the contrary, a question has arisen whether Gen. 1:1 does not actually imply the reverse. The sentence is of unusual Hebrew construction. And it has been boldly asserted that the correct meaning is that given by the Chicago translation: "When God began to create the heavens and the earth, the earth being a desolate waste, with darkness covering the abyss and the spirit of God hovering over the water, then God said, 'Let there be light!' " That is, matter was not created but was pre-existent. The world is of dual origin: a shapeless chaotic mass of matter, on one hand, and God and his work on the other. Unfortunately, further references in the Old Testament to the origin of the world fail to clear up the problem, and we are compelled to leave it in this uncertainty. But the situation does not qualify the major emphasis which we have sought to make at this point. For even if Israel did actually think of matter as eternal and pre-existent, still there is nowhere any suggestion of stigma upon it as matter. Instead it was worthy to be the medium and content of God's work of creation, so that in the end the complete work was "very good."

But the thought carries still further. It deserves repetition that man as a creature of flesh bore thereby no stain of uncleanness or unworthiness. Of man's sinfulness we must speak in a moment, and it was very real for Israel's thought. But it did not derive from his fleshly being. God had made man, and in those primeval days of more than Elysian bliss he had associated freely with our first parent, a being of just our nature. But, further, God had given to the first couple the injunction: "Be fruitful and multiply and fill the earth, and have dominion." It is a command that remained basic in subsequent Hebrew life. However black the present and future, the devout Israelite might not seek racial release by abstention from begetting children and through them children's children. Jeremiah, it is true, had taken that course, but to such extent he stood apart from his people. God had commanded, "Be fruitful and multiply." Apart from some practice of ritual fasting and other restraint, there was no asceticism in Israel, with but the exception of the Essenes, who fall in a period so late that they may not be cited as typically Hebraic. Celibacy and a special "immaculate conception" are ideas that have come into our religious tradition from sources other than the Old Testament. For Israel, every conception was immaculate; it was instituted of God and, to their simple scientific ideas, was in detail a direct gift from him. True, they knew well the biological sequence; nonetheless, it was the Lord who gave conception or, it might be, withheld it. Children were a blessing of the Lord and a sign of his grace. Yet every Bible reader will in this connection think of the contrite confession in the Fifty-first Psalm:

> For I was shapen in iniquity
> and in sin did my mother conceive me.

It is a passage that has been responsible for much distorted thinking about biblical ideas. But even if we take the passage in an individual sense and context, we must nonetheless note that it is unparalleled in the Old Testament, so that we should be compelled to understand it as a piece of poetic hyperbole. But commentators, recognizing this, wisely understand a national meaning. Just as the poet in Isa. 43:27 speaks of original national sin, "Your first father sinned," so here the devout writer thinks of himself as heir of his people's proneness to disobedience. It is well said, "The mother here is Mother Israel."

The bases of these exalted concepts of man and the world are not such as to permit of conclusive analysis. Indeed, we seem here to deal with a mood rather than with a reasoned position; for Israel's thinkers were deeply conscious of the darker side of human nature. They had painful occasion to know the badness of their environment, both physical and racial. Nonetheless, they held firm the faith that man is a being essentially of noble nature set in a world that is essentially good. It has been our habit to comment on the liberty of the Greek mood that looked the gods in the face in a relationship similar to that between equal humans. And what was it that brought the Greeks to this? Was it that they, too, were Mediterranean folk, who reveled in the long and cheerful sunshine of the region and that they, like Israel, were a mountain people, living a socially atomistic life in their secluded valleys? Are we, then, to search in environment rather than in racial heritage or reasoned processes of thought for the source of such ideas of God and man? However that may be, it is apparent that Israel's position here transcends that of Greece in that her God was exalted far beyond the human weaknesses of the Greek deities. But environment does not tell all, for Israel was unique in the Orient. The Syrians and Moabites also were mountain dwellers in the Mediterranean world, and there is no need to delay over the inferiority of their religious achievement. We are driven to hold that the Hebrews' concept of man cannot be understood in isolation, but only as a part of their whole remarkable system of thought. They recognized that man is superior to the brutes—even the tempered pessimism of Ecclesiastes cannot hide his admission of the fact—and then, realizing a strange quality in human character that is more than biological and that for them, as we shall presently see, was nothing less than a divine endowment, they were brought to the conclusion that man's nature somewhere between the brute and the divine could be only "a little lower than God."

Yet, notwithstanding his exalted origin and nature, man was, for Hebrew thought, a sinful and sinning being. In these paradoxical extremes we sound the depths of Israel's concept of man. Nowhere has there been such sense of the depravity of sin as among this people; and we in turn have entertained a comparable view only by virtue of our Hebraic heritage. The sinfulness of sin, if one may clarify through the obscurity of redundancy, was the counterpart of the transcendence of God. Here again is an eloquent paradox. All Israel's thought traces back ultimately to her great confession, "The Lord Our God, the Lord is one." The idea of sin was very old in the Orient, as doubtless in human life long prior to the rise of the earliest oriental cultures. But there is a great gulf between that and Israel's thought. The simpler notion is of action which displeases the deity. And when that deity is merely the enlarged stature of a man, with much of human caprice, then sin can have little if any of moral relevance. At the most, the general Orient had moved noticeably in the direction of a transcendent concept of sin. But for Israel sin was offense against a supernal holiness and righteousness that far transcends our highest attainments or even understanding. True, this holiness was a Person: for Israel other thought was impossible; but his exalted nature suffused all their thinking, transforming personal affront into moral evil. There remained the personal relationship in even the deepest individual experiences of guilt; the great penitential confesses:

> Against thee, thee only, have I sinned,
> and done that which is evil in thy sight [Ps. 51:4].

And another psalmist, expressing human fallibility, says:

> Thou hast set our iniquities before thee,
> our secret sins in the light of thy countenance [Ps. 90:8].

By contrast with the pure light of that ineffable presence, "All our righteousnesses are but filthy rags."

And there, in such paradox, is Israel's thought of man. He was made in the image of God, but a little lower than he, worthy to companion with him, but yet so far removed that the highest human attainments, even the best aspirations are acceptable only by divine grace. The paradox merits repetition; for in it, beyond a doubt, lies the source of Israel's best and highest thought and her unceasing moral striving. Yet we must set limits and guards to the concept, for emphasis on the transcendence of God has led into devious ways in the history of theology, not least within our own times. God was exalted, yet he was not separated from man. God and man were alike in nature. Even if man's frailties were such as to make the resemblance a caricature, nonetheless, he was in the image of God. God is in the heavens; God is far other than man. But it is entirely false to Old Testament thought to introduce into the statement that adverb favored in recent theological speculation and say that God is "wholly" other. Israel's thinkers would have repudiated such an idea with indignation. There were exceptions, it is true, such as are represented by Eccleasiastes and the "friends" in the Book of Job. But the cynicism of the former resulted in a grotesque caricature; and the latter are properly held up for censure, by the great author of the dialogue, as a little weak in their logic.

Current theology undertakes to explain all sin as an expression of human pride. Whether or not such would be true of later thought, it can be posited of Old Testament speculation only by a rationalization. One may take the position that frail man can wilfully transgress the commands of a holy God only through a mentality distorted by exaggerated self-importance. But certainly the Hebrew thinkers did not hold this view. They knew human pride and properly deprecated it. Yet for them sin was primarily rebellion, either wilful and deliberate or unconscious through "forgetting" God by absorption in other interests.

Such being man's nature, what did Israel think of his destiny? One answer we have already noted. Ecclesiastes admitted no outcome but complete despair. Man dies like the brute—and that is the end! Even while he lives he is able to accomplish nothing, so that the best answer to the problem of life is "Live it as comfortably as you can; and don't think much about it." But it is obvious that such a view would not satisfy the great stream of Israel's thinkers whom we may call with admitted inaccuracy "the orthodox." In time they came to accept the belief long cherished in Egypt and doubtless well known throughout Israel that death is not the end but the beginning. It is a portal through which man goes out into a larger life. This came so late in the Old Testament period that little can be said about it. One of our very few treatments of the theme speaks briefly of "everlasting life" (Dan. 12:2); another summons: "Awake and sing, ye that dwell in the dust" (Isa. 26:19). And beyond that we cannot safely go without danger of reading in the ideas of later times. It is an enticing question why

Israel continued so late to reject the faith she had long known. We do not know; but it is suggested that the reason lay in an intimate relationship with the pagan cults against which earlier Israel had been compelled to struggle.

For Israel, through the greater part of the Old Testament period, man's destiny, then, was a mundane affair. His personal good was to be found in this life, and his achievement, whatever it might be, related only to this world. He found a sort of survival, however, in his family. So it was that children were prized even more than is common in human society. The tribe and nation also were vehicles to carry his significance into far-distant times and, as such, commanded his loyalty. The idea is not strange to us, unless in its formulation; for it is essentially the motivation that in our age impels hosts of men to give themselves freely on the battlefield: they do so for an idea, for the survival of human freedom, that is, for the persistence of our culture with its possibilities and promise of a much better culture arising therefrom. But apart from such hopes, the Israelite sought meaning and satisfaction within the days of his own years.

The wholesomeness of Israel's thinking insured that basic in the conception of the good life was a sufficiency of material things. The Hebrews were no starving saints or unwashed ascetics. They accepted the good things of life with zest. The emphasis of the prophets and other religious leaders on intangible values must not obscure for us the fact that all alike recognized the indispensability of at least reasonable physical provision, if life was to be satisfying. This was the hope and promise of the land into which the nation had come by divine promise: it was "a good land, a land of wheat and vines and figs and pomegranates, a land of olive trees and honey; a land in which thou shalt eat bread without scarceness: thou shalt not lack any good thing in it; a land whose stones are iron and out of whose hills thou mayest dig copper" (Deut. 8:7–9). Poverty and suffering could be borne through faith in unseen realities, but they were not desirable. Equally a desire for great wealth was only seldom encouraged. The enthusiasm of the historian of Solomon's reign appears to measure the king's happiness in direct relation to his wealth. Similarly Job's prosperity is presented as an item of his good fortune, though literary needs may here have enhanced the mood. Elsewhere we find rather an ideal of moderation. One writer deprecates alike wealth and poverty (Prov. 30:7–9); and the Deuteronomist's attitude just now cited must be qualified with his warning: "when thou hast eaten and art full, then beware lest thou forget the Lord thy God" (Deut. 6:11–12; cf. 8:11 ff.). Such an ideal of the happy mean in all life was expressed by Ecclesiastes; we can imagine he wrote it with his tongue in his cheek!

> Be not righteous overmuch, neither make thyself overwise; why shouldst thou destroy thyself? Be not overmuch wicked, neither be thou foolish; why shouldst thou die before thy time? It is good that thou take hold of this and withdraw not thy hand from that [Eccles. 7:16–18].

But it is possible that older Hebrew ideas have at this point been crystallized by the impact of Greek thought.

Then, as we have seen, for the Hebrew, life was not full and complete unless he was husband of a good wife and with her parent of several children; indeed, we should rather say, of many children, for one poet voices the common ideal thus:

> Lo, children are a heritage of the Lord . . . .
> As arrows in the hand of a strong man
>   so are the children of youth.
> Happy is the man who hath his quiver full of them [Ps. 127:3–5].

Of the quality of a good wife we are left in no doubt. She is sensible, industrious, thrifty, a good manager; and, not least, she rises early, apparently in order to let her husband sleep in! (Prov. 31:10–31). That she is also a good mother in much the sense that we understand is admitted.

As a final element in his happiness, one hoped for a long life. All this is nowhere more eloquently set forth than in the first speech of Eliphaz in the Book of Job:

> He will deliver thee in six troubles
>   yea, in seven there shall no evil come nigh thee. . . . .
> At destruction and dearth thou shalt laugh;
>   neither shalt thou be afraid of the beasts of the earth. . . . .
> Thou shalt know that thy tent is in peace;
>   thou shalt visit thy fold and shalt miss nothing. . . . .
> Thou shalt know also that thy seed shall be great
>   and thine offspring as the grass of the earth.
> And thou shalt come to thy grave in a full age,
>   as a shock of grain cometh in its season [5:19–26].

But obviously the good life entailed as well rigid standards of ethics. We have several summaries of these, more or less partial. Those in Psalm 15 and in Job, chapter 31, are famous; the latter has been highly praised. A more brief statement will serve our present purpose:

> Blessed is the man who walketh not
> in the counsel of the wicked,
> nor standeth in the way of sinners,
> nor sitteth in the seat of scoffers;
> but his delight is in the law of the Lord [Ps. 1:1–2].

An adequate statement of Hebrew ethics would take us far. Briefly, we may say that the good man was honest, industrious, generous, and kind; there is no need to list his negative virtues. But we should recall relative to his gracious qualities that "the merciful man is merciful to his beast." The ideal was broadly conceived and applied; and in this consideration for the dumb beasts that serve man so faithfully and well we have a note that unobtrusively yet significantly is sounded several times in Israel's literature. But it is obvious that this summary, with whatever apologies for its compact character, fails so much as to suggest the distinctive feature of Hebrew ethics. The good man found his place as a member of a good society. For in Israel's thought society, not less than the individual, had a character of its own and entailed thereby its reward or retribution. A person's welfare and happiness were thus bound up in the status of his group. His own merit or lack of it had relevance for the general character, as his activity had power to shape it. Yet it was society that determined his fate. Even outstanding personal character could not absolve him from society's doom or debar him from sharing in its welfare. We shall see presently how the individual gradually emerged to a relative independence, yet to the end Israel's ethical thought remained highly socialized.

Of the culture of the mind less is said. Yet we should err if we then concluded that Israel was indifferent to it. On the contrary, it is an ideal highly praised. We think of Solomon, intrinsic in whose greatness was the fact that the Lord gave him "largeness of heart as the sand that is upon the seashore." The prophets and other re-

ligious leaders were so engrossed in their campaign for reform that
they say little of this quality which actually takes so large a place
in their own lives and activities. But in the Wisdom Literature the
appeal of learning and the life of the mind is clearly and forcefully
presented. The outlines of this intellectual culture we have in part
seen already, and more must be added presently. But we may summarize this secular aspect of the good life in a, perhaps, dangerously concise phrase, that Israel along this line thought of it as
that of the cultured gentleman—in much the sense that we give to
these words in their better connotation: a man of easy circumstances, of good home life and unimpeachable integrity, gracious to
his acquaintances, and possessing opportunity for satisfying intellectual pursuits.

Yet it is apparent that to leave the description with this would
be a gross misrepresentation of Hebrew thought. For the good life
was basically and supremely the religious life. All we have said
takes its place in this larger whole. Again we may cite a famous
summary; the ideal was for man "to do justly, to love mercy, and
to walk humbly with his God" (Mic. 6:8). It was the religious
orientation that brought meaning and abiding satisfaction into life.
The fear of the Lord was the beginning of wisdom—of the finest
values of life. In his faith in God the devout Hebrew found the final
answer to life's enigma: a conviction that he was individually of
worth in the eyes of God, hence might expect divine guidance and
help, a faith which meant a rich experience of mystic relationship
with the divine, a faith, too, in God's plans and purposes for the nation and for the world through which the individual participated in
issues far transcending his transience and found meaning in an
eternal cosmic process. Certainly we must not look for such a faith
in every ancient Hebrew whose thoughts we can scan; the ignorant peasant out on the hills of Israel could scarcely be expected to
shape his world view in such terms. But here we are concerned primarily with the best that Israel attained. And we shall see more of
this cosmic outlook in a few moments.

Such was the good life. And denial of it in faith and conduct was
sin. In turn, salvation, apart from its national connotations, was
the attainment of this life. In much of Hebrew thought there was
little if any of the mystical element which Christian thinking has

attached to the experience of salvation. The directness and simplicity of Israel's thought insured that for most of the Old Testament period conversion and salvation alike were matters of volition. If one were a sinner, then the rational thing was to change his conduct. "Cease to do evil; learn to do well," Isaiah had demanded (Isa. 1:16–17). "Turn ye, turn ye from your evil ways; why will ye die?" was a later formulation of the same idea (Ezek. 33:11). Apparently it was as simple and easy as that. Yet Israel's thinkers realized well the constraining power of ingrained habit. It was as inescapable as the leopard's spots or the Ethiopian's skin (Jer. 13:23). Israel's doings would not permit her to return to the Lord (Hos. 5:4). "Every imagination of the thoughts of the heart" of man in some circumstances "was only evil continually" (Gen. 6:5). The sin of the Judeans was written with a pen of iron upon the tablets of their heart (Jer. 17:1). Circumstance and heredity likewise exerted a conducive influence upon conduct. When Israel came into the land, their relations with the Canaanites became a powerful inducement to participation in the pagan cults: when they had eaten and were full, then it was more than possible they would forget the Lord their God (Deut. 6:11–12).

Hence it was that through the course of centuries Israel's thinkers were impelled to a more profound understanding of the problems of human conduct. More and more they realized that it rises from the deep springs of the personality, not out of some casual circumstance. The generous man does generous things, while the churl will be churlish (Isa. 32:6–8). In Old Testament phrase it is a question of the human "heart." The classic expression of the problem is that by Paul in the seventh chapter of the Epistle to the Romans: a sense of futile strife with one's self voiced at length in the despairing cry, "O wretched man that I am, who shall deliver me from this body of death?" But Paul's utterance, though evidently rooted in his own experience, was by no means novel. He was in this regard, as in so much else, the direct heir of his Jewish ancestry. For the thinkers of the long post-Exilic period turn on various occasions in diverse times to the glowing hope of a day when the Lord should change men's hearts and enable them to do the right.

I will sprinkle clean water upon you and you shall be clean; from all your filthiness and from all your idols will I cleanse you. And I will give you a new heart, and will put a new spirit in you. I will take away the stony heart out of your body and will give you a heart of flesh. And I will put my spirit within you, and cause you to walk in my statutes. Then you shall keep my ordinances and obey them [Ezek. 36:25–27].

In this time, too, was voiced the ideal of the law written on the heart, than which there is no more profound understanding of the regeneration of human life.

I will put my law in their inward parts and will write it upon their heart. And I will be their God and they shall be my people. They shall no more teach each one his neighbor and his brother, Know the Lord, for they shall all know me from the least of them to the greatest. For I will forgive their iniquity and their sin I will remember no more [Jer. 31:33–34].

There in notable formulation is Israel's doctrine of the grace of God. In earlier thought the Lord had been a temperamental being whose sense of injured dignity might be too deep for mollification. Forgiveness was a conjectural matter. We are familiar with the threat that the sins of the fathers should be visited upon the children to the third and fourth generation—although in fairness we must remember that these were the recalcitrant, or, in biblical phraseology, "them that hate me." The prophets likewise speak of sins that will not be forgiven as long as their perpetrators may live (Isa. 23:14); or they regard divine forgiveness of the repentant as problematic: "It may be that the Lord, the God of Hosts, will be gracious to the remnant of Joseph" (Amos 5:15). But with the maturing of Israel's thought the emphasis was upon the unbounded grace of God. "Like as a father pitieth his children, so the Lord pitieth them that love him, for he knoweth our frame, he remembereth that we are dust" (Ps. 103:13–14). Still more: not alone was he ready to forgive the penitent, but he was himself the enabling power to vitalize human penitence; in just the sense that the words came to hold in a later time, he saved his people from their sins.

Along these several lines, then, we find Israel's concept of divine salvation. With a wide scope of detailed concepts, it was in essence to live in the grace of God. And this experience was of unmeasured possibilities.

The patriarchal stories preserve records very familiar to us of favored individuals who in some peculiar way walked with God and were accepted into an intimate relationship. Abraham even yet is reputed as "the friend of God." With him Moses also talked as a man talks with his friend. But it is notable that such experiences were confined to the legendary past. In the clear light of history we deal with a different experience. The spirit of God might "rush upon" some chosen and worthy individual and equip him for notable service. Such was the qualification of the national champions in the Book of Judges. A comparable experience is implied in stories of the tenth- and ninth-century prophets. They were "men of God," an appellation that in its Hebrew possibilities as well as in the episodes related of them carries evidence of their exceptional status.

It is worthy of note, however, that even these sources are not untouched with legendary embellishments. We come rather to Israel's true concept of the nature of a "walk with God" in the careers of the writing prophets. It is important to realize that the prophetic experience was essentially one of personal relationship with the divine. In the quiet of his inner life the prophet heard the words of the Lord; he lived under a sense of the divine choice and commission and of an intimate relation that brought him guidance, and support, and utterance, through the common days of his career. Illustrations are too familiar to require long delay. We think of Amos' experience of being "taken" from his peasant's work and sent to prophesy to Israel; of Micah's being full of the spirit of the Lord; of the occasion when the Lord spoke to Isaiah "with strength of hand" (Isa. 8:11). But the career of Jeremiah is peculiarly rich in this regard. It is clear that the account of his call to his high office as recorded in chapter 1 of his book is to be understood in the light of what we know of the awakening of a thoughtful adolescent to the personal religious realities and tasks of life. And the famous passages of the book which reveal his inner doubts and struggles through his active years again are intimately related to present-day religious experiences.

Briefly, then, Hebrew thought at its best, we may say, understood that the individual can hear the voice of God deep in his own consciousness and may, through the unexplored mediums of the mystical experience, commune with him in silence. Such is clearly the view of the psalmists also; from a host of relevant passages we cite only the confession of the author of Psalm 73. He was deeply perplexed and troubled by the seeming injustice of God's rule of the world; the arrogant wicked lived in bounty, while the just were plagued all the day long and chastened every morning. Consideration of this was too painful for him, he says, "until I went into the sanctuary of God and considered their latter end" (vs. 17). And there satisfying answer came to him, not by audible voice, we are to observe, nor heaven-bent theophany, but in quiet meditation on the realities of religion and of life.

With the passage of time, however, and under stress of social and national crisis which always fosters apocalyptic expectations, wishful thinking turned back to concepts not unlike those found in the patriarchal stories. It is no accident that the pseudepigraphic literature is fathered on the heroes of that remote time, for it seeks to revive the largely abandoned, supernatural concept of God's dealing with man. Once again we find favored individuals who stand in a special, almost superhuman relation to God; to them come angelic ministrants with messages direct from the heavenly throne and to them are given visions of the heavenly world and glimpses of divine plans. This type of thinking, rather than the concepts of the great prophets, when carried over into later religious ideas, has continued until the present to make a peculiar appeal to minds which for lack of knowledge of the history of ideas, or for whatever other reason are susceptible to cabbalistic computations and imagery.

There remains yet the question of Israel's understanding of the problem of evil. How is it that suffering and sin exist in a world created by a good and all-wise God? The Hebrew answer is familiar, for it is provided by the famous story of the fall of man. God put the first pair in the sacred garden, giving them wide privileges but strictly restraining them, "Of the fruit of the tree which is in the midst of the garden ye shall not eat, neither shall ye touch it lest ye die" (Gen. 3:3). And they went straightway and did just that! They were seduced by the wicked snake, it is true; but nonetheless they had the power to refuse: the snake merely persuaded them. There we have human freedom, pure and unalloyed. And out of it came all our ills, so the writer tells us. But something else came also, for this mysterious tree was "the tree of the knowledge of good and evil."

It is idle to seek to exhaust the depths of the concept here. But it is clear that this is the Hebrew form of a widespread myth of the theft of divine prerogatives and their appropriation by man. Most of us are familiar with the Greek form of the story. Prometheus stole fire from the gods and gave it to man: but for this he was chained to a rock in the Caucasus while an eagle ate incessantly at his living liver. But the idea certainly did not originate with the Greeks; it is oriental. Ea's befriending of man and the concept which developed in course of time of Osiris as the patron of civilization who suffered at the hands of Seth are treatments of the same problem. The East and, in particular, Israel's thinkers speculated on the mysterious quality that sets man apart in all creation. He possesses the fire of the gods—or better, in Hebraic phrase, he has secured knowledge of good and evil. For this he suffers. Through this he sins. Yet otherwise he would be less than man.

To be human demands freedom; we must assert our will and purposes, if need be against all creation, saying only, "This is my way." What monstrous arrogance; ludicrous finitude claiming to direct its steps in a vast and mysterious universe! Who but God himself can know enough to decide his course of action? But it is just this that the Hebrew thinkers asserted of frail and finite man: he is made in the image of God. He is a free person, with all that such blending of finitude and freedom entails in the way of error and iniquity and pain.

But indeed the great thinker who wrote the Dialogue of Job pushed the matter still further. The exegesis of this book is still beset with acute difficulty; there exists no consensus as to its main purport, and not least the figure of the intermediary between God and Job remains shrouded in uncertainty. But in any case it would appear that the author advanced the bold concept that God himself suffers. Pain and woe are in the deepest nature of things. To live is to suffer; and the more intensely one participates in life's highest, the more he is susceptible of pain.

Yet there could have been but a few choice intellects that penetrated to such understanding. For the rest it was much that they
recognized so clearly how large a part of the woe that has black-
ened human history is of human creation. Certain individuals
through their wilful sin or by foolishness bring suffering on themselves, soon or late, and also on others. The sin of Adam left an
entail for all his descendants; that of David brought plague on the
people (II Sam. 24:15). The profound truth of vicarious suffering,
so notably portrayed in the Servant Songs (Isa. 50:4–9; 53:2–9),
was deeply interwoven into Israel's religious thought. Further, a
disciplinary function of suffering was recognized: it was sent not in
punishment but for guidance. The author of the first speech of Elihu reveals deep understanding when he remarks of the sufferer:

> He is chastened also with pain upon his bed
> and continual strife in his bones. . . . .
> If there be with him . . . . an interpreter
> to show man what is right for him,
> then God is gracious to him . . . . [Job 33:19–24].

Yet it was characteristic that all this should have been set in a cosmic system responsive to the conscious decision of a personal God.
When the nation sinned, God sent defeat and other disasters: such
is the clearly enunciated teaching of the Book of Judges, and such,
too, is the warning of the prophets. God apportions good or ill in
accord with human conduct. But the realism of the Hebrew mind
insured that such oversimplification should not finally suffice.
Presently men came to see that the facts of life are far too complex
for any such formulation. The considerable body of literature that
deals with this problem is familiar to every reader of the Old
Testament. Notably certain psalms sought a deeper explanation
that would accord with experience. Some of these efforts do not
impress us; they are little more than a reaffirmation of the dogma
that retribution overtakes the wicked in this life; they concede
only that the mills of the gods may grind slowly. The conviction of
the author of Psalm 73, from which we have already cited, is:

> Surely thou dost set them in slippery places. . . . .
> How are they become a desolation in a moment!

But the effort to find a satisfying response to the troubles of the righteous was somewhat better. This same poet goes on:

> Nevertheless I am continually with thee;
> thou dost hold my right hand.
> Thou wilt guide me with thy counsel
> and afterward wilt receive me with honor.

The classic treatment of the problem, as everyone knows, is in the Dialogue of the Book of Job. The author represents Job as moving on through despair and resentment to a dawning concept of the place of suffering in the world and to faith and hope, at length expressed in the notable words of chapter 23:

> He knows the way that I take;
> when he has tried me, I shall come forth as gold.

Israel did not evolve some logical formulation which might be considered a complete explanation of suffering. But with their conviction of the moral reality in the universe and their recognition of unseen but transcendent values in life, it was not strange that at the farthest outreach of their thought these thinkers should assert a solution in the direction of such values, even if they, as we also, could not formulate precisely the nature of that solution. More simply, Israel's answer was in her religious faith.

Still the understanding of human freedom was not so simple as our statement might indicate. We recall the experience of the Pharaoh of the Exodus, who doubtless would have released his Hebrew slaves, but always at the critical moment the Lord hardened his heart. And lest there be doubt of the divine interference, the Lord is represented as explaining, "In very deed for this cause have I caused thee to stand to show thee my power and that my name may be declared throughout all the earth" (Exod. 9:16). The king was not free; his decisions were determined by God in the interests of ultimate divine plans. A writer in the Book of Proverbs, indeed, gathers up such speculation into a general statement:

> The heart of the king is in the hand of the Lord;
> as watercourses he turneth it whithersoever he will [Prov. 21:1].

That goes far in a doctrine of determinism. Jeremiah's oracle in the potter's house, also, is famous for its similar interpretation.

The Lord was the great potter, shaping the nations to his desire (Jeremiah, chap. 18). And the vision of Micaiah ben Imlah is likewise to be considered. He claimed to have witnessed a lying spirit going out from the presence of the Lord, which now, he charged, was misleading King Ahab's official prophets in order to seduce him to his death (I Kings, chap. 22). The philosophy of Ecclesiastes, too, will suggest itself at this point; his cosmic wheel of fate by the revolutions of which all events come round in their proper sequence is patently a theory of determinism. Yet all these, and the rest of similar sort that may be adduced, are subject to qualification. Certainly Ecclesiastes considered himself free to choose when he undertook his experiments relative to the worth of life. It is claimed, in fact, that his discussion throughout is aimed at asserting human freedom. But, however that may be, there can be no doubt that he regarded man as somehow standing outside the universal process and able to survey it critically in full intellectual freedom. He realized the compulsive force of circumstance, but in some way, for him, man was free to choose his course even though not able to achieve his ends. It is notable, too, in regard to the stories of the Pharaoh and of Ahab that the monarch's normal freedom is clearly implied. Why did the Lord go to all the trouble of sending a lying spirit if he could instead merely have decreed that Ahab should think it right to go to Ramoth Gilead? And the interference in the Pharaoh's decisions was obviously an abnormal, divine act. The situation seems to clarify itself thus: with their notable realism, the Hebrews regarded human freedom as obvious and axiomatic. Yet, having said that, they recognized that they had not exhausted the problem. For they held firmly to a divine purpose and process in history. And history is only human life in the large. Hence if God is shaping human ends, he must at times interfere in individual thought and will. For one phase of this there was a ready explanation; the prophets by profession sought to subordinate their minds to divine impulse. Hence God could through them intervene in human affairs. For the rest no clear answer was given as to how God could direct history. The important matter, however, is that, while holding firmly to a belief in human freedom, Israel nonetheless realized that it was a complex and contentious problem.

But it will be recognized that about this point a more comprehensive issue was forcing itself on Hebrew thought. The question as to why the mind takes a certain course in given circumstances is the open door to the entire psychological problem which we have been prone to regard as a contribution of the Hellenic genius. Yet Israel's thinkers by and through their own intellectual habits turned their inquisitive eyes backward upon themselves to inquire how their minds behaved.

With their characteristically direct approach to reality, they never seriously doubted the validity of human mental processes or the power of the mind to apprehend truth. They were familiar with the fact of deception, both of the ordinary sort, where some malicious individual presents as truth what actually is false, and of the more insidious kind referred to just now that was attributed to the interference of an unfriendly spirit. This latter, it will be recognized, was a subjective experience. And it is well to realize that in this they were dealing with experiences common to us as well. Our thinking, at times even our senses, can play most callous tricks on us, so that we are positive of having seen or heard things that in reality never occurred. For us a solution may be sought in psychology; the Hebrews found it in external spirits. The observation is the same; the explanation differs. To this extent, then, the Hebrew thinkers were ready to concede a dubious character to human processes of knowledge. But, in the ordinary, one might trust the evidence of his senses and the concepts which his mental processes deduced from sense experience. Knowledge was basically a matter of sense perception. But again Israel avoided oversimplification. The prophets speak much of a knowledge of God—it is a great phrase with Hosea in particular—yet they had left far behind the simple faith that he was to be experienced by ordinary sight and hearing. Nonetheless, the senses, along with the mental processes that compound experience into knowledge, provided for the Hebrew an indubitably valid understanding of reality—up to the point of the limitations of these; for there were areas of truth that for one reason or another lay outside the normal knowing process.

The Hebrew psychological system is familiar, perhaps dangerously so, for it has been misinterpreted. The threefold division into body, soul, and spirit, apparent in the New Testament, seems to carry back into the Old as well, for one can easily assume that it is met with in the creation stories, to speak of no other. And beyond dispute Hebrew has different words corresponding to these assumed entities. Yet there is also through the Old Testament frequent reference to organs or parts of the body to which are ascribed special functions, or, in some cases, near-independence, in human consciousness and action. It is an idea that again points us to the New Testament, for it is suggestive of Paul's famous debate among the members of the body as to relative importance (I Cor. 12:12–26). But actually the concept of personality was by no means as chaotic as this would suggest. There is no doubt that all members were subordinate to the central consciousness, whatever that was. Yet the function of the organs calls for some attention. A remarkable fact is that no mention is made anywhere of the brain. In those days when heads were somewhat commonly smashed, the Hebrews must have been familiar with the strange jelly-like matter that fills the skull; but the odd fact is that they never ascribed any function to it or even considered it deserving of a name. Perhaps this was because it seems a thoroughly passive substance; in any case, as a modern commentator has facetiously remarked, the Hebrews had no brain! But they speak frequently of the heart, which is sometimes clearly the organ we mean by that word, but often is only vaguely one's insides. To this they attributed much of the function of the brain. But the liver also, the kidneys, and the bowels were for them important centers of human consciousness and volition. It is commonly held that some or all of these were associated with the emotions, and, while there is in this a measure of truth, yet the contrast of mouth and kidneys (Jer. 12:2) paralleled elsewhere with that of mouth and heart (Isa. 29:13; Ezek. 33:31) reveals the looseness of the concept. Further, we recall the familiar passage: "My kidneys also instruct me in the night season" (Ps. 7:9).

It becomes apparent that there was no clear division of organic functions. And while the difference of the emotional, rational, and volitional aspects of consciousness were to some degree recognized, there was no clear analysis, if even any admission, of the desirability of such analysis. This deficiency, as it must seem to us, was in actuality related to Israel's major attainment in the understanding of personality. For it is evident on closer study that the threefold division of the personality is likewise more apparent than real. While it is true that the Hebrew word translated "soul" commonly denotes the appetites, and in other cases the physical life, and while that rendered "spirit" can mean something approximating our idea of personality, actually such distinction is not consistent, if indeed it was ever consciously applied. At the most the terms signify not different entities but different aspects of the personality; and even so they were in later times treated as practically synonymous. And thus man is of two, not three, aspects: the body, which is the organism in its physical being and functions, and the soul-spirit that accounts for all the rest, comprising as it does whatever rises into consciousness—for the Hebrew had another explanation for what we are accustomed to speak of as the subconscious. But between these two there is no separation or antithesis; they are but complementary aspects of a single whole. The human personality is a single, indivisible unit. It has been well said that, for the Hebrew, man is not an incarnate spirit—that is a Greek idea; he is an animated body. Israel admitted no dualism of mind and body with a sort of antithesis and rivalry between them; but man was one single unified organism and personality. As we have seen, these ancient thinkers were fully aware of the conflict that perpetually is joined within the human consciousness, our nobler impulses forever struggling against the selfish and bestial in our nature. In later times the biblical phrases *yetser tobh* and *yetser ra^c* (the good will and the bad will) were much in use in discussions of man's contradictory instincts. But Israel's thinkers refused to solve the problem by the simple device of postulating a divine origin for the one and a material or diabolical for the other. For man was one; and his conduct, be it high or low, was his own to determine in accord with the dictates of his whole nature.

Important as was Israel's attainment in her conviction of the unity of the human personality, it must yet be freely recognized that her psychological interests did not carry into a study of the responses of the organism. Of the nervous system they knew nothing; to the complicated interrelation between body and mind they gave but elementary attention. It is to be admitted that Is-

rael's genius was not scientific. For the science of the ancient East
we must look to Egypt and Babylonia, from whom Israel took her
concepts, modifying them profoundly, it is true, in their religious
aspects, but making little change in their scientific content. The
Hebrews' achievement in their own peculiar sphere was so notable
that the most ardent Judeophile need not hesitate to concede the
vast areas where Israel accepted a status of secondhand scholarship.

Yet, however this may be, there is an aspect of the Hebrews'
knowledge of psychology that calls for no apology. That is their
understanding of human motivation and its emergence in conduct.
It is typical of the attitude of the Old Testament as a whole that
the rampant wickedness of the time of the Flood is traced to "the
whole imagination of the thoughts of the heart" of the people of the
time. And it is to this quality that the narratives owe much of their
contemporaneity, a psychological interest which, while admittedly less than that of modern storytellers, is a worthy antecedent.
The heroes of Hebrew story walk before us not as painted figures
of imagined perfection; their biographers reveal with ruthless can-
dor their foibles and selfishness. Sometimes it is by a revealing incident, commonly, however, by a telling analysis of what the subject of the story "thought in his heart"—but, by whatever means,
the writers succeed in portraying the inmost nature of the men and
women who under their hands move across the scene before us.

This sense of the centrality of character and the ability to sketch
and develop the characters of their heroes is one aspect of the notable excellence of Hebrew narrative. A high place must be accorded the story of Joseph, who in a spirit of revenge, it might seem,
dealt harshly with his brothers, but whose real magnanimity the
evolution of the plot reveals. It reveals another feature also in
the reiterated inquiry for "that old man your father," still more in
the impressive episode where he makes himself known to the
brothers: his first words were, "I am Joseph. Is my father yet
alive?" The writers tell us, too, of Abraham, "the prince of God,"
who yet was so frightened in a crisis that he had his wife screen
him with a lie—or was it only half a lie? And Moses, the paragon
of meekness as well as of piety, lost his temper and so was debarred from entering the land. King Saul of the independent spirit

that would not be servile to any priest-prophet however revered gradually deteriorates before our eyes through a mental breakdown. The vital David, hero of Israel, of whose shortcomings the less said the better; pompous Solomon; Rehoboam, whose dream was to make himself a despot; Elijah, the perpetually untamed Gileadite; imperious Jezebel, defiant to the last; the headlong Jehu, whose murderous impetuosity simmered down into mediocrity—striking individuals as they all are, their records are not less noteworthy for the insights of the nameless men who penned them.

However, with such psychic equipment as we have sketched, man, according to Hebrew thought, undertook the joys and tasks of life and confronted its problems. Knowledge, then, was a direct experience or, at most, a result of experience, that brought the individual into direct contact with objective reality. Epistemological dualism was unheard of; man could and did know reality by immediate contact. Yet the limitation of knowledge, that is, the limitation of the human potentiality of knowledge, was fully recognized. In considerable part this was apparently nothing but a reflex of the imperfect science of the time. Man was surrounded by a vast and mysterious world that he possessed no method or means of investigating. There was no answer to the problems of the heavens above and the teeming phenomena of the world beneath but the leap of the mind into speculation which had already produced the multiform vagaries so ably surveyed in the chapters by Professors Wilson and Jacobsen. But Israel grew noticeably weary of the uncharted areas of pure imagination, as much of this gradually came to be considered. Ecclesiastes, we have already pointed out, displayed a really scientific mood, even if his methods must be adjudged crude. Israel's contact with Babylonian astronomy likewise was mentioned above; hence Ecclesiastes' investigation must not by any means be thought of as a pioneer scientific venture. But it is close to that in its application of an empirical method, however imperfect, to the problems of psychology and philosophy.

His results were none too impressive; and certainly we may describe them as unhappy for himself, for they served only to corroborate his conviction that "all is vanity." But in how much worse position he was when he attempted the whole problem of man and the world! To his credit as a thinker, he claimed no success. On the contrary, he felt himself narrowly confined in an intellectual ghetto from which there was no egress: in simple terms, he was ignorant of the nature of things; he knew it, yet saw no way of correcting it. His failure was so complete that he came to believe he suffered from some personal obstruction. It was God himself who, jealous of his prerogatives, was withstanding the free course of human investigation. It is a mood closely parallel to that of the Tower of Babel story, except only that Ecclesiastes is not inhibited by the piety of the other; he would push into the abode of the divine, restrained only by misgivings for his safety. He wants most of all to know and understand. It is to his credit that a considerable part of his pessimism is directly due to intellectual frustration. We shall doubtless feel somewhat qualified respect for his explanation of this situation; yet we may not be too severe in our disdain, for, like most thinkers, he merely took over uncritically considerable of the thought of his time. Ben Sira expresses well a characteristic attitude, "Seek not out things that are too hard for thee . . . . but what is commanded thee think thereon . . . . for more things are showed thee than men understand" (Ecclus. 3.21–23). "The heaven and the heaven of heavens belong to God," another writer asserted, "but the earth has he given to the sons of men" (Ps. 115: 16). To pry into the secrets of the divine was blasphemous impiety. The view was fostered by the conviction that knowledge is power; there were realms of truth reserved for divine exploitation, by virtue of which superhuman wonders were wrought; but for man to appropriate such was cosmic larceny! Out of this attitude grew Israel's conscience against traffic with magic-workers of whatever sort, a restraint that seems to carry a reminiscence of the primeval tragedy when our first parents took sinfully of the forbidden tree of knowledge.

The orthodox attitude, then, was that God had revealed to man as much of the ultimate nature of things as was good for him. Indeed, even the commonplace knowledge of practical things such as for us lies close to scientific discovery was, for the devout at least, also a matter of divine revelation. One writer, we saw, tells how the practice of the peasant in his tillage and care of his crops was taught to him by the Lord (Isa. 28:23–29). It is a view which, obviously, looks back to the primeval myth of the divine schooling of man in the ways of civilization, and forward to the whole basic theory of the wise men, of which more in a moment. Yet we must not confuse the present issue with this inclusive belief, for we are concerned now to understand Israel's concept of the knowing process. That most of it was by normal sense and intellectual activity has already been emphasized. But we are concerned to see that a knowledge which lay beyond human capacity was, according to accepted dogma, given by direct divine intervention. And the mediums, it is apparent, were primarily priest and prophet.

In the priesthood there was a growing tradition of religious precepts that were accepted as of divine origin and authority. But, when we push the matter back to the rise of these directives, we come face to face with the basic character of the priest as the personal attendant and minister of the god. He was precisely on a par with the servants and attendants of noblemen and royalty; in just the same way he ministered to the god. The fact that his lord was a presence at most visible in the image made no difference in the basic concepts. Like the cupbearers and other valets of the ancient world, his close association with his lord gave him opportunity to learn his character and his will. But it will be apparent that the valet had the advantage that his master could and did speak to him by an audible voice. Denied this direct revelation of the god's will, the priest depended on some ancient theory equivalent to our adage that actions speak louder than words. He learned from what the god did. Stories such as the sudden death of Uzzah when he touched the ark or of the tragedy of Aaron's sons when they offered "strange fire" are eloquent of the growth of the priestly tradition. Briefly, the priest secured his revelation by the astute use of his normal wits!

The method has illuminating illustration in the procedure of the Babylonian augurs, who, it would appear, worked out an organization for report of unusual occurrences to central priestly agencies, so that if even a fox jumped into a vineyard, the fact was solemnly recorded as data in accord with which, first, to relate important events and, later, to predict them. If we might concede the priests' theory that "coming events cast their shadows before" in signs and portents, then it would appear that the augur priest was an ancient scientist, carefully gathering his data, discovering their meaning by observation, and then proceeding to the conclusion that similar phenomena have always a similar result. This characterization is further enhanced by the activity of the magician, illegitimate priest as he was, who is commonly recognized to have been in some way ancestor of the modern scientist.

Similar was the means of revelation through the wise men, as they themselves would have admitted. They were primarily students of the course of human life. Their observations were made by completely normal human faculties, and their conclusions were deduced by ordinary processes of thought. But the prophet, as distinct from both priest and sage, received his revelation deep in his own consciousness by means that for him were genuinely supernatural. He did not deprecate the normal use of the mind; on the contrary, his criticism not infrequently was that the people did not observe and think. But he held fast the conviction that there is a means of valid knowledge quite independent of sense experience. True, the terms employed in regard to prophetic visions imply a belief in a sort of sublimated use of the senses; the prophet passed into direct contact with the unseen world of spiritual reality and there received knowledge by seeing and hearing matters that were not discerned by the ordinary senses. Still, it is freely recognized that we caricature the career of the prophets if we demand an ecstatic experience as prelude to every utterance; our sources for the activities of the great prophets lead us to believe that it was actually quite rare, if not for some of them nonexistent. Nonetheless, the prophets were obviously sincere in their claim that their message was received from the Lord. The conclusion, then, is inescapable that they believed fully in a process of knowledge quite divorced from sense experience but operative through channels of consciousness that we may loosely speak of as thought and feeling. It was very close to what is now sometimes called intuition. The importance of this in Israel's religious apologetics has already been noted. But also, evolving from the prophetic experience, a sense of personal relationship and communion with the divine became almost a standard feature of Jewish religion. It is deserving of the emphasis of repetition that such suprasensuous knowledge was accepted as a valid experience of reality.

Precisely this epistemological problem is one of the issues in the debate of Job with his friends. Stung by his own unmerited suffering and the shallow advice of the friends, Job breaks out in blasphemous denunciation of the ways of God, calling him to account before human standards of right. But in despair of justice he questions, "How can man be just with God?" Typical of the friends' position throughout, but also of orthodoxy in all ages, Zophar retorts:

> The deepest things of God canst thou find out,
> canst thou find out the Almighty completely?" [Job 11:7.]

Such, too, is the theme of the pious reflections in the speeches of Yahweh. The might of the divine creation and rule of the physical universe overwhelm the inquisitive Job so that he contritely passes judgment on his questionings.

> I have uttered that which I understood not,
> things too wonderful for me which I knew not . . . .
> wherefore I abhor myself
> and repent in dust and ashes [Job 42:3–6].

Yet it is a very different Job who is presented by the bold spirit who penned the matchless words of the Dialogue. For Job in his thinking is a naturalist; he demands a meeting with God, where, armed only with his human intelligence, he may talk with him as one talks with a friend. He fears the might of God and wishes for an intermediary to preside over his high debate; he despairs of such a meeting this side of the grave; but soon or late, wherever he may come before him, Job is confident that he will find God a being of manlike rationality.

> Would he contend with me in the greatness of his power?
> Nay, but he would give heed unto me.
> There the upright might reason with him,
> So should I be delivered forever from my judge [Job 23:6–7].

But all this, for the friends, is shocking irreverence. For them the nature of God is

> Higher than heaven, what canst thou do:
> Deeper than She³ol, what canst thou know? [Job 11:8–9.]

Nonetheless, they claim a knowledge of God—it is so armed that they accost Job with advice as to his recovery of divine favor—and its source is clear. Like many persons from that day to the present, they believed that, by setting the acquisition of knowledge in the remote past, they not alone enhanced its authority but at the same time bridged the gulf that separates from the unseen. For them there was a valid knowledge of God handed down from remote antiquity: accept this, they said, and learn of him! Yet they boast themselves as independent investigators; they have examined the dogmas they unload on Job and found them true (Job 5:27). But, like exponents of modern authoritative systems of theology, they exercised their criticism well within the limits of the system and then claimed that their research confirmed the faith once delivered to the saints. But Job will have none of it! Hard and inescapable facts have destroyed his former credulity. Now he is launched on the wide seas of uncharted truth, guided only by his human faculties. And Eliphaz rebukes him: "How hard is thy heart and how haughty thine eyes!" (Job 15:12–13.) In such free questioning he is setting his spirit against God. Job, he charges, denies the possibility of a knowledge of God, whereas the notable fact is that he himself is in essentially that position; he is Barthian in his repudiation of the adequacy of the human mind for a knowledge of God. Then, true to such orthodoxy to this very day, having repudiated the guidance of intelligence, he has no protection against credulity. Like devotees of certain of the dogmatic religions of our time, he is positively gullible in his acceptance of the supernatural; even his absurd ghost story is for him valid revelation of a truth so trite that any common man in the street might have told it to him, a truth which, however, he believed the human mind could not itself apprehend! The crux of the dispute, it will be seen, hinges about the so-called "will to believe" from which into superstition there exists a "facilis descensus Averno." Job, though not less a man of faith, demands a respectable basis for his belief.

Now, it will be apparent that Job—no, rather we must say, the great unknown thinker who composed the Dialogue—was in his mentality a man of the modern world. He demands that thought proceed from fact to sound conclusion: only so can knowledge be

gained. Indeed, it is a formulation of just this principle and its application to theological speculation which constitutes one of the astonishing, though commonly overlooked, features of this remarkable poem. Job, as we have seen, repudiates the traditional lore
which the friends pour on him in too generous measure. And why?
Because they do not practice sound and honest thinking! To that
very speech in which Zophar had raised the issue of a knowledge of
God, Job replies:

> Hear now my reasoning
>   and hearken to the argument of my lips.
> Will ye speak unrighteously for God
>   and talk deceitfully for him?
> Will ye show partiality for him?
>   Will ye argue on his behalf?
> Will it be good that he search you
>   if as one trifles with a man ye trifle with him?
> He will surely reprove you
>   if in secret ye show partiality.

"In secret," that is, in the secret of their own consciousness, under
the cloak and restaint of piety, they were deceiving themselves
with shoddy reasoning which was nothing less than applying inferior categories of thought to religious problems. Briefly, we have
here the charter of the entire modern critical mood and movement
in religious thinking.

But we err if we suppose that with this illustration we exhaust
the matter. On the contrary, there is evidence of a pervasive recognition of the demands of sound principles of religious thinking. I am
indebted to Professor Meek of the University of Toronto for an
illustration from that most orthodox of documents, the Book of
Deuteronomy. In our common translation (American Standard
Version) the passage runs: "Take heed to yourselves lest your
heart be deceived and ye turn aside and serve other gods" (Deut.
11:16). Professor Meek has translated ". . . . lest your mind become so open that you turn aside. . . . ." It is a valuable insight;
for, while the verb is not the common one "to open," yet it is closely related and ultimately means the same. So the passage, just as
Professor Meek has rendered it, is a warning against too great
openness of mind, a loose and easy tolerance that fails to distin-

guish things which look alike but in essence are quite different. Religion and ethics, the author seems to say, demand for their highest expression careful and precise habits of mind. How much of the long story of Israel's religious advance is gathered up in the attitude here briefly glimpsed!

But this same verb is the root from which one of the common words for the "fool" is derived. This famed but unfortunate character of Old Testament pages, whom the sages would instruct, from whose blunders they would warn the young, is in reality, then, nothing more than a simple-minded fellow whose worst quality is just that he does not know and does not practice sound thinking. And such principles are well suggested by the antithesis set forth by the wise men themselves: "The simple believes everything, but the prudent gives thought to his course" (Prov. 14:15). He thinks about the way he is going, about the observed facts of life and all that may be rightly deduced from them as to ends and means. For we have seen enough to realize that for Israel's thinkers the first step in sound methods of thought was the accumulation of relevant facts. They did not, it is true, give us treatises on correct methods of analysis, classification, and appraisal of those facts and proper deduction from them. But it is clear that they knew and practiced such procedures even though their methods had not attained the perfection implied in self-conscious organization.

Such then was Israel's treatment of the problem of knowledge, both secular and religious. Much of it was a new thing in the history of human thinking, and not a little has been of profound significance in the sequel. Yet, reverting to our main theme, there remains an aspect of the Hebrew thought of man and his place in the world that can be regarded as little less than astonishing. Its far-reaching importance has received too slight attention even from biblical specialists.

The Orient had long concerned itself with the pursuit of "Wisdom," an entity which, at first highly utilitarian, presently came to comprise the total of the intellectual culture of the age. The wise man was the educated as well as sagacious man. The Hebrew sages were fully conscious of the activity and results of their colleagues; from quite early in the history of Israel's life in Palestine we begin to hear of the importance of the "wise" who must be regarded as in some way a bequest of the great Canaanite civilization. And there is a revealing passage in the account of Solomon's wisdom that compares him with famed sages of the non-Hebrew world:

Solomon's wisdom excelled the wisdom of all the children of the East, and all the wisdom of Egypt. For he was wiser than all men, than Ethan the Ezrahite, and Heman and Calcol and Darda, the sons of Mahol; and his fame was in all the lands round about [I Kings 4:30–31].

Yet Israel's wisdom movement traversed a history parallel to that in "the lands round about." From an early engrossment in practical ends it was compelled by force of circumstance to consider wider implications and values. Yet even the cultural interest from Solomon's time onward continued to be, so our too meager evidence would indicate, largely utilitarian. It was the Exile, that most profound experience of the Hebrew people, which, touching and transforming all aspects of Jewish life, compelled a new and deeper concept of wisdom. Highly revealing for us, then, is a lyric passage dating from somewhere in this late period:

Happy is the man that findeth wisdom
and the man that gaineth understanding!
For the gaining thereof is better than the gaining
of silver
and the profit thereof than fine gold.
She is more precious than rubies
and all the things of desire are not comparable
to her [Prov. 3:13–15].

The striking feature of this is the repudiation of precisely those good things which earlier sages had accepted as the ends of life: gold, silver, rubies, things of desire. Since the days of the Egyptian sage Ptahhotep these had been prized as the mark and content of life's worth. But here some Hebrew thinker—rather, it appears, the entire late school of Hebrew sages—asserts boldly that there is something else in life which far transcends them, or through which at most these can best be enjoyed. It is evident that, in rejection of tangible good, the writer speaks of the unseen, finer things of life, all the beauty and goodness and intellectual elevation which redeem us from our brute heritage. But in view of the oft-emphasized aphorism that the fear of the Lord is the beginning of wisdom, it is certain that the author thinks of religious faith and conduct as holding also an honored, if not primary, place among such human treasure. We should greatly err if we were to claim that at this point the idea first dawned on human thought through the insight of this Hebrew poet. But it does mark clear gain to have it formulated and emphasized as here.

However, we move on to a striking development of the theme. All students of the Old Testament are familiar with the words

> The Lord possessed me in the beginning of his way
>   before his works of old.
> I was set up from everlasting, from the beginning
>   before the earth was.
> When there were no depths I was brought forth
>   when there were no fountains abounding with water. . . . .

And so the writer runs on through a poetic survey of the wonders of creation, to the concluding thought:

> When he established the heavens I was there . . . .
>   when he marked out the foundations of the earth:
> then I was by him as a master-workman
>   and I was daily his delight
>   rejoicing always before him
> rejoicing in his habitable earth,
>   and my delight was with the sons of men [Prov. 8:22–31].

It is wisdom that speaks: wisdom which just now we have seen to be the finest attainment of human aspiration. But this same wisdom here declares herself as pre-existent, associating with God in creation, so that without her "was not anything made that was made."

Much energy has been wasted in speculating as to whether the writer here conceives of an actual person associated with God before the world was and how such heresy could ever have been expressed by a devout Jew. But is it not so obvious as the nose on a face that in this poetic passage the writer is employing imagery to express an idea which he hoped others would have enough intelligence to grasp? This mysterious pre-existent personification is nothing but an aspect of the character of God; by virtue of his being this sort of a God he made the world. He took, we might say, this attribute and built it into the nature of things as they are, most

of all into the being of man. Here is the answer to the baffling fact
that the writer has used the same word for the human quality and
for this supernal, pre-existent reality. They are, he undertakes to
say with emphasis, one and the same thing. It is human because it
was first divine and was so made a pervasive quality of God's
whole creation. All our best achievements, all our highest hopes
and aspirations, all that the mind and soul of man has attained or
even dreamed, this ancient thinker asserts, is in accord with the
deepest nature of things. For the ultimate reality in the physical
world is the wisdom of God!

Now, it will be apparent that we have here a remarkable parallel
to the notion of universal ideas that took so important a place in
Plato's speculation as well as to the Stoic thought of the pervasive
divine reason. But what does the similarity signify? For we have
already pointed out that the biblical passage is late, and, though we
cannot date it within a couple of centuries, there is no good basis
for denying that it is not earlier than Plato and may easily be as
late as Zeno. Once more, then, we confront the perplexing question of a possible Greek influence upon Israel in one of its most
notable attainments. But the answer is even more clear than in our
previous dilemma. If borrowing is to be asserted—observe, *if* it
is to be—then the direction was clearly from East to West, not
the reverse. For this concept is so firmly rooted in the thought of
the ancient East, which had speculated for many centuries upon
divine wisdom and the divine word, that there can be not a doubt
this notable exposition of the theme in the Book of Proverbs is
Israel's own. The Hebrew thinkers have here, as so often, sublimated and transcended their oriental heritage, making it their
own and making it a new thing in the process. But they needed no
Greek, not even Plato, to teach them about the wisdom of God.

But we have not yet exhausted the concept. We turn again to the
great poem in Proverbs:

> Doth not wisdom cry
>   and understanding put forth her voice?
> On the top of the high places by the way,
>   where the paths meet, she standeth,
> beside the gates, at the entry of the city,
>   at the coming in at the doors, she crieth aloud:

"Unto you, O men, I call,
  and my voice is to the sons of men.
O ye simple understand prudence,
  and ye fools be of an understanding heart. . . . .
Receive my instruction and not silver,
  and knowledge rather than fine gold.
For wisdom is better than rubies,
  and all the things that may be desired are not to be
  compared unto her" [8:1–11].

Wisdom we first saw as a human attainment, then as a cosmic quality immanent in the world and in human life. Here we discover the nexus of the two. In poetic terminology, she stands in the busiest concourse of human affairs, wherever man may be, and there accosts all and sundry. Receive instruction; choose the better things of life; final satisfaction cannot be found in material things but only in the uncharted region vaguely known as the spiritual realities of life. This pervasive, immanent quality of life and the world has been ever active in human life, individual and collective, in leading, persuading, and inducing men to higher and better things. Through this function of the divine wisdom immanent in man the whole long story has come about of our groping progress from our brute ancestry, our slow attainment of civilization, and our unceasing outreach for ever better things in thought and practice.

Here, then, is the ultimate nature of man. He was made in the image of God and but little lower than God; but also he is infused and impelled and fashioned by the wisdom of God himself. By nature man may be related to the brute, but vastly more significant is his kinship with God and participation in the wisdom of God. Here is that concept familiar in the words quoted by a later thinker: "In him we live and move and have our being." All the talk of certain modern schools of theology about the lost condition of man apart from God would have been to the Hebrew thinker just so much crackling of thorns under a pot. For him such a being never has existed. Always from the first to be human was to possess the divine wisdom. And the difference among men, the distinction of wise and fool, of righteous and sinner, has been in the measure with which the individual has heard and then given willing obedience to the appeals of wisdom.

And here is the notable supremacy of the Hebrew thought above its apparent parallel in Plato. His was a republic for philosophers; these only could enter into the accumulated heritage of finer racial treasures. But for the Hebrew thinker the appeal of wisdom was to all men wherever and whatever they might be; in particular it called to the simple and foolish for whom Plato would have had only a place of menial service.

Yet there is still more for our purpose in this concept. It is apparent that here is the bridge between the human and divine; by this means God and man have come into relationship. All that we have achieved as we have left behind our savage origins and have climbed higher and yet higher in civilized life has been through the leadings of the divine wisdom. And this, it is to be noted, came not through some heaven-rending voice or aweful theophany, but within the individual consciousness, as our better nature, comprised of the indwelling divine wisdom, strove against our brute ancestry, ever warning: "Receive my instruction and not silver and knowledge rather than choice gold." The whole of history is thus gathered up for the Hebrew thinker in a single formula. And here is the doctrine of divine revelation. It has all come by this quiet, unspectacular, but effective means. Man is but little lower than God; and the divine in us has been slowly overcoming the bestial.

CHAPTER X
MAN IN THE WORLD

THE concept of the wise men, that there is pervasive throughout the world and immanent in man a mysterious urge toward better things which they called the Wisdom of God, had a long sequel in the history of our thinking. It was taken up by the authors of the Books of Ecclesiasticus and the Wisdom of Solomon. The former identified the divine wisdom with the Torah. In this we are not to see an excess of legalism but, on the contrary, his high appraisal of wisdom: it contained all the best in human life; it was the revelation of God. But, since this latter function was fulfilled by the Torah, then the conclusion was inescapable that the two were one and the same.

The author of the Wisdom of Solomon gave the concept a different turn, not less significant for our purposes, although at first glance one is prone to dismiss him in disappointment, for he adds little to the thought of Proverbs, merely incorporating certain Stoic phraseology into his discussion. Yet the meaning of this will be recognized. The author, and perhaps Jewish thought in general at that time, recognized the intimate relationship of the age-old speculation of the Orient to that of Greece; both had come to express in differing terms but in essential unity the conviction that human life is infused with a pervasive entity which is more than human, finding its ultimate origin and nature in the being of the universe.

But, further, the thought in the Prologue of the Gospel of John is almost in its entirety a recapitulation of the description of wisdom in the Book of Proverbs. True, the latter does not emphasize the life-giving powers of wisdom, though this is not foreign to its thought, and some passages approximate such statement (3:18, 22; 4:13, 22; 7:2; 8:35). Likewise, Proverbs does not employ the symbolism of light; but how negligible is this difference becomes apparent in the fact that the writer's prime concern in the description of wisdom was with human enlightenment. And as the

Christian writer advances to his doctrine of the incarnation, he goes beyond Proverbs, but still only in application of the principles contained in the latter. There is no need to seek in Greek speculation for the origins of the Prologue, for it is practically all contained in the writer's Jewish heritage, whether or not his thinking was stimulated by the Greek ideas. But Christian indebtedness to the great Jewish philosopher in the Book of Proverbs does not stop here; his thought has penetrated the very center of Christian theology. When Paul speaks of Christ as the power of God and the wisdom of God (I Cor. 1:24), when he presents him as the medium of creation (Col. 1:16), when he mentions wisdom, understanding, and knowledge as divine gifts to the believers, and when he formulates his doctrine of the pre-existent Christ who emptied himself to live among men (Phil. 2:6–8), it is clear that he is carrying over the thought of Proverbs into his concept of the person of Christ. And through him it has permeated subsequent Christology.

It is clear, however, that the idea of Ecclesiasticus confronts us with a new aspect of Hebrew thought. And a moment's consideration shows that the mood of the Wisdom of Solomon, also, and back of both the notable thought of Proverbs, carry the same implication. A pervasive quality in human life which everywhere sets before all men a standard of better conduct and ideals—here is clearly that concept which has played a very large part in the social and political life of the Western world under the name of natural law. It is commonly attributed to Greek speculation, and beyond a doubt it was given notable discussion by them. Yet the mere formulation of a definition shows that it was well recognized among the Hebrews; the course of our thought already has come upon it but now demands serious study of the matter.

Natural law has been described as "a supreme unifying, controlling power manifesting itself in the universe at large. In so far as men are men they possess common elements; and in their political and social life those elements inevitably emerge and are recognizable in custom and law. . . . . Such natural law represents the permanent portion of human law in general, and it is prior to and superior to positive legislation, which is only a supplement thereto." It will be observed that the idea, then, looks in two directions.

It comprehends the universal elements in the laws of all peoples, in "positive law" according to the terms of the definition. But beyond and subsuming this is the invisible, unwritten law, the universal sense of right which has reality only in human thought and ideals but expresses itself in a mood of judgment upon positive law as well as in just and right action that transcends legal requirements. It will be apparent, then, that Ecclesiasticus' identification of the divine wisdom with the Torah is a statement of the anterior relation of natural law. For him it has absorbed positive law: the social and religious legislation of Israel rests upon, rather is identical with, universal principles, universally recognized wherever men pay heed to the leadings of wisdom. But Prov. 1–9, Ecclesiasticus, and the Wisdom of Solomon are all late bodies of literature; even the first is certainly well within the period vaguely spoken of as post-Exilic. Yet it is important to keep in mind the situation already emphasized—that the speculation of Proverbs is rooted deep in the Orient: it is thoroughly Hebraic. And although the other two come from a time when Hellenism was admittedly making a profound impression upon Jewish life, marks of which are obvious in the Wisdom of Solomon, yet they likewise are of the Hebrew genius and stream of thought. The concept of natural law here expressed is Israel's own achievement; its relation to that of Greece must be sought in other directions than one of dependence. And evidence is abundant that Israel recognized and discussed the matter in times when it lies beyond reasonable consideration to postulate influence from the West.

Israel was early impressed with the regularity of nature, as doubtless even primitive man likewise. The personal concept of the world and its phenomena then prevalent would seem to weaken this conviction, introducing an element of volitional caprice. But observed facts could not be evaded even on the grounds of religious presupposition; for whatever reason, nature was notably regular. In Israel's orthodox thought this was an evidence of the grace of God: he chose so to order his world for the benefit of man. The promise was of divine grace that,

> While the earth remaineth,
> seedtime and harvest, cold and heat,
> summer and winter, and day and night,
> shall not cease [Gen. 8:22].

The same thought, qualified only by some doubt of the accuracy of our received text, is expressed in Job 10:22. Some unknown writer, commenting on the gloomy land of the dead, mentioned as one of its most terrifying aspects that it had no order. The implication is clear: by contrast, the regularity and system of the known world making possible planning and purpose in human life instead of rendering it the bauble of caprice—briefly, the fact that this writer recognized the world to be an ordered cosmos made it for him a land of the living. Somewhat similar was the idea formulated by Jeremiah in his exhortation of his contemporaries:

> Let us now fear the Lord
> who giveth us the rain
>   the early and the latter, in its season;
> who preserves for us
>   the appointed weeks of harvest [Jer. 5:24].

Even the animals, it was believed, obey a law immanent in their being:

> The ox knoweth its owner
> and the ass its master's crib [Isa. 1:3].

> The stork in the heavens
>   knoweth her appointed times;
> the turtledove and the swallow and the crane
>   observe the time of their coming [Jer. 8:7].

Yet we do well to apply these utterances cautiously; for the two latter are used in rebuke of the speakers' contemporaries, who, it is alleged, follow no such immanent principle. And Jeremiah's exhortation that ascribes the cycle of the seasons to divine activity is prefaced with the flat statement that his contemporaries pay no regard to this view. And, indeed, our knowledge of Israel's concept of the source of fertility shows that the belief in Yahweh as the giver and guardian of the increase of flock and field was hard won only through the struggle of a succession of prophets. From the time of the entry into the land, the people had accepted somewhat fully the Canaanite theology which credited Baal with this bounty. The theological framework of the Book of Judges would have us believe that prophetic opposition to such infidelity arose contemporaneously—and the claim is plausible—but the earliest actual incident on which we can depend is the conduct of Elijah through the drought and the culminating contest on Mount Carmel (I Kings 17–18). It is apparent that the theme of this story is the power of the Lord to withhold the rains and then to give them when the repentant people recognize the futility of faith in Baal.

However, a hundred years later, as attested by the utterances of Hosea, and still later, by those of Jeremiah, the faith in Baal as the source of fertility was still so prevalent as to amount practically to the popular religion of Israel. And this situation becomes meaningful for our present problem in the light of the well-known cultus of Baal. The annual cycle of rites commemorating the death, and then the resurrection, of the god, it is freely recognized, were magical. This stratum of Israelitish thinking was at the far extreme from the sense of an ordered regularity in nature expressed in passages of which those cited above are typical. For the popular belief was that the magical rites were essential to the alleged resurrection of the god, that is, to the regular cycle of the seasons. Far from believing in a fixed order of nature, the people conceived the only fixity and dependability to consist in a world of magic, for the operation of some part of which they possessed the secret. And, in this sense, they themselves were custodians of nature and its changes. Without their co-operation, neither magic nor the gods nor any other conceivable power would bring back the season of growth and reproduction.

This conclusion seems to carry us still farther from any sense of order in nature. Yet a moment's consideration dispels the illusion. Results in the form of fertility could and would come only as men voluntarily chose to perform the necessary magical rites, but the fact to be firmly grasped is that the world of magical powers stood constant, whether or not man invoked it. It would always react in one certain way to the performance of the proper rites. In that fact, as it was believed to be, lay the constancy and predictability so notably lacking from the capricious gods. Further, this power was probably thought of primarily in impersonal terms, although there was a steady tendency to identify it with one or another of the gods—in Israel, obviously, with Yahweh. It was greater than the gods, for the distinction of Thoth in Egypt and of Ea in Babylonia was that these each possessed powerful knowledge. The reply of Ea to Marduk's frequent consultation is familiar to every student of the ancient East: "What I know, thou knowest also, my son. Go"—and then there follow specific instructions for magic rituals. These gods knew how to invoke and vitalize this immense world of force that was not of themselves or of the other gods but could be employed by them for chosen purposes.

The prevalence of such concepts in Israel is apparent, then, in the vogue of the fertility rites. But it was by no means confined to the common popular level with which we associate this cult. It pervaded a wide area of Hebrew thought, even making its impress upon what we may call the orthodox religion. A notable illustration of this is the concept that the prophets were magicians. Such is clearly the implication of Elijah's conduct in the raising of the widow's son (I Kings 17:21), as of Elisha also in the parallel incident (II Kings 4:31–35). Their procedures were patently magical. Such, too, must have been the understanding of Jeremiah's famous symbol, where in the presence of dignitaries of the city who had been invited to witness the ceremony, he solemnly broke a pot and declared that in such manner the Lord would break Jerusalem (Jer. 19:10–11). It is difficult to conceive of action which for his audience would more clearly declare itself as magical: this was no innocent speaker telling of things which he believed would come to pass. He was working in occult powers and, by his own volition through his ritual of smashing, was bringing about that smashing of the city, which he foretold. How far Jeremiah himself shared this view it is difficult to say. Much can be adduced on the negative side; but if he was not at least a little interested in posing as the wonder-worker, then he was notably inept in his choice of symbols.

And what, then, of the prophetic symbolic acts as a whole? A careful examination leads to the conviction that they were not the innocent illustrations they are commonly supposed to have been. Ezekiel's drama of the captured city (4:1—5:3; 24:1-11) and his numerous similar performances, although regarded by the populace as merely good entertainment, had, for the prophet, as for several of the ancient commentators on his work (e.g., 4:4–6), some positive worth in accomplishing the ends he predicted. The prevalence of such belief among the populace is attested by the plea of the officer who went to bring in Micaiah ben Imlah at the request of King Ahab. He told how the court prophets had promised a happy outcome of the projected campaign against Ramoth Gilead and continued: "Let thy word, I pray, be like the word of one of them, and speak thou good" (I Kings 22:13). Now it is apparent that he had no thought of Micaiah's deceiving the king with pleasant assurances which could prove only delusive. On the contrary, he was clearly requesting that the prophet would speak the powerful word which would insure success for the project. For him, Micaiah was no mere predictor; as prophet he was in control of the mighty forces with which man's life is surrounded and could with a word direct them to chosen ends. In just such a role of wonder-worker Isaiah presented himself in his challenge to King Ahaz to ask a sign in the heavens above or deep as She'ol beneath (Isa. 7:11). The words of the offer indicate that even if the king should demand a repetition of Joshua's famous miracle at Ajalon (Josh. 10:12–14), Isaiah considered himself possessed of the power to perform it! Such, too, is the view of the later writer who relates the prophet's dealing with the sick Hezekiah: the shadow of the sun dial went back (Isa. 38:8). In all such cases the intimate relation between the prophet and the Lord is apparent in the story, and undoubtedly this was the orthodoxy of thought as it developed. These wonders were the working of the Lord through his representative. Yet this will not explain all the incidents. The stories of prophets of the ninth century and earlier reveal a basic concept of their office only by later thought reduced to that of spokesmanship for the Lord. In the phraseology of this time the prophet was a "man of God"; and the Hebrew idiom is much richer than this English equivalent. It is harmonious with the significance of these stories that the prophet could in his own right perform wonders; he controlled superhuman forces.

The close relationship of this thinking with the pervasive faith in the power of the blessing and the curse is immediately evident. Once again these powerful formulas were commonly pronounced in the name of the Lord, yet their more remote sanction speaks through many passages. Doubtless it would be of little cogency to point out that in some cases there is no invocation of divine action; this could well have been implied. But equally, if one is to argue along this line, it is possible that such invocation, when employed, is secondary and represents only a later usage. However, blessings such as those of the patriarchs, which it is apparent "fulfilled" themselves in the course of Israel's history, leave the strong impression upon the reader that here was magic pure and simple. The old dignitary was pronouncing formulas which in and of themselves would work out, even across centuries, the destiny of the nation or of its separate tribes. Now, if this be correct, it is a matter of high importance to our quest, for, in addition to demonstration of the might and prevalence of magic in the being of the world, it shows that it was also to some undetermined extent the ruler of human destiny. This is almost equivalent to a concept of fate, save only that it may have been less inexorable in its control of man's life.

Intimately related to the blessing and curse in both genius and sanction was the oath of attestation. It too possessed potentialities of results in far distant times. From the wealth of illustration we cite only the dire result of the breach by King Saul of Joshua's oath to the Gibeonites (II Samuel, chap. 21), and the nation's faith that its possession of the land was in fulfilment of the oath sworn to the patriarchs centuries before. But this oath was sworn by the Lord! Here is an astonishing situation. Oaths and agreements between men were commonly attested in the name of the Lord—or such became the usage; he was invoked to watch over the spoken word and insure its faithful performance. On the surface, this appears to be a recognition of Yahweh as himself the source of justice and, at the same time, immanent in the pervasive sense of justice. Yet, even so, the act was patently not religious. There was in these cases no supplication, no securing of divine sanction, no waiting upon the will of God. Man spoke and God was obliged to fulfil. It is clear that such was magic, however it may have been cloaked with pious words. But in cases where the Lord himself swears, there is not even a semblance of evasion of the issue. Of course, the devout author of the Epistle to the Hebrews reasons that "since he could swear by no greater, he swore by himself"; but this is decidedly thin as historic exegesis. More convincing would be the claim that the divine oath was but an unthinking carry-over of human practice. Yet even this is not convincing; surely the biblical writers

were not so consistently stupid as this would imply! There is no
good reason to evade the conclusion that Israel conceived of God's
oath as more binding than his promise, for precisely the same reason as in parallel human agreements: because there was a power
watching to compel fulfilment! Obviously such power was not
personal; that would be to create a hierarchy of the gods with
Yahweh in a menial position. It was force. And Yahweh was subject thereto!

Astonishing as this conclusion may well be, there is related a
strange incident which, to say the least, suggests some corrobora-
tion of the belief in a supra-divine world of power. When the al-
lied armies of Judah and Israel had ravaged the land of Moab, had
shut up its king in his capital, and were pressing the siege, the king
in despair "took his eldest son who was to reign in place of him,
and offered him for a burnt offering on the wall; and great wrath
came upon Israel, and they departed from him and returned to
their own land" (II Kings 3:27). It is freely admitted that the
meaning of the incident is obscure; but a process of elimination
indicates an interpretation.

First, the account cannot mean that "there was great wrath in
Israel" so that in disgust with the proceeding they went home.
Such meaning would have demanded a different Hebrew preposi-
tion. Besides, it is inconceivable why they should go home as a
result of "great wrath"; this would rather have roused them to
vengeance. Then, this wrath that came upon Israel and compelled
them to go home could not have emanated from the Moabite god,
for he was broken and overwhelmed: he had been doing his best,
apparently, in defense of his people, yet the Hebrew warriors continued victorious. Besides, these were operating in the name of
Yahweh; he could well be depended upon to deal effectively with
any bad temper on the part of defeated Chemosh. And it is out of
consideration that it was Yahweh's wrath that sent his people
home. Why should he have been stirred against his own armies by
a pagan act of a pagan king? There is no apparent escape from the
view that the "wrath" emanated from some source other than the
gods concerned. Further, this source was so mighty that the devotees of Yahweh, operating under notable marks of his approval
(vss. 9–20), abandoned their success at the moment when final vic-

tory was within reach, and went home. The sacrifice of the heir-apparent was a mighty magical rite, against which even Yahweh was impotent.

But, indeed, all this is less heretical from accepted "critical" views than may perhaps appear. For the concept of what we have come to call the taboo is just the thing we have been describing. There, too, a tendency existed to draw its operation into the realm of Yahweh's authority. The *herem* upon Jericho was pronounced in his name and was guarded by him (Josh. 6:17, 7:11–12). The temerity of Uzzah was punished by Yahweh himself (II Sam. 6:6–7). The sin of Nadab and Abihu brought consuming fire from him (Lev. 10:1–2). Yet it is but the orthodoxy of scholarly opinion that the realm of the holy was one of impersonal force that operated automatically and independent of divine volition. And the carry-over of such ideas into the priestly legislation, the natural custodian of concepts of and dealings with the occult, is well illustrated by such a ritual as that of the heifer whose neck was broken in an untilled valley where ran a perennial stream, every detail of which declares its magical character (Deut. 21:1–9). But, as is well known, magic persisted to find expressions in the Psalter likewise.

To recapitulate: there are various lines of evidence that Israel believed in the existence of a power supreme above gods and men, which could be employed in some undetermined measure by both, through rituals and formulas of the sort that we call magical. While not primarily ethical, it possessed qualities that are of some such implication. Its dominant feature was constancy. Over against the uncertainties of capricious deities, it was always the same. Those who knew how to employ it could always depend upon its effectiveness. One aspect of this approximates moral quality: it was guardian of the solemn agreement; this suggests the attribute of truth, but in reality it was probably no more than a manifestation of the constancy already mentioned.

Such as it may have been, then, here was Israel's simplest concept of natural law. It was a force operative upon gods and men which could enjoin truth and faithfulness to covenant. It did not compel, however; and, presumably, divine freedom was not impaired. One might freely ignore this world of force and shape his conduct indifferent to it. But, like a moral order in the universe, or like law in human society, it imposed inevitably the consequences of defiance, and through their unpleasantness induced conformity. Its remoteness from the orthodox faith and its intimate relation to earlier forms of belief declare themselves. Still it is to be noted that the divine oath, for example, was emphasized by the relatively late and highly developed Book of Deuteronomy. Further, manifestations of these beliefs are found in the prophets and in the ritual literature through various periods down to the close of the Old Testament. Thus it is clear that a certain dualism ran right through Israel's concept of the world. Side by side with a dominant and growing faith in the universal rule of Yahweh, there existed this belief in a realm of magic that lay outside his power. But, indeed, this is not remarkable, since precisely this situation persists to the present. Large numbers of more or less devout people, and even certain branches of the church, cling to beliefs and practices which are essentially magical and hence deny the supremacy of God. So while we recognize a contradiction in Israel's thinking, here we can only trace the expression of the concept of a moral order in the world without trying to resolve the problem of how completely it commanded the best Hebrew thought. But certainly this growing sense of moral government was intimately a part of the faith in the universality of Yahweh's rule as a God of righteousness.

What Israel's original concept of government may have been, it is difficult to say. The earliest rule by the elders of the community and the essentially democratic freedom inherited from nomad society would seem to imply a respect for inherited custom and some more or less crude sense of justice. Certainly the traditions that are presented in the Old Testament as the early history of the nation reveal a sense of law beyond and supreme above mere individual whim. But the validity of such representation is precisely our problem. It carries some plausibility. But, on the other hand, the older strata in the Book of Judges, which are among our earliest genuinely historic sources for Hebrew society, provide disturbing considerations. A later writer generalizes about the period that "there was no king in Israel; every man did that which was right in his own eyes" (Judg. 21:25; cf. 18:1, 19:1), an explanation which, in its context, means nothing but social anarchy. And certainly the conduct of the Danites at Laish, their treatment of Micah, and the whole incident of the Levite's concubine and its sequel (Judges, chaps. 18–21) speak eloquently of a complete lack of moral restraint. The standard of conduct was desire, and the means to attain one's ends was physical, then political, power. The life of the strong was the happy life, since it was one of realized desire. The folk tale of Samson, whatever else it may originally have been intended to teach, certainly expresses an ideal of the time; he was such a one as the writer wished he might have been: able to buffet and toss about his foes, to make sport of their retribution and plots, to take what he would, and consort with harlots at his desire. Such was a real life for a man! And there clearly we have the "natural law" of the time of the Judges: it was the law of the jungle.

We may not suppose that these heroes themselves critically evaluated and, with ethical self-consciousness, chose such courses. But Israel's thought on the problem certainly dates far back into an early period, for even in these stories, notably those of Samson and of Abimelech, judgment is passed upon their principals' conduct. But it was in a later age that thinkers set this sort of "natural law" over against principles of equity and voiced their condemnation. Yet for the time of the Judges, we may with confidence assert the prevalent thought was that might constituted the one socially valid norm, qualified only by the restraining magical powers of the oath (Judg. 21:1–7) and certain established usages, such as blood revenge, and also possibly some tribal and family custom. We may still refuse to accept this view in its completeness; doubtless our understanding of the beginnings of Israel's religion compels the postulation of better ideals even through this rough period. But the evidence is such that we must then conclude that they were an esoteric concept practically impotent for society as a whole.

Nor can we trace the causes and the course of evolution of a public sense of law but only point out a few relevant facts. Israel inherited the law of the Canaanites, and her life among their relatively cultured communities must have exerted a moderating influence upon primitive violence. The kingship, too, in spite of the obloquy it receives from certain biblical writers, clearly entailed a national law that all must recognize. Such is the implication of the comment on the period of the Judges just now quoted; such, too, is the impression we derive from glimpses of David's judicial administration. It is significant, also, that in this period we find voiced a strong sense of the restraining power of social practice and norms: "It is not so done in Israel" (II Sam. 13:12).

Yet it must be recognized that the supremacy of positive law was deeply imbedded in Israel's concept of the monarchy. Since the kingship was historically a projection of the rule of the Judges, it was inevitable that an ideal of the finality of power should carry over into the conduct of the kings. Such is the summary of royal prerogatives attributed to Samuel when the people proposed a monarchy; he warned, "the king . . . . will take your sons and appoint them to himself for his chariots and to be his horsemen, and they shall run before his chariots. . . . . He will take your daughters to be perfumers and cooks and bakers. He will take your fields and your vineyards and your olive yards, the best of them, and give them to his servants" (I Sam. 8:11–12). The passage, it is recognized, is late, but its evidence for the character of the Hebrew monarchy is not less reliable, for this is how we see it actually working itself out. The oriental ideal of the absolute monarch who "could do no wrong" invaded Israel's court in the days of David, if, indeed, it was not already manifest under Saul; it became supreme through Solomon's reign; it was the impelling principle in Rehoboam's folly at Shechem (I Kings 12:14). And though it suffered a solemn check in the revolt of the northern tribes, yet even these devotees of freedom soon found themselves under a ruling class even more irresponsible than that in Jerusalem. We need here cite only the Naboth incident (I Kings, chap. 21) and recall the social oppression against which the prophets of the eighth century spoke to realize that Israel, north and south alike, gave itself officially to the theory that power is irresponsible, since it is the ultimate source of law. The political aspect of this and the struggle for responsible government we must postpone for a later section; our interest now is to see how completely positive law possessed the ruling classes in the two kingdoms.

Two incidents of the period of the kings are highly significant of thought in the time. They are the Bath-sheba and the Naboth episodes. In their highhanded indifference to human rights and in their bold arrogation of absolute royal authority, they are intimately related. But both are highly important also as steps in the rise of Israel's sense of a higher law, for in both a prophet intervened to rebuke the monarch in the name of the Lord. More simply, he denied the king's claim of final authority and announced instead the supremacy of the will of the Lord, a law that bound the reigning monarch not less than his humblest subject.

This is the background of the work of Amos, whose significance for this line of Israel's thought has already been suggested. We saw that his enlarged concept of the nature and authority of God evidently was rooted in a feeling of common human rights, pervasive beyond the political and religious boundaries of the time. This principle was for him embodied in the person of the God of Israel. But in at least one notable passage he implies the existence of such a force for good existing in and of itself. He says: "Do horses run on the rock, or does one plow the sea, that you should turn justice into gall and the fruit of righteousness into wormwood; you who rejoice in a thing of naught and say, 'Have we not taken to us horns by our own strength?' " (6:12–13.) A certain propriety of conduct, he says, is freely recognized in common affairs, but in religious matters his contemporaries outrage the common sense of mankind with their moral and religious aberrations. Ordinary human good sense, he implies, ought to lead one to just conduct and right religious attitudes.

Israel's thought was in general so highly personalized, so fully drawn into the belief in a universal Person who pervaded all and was the moving force in all, that it is important, before we turn to examine the implications of this, to recognize fully the existence of a more humanistic concept of natural law, such as Amos entertained along with his deep faith in divine activity. Even more notable in this regard was the wrestle with the problem of theodicy, which, it is apparent, implies a standard independent of God and in some way beyond him—a standard to which his conduct is amenable just as that of man. It is scarcely necessary to mention that the Old Testament, particularly in its later expressions, was much concerned with this problem of the justice of God's rule of the world. Obviously it was paramount in the strange theology of Ecclesiastes. His God was judged by human standards of right and was found wanting. He had guarded his privileges in a most selfish way; further, his major concern seemed to be his own enjoyment, while man, striving and seeking, was circumvented at every turn by this cosmic might, and granted only minor concessions in order to keep him occupied. Man's chief concern in relations with him should be to guard his steps and be cautious of his words, for rash words may get one into untold trouble. Where Ecclesiastes found basis for his theory of ethics in such a philosophy is not stated, although it becomes apparent by careful study. True to the tradition of the wisdom movement, his thought was thoroughly humanistic, rooted in certain convictions as to the nature of the good life and the desirability of specific courses of conduct. He sought to know whether there was any good thing for man; and his conclusion was that the good thing was what would provide abiding satisfaction. So he gave himself to all sorts of conduct without let or hindrance from traditional scruples. Yet it is notable that through this experience, dominated as it seems to have been by a self-interest as crass as that which he ascribed to his God, he paid unconscious tribute to common social ideals of justice and humanity. He was concerned about the rampant injustice of his time, although he put the matter off with the reflection that nothing could be done, for the total of human misery was a constant quantity. He remarked on the selfish hierarchies of officials, each preying on the one below, and, finally, all on the poor peasant. He spoke with apparent censure of the ways of absolute monarchs, before whom subjects could only cringe and watch astutely for opportunity to serve themselves at their expense. By contrast he praised the poor but wise youth, fated to continue to the end in his lowly state, yet better than the powerful monarch whose self-serving would leave at his death not a single person to mourn his going. The wise man who delivered his city by his wisdom when military might had failed: there was something that Ecclesiastes could and did respect. He was a man of deep social feeling, which indeed was a fruitful source of his pessimism by reason of his despair of improving matters. Indeed, at this point he confronts the central problem of a theory of natural law, the existence of conflicting standards of conduct. These selfish rulers acted in accord with universal human impulses. But Ecclesiastes had no thought of commending them on this ground and condoning a return to conditions of the days of the Judges. For over against such norms of life there existed also an instinct for better things, a sense of justice rooted not less deeply in human nature. It would seem, then, that these concepts lie close to the basis of Ecclesiastes' whole system of thought. His norm was the common human feeling for justice, though only vaguely defined. By it God himself must submit to judgment.

But the treatment of this theme in the Book of Job is notable for its projection of the antithesis of might and right into the conduct of God himself. In varying expression this is found throughout the book. The speeches of Yahweh spend their eloquence in emphasis upon the irresponsible might of God. His power is such and the complexity of his working so far beyond human understanding that mere man may not question his ways. The inquiring spirit can in the end only confess his temerity:

> . . . . I have uttered that which I understood not,
> things too wonderful for me, which I knew not. . . . .
> Wherefore I abhor myself,
> and repent in dust and ashes [Job 42:3, 6].

The Elihu speeches are not far from the same position: God "giveth not account of any of his matters" (33:13). Still, these writers are not unconscious of the problem; they undertake to demonstrate that God will not do wickedness (34:10 ff.) and are shocked that Job, presumably, claims his righteousness to be greater than God's (35:2). In this regard, the Elihu speeches reveal the familiarity with the Dialogue for which they are well known. For Job's moral independence outraged the traditional piety of the friends. He refused to bow in contrition before transcendence; on the contrary, he asked insistently: "Why should God do this?" For him it would not suffice that absolute might sat enthroned at the center of the universe; such power must itself answer to common standards of equity, not less than the lowliest man. On this basis Job sought a meeting with his great adversary where he might argue the justice of the issue:

Behold now I have set my cause in order;
I know that I am righteous [Job 13:18].

Even more to the point is his querulous taunt of cosmic might,
which he implied should be at least as just as man:

Is it good to thee that thou shouldst oppress,
that thou shouldst despise the work of thy hands?
Hast thou eyes of flesh,
or seest thou as man seest?
Are thy days as the days of man,
or thy years as man's days,
that thou inquirest after mine iniquity
and searchest after my sin
although thou knowest that I am not wicked?
But there is none that can deliver out of thy
hand [Job 10:3–7].

Such was Job's constant complaint: he had done no wrong, yet
affliction came upon him. Little wonder that his bold spirit went the
full length in condemnation of divine irresponsibility before at
length he recoiled from his own excesses, realizing that his life was
not all recorded in terms of misery:

Thou hast granted me life and lovingkindness;
and thy visitation hath preserved my spirit [Job 10:12].

Yet at the depth of his black mood he exceeds even Ecclesiastes in
denunciation of an unethical God:

As for strength: he is mighty;
as for justice: who can call him to account?
I am upright; I do not regard myself;
I despise my own life.
It is all one! Therefore I say
upright and wicked alike he consumes [Job 9:19, 21–22].

But the great difference between Job and Ecclesiastes was that the
former clung to his faith and worked through to a reasoned position where he could hold that the principles of right which he
honored as a man rule correspondingly in the conduct of God.

Yet it will be apparent that, however attractive such views may
have proved for the philosophic temper of the wise men, the great
mass of Israel's thought, if we may judge by the prominence given

it in the literature, went on the conviction that the source of ethics was in the nature and will of God. And the nexus of the two seemingly contradictory views is revealed by the great thinker to whom we have already frequently turned—the author of chapter 8 of the Book of Proverbs. In his concept of wisdom as the vitalizing power in man's restless urge toward better things, which yet was with God before creation and by him was implanted in the nature of things, there is, we have noted, the clear implication that in such wisdom man gains his truest insight into the essential nature of God. The Hebrew philosopher would have agreed heartily with Socrates in an answer to the latter's famous question. Right was not right because God willed it; he willed it because it was right. For his nature was righteousness.

It is, then, along the line of the growing concept of the universality of the rule of Yahweh and the enlarging of ethical thinking within Israel's religion that we are to trace the advance of a sense of universal standards of right. And the triumph of this concept, apparent in the prophets' condemnation of injustice within Israel, is nowhere better manifested than in the revulsion they felt toward the irresponsibility of the aggressive empires. Isaiah held up to scorn the boast of the Assyrian:

> By the strength of my hands I have done it,
>   and by my wisdom, for I have understanding.
> And I have removed the bounds of peoples
>   and their treasures I have robbed;
>   and as a mighty one I have brought down those en-
>   throned
> My hand has found, like a nest,
>   the wealth of the peoples;
> and as one gathers eggs hidden away
>   all the earth have I gathered.

But:

> Does an ax boast against the hewer,
>   or a saw make itself greater than its user? . . . .
> Therefore will the Lord send
>   upon his fat ones leanness [Isa. 10:13–16].

Not less effective is the brief note of Habakkuk in his account of the violent aggression of the Chaldean foe, the culmination of whose reprehensibility was that

from himself proceed his standards of right and dignity . . . .
that reprobate, whose own might is his god! [Hab. 1:7, 11.]

It is important to realize that in these concepts Israel's thought
of natural law attained its characteristic form. The notion of a
universal directive force, perhaps impersonal, but in any case independent of the power of the Lord, was but incidental. Emphasis
upon it has been necessary in order to insure it adequate attention
as a genuine phase of the total of Hebrew thought and to show the
measure of its ultimate attainment; for the conviction that Israel
regarded the world and all within it as dependent upon the will and
activity of God has become axiomatic in our minds to the exclu-
sion of other possibilities. Nor is this a serious error, for the outstanding aspect of Israel's thinking about the world was its per-
sonalism; and not least in their thought of a universal law valid and
operative in the lives of men did the Hebrew thinkers postulate the
personal reality and activity of their God. The supremacy of this
faith among the prophets is obvious. But likewise it was the view
of the wise men. The "wisdom of God," of which they made so
much, was not a detached, impersonal entity; it had emanated from
God: more simply, it was God himself at work among men.

This, indeed, is the distinctive contribution of Israel's thinkers
to the discussion of natural law. For them it was not an irresponsible force that in some blind way, however benignly, influenced human impulses. It was God in his holiness and righeousness revealing to sinful man his will and their high destiny and only happiness
in obedience thereto. From this there resulted all that is characteristic of Hebrew ethics: its white heat of urgency, but also its tran-
scendentalism that set righteousness far beyond human attainment
yet held it as a compelling ideal toward which one must strive and
aspire. The moral passion of the prophets has become axiomatic;
they were concerned with human well-being, it is true, but no such
urgency of appeal could have arisen from human considerations.
The compelling force that took possession of them "with strength
of hand" was the holiness of a personal God who was very near
and who sat in judgment upon the unrighteousness of man. And
this for Israel was natural law! It was something more than a
"supreme unifying, controlling power manifesting itself in the
universe at large." It was God himself in his supremacy and holiness saying, "This is the way; walk ye therein."

The role of this concept in shaping positive legislation as well as in criticism of existing laws will be immediately apparent. Nonetheless, it is a noteworthy fact that, until comparatively late times, ethical speculation and sanctions had no recourse to codified law. The ultimate source of right and justice reposed in unwritten codes: more plainly, in the instincts and impulses that stir in the hearts of men. Doubtless the monarchs and other practical folk were ready in citation of the codified legislation of the land, but, for those who gave thought to the matter, the final rule of the hearts of men lay far deeper in a universal norm. The function of this in the legal history of Israel is evident in the work of the prophets. It stirred, too, as an uneasy conscience in the several reforms of the period of the monarchy, even if these were largely cultic. Also, the Book of Deuteronomy is, per se, eloquent testimony to the reality of the movement, for, though it purports to be a "second law," it was in reality a revision of the ancient social legislation that in considerable part Israel had taken over from the Canaanites. So we may safely conclude that an independent attitude of criticism toward the law of the land was widespread among thoughtful men. But, excellent as this is for our present purpose, a further issue forces itself upon the attention. Natural law can exist at all only if it is universal. The crux of the problem is how far Israel's thinkers applied their accepted standards to the laws of foreign nations, or believed that among those peoples there was a stirring such as manifested itself in Israel's own thought.

Investigation of the question is beset with the obvious difficulty that Israel's writers were primarily concerned with Israelite standards and conduct; to the life and thought of foreigners they gave but minor attention. But at least the first eleven chapters of Genesis promise material for our purpose. The heroes and other characters of this narrative may in some measure have been regarded as remote ancestors, but certainly they were not Israelites; and from the stories certain relevant facts stand out. The authors have not the least doubt that God was known among these non-Hebraic peoples, through revelation of a sort similar to or identical with that later given to Israel. His will was their ultimate law, upholding those standards later established in Hebrew society. Cain should not have killed Abel; the rampant "violence" of the time of the flood cried out to high heaven for retribution; the life and conduct of Noah was a standing rebuke to his contemporaries; the builders of the Tower of Babel were guilty of arrogance; etc. Further, the distribution of the peoples of the earth is represented as being in accord with divine purposes; even if not ethically determined, at least it was an expression of that impulse which the writers believed to be the ultimate authority in human life.

Comparable are the results that may be deduced from accounts of Israel's relations with foreign powers. The Egyptians should not have oppressed the Hebrews; the hard labor of the slaves raised a cry to heaven which in turn brought divine retribution in the plagues and the incidents of the Exodus. The lawless oppressions of the Assyrians and Chaldeans were denounced; these peoples outraged all human standards—and made a virtue of it. And for the smaller nations near Palestine, the threats contained in the first and second chapters of the Book of Amos took their rise in a reaction against unhuman conduct; these peoples had practiced barbarities against helpless neighbors, they had forgotten "the brotherly covenant," they had enslaved whole peoples, they had been implacable in their hatreds. On the other hand, the implications of the Servant Songs, and of passages that picture a great movement of Gentile peoples to Jerusalem for worship, as well as the claim in the Book of Malachi that from the rising of the sun to its going-down the Lord's name was great among the Gentiles, all alike indicate recognition of a common human bond among all peoples that rendered foreigners amenable to the same high appeals and impulses as native Hebrews. It will be recognized that we lack formal discussion by Israel's thinkers of the universality of basic ethical standards; to that extent we are doubtless justified in concluding that the problem was not fully realized. But at least it is clear that they assumed, even if uncritically, the world-wide rule of those standards of right which they themselves honored. The words of Paul again may be quoted as expressive of his people's traditional thinking: "For the wrath of God is revealed from heaven against all unrighteousness of men . . . . because that which is known of God is manifest in them, for God manifested it unto them."

Yet the problem of natural law looks in still another direction, for within Palestine, through the centuries of Israel's occupation, there were notably two groups that provide test cases of Hebrew consistency; they were the foreign immigrants and the slaves. The underprivileged condition of both is apparent to every casual reader of the Old Testament. Of the former, however, it can be affirmed that progressive thought refused to leave them to the whims of popular bigotries and suspicions. The concern of the authors of Deuteronomy for the "sojourner" is a notable feature of the book. The prophets likewise urged consideration and fellow-feeling toward this noncitizen populace. But it was the Priestly document that took the final step of legislating equal rights and equal responsibilities for the *gerim:* "You shall have one law for the home-born and for the stranger who sojourns among you" (Exod. 12:49). The late date commonly ascribed to this legislation and its high authority in post-Exilic Judaism raise the prescription to a high significance.

The problem of the slave is not so easily handled; for the thinking of today, the widespread and legalized practice of slavery constitutes a very black stain on the social attainments of ancient Israel. And, to make the matter worse, no protest was raised against the institution per se, demanding the equal freedom of all men. Jeremiah, for example, was indignant because recently liberated slaves were illegally repossessed, but he says not a word to the effect that their ever having lost their freedom was a mark of the iniquity of his contemporaries (Jer. 34:8–22). Yet the facts are not so damning as all this may suggest. Slavery in the primitive days of Israel's history had humane features. The foreign slave, who was generally a captive in war, owed his life to the institution; apart from it he would almost certainly have been slaughtered at the time of his people's defeat. The enslavement of Hebrews had an economic basis; one accepted slavery when he could no longer win a livelihood. The condition insured at least subsistence, and to this extent it may be considered, like the institution of blood revenge, a progressive social measure for its time.

The ethics of Old Testament slavery thus depended in large measure upon the character of the slaveowner; and there is abundant evidence to show that, in general, the slave enjoyed a status far above what the term suggests to us. Social distinctions are moderated in the simple, immediate relations of rural life. Master and slave, associated together as they were in tasks and adventures in the field, developed some sense of comradeship. A revealing incident, frequently cited in the study of Hebrew slavery, is that of Saul's consultation with his slave when the two had been for several days searching for lost asses; and it was the slave, not Saul, who had money in his possession to pay a fee to the "man of God." On the other hand, there were, as always, brutal masters who on occasion beat their slaves even to the point of death.

But the important matter is that Israel's conscience did not lie supine under these conditions. Legislation was enacted to protect the slave, and in the great legal revision represented by our Book of Deuteronomy these provisions received notable strengthening. But even more indicative of a Hebrew conscience toward this matter is the ground ascribed for such consideration: "You shall remember that you were a slave in the land of Egypt, and the Lord your God brought you out." "Keep the sabbath day . . . . that your male slave and your female slave may rest as well as you." It is to be observed that provision is not specifically for fellow-Hebrews but for any slave.

And its *raison d'être* expresses clearly a sense of common human unity: briefly, a respect for fellow-humans as persons. Beyond this, Hebrew thought on slavery did not go. But it is to be recognized that in this attainment there lay the germ of all future advance. While admitting freely Israel's failure to repudiate slavery, there are then three points to be kept in mind: Hebrew slavery was relatively humane; it was regulated and guarded with increasingly humanitarian legislation; and, third, the slave was recognized as possessing certain inalienable rights on the grounds of his being human. The situation was such that we need not hesitate to include it as an aspect of Israel's thought of natural law.

In course of time that body of literature which we know as the Pentateuch assumed its final shape, and apparently by the fourth century B.C. was "canonized," that is, it was accepted as of divine origin and authority. Through the various circumstances that determined its composition there were included certain social codes and much ritual direction, both of which had enjoyed a long history and operation. But now they were endowed with a halo of sanctity. For devout thought, all alike became *ipsissima verba* of the will and revelation of God and, as such, of ultimate authority over human conduct. In this fact, then, we are to see the confluence of the two streams of Israel's law and the termination of the antithesis that marks this line of thinking. Living under foreign rule as they did, subject also to the whims of fallible leaders of their own, the Jews never escaped, in actuality, the problem of positive law; but, for orthodox thought, in the Pentateuch natural law had absorbed and sublimated positive law.

Still, the concept of the unwritten law and its authority continued. It found notable expression in the oral tradition that eventually was codified in the Mishnah. Criticism may smile indulgently at the palpable deception in the claim that this was given to Moses at Sinai along with the Torah, but if we would read the meaning of figurative language, it is apparent that this was but an expression of the sense of a pervasive natural law: the religious impulse and revelation with which the name of Moses was associated was too great to embody itself in written form—not even the Torah was adequate; but it reposed ultimately in the divine impress upon the heart of man. Even in the Old Testament itself, and apparently from a period when the Torah had attained sanctity in Jewish thought, the supremacy of the unwritten law is notably expressed. There are several passages which voice the hope for the future that Israel should then be cleansed of its propensity to sin and transformed into a righteous nation. The following is especially deserving of attention:

> Behold the days come, saith the Lord, when I will make a new covenant with the house of Israel, and with the house of Judah, not according to the covenant that I made with their fathers. . . . . but this is the covenant that I will make with the house of Israel after those days, saith the Lord: I will put my law in their inward parts and in their hearts I will write it; and I will be their God, and they shall be my people. And they shall teach no more every man his neighbor and his brother saying, Know the Lord; for they shall all know me from the least unto the greatest of them [Jer. 31:31–34].

The law written on the heart, not an external law, should rule men's lives. But it would be a gracious rule: not compulsion, not an infringement of man's freedom but its fulfilment. Men would do the right because they most wished so to do. They would recognize the beauty of goodness, won by its inherent attractiveness. Here is the culmination of Israel's thought about natural law: a glorious day should dawn when man's jungle impulses would atrophy, when right would triumph deep in human nature, and society would pursue its happy course in a state of "anarchy," of "no law," because everyone would do the high and noble thing through his love for it, in obedience to the unwritten law inscribed on his heart!

There remains yet one difficult problem of this line of thinking. When the Torah was canonized and the law of God thus became ostensibly the law of the land, there could be no clash between conscience and authority. Yet it is apparent that such a situation never became an actuality of Israel's life. Even in the period when Jerusalem was under the high priests, the Jews were nonetheless subject to foreign rule; and even if we concede for the sake of argument what notably was not true, that all the officials of the theocracy were high-minded men, still the people were never remote from the problem of what to do in face of a bad law. And even more was this true of earlier ages. A devout answer is immediately at hand. In the words of the apostles faced with some such dilemma, one "ought to obey God rather than man."

Yet the issue is not quite so simple. Paul formulated the crux of it in his seemingly antithetic saying that "the powers that be are ordained of God." Apparently the words of Jesus relative to payment of tribute bear a similar interpretation. "Render unto Caesar the things of Caesar." Both imply recognition that government performs an indispensable function. Without ordered society the bare essentials of civilized life are not possible. Even a bad government provides some measure of security and settled procedure. What then? Are we to weaken the pillars of society by a course of flagrant disobedience of laws that we consider wrong? Or shall we take the opposite course and outrage conscience by supporting a wicked government in the interests of stability? Is there a middle course, and what and where are its bounds?

The revolts instigated by the prophets, notably that of the northern tribes in the time of Rehoboam and of Jehu a century later, were frank acceptance of one horn of the dilemma: direct action for the overthrow of an evil ruler is in harmony with the will of God. But it is notable that subsequent thought repudiated this policy and sought reform within ordered society. The Maccabean revolt, commendable as it seems to us, was likewise given scant honor by the contemporary author of Daniel; it was only "a little help."

This comment may suggest the answer which Hebrew thought finally accepted. For it is apparent that, in repudiating the prowess of Judas and his outlaws, the writer looks rather for divine deliverance. And certainly this is in harmony with the entire apocalyptic movement and with most of the later political thought as it is expressed in the Old Testament. The Lord stirred up the spirit of Cyrus to deliver his people; he showed mercy by inclining the hearts of the kings of Persia to the needs of the Jews in Judea. On the other hand, Daniel and his companions in the Babylonian court "purposed in their heart that they would not defile themselves"; the three who refused to worship the great image were thrown into the furnace. Daniel himself continued his daily devotions in the face of royal prohibition; and in every case deliverance and advancement came to the faithful by supernatural means.

The conclusion is fairly clear. Jewish thought favored an honest acceptance of government, whatever it might be, and loyal conformity to promulgated law, but only within the limits of Jewish conscience. Where law and religion clashed, then the Jew was to honor his religious duty at whatever cost, encouraged, it may be, with the belief that this course would prove in the end wisest even from the practical point of view. Yet such conformity to the rule of government did not mean indifference to public standards of right. But change of government, in that age when it could be brought about humanly only through violence, was regarded as properly in the hands of God. He set up kings and he removed kings in accord with his eternal purposes. One must endure evil days sustained by the conviction that it was the will of God. And, at the worst, oppression was but a transient affair, for soon the kingdom of the saints would be established.

At this point there emerges one of the notable features of Israelite literature and thought, its treatment of history. A moment's consideration shows that history is the theme which permeates the Old Testament almost throughout: history told from a determined point of view and with a set purpose, but, nonetheless, great history. Even such ostensibly prophetic works as the apocalypses may be regarded as of historic temper, for their concern is with the course of mundane affairs. The theme of the Hebrew historian, it is true, is Israel's career, but this is told in a world setting. In a limited way it is world history to which the Hebrew writers introduce us; indeed, the first ten chapters of Genesis attempt nothing less than an account of the entire human career through its early ages, and they culminate in a survey of the peopling of the whole known world of the writers' times. From this point onward the story narrows to that of Israel, yet, whether by the demands of the narrative or through the writers' interests, the reader is kept conscious of the movement of affairs in the world beyond Palestine. Through a long section the immediate background is Egyptian history; and the proximity and importance of Egypt echo repeatedly through the subsequent story. The little neighbors of Israel take their place in the account. Presently Assyria becomes the dominating theme, then Babylonia and Persia and the Macedonian kingdoms. A recent popular treatment of the "science of history" gives three features of modern historical method. The historian, it says, undertakes "to ascertain his facts, to explain them, and to give them significance by fitting them into a general scheme." This third was richly exemplified by the Hebrew historians. Their theme is Israel's history in Israel's world. And it is deserving of remark that in this they were bringing into existence a new thing. Only in a remote way as expressed in certain myths had civilization to this time witnessed anything of this sort. And notwithstanding the repute of Herodotus and the subsequent Greek historians, one goes all the way to Nicholaus of Damascus to find anything deserving of comparison with this aspect of Hebrew historiography, and even then the famed "Universal History" is too little known for us to assess its advantages, if any. And we should remember that Nicholaus was an Oriental! It will bear consideration whether later interest in world history is not directly the heir and consequence of the Old Testament. The importance attained by the Old Testament in Western thought through the medium of Christianity provides a connection which raises the question well out of the region of the absurd.

The limitations of Hebrew history-writing as judged by present-day standards are fully apparent. Notably it is lacking in a sense of economic and social forces. Its perspective is badly out of balance at times, relating colorful personal incidents at length while dismissing briefly, or even omitting entirely, events of major importance. But no one, himself possessing a sense of historic development, will long delay over these failings; rather he will give generous praise that, beginning something new in human culture as these men did, they achieved such excellence.

Probably the weakest point in their procedure was the treatment of sources, specifically their deficiency of critical appraisal. Some of them wrote of their own times, relating events which they knew in large part at first hand; others made use of written sources, which they have frequently cited by name; elsewhere the account relates oral traditions, the nature and source of which we can only speculate upon. Excellent as is much of the result—even that based on tradition has earned a higher respect than was once conceded it —nowhere do we find the writers passing critical judgment on their sources and rejecting the improbable or unattested. This may be due to their method; as in other expressions of Israel's thinking, it may be that they prefer to omit all reference to procedure and center attention on results. Yet the indiscriminate relating of the miraculous and even legendary in the Elijah and Elisha stories, for example, along with patently reliable accounts such as the episode of Naboth's vineyard or the Battle of Ramoth Gilead, indicates rather a failure to distinguish. On the other hand, fairness demands that we recognize the straightforward naturalism which characterizes contemporaneous histories such as the memoirs of Nehemiah and the account of David's reign. Their freedom from wonder elements and mythical elements sets them apart from much oriental narrative. It is apparent that here the writers limit themselves to what they knew to be rigidly true. Such also, it is clear, is the method in the greater part of the court history in the Books of Kings. In these passages we see Hebrew history-writing in its highest attainment.

And certainly if for a moment one turn from the science to the art of the historian, these authors must be accorded a place among the best, save only for a deficiency of the sort already mentioned—

some weakness in scope and balance. All alike manifest that high feeling for narrative which is the remarkable quality of the Hebrew literary genius. Hebrew historiography is marked by an instinct for essentials of the human story, a psychological insight, a sense of the dramatic, and a feeling for individuals in the movement of history that infuses dry and sometimes drab events with the quality of a good story. And all together compound into history as it ought to be written!

But it is the historian's work as expression of his thinking with which we are now primarily concerned. And Hebrew history is rich in relevant results. Of Israel's sense of significance in history it may well be remarked that to maintain such an attitude is to survey life *sub specie aeternitatis.* Here was no engrossment in the moment but full recognition that human life is a great stream of which the present is only the realized moment; its long course stretches out of the far past into an eternal future. Such a concept sets the individual and the nation in a perspective which at once humbles and exalts. It was no accident that the supremely religious peoples of all time were likewise our first great historians.

It will seem a case of laboring the obvious to remark that, for Israel, history was reality, a comprehensive reality that raised it to the highest importance. Yet certain trends in recent thinking absolve the comment of mere verbosity. Israel knew nothing of a suprahistorical plane where the true reality of events was being enacted, while all below was sham and make-believe. There was a realm of suprahuman reality, they would have affirmed, that periodically in notable fashion and perpetually in more normal ways was breaking into the stream of human events and shaping them. But all this by its occurrence became historical; it was a part of man's career, rather of the story of God and man, for that was the Hebrew's concept of history. And all that happened on this earth, whether events which an uncritical piety ascribed to divine intervention or at the other extreme the machinations of the wicked —all alike were part of the long stream of man's experience and of importance as taking a place in the ultimate shaping and ultimate meaning of man's life and God's purposes. The naturalism of the Hebrew mind is nowhere more manifest than in his realistic attitude to history.

Just there was the crux of the matter for Israel's thought: history had meaning. On this ground it contained important lessons for current life. The wise men deduced their teachings from it; and religious thinkers of one school or another recounted the nation's past for the value it could contribute toward shaping the future. Some of the defects of the historian's method are traceable to the fact that his interest was not so much in recording events as in explaining them. And such a temper can mean only one thing: Hebrew history was primarily a philosophy of history.

Such evaluation of our Book of Judges is very familiar. The so-called "Deuteronomic framework," in which the successive stories of ancient heroes is set, reiterates that Israel's political difficulties in those turbulent days were directly due to the nation's religious infidelity. But this is not all, nor even the most significant part, of the Hebrew philosophy of history. It becomes apparent that all—the story of primeval man, the experiences of the patriarchs, the Egyptian episode, the conquest, and on through age after age to the closing years of the Old Testament period, when the great empires pass in hasty survey in the symbolic imagery of the Book of Daniel and events hasten on to their culmination in the kingdom of the saints—all is related as possessing a meaning which the authors imply they have grasped and on occasion are not unwilling to divulge.

We have been obliged frequently in this study to remark on the uniqueness and originality of Israel's achievement. If the comment should grow tedious, we must blame, first of all, the Hebrews themselves that they were a people of such vigorous independence. For once again the remark is in order. In Israel's philosophy of history there entered human culture a new idea that was destined to have far-reaching results all the way down to our own days. It was new in its attainment of a level elevated beyond parallel, although Professor Jacobsen has pointed out to me that the beginnings of such thinking can be traced in Babylonia. But philosophy of history as the Hebrews conceived and developed it had never been known in all the centuries of the great civilizations which preceded them. And it long remained uniquely Israel's contribution to the course of thought, for Herodotus' attempt is scarcely more impressive than that of the Babylonians; nor do his successors in

Greece or Rome rise to the level of rivalry. But through Euse-
bius this heritage of the Old Testament came at length to the
Western world and, in the course of time, to its notable development in the interest and thought of our own times.

The objectives of the Hebrew philosophers of history were to
discover principles which determine the course of events so that
these might serve as guides for their contemporary world. The similarity of this to the studies of the wise men shows the error of
separating the Hebrew intellectual world into rigid compartments.
Israel's thought life was one and indivisible.

These principles of history were of two sorts. On one side were
the will and purpose of God; over against him was man with his
purposes and his independence. The two commonly clashed, and
never were they in complete harmony. History, then, was to be
explained in the ebb and flow of these forces. So far, so good. But,
on the human side of this rivalry, the statement seems to say nothing at all, for everyone recognizes that man's striving for the
things he wants, subject only to some weight of circumstance, has
molded the course of events. But the Hebrew scholars carried the
analysis further. Man's purposes were a chaos of ambition, revenge, lust of power, economic needs and the demands of security,
along with much magnanimity, ethical idealism, consideration for
the weak and underprivileged, and a whole range of desire and conduct gathered loosely under the term "righteousness." Out of this
medley of purpose came the uncertain results of individual, national, and social achievement and the long story of civilization in
its totality. But God's purposes were one. Also, God was righteous
and God was supreme. Here is the great conviction of Israel's
thinkers. History is not the meaningless clash of human passion
that it may sometimes seem or yet the plaything of blind force;
God is ruler of all, and he is shaping events to his far-off purpose.
Through the strange interplay of human freedom and divine sovereignty which the Hebrew thinkers affirmed, he was molding human life to his own will. History is a tale of progress! The Hebrew philosophers would have made no delay in answering the
moot question of today, "Is progress a reality of human history?"
For them the answer was clear and obvious. The course was devious; the stream frequently turned back upon its general course;

there were eddies and cross-currents, backwaters and pools; nonetheless, the stream flowed onward toward its determined end. Human perversity might delay the divine plan; it could not defeat it. But ever since the world was, God has been working his supreme purpose; and it will surely come. Though it tarry, one must wait for it; for the vision is for the appointed time—and the just shall live by his faith.

The eternal purpose was realizing itself through men chosen of God: more strictly men who, like Isaiah, heard the divine challenge, "Whom shall I send and who will go for us?" and then responded, "Here am I; send me." Through them there came into existence the chosen nation; but even within its history the same process went on of divine selection and, in case of unworthiness, of rejection. The supremacy of God was such that he could use even the devices of the wicked to further his ends. Assyria in all its imperial pomp served but as the tool in divine hands. And the other arrogant powers, of whatever name, one after another while boasting their might, were but tolerated to give way at length before the rule of God. History was moving on to a glorious culmination.

It is one of the astonishing features of Hebrew thought that a nation who suffered as they did, who on several occasions almost perished under brutal conquerors and oppressors, yet were supremely an optimistic people. They never lost hope. Jeremiah, buying a field and carefully laying away the deed at the height of the Babylonian invasion of Judah, is a true symbol of his people. For in dreary days they shaped their glowing dreams. They held stubbornly to the conviction that beyond the time of trying there lay an age when Jerusalem should become the city of righteousness, the faithful town, and Zion should be redeemed with justice. Though the present was in the grip of circumstance as stern as though ruled by a great beast, yet if one would but look with understanding, he could see in anticipation the beast slain and its body destroyed and given to be burned; and then sovereignty and dominion and the greatness of the kingdom under the whole heaven would be given to the people of the saints of the Most High—"his kingdom is an everlasting kingdom and all dominions shall serve and obey him."

It may not be denied that many of these dreams of the future are cast in a nationalistic frame. The kingdom of the saints was to be a kingdom of Jewish saints. And the glorious culmination of all history, for too many a dreamer of the ancient ghettoes, was to consist in Jewish rule of the world, conceived, it must be admitted, in typically imperialistic terms:

> Thy gates, also, shall be open continually;
>> they shall not be shut day or night,
> that men may bring unto thee the wealth of the nations . . . .
> for that nation and kingdom that will not serve thee shall
>> perish,
> yea those nations shall be utterly wasted [Isa. 60:11–12].

Yet we must bear in mind two facts: the Old Testament by virtue of the diversity of its authorship—in less agreeable terms, the spurious origin of very many of its passages—is a cross-section of the total mind of Israel, high and low alike; but the significant matter is not how some of these thinkers conformed to the ideals of their world but rather the astonishing way in which many of them transcended it. We shall have occasion presently to note the height to which their universalistic hopes attained. However particularistic certain passages may show themselves in their concept of the future and the culmination of the historic process, we must read them in their total context and as illumined and sublimated by the ideals of men of wide vision who were actually the point of significance in ancient Israel. Stripped of their imagery, then, and interpreted in their truest Israelite context, the Old Testament dreams of the end of history mean simply that human life is a progress to better things. Ultimately right will triumph and will be the rule and law of all mankind.

CHAPTER XI

NATION, SOCIETY, AND POLITICS

THE Israelites thought of themselves as a nation centered about a fusion of the ideas of their common ancestry and of the covenant with their God. Neither of these is as simple as it might appear. According to the tradition, God had called Abraham from Ur of the Chaldees, had led him to Palestine, and there had promised him a numerous offspring who should become a mighty nation and possess the land in which he was then a foreigner. The promise was renewed on various occasions, notably in the great experience at Sinai, and its character as a covenant with dual responsibilities became clear. In simplest terms, Israel was to be the people of Yahweh, and he was to be their God. Their allegiance implied rejection of all other gods and service of him alone in ritual and in national and social obedience. On the other hand, he, as their God, was responsible to fulfil the promise to give them the land, to make them a great people, and to bestow upon them material bounty, physical well-being, and spiritual content.

But difficulty arises when one seeks to trace these ideas back into the nation's early history. Once more exploring the evidence of the old sources in the Book of Judges, to our astonishment we find neither of these supposedly basic notions of Israel's common life. Unquestionably there was some unifying bond among the clans and tribes of that time; equally it had resemblances to both these ideas; yet it was far short of either. Israel's sense of a common interest by which various groups united in face of danger was evidently a conviction of essential unity such as would imply, especially for that time and region, a common ancestry. But nowhere is it mentioned, even in vague terms. It may be that the omission is due to circumstances which rob it of significance, yet the fact that the older sources in Samuel manifest the same oversight and that one goes on as far as the prophetic histories and then to the writing prophets for indubitable evidence of belief in a common ancestry strengthens the suspicion that things were not what later writers

326

would have us believe. Further, while the names "Israel" and "Jacob" are familiar designations for the nation and descent from Jacob is spoken of, mention of Abraham outside the Pentateuch is astonishingly rare until a quite late time. Since the old narrative documents incorporated in the Pentateuch commonly designated J and E, according to orthodox criticism were already in existence before the age of the prophets, it is strange that these writers should pass over the impressive account of Abraham's call and the promise to him. References to the nation's history commonly reach back to the oppression in Egypt and the Exodus, in some cases to the career of Jacob; but back of that all is blank. The meaning of this situation is difficult to appraise. One solution might be that the J-E stories of Abraham represent a little-known tradition which only through the growing prestige of the proto-Pentateuch won general acceptance about the time of the Exile, but familiarity with the story of Jacob was somewhat old.

However this may be, it is apparent that descent from Jacob could have been just as satisfactory as a basis of national coherence as an Abrahamic theory. Even accepting this presumably lesser view, complications are not yet at an end; for it was freely recognized by Hebrew writers that even this theory was threadbare; we are told in no uncertain terms that the nation was not of common ancestry. A great mixed multitude went with the Hebrews out of Egypt and clearly amalgamated with them. In the conquest large numbers of Canaanites were not exterminated—not even conquered; but the Canaanites dwelt with the various tribes to the day of the historian (Judg. 1:21 ff.). Eventually Solomon enslaved the last of them, but in the meantime the result of their living side by side was frequent intermarriage, as the laws make clear. Yet such mixing of the blood of Israel was not in defiance of public conscience; it was condoned and legalized. The story of Ruth the Moabitess is symbolic of a free intercourse which the ancient writer finds no basis for criticizing. The prohibition of admission of Ammonites and Moabites into the assembly of the Lord unto the tenth generation (Deut. 23:3) carries clear implication that they were acceptable after this long probation and that others came in more freely, as indeed is stated of Egyptians and Edomites in the sequel to this passage (vs. 8). Even the relatively late Priestly document provided that the sojourner who consented to be circumcised would be not alone permitted to eat the Passover but accepted as of the status of the native-born. The doors were thus thrown wide open to proselytizing, and its prevalence in the centuries about the beginning of the Christian Era is well known.

The implication is apparent. The Israelites recognized, just as modern historians also, that as a nation they were highly composite; lineal descent from Abraham or from Jacob was a pleasant fiction to which some central reality was attached, but it was in no sense the test of membership in the commonwealth of Israel. This depended rather on personal faith and conduct. The foreigner who submitted to circumcision and who manifested loyalty to Israel's faith and institutions became a good Israelite; to employ a famous phrase of a later writer, he was grafted into the stock of Abraham. Paul was once again expounding the best thought of his people when he distinguished between Israel after the flesh and after the spirit. In final essence membership in the nation Israel was a spiritual matter; it was a question of loyalty. A phrase in the Song of Deborah expresses the final essence of Israelite nationality: Israel was "the people of Yahweh."

The problem of the covenant is similar. It became so popular in later literature of the Old Testament that even critical scholars indorse the delusion that Israel from the first shaped its thought on the basis of a covenant with Yahweh. Yet the fact is that the idea is absent from early sources. The Song of Deborah speaks at the most, in the phrase just now quoted, of "the people of Yahweh" (Judg. 5:11). The word *brith* ("covenant") occurs, it is true, in an unquestionably early source in the Book of Judges; but it is in the name, or title, of the Shechemite god, Baal Berith (Judg. 8:33; 9:4). Yet this may not be invoked as collateral support of the idea of Israel's religious covenant, for the title may mean no more than that this god was patron and guardian of agreements. More to the point is the occurrence of the word in connection with Israel's sacred ark in the account of the capture of this by the Philistines (I Sam. 4:3–5) and of its transfer to Jerusalem in David's reign (II Sam. 6:17). Yet this is meager and questionable evidence for the theological idea commonly postulated. Specific

mention of Israel's covenant with Yahweh occurs first in the
Book of Hosea, two of which allusions are evidently genuine
(Hos. 6:7; 8:1). The idea is absent from Isaiah and Micah but
is referred to a number of times in the utterances of Jeremiah;
then, as is well known, it becomes one of the great emphases of
Deuteronomy. When we recall that Hosea lived not long after
the ascribed dates of composition of the J and E documents, the
situation becomes relatively clear. The notion of a covenant between God and Israel was introduced by these "prophetic histories"; it was indorsed by Hosea, adopted by Jeremiah, and in
Deuteronomy became an essential element of Israel's theology.

But the objection obtrudes itself that specific mention is not the
whole story, for the covenant is implicit in much of the early
thought: in the rallying of the tribes in Yahweh's name in the time
of the Judges, in their consciousness as "the people of Yahweh,"
and much else of the sort. To this one can but give hearty assent.
Certainly the J and E writers and their successors who made so
much of the idea did not create it out of pure imagination. The
concept was implicit from a very early period. But such implication sets the whole notion on a very different basis from that usually
ascribed. For it destroys the uniqueness of Israel's claim and
makes the notion of divine covenant a normal feature of oriental
religious thought. The relation of Yahweh to the scattered tribes
of the Judges' time was, so far as we can see, purely that of the
national god. There is no reason to postulate any essential difference at this time between the attitude of Israel to her God and that
of Moab or Ammon or Edom or any other nation to Chemosh,
Milcom, or whatever other appropriate deity. The idea of a national god carried in it the concept of a covenant between the god
and his people. It was Israel's uniqueness to develop this into the
notable form and religious worth of her doctrine of the divine
covenant. This became in turn a very powerful motivation; nonetheless, the covenant was secondary in Israel's religious and ethical
evolution.

Somewhere along this line of development of the pagan national
god idea into the ethical doctrine of the covenant there entered the
concept of the divine choice of Israel that was destined to become
the distinctive feature of the nation's thought of itself. Again we

are to see it as implicit ever since the simplest forms of the belief in a national god; but, like the covenant idea itself, it attained an exaltation such as to make of it a new thing. The simplest statement, and perhaps the original, of the doctrine is the story of the divine call of Abraham (Genesis, chap. 12); but altogether its greatest formulation is in the Book of Deuteronomy, where it is presented as an act of God's free grace. Because of his love for Israel he chose them when they were few and the smallest nation of the earth—they possessed no merit, they had no claim upon God: of his free will he bestowed upon them his love and chose them as his own people (Deut. 7:6–8). It must be recognized that in this, not less than in the concept of the covenant, there was profound ethical content which religious leaders were not slow to apply for the vitalizing of the religion of nation and individual, several of them commenting on the astonishing fact that Israel was a peculiar treasure of God.

Here was the essence and being of Israel's sense of uniqueness. Her God had chosen her out of all the nations of the world and had entered into an intimate relation with her, such as no other people enjoyed. Such consciousness of peculiarity pervades the Old Testament. One cannot but be impressed with its clear expression in a document so relatively early as one of the Balaam oracles: "Lo it is a people that dwelleth alone and is not reckoned among the nations" (Num. 23:9). Here is expressed precisely that sense of difference in which anti-Semitism through its whole long course has found its real origin and provocation and which to this day continues, among the ignorant or bigoted, to make the Jewish people an object of suspicion and persecution.

But all nations to some extent consider themselves unique. Some of the most notable expressions of this in all history have been manifest in the tragic events of recent times. But, too, these exaggerations have sufficed to reveal similar arrogance in our own thought. Israel's faith in herself was basically but a manifestation of this universal human trait. She, too, believed in a unique character and a glorious destiny; she clung to hopes of world leadership, if not actually political or military domination. Yet we understand the Hebrew doctrine of "the peculiar people" in terms not of its identity but of its distinctive feature, and this is not far to seek. The vital root, as well as the essence of the Hebrew sense of difference, was the uniqueness of Israel's God. One of the poets well expressed this, remarking of the hostile gentile nations: "For their rock is not as our rock even our enemies themselves being judges" (Deut. 32:31). It was a profound insight. Whatever hypercriticism may say of the arrogance of the dogma of the divine choice and the peculiar people, it cannot be denied that at this point we touch solid reality. Israel's God was vastly different from the deities of all other nations, and Israel was, as a fact of history, the people of God. It was Israel's proper realization of this superiority and of her own uniqueness in her faith and worship of this God that constituted her separateness. No other course was possible but that Israel should "come out from among" the nations and be separate unless she would be recreant to her spiritual heritage and apostate from her best self.

Nevertheless, in spite of the interpretations offered by liberal thought, ancient or modern, the doctrine of divine choice did in actuality work out as a prolific source of national arrogance. How could it have done otherwise, the Hebrews being of a human fallibility such as our own? Yet there were not lacking thinkers who pointed out the more profound meaning of their special relationship in a special responsibility. A writer in the Book of Amos has the Lord warn Israel:

> You only have I known
> of all the clans of the earth;
> therefore will I visit upon you
> all your iniquities [Amos 3:2].

The meaning of the divine choice of Israel as better minds came to understand it was revealed in the call of Isaiah. In his great initial experience as a prophet he heard the voice of the Lord, not in a personal call to himself, but in a general appeal: "Whom shall we send and who will go for us?" And Isaiah's call lay in the fact that, having heard, he responded: "Here am I; send me." The Lord's work waited to be done; who was able and willing to undertake it? That was the essence of Isaiah's call—and of the call of Israel as well. The divine election was not for privilege or arrogant separateness but to service. The Lord's work waited to be done!

The greatness of the Servant Songs of Second Isaiah in this regard is so well known that exposition is unnecessary. Israel's divinely appointed destiny was that she should be "a light to the Gentiles." The same thought is vividly enforced in the story of the recalcitrant prophet Jonah. And numerous other passages cherish this vision of Israel's high call and responsibility. In her knowledge of God she had a treasure of such serene exaltation that she might not, at peril of her soul, retain it as hers alone. The greatness of her experience compelled that Israel share her best with all.

The place of foreign nations in Hebrew thought is the counterpart of the doctrine of the peculiar people. The bitter hatreds, the imprecations, the ruthless slaughters that are recorded in many a page of the Old Testament, call for no recapitulation but only understanding of the brutal world of which Israel was a part. Even the Psalter, the voice as it is of Israel's deepest spiritual experiences and aspirations, has many a passage less in intensity but of similar mood to the terrible curse:

> O daughter of Babylon who art to be destroyed . . . .
> happy shall he be that taketh and dasheth
> thy little ones against the rock [Ps. 137:8, 9].

Yet better things are apparent even from the days of the conquest, when Joshua spared the Gibeonites. The kings readily and frequently entered into friendly relations with neighbor nations. However, the function which religion strangely has very often served of creating divisions and animosities was manifest as early as the time of Elijah, when the prophets denounced and threatened Ahab for leniency toward the defeated Ben-Hadad. But our interest is in the attitudes of the religious group after doctrines of the covenant, the divine election, and the peculiar people had taken firm hold of their thought.

The separatism induced by the religion of even some of the best thinkers in the time of the kingdoms is apparent in the attitude of Isaiah, for example, who definitely feared contamination of the religion of Yahweh by close relations with foreign nations. The high emphasis given this warning by the Deuteronomic school is familiar to every student of the Old Testament. Still a more liberal mood existed even in that time, as evidenced by Amos's famous pronouncement as to the equality of Philistines and Syrians with the Hebrews in the sight of God (Amos 9:7).

Both these attitudes found yet more pronounced expression in the later time. The separation of Judah was a prime policy of Nehemiah and Ezra and became an aspect of the thought of the following centuries. Yet a full understanding of the situation qualifies in a marked degree the obloquy which the modern temper has been prone to offer all these. Certainly Nehemiah and Ezra, and presumably the leaders of the ritual movement likewise, took their course through an apprehension as well based as that which had functioned in the days of the prophets. The paganism of the Jewish group at Elephantine, a fair index as it probably is of the religion of most Palestinian Jews of the fifth century B.C.—and certainly we cannot postulate a better attainment of the neighboring Samaritans—constitutes vivid commentary on the work of the Jewish reformers. It was against such conditions that they set up their stringent restraints. And, to be fair to them, what other course was practical? A genial affability would have resulted, beyond a doubt, in that contamination and dissipation of Jewish religion which they feared. And Judaism through the remaining pre-Christian centuries, even when the state became strong in Palestine, lived in immediate contact with self-confident heathenism. The reality and persistence of its problem are apparent to one who will read with insight the restrictions in the tractate, Aboda Zara. Yet, as symptomatic of the mood of Jewish religion when its very existence was not imperiled, it is to be noted that the Priestly document is in some regards the most liberal strand in the Pentateuch. Its provision for admission of loyal sojourners into Judaism has already been noted.

The universalism of Second Isaiah has already been mentioned. Dreamer as this poet was, he could well picture glowing ideals which the practical men of affairs might struggle toward only as time and circumstance would permit. The truth of his vision and the greatness of his achievement are not disparaged when it is recognized that his dreams were impossible of realization in that time. They were the seed of the future, which in fact did produce bounteous harvest. But their time of fruitage was not in his day. Still, initiated by his utterances, there ensued, as President Morgenstern of Hebrew Union College has pointed out, a notable mood of universalism in Jewish thought from which there are numerous passages of broad humanitarianism in the latter chapters of the Book of Isaiah and in the Minor Prophets. The length to which these thinkers went may well surprise us. They seem frankly to have abandoned all claims of Jewish privilege, holding only for a faithful loyalty to Israel's God. In every nation, they believed, there were those who served the Lord, and his name was honored throughout the world. The foreigner, also, who joined himself to the Lord to minister to him and to love his name would come to the temple in Jerusalem with all the rights of native-born Jews and there would rejoice in worship in the house that would be called a house of prayer for all peoples. This movement seems to have been most powerful in the sixth and fifth centuries. Then the success of the reform of Ezra changed the aspect of Jewish thought; but not its essence, for the ideals of this expansive period lived on to moderate the stringency of ritual particularism and to offer promise of wider vision when the destined moment should arrive.

Discussion of this topic would be incomplete without mention of the work of the wise men. They were characteristically international in their attitude. They were the scholars of the ancient world, and scholarship is always larger than nationalism. The theism of the Hebrew wisdom movement has already been described. Like the scholars of the Renaissance, these men saw no contradiction in being at the same time humanists. Their work in reinterpreting the dogmas of orthodoxy and in mitigating its rigidity will come to mind with the mere mention of Ecclesiasticus, the Wisdom of Solomon, and the work of Philo.

But while these questions were demanding solution, other aspects of Hebrew corporate life likewise posed acute issues. The nation, in its internal aspect, that is, as society, underwent profound changes which precipitated problems for the Hebrew thinkers.

We do not know the cultural background and ethnic origins of the tribes that took part in the movement which we know best as Joshua's conquest of Palestine, yet the influence of the Arabian Desert was strong upon them, if we may judge from such information as we possess of their social life in the immediately following period. And certainly nomadic influence continued a potent force in Israel's life, reinforced by the steady infiltration of desert wanderers who entered and lived much as Abraham had done many centuries before. The process has continued to the present; the black tents of the nomads pitched in convenient spots as far west as the shoulder of Carmel at the entrance to the Plain of Accho are, for those who can understand, among the revealing sights of modern Palestine.

Life in the desert, with its loneliness, its sparseness and transience resulting in insecurity, has through unnumbered centuries induced characteristic social forms. Life centers itself in the tribe and clan: outside, insecurity quickly attains the point of extinction. Survival is a matter of social strength. There result the characteristic features of nomadic life—group solidarity, blood covenant, blood revenge, and hospitality. The persistence of these into Israel's life in Palestine is evidenced by many incidents and allusions of which it suffices to mention the national consequence of Achan's trespass and the execution of his entire family with him (Joshua, chap. 7); the hanging of the seven descendants of King Saul to relieve the drought that afflicted the land, so it was believed, because of the king's wrongdoing (II Sam. 21:1–11); also the numerous instances of blood feud (e.g., II Sam. 3:27–30; 14:5–7) or of blood guilt (e.g., II Sam. 25:33; I Kings 21:19). Notwithstanding the persistence of these attitudes, especially among certain groups, altered conditions of life in Palestine soon began their moderating influence. The solidarity of the social group is not typical of peasant life. On the contrary, the tiller of the soil is by nature a stubborn individualist. Further, agricultural life, centering as it did in the country villages or, during times of danger, in walled towns, conduced rather to community than to communal life, with foreshadowing of even city organization. Still, the old patriarchal institutions were not completely unsuited to land tenure, and through these early centuries the idea of family possession took such firm hold as to be written into the laws and to provide the background for the colorful incident of Jezebel's theft of Naboth's ancestral property. The revolution in Hebrew society, which presently came about, for it was nothing less, was inaugurated by King

David. When he captured the Jebusite stronghold of Jerusalem and made it the capital of his united kingdom, he set in motion forces of which clearly he had no conception; and, although in his own person he soon succumbed to certain of them, he could not have anticipated the distance to which they were to carry Israelite society.

Briefly, the process was the urbanization of Hebrew life. The term is a deliberate overstatement, for, to the end, life in Palestine remained basically agricultural. Yet the change that began with David, confined as it was first to Jerusalem and then to other cities and royal residences, in course of time transformed Hebrew society, leaving only vestiges of the old institutions. The change began with the court. The king surrounded himself with a coterie of supporters and military officers, then presently with a considerable and growing harem which in turn attracted hangers-on—in more respectful terms, courtiers—who lived by the favor of the king and by their own shrewdness. But the court and camp were not insulated against the city. David and his men were hardy outlaws who knew the wild lands of the Negeb better than the graces of city life. But with their success they found themselves the "upper class" in an old city whose institutions and habits long antedated the coming of Israel into the land. The luxury and indulgence of city life soon softened the hardihood of the king, certainly, and, it is fair to conclude, of his followers also. But the city had its aristocracy also and its classes in descending order. And apart from the old military clique of the Jebusites, which evidently was wiped out or absorbed by the Hebrew captors of the city, it was a loose organization based on commerce, industry, and probably religion.

Under Solomon the influences of court and city flourished. Indeed, the fame of his days is to be understood largely in terms of the development of urban life. His immense building program laid the ground for a huge class of temple and palace officials and servants. Not less indicative of the changes taking place were his commercial ventures; royal monopolies they were, but still indicative of what was to continue in some form through the following centuries. The king's mining and smelting activity in Edom was likewise adapted to alter deeply the outlook and structure of his kingdom, a result that we dimly discern through the biblical historian's enthusiastic account of the wealth of the age. With this there went political changes that must be surveyed more systematically in a moment; for the present we are concerned primarily with the practical enslavement of hosts of Hebrew tribesmen. We are told that they were only Canaanites whom the king so employed, but elsewhere it is made clear that his own fellow-Hebrews were by no means exempt.

The outcome, as everyone knows, was the revolt under Rehoboam. The northern tribesmen demanded restoration of their ancient rights. On the king's refusal they set up a state which at first seems to have fulfilled their objective of freedom from city domination and from an oppressive court, but within half a century matters in the north were every whit as bad as in Judah. The same forces—commercial and industrial development and the inescapable trends of city life—operated in both. Samaria was as Jerusalem. North and south alike, the ancient social structure was breaking down, and life was conforming to its new facts. The culmination came in the eighth century. The immediately conducive forces were the hundred years' war with Syria and the ensuing tranquillity of the time of Jeroboam II. The social features of the time are familiar to every student of the prophecies of Amos, Hosea, Isaiah, and Micah. At one extreme was a selfish and indolent group of courtiers and idle rich living their parasite life of drunken revelry; at the other, the peasantry and poorer workers whose slavery was not merely that of an income below a living standard but sank even to the unqualified legal sort. And between these upper and lower levels a numerous class of greedy business folk cheated and swindled one another and whoever else might fall within their power. Little wonder thoughtful persons of the age looked back to the good old days of simplicity. Israelite society had departed far from the rude equity of its times of patriarchal institutions.

The fatalism of the Orient and social despair such as that voiced by Ecclesiastes in a later age did not preclude efforts at reform. It would have been strange if there were not at that time some who as in every age advocated a solution by the simple process of turning back the clock. The good old days were those of rustic, or even nomadic, society; then away with the city and all its distortions! The Rechabite movement, while not founded in a mood of reform, clearly did mean, however, for the Rechabites themselves deliverance from current evils by the too easy course of denying civilization. "Remain Bedouin," Jonadab ben Rechab had commanded his descendants; and, faithful to patriarchal authority, they followed this plan for centuries. It is rather more surprising to discover that this attitude found acceptance even among the prophets. It was Elijah's temper; Hosea held up the ideal of a time when Israel should once again live in tents; and some writer whose words we have in the seventh chapter of the Book of Isaiah apparently believed that the land's reversion to wilderness and its inhabitants' return to hunting would solve the problems of his time. But civilization cannot be voluntarily thwarted, nor can its evils be escaped by evasion. Israel's thinkers were not all Gandhis. Some believed in direct political action; it is noteworthy, however, that after the revolt in the days of Rehoboam this method was tried again only once. But then, Jehu's conduct, though instigated by the prophets, was roundly denounced in the sequel.

Two other solutions were advanced by different groups. It was characteristic of Israelite life that the liberal-minded did not throw up their hands in despair, nor yet accept the situation with pseudo-pious resignation. They confronted it as a social situation that cried out for action. In this they were not without antecedent. Urukagina in Shumer had sought reform through legislation many centuries before, and six hundred years after his time Hammurabi of Babylon had renewed the effort. The musings of the Egyptian seer Ipuwer evidenced the same social stirring, although in the end his prophecy dissipated itself largely in wishful thinking; but the author of the speeches of the Eloquent Peasant was of more vigorous mood. Nonetheless, the contribution of the Hebrew prophets toward social reform was such as to set them in a class apart. In their compelling earnestness, in their intensity of conviction, in their penetrating insights and ethical elevation, they were a crowning glory of the cultures of the ancient East; and they retain to this day a high place among the great of all ages. The prophets' solution of the social problem was simple, yet incisive. Social betterment is to be brought about by personal reform. Remake the selfish and dishonest, and you will have an ideal society: Jerusalem will be redeemed with righteousness and then become a faithful town.

Now it was no accident that the prophets threw the social problem back upon the individual's character. For by their genius they were individualists. And one of their great contributions to Israel's thinking was in this regard. While undertaking to combat the results of Israel's long development away from the nomadic social structure, they actually contributed the final element in making a return to the old thinking forever impossible. The individual had been emerging from his absorption in the group ever since the days of the first settlement in the land, but the prophetic experience provided new impetus for the developments. The essence of prophecy was its personal relation with God. The prophet received his messages, so he was convinced, not out of law or tradition, but through his own individual experience in which he heard the Lord speaking to himself. Accordingly, he stood before king, priest, and people and, on his own unsupported conviction that he as a person possessed invaluable truths denied to all others, hurled his denunciations and directions in opposition to accepted standards and conduct. The prophetic experience, not less than the prophet's words, became the basis of religion of the later age, in time absorbing into itself other expressions of piety. The personal quality of the Psalms which has made them to this day the great classic of inner religion is but the extension to every devout believer of the prophets' experience of the reality of God in individual life.

Such, then, is the meaning of the prophets' advocacy of reform through personal regeneration. Still its real worth we grasp best, it may be, by reference to the hope voiced in a late time. For the doctrine of the law written on the heart (Jer. 31:33) will be recognized as nothing less than the hope that this experience known first by the prophets should in time become the possession of every faithful soul.

It was the weakness of the prophetic program of reform that, in modern phrase, it lacked teeth. The appeal to the thought and conscience of his audience, while ultimately the only means to the reform of thought or conduct and justified in the religious history of succeeding centuries, was for the time of the prophet himself largely futile. It is always difficult to the point of impossibility to appraise correctly a contemporary who departs from accepted procedures. The prophets met with little success; the majority of their compatriots thought them misguided nuisances. Their reforms did not come about, save only after centuries and then imperfectly. But the legislator is a man of a different approach. He intends, and he takes steps to see to it, that his policies shall be put to practical use. Nonetheless, the reforms of Asa, Joash, and Hezekiah accomplished nothing of social significance. Their objectives were cultic, not ethical, an illuminating fact in itself as showing that social ethics had not yet seized the conscience of the rulers. But not so the reformers to whom we are indebted for one of the truly great bodies of Israel's literature, the Book of Deuteronomy. This is, as the name happily indicates, a recapitulation—better, a revision—of the old social legislation of Israel. It is relevant to our present interest that the date commonly assigned to the basic core of the book is late in the eighth century or sometime in the first three quarters of the seventh; consequently, it was aimed at ameliorating contemporary conditions of the sort sketched above.

These legislators were profoundly conscious of the social problem. Their revision of the old laws in favor of the poor and underprivileged provides many interesting features. The recension of the Decalogue (Deut. 5:6–21), while perhaps not properly a part of the original work, is drawn into its temper. In contrast to the familiar law of the Sabbath that enjoins observance because the Lord rested on the seventh day and hallowed it, the Deuteronomic law gives as the reason a recollection of the enslavement in Egypt and consideration for the manservant and maidservant so that they may enjoy a Sabbath's rest as well as their master. In the code proper the old agricultural prescription for a sabbatic year of fallow is transformed into a year of cancellation of debt, or it may be only a year of grace from its collection. The tithe of the third year is to be laid up in a city where the Levite, the sojourner, the fatherless, and the widow may come and partake freely. In the communal festivals of the religious seasons and the payment of tithes, these same classes of indigent, along with the male and female slaves, are to share in the rejoicing, apparently provided for by the bounty of their more fortunate neighbors. Notable, too, is the new regulation of slavery. For the first time the Hebrew woman slave is permitted to share in the manumission at the end of six years of service. Still more striking, liberated slaves are to be given generously of their masters' produce, a clear effort to meet the situation where formerly the slave, after his years of service, went out into society as poor as he had been six years before and hence liable soon to lose his freedom again. Significant is the fact that this generosity is not to be in niggardly spirit, for "thou shalt remember that thou wast a slave in the land of Egypt, and the Lord thy God redeemed thee."

How far these expedients were effective in relieving the suffering of the time it is not possible to calculate. At the worst they promise as much as our modern expedients of soup kitchens and bread lines in time of economic stress. The malady was too deep for superficial treatment, however. Poverty has origins and causes which it ought to be possible to isolate and perhaps remedy. It is not less than astonishing that these social thinkers of twenty-five centuries ago recognized this fact. In addition to the palliatives just now sketched, Deuteronomy goes to the heart of the matter with a frontal assault on the problem of poverty. The solution offered may seem nothing but a pietistic leap into supernaturalism: "There shall be no poor with thee . . . . if only thou diligently hearken to the voice of the Lord thy God to observe to do all this commandment which I command thee this day" (Deut. 15:4, 5). Yet the statement deserves further examination. In its context, "all this commandment" was a comprehensive program; it was nothing less than full social equity. There are probably few today who would deny that if all would "diligently observe to do" such a command, poverty in a land of plenty would shrink to terms descriptive of relative bounty. The crux of the matter is how to implement such a principle. The writer hints at a partial method in his repeated exhortations to consideration for the underprivileged. But the conditions of the eighth and seventh centuries B.C. did not obtrude upon the writer's attention the complement of this in a total social program.

It will be apparent that by this time the old social solidarity of the days of the conquest was extinct, save for some vestigial ideas. It is not at all surprising, then, that the concept of individual responsibility in religion was formulated in definitive statement, first briefly by Jeremiah, and then somewhat more fully by Ezekiel. It would seem that Ezekiel was in this, as in so much of his prophetic teaching, directly indebted to his older contemporary, his own contribution being merely that of expressing the idea in a form that seized upon general thought. The circumstances conducing to the enunciation of the doctrine at this time can be conjectured, if not certainly identified. The impelling consideration for both prophets seems to have been the disintegration of the nation. which obviously threw the individual out into relief. More specifically, the warnings and reproof of the succession of prophets through several centuries, often directed immediately toward personal conduct and always implying such application, had borne fruitage in a realization that the individual's righteousness depended, not on his membership in the nation, but on his response to the prophet's message. A group of immediate followers and friends of the prophets, their disciples, to use Isaiah's word (Isa. 8:61), successors to the older protomonastic organization of the "sons of the prophets," had embodied the thought in living form as a sort of "church" within the state. In this there was visibly existent precisely that individually centered society, in embryo, which the teaching of Jeremiah and Ezekiel indicated as the hope of survival beyond the imminent ruin of the nation. Their thought may well have been fertilized also with a realization of the unequal responsibility for this catastrophe, such as would compel consideration of corresponding recompense. But, finally, much depended on the personal characters of these two prophets. Jeremiah was a deeply sensitive man, who wrestled with a sense of personal injustice; and Ezekiel was moved by a feeling for the individuals for whose safety he was by his office responsible.

Notwithstanding its long antecedents, Ezekiel's formulation of the doctrine of individualism in religion was still sufficiently new to provoke the excesses that usually attend novelty. Certain commentators in his book have stereotyped it into essentially a mechanical procedure that automatically works retribution or reward in accord with the individual's conduct (Ezek. 18:5–32; 33:12–20). No regard is shown for the conditioning of heredity, habit, and circumstance, which other thinkers had considered; but the judgment is flat: if one does such and so, he is wicked; he shall die!

However, the concept of the primacy of the individual in religion worked out in a much more wholesome way than these passages might indicate. And the whole problem of the antithesis and interrelation of society and individual, which has so recently been an issue of the first importance in world-wide politics and must continue with us for many a day, was given very sane treatment in the course of Jewish history. Enough of the traditional emphasis on the supremacy of society persisted, if only as an influence, to insure avoidance of the atomism which has cursed our society. Judaism was, and remained, a community, expressing its characteristic life and convictions in social institutions. But yet the individual was never submerged. The long list of brilliant names in every walk of life that embellish Jewish history to our own day are sufficient testimony to the vitality of individualism within Judaism. Yet they were rooted and nurtured in the Jewish community. They were its expression and outreach; and, in turn, it gave them a concrete loyalty, a vitalizing devotion, and a transcendent purpose.

The development of Israel's politics paralleled closely that of her social thought. In several cases the same documents or recorded incidents have relevance for both.

Here, too, the deficiency of our knowledge of the invading Habiru clansmen qualifies the approach to the question. The Amarna letters mention certain chieftains of the invaders, but the means of their appointment and the nature of their office we do not know. One might invoke Bedouin rule as parallel, but the better course is to drop the problem for lack of evidence and go on to our earliest sources for Israel's life after the settlement in Palestine. These reveal clan and community organization under elders who apparently exercised judicial as well as executive functions. It was a primitive democracy, uncritical and unconscious, for there is no ground to suppose other than that every senior member of the group was admitted to the governing body purely on the basis of his age. The decisions of these were apparently reached through free discussion of a most informal sort. The operation of such a ruling group is pictured in the story of Boaz' negotiations for the redemption of Naomi's property (Ruth 4:1–12); the narrative is presumably from a comparatively late time, but the councils of elders persisted in the smaller communities right through Old Testament history, so there is ground for believing that the author relates practice with which he was familiar.

But the stress of circumstance compelled the coalescence of the smaller groups of clans and tribes into some approximation of a national unity. This is the story of the rise of successive "judges" and of their rule. Their election to leadership again exemplified primitive democracy. The basic fact was their ability to lead and to deal with the crises of the moment. This was variously manifest; at times through known repute, as in the case of Jephthah; again by spontaneous response to the situation which lifted the erstwhile peasant out of his mediocre role into an exhibition of power and decision that doubtless surprised him not less than his associates. Probably physical prowess was in some cases the desired qualification. The point that concerns us is that, by whatever means, the "judge" won the free consent and loyal following of the clans, so that they accepted his command and under him went against the foe.

It was inevitable that success such as is related of these champions would give them lifelong prestige, and so they "judged Israel" variously for ten, twenty, or forty years. But in only two cases is a tendency revealed to turn this advantage into hereditary rule. It was offered to Gideon, but he refused. Observe, it was *offered* to him: the initiative was with the people. The terms of the refusal, too, are of interest. He replied: "I shall not rule over you, nor shall my son rule over you. The Lord shall rule over you." If we may beg the doubtful question of the genuineness of the passage, we may recognize in it again an expression of primitive democracy. The unifying bond as well as guiding principle of the tribes had been their loyalty to their God: neither monarch, priest, nor organization had held them together, but all responded when their God spoke through the one chosen by him to save his people. And Gideon, recognizing well that spiritual bonds are mightier than political regimentation, desired to leave matters as they were. However, his son Abimelech felt no such restraints. He was a typical self-seeking upstart of the sort that has made history—and trouble—through many a century, and his story runs true to the type as known in our own days. First he secured by specious argument a following in the city of Shechem and then broadened and supported his rule by violence—until at length violence in turn happily removed him. But in the meantime his venture was symptomatic of the situation. So it is not at all surprising that presently another popularly chosen leader, after succeeding in the crisis that had called him forth, was frankly acclaimed as king, perhaps through the scheming of his friends; but also it is entirely possible that he was chosen by spontaneous action of the associated tribes who actually felt, as is recorded in a late account of the incident, that the exigencies of the disordered time required them to have a king as did other nations. In any case, Saul was "the last of the judges and the first of the kings." Whether or not it was envisaged at the time of his choice, he came to believe that hereditary right lodged in his family. And, in point of fact, his son did succeed him.

Saul maintained simple state at his country capital. He was more a rustic squire than a nation's monarch. He was highhanded and arbitrary at times, yet not more so than many a father unfortunately has shown himself in his own family, and he manifested little inclination to enlarge the prerogatives of his office by encroachment on traditional rights of his people. He did, it is true, refuse to be a mere underling of the old "kingmaker," Samuel, for which he merits general respect. Somewhat more insidious, however, were his attempt to establish the ascendancy of the throne over the priests and his jealous concern for his family's succession as revealed in his rebuke of Jonathan's friendship for David. But, on the whole, his behavior was well within what we may with some exaggeration call the constitutional rights of the monarchy. In the light of developments we can see, as did some ancient writer (I Sam. 8:10–18), that in himself, ex officio, he embodied a stern threat to Israel's political institutions such as to constitute virtually a revolution. But of this Saul personally was largely innocent.

David began well. He likewise was a popular chieftain who by a combination of personal and national exigencies emerged into such importance that he also was offered, and accepted, the throne. The menace from the Philistines was acute. After the disaster at Mount Gilboa, they were in practically undisputed control of all western Palestine; the Israelites lived by their grace. A hardened outlaw loyal to his people, such as David had abundantly shown himself, was just the man for the time. The popular choice was wise, and events soon went far to justify it. His phenomenal success in reversing the ascendancy of the Philistines, in seizing the famous fortress of Jerusalem for his nation's capital, and in extending his sway and influence until he was the mightiest monarch between the Euphrates and Egypt transformed the face not alone of the Hebrews' cultural status but of their politics also.

Yet David never escaped his origin—as, who ever does? Something of the soil and of his hardy life clung to him through all his changed condition as a great monarch in an ancient capital. He had risen from the peasantry, and to the end he understood his people and was properly restrained by his knowledge of their stubborn love of freedom and by the nature of his own position as dependent upon them. The sinister forces that played upon the throne in Jerusalem are best seen in the perspective of the entire united monarchy, extending as it did only into a third reign.

An ominous feature, intelligible only in the light of later history, appeared when David abandoned the command of the army in the field, remaining behind in Jerusalem while Joab conducted the campaign. It will be recalled that this was the background of the nefarious Bath-Sheba episode. Also it was at just the parallel point in their history that the obvious decay of the Ottoman dynasty set in. But even more pernicious was the influence of the harem—that breeding ground of seditions and knavery, as well as the source of the monarch's personal demoralization, in every oriental court through history—which was firmly established by David and much enlarged by Solomon. It was a harem intrigue that determined the succession of Solomon. And Solomon's son, who at length wrecked the kingdom, was of the second generation of moral decline that this institution had fastened upon the Jerusalem court.

But other and less reprehensible influences were beating upon the king. Success tries the mettle of any man; and David had succeeded beyond fond dreams. Did he ever in self-consciousness recall his simple days as a shepherd boy near Bethlehem and wonder what his old father would think if now he could look in on the estate of his royal son? In any case, ease, luxury, and wealth that in Solomon's days attained a relatively fabulous level, public respect that became adulation, full opportunity to indulge his whims such as easily descends into self-indulgence, and not least the position of king per se all combined to set the king apart from the simple state of the nation's leaders of only a little before. The mystic concepts of the monarchy expressed in various forms in the Orient from the divine kingship of Egypt to the mighty monarch, the darling of the gods, as conceived in Mesopotamia, and further the interrelation of king and dying god through which the monarch in some way was the life and being of his people: these were entailed in some relevant way when Israel set up one of her sons as king. To the concept of the king as a being, in his religious significance, apart from and above his people, we have numerous allusions: Jeremiah refers to public lamentations at the death of a king such as clearly relate them to the ritual of the fertility god (Jer. 22:18). The seemingly innocent story of Abishag, who was to warm the aged David (I Kings 1:1-4), is suspiciously reminiscent of widespread practices in which the ebbing virility of the old monarch was put to the test, since in his person he embodied the vital forces of the nation. The prevalent school of interpretation of the Psalms would see much of this testing of the king in the plaintive cries of many of these devout poems. Clearly, too, the monarch was regarded in some mystic way as a person more than normal because of the fact that he was the anointed of the Lord. The application of the holy oil transformed him into another man (I Sam. 10:6) so that he came to stand in an intimate relation with God almost of sonship (Ps. 2:7) and certainly of close association (Psalm 110).

It was, then, not merely from personal ambition which doubtless functioned, nor because of an exaggerated self-importance induced through unaccustomed flattery, that these kings moved steadily in the direction of arrogation of absolute powers. The development was almost forced upon them; it was inherent in the oriental kingship.

Symptomatic of this was the accession of King Solomon. The earlier kings had been chosen by the people; for even the usurper Absalom the fiction of popular choice was maintained (II Sam. 16:18). But Solomon was appointed by his father, under pressure from the harem. The old king had in his forty years of rule moved so far from principles fully accepted at his accession that he either forgot or chose to ignore the rights of his subjects. The succession had become a prerogative of the royal family. Yet there were danger signals for any ruler not blinded with an exaggerated sense of his regal rights. When David was returning from his brief exile during the sedition of Absalom, there went up the ominous cry destined to be heard once more in a crisis of Israel's history: "We have no portion in David, neither have we inheritance in the son of Jesse. To your tents, O Israel!" (II Sam. 20:1.) The kingship, whatever the entourage in Jerusalem might think, sat light upon the free men of Israel; and David knew it. He realized the acuteness of the crisis; his prompt action throttled the separatist move and delayed its maturing for another generation. Rehoboam became heir of a problem that he was vastly less fitted to meet than his grandfather had been. Yet, even with full recognition of the folly he manifested, one cannot but feel some sympathy for him. He was a victim of circumstances. How could he, grandson of the harem and its nefarious political influences, have regarded the plea of the peasants as other than an infringement of his sacred rights? The dogma of the divine right of kings had grown apace through Solomon's reign. It is evident in his irresponsible treatment of affairs of state: his public corvee of Israel's free men; his extravagant court supported at the expense of the nation; his administrative division of the land in disregard of traditional tribal bounds; and his whole ingrown life in a court that defied the realities of Israel's basic peasant economy and spent its days in the grand style, with feasting, royal processions, and dilettante scholarship in a setting of magnificent architecture, erected by Israel's peasants, and with women enough for all and to spare.

But we are indebted to Rehoboam for his clear statement of the issue. He had consulted with the older counselors, who apparently retained some sense of political realities, if not actual memory of events in the reign of David; but he accepted the view of the young fellows of the court, his boon companions reared, like himself, in the diseased artificiality of the harem-infested court and doubtless for long anticipating the day when with his enthronement they should do as they pleased. The serious request of the people of the north who lived on the land, far from the blandishments of Jerusalem, was "Lighten now the severe service exacted by your father, and the heavy yoke which he put upon us; then we will serve you." Rehoboam replied: "My father chastised you with whips; I will chastise you with scorpions." So there it was. Had the people rights? Or only the king? The revolt of the northern tribes was an assertion of the sovereign freedom of the common people. The king stood firmly for the divine right of the king to rule his subjects as he chose. He was above the law: he *was* the law, and they had no rights beyond. For many today this claim is associated with the Stuart kings of England; but James I in his *New Law for Free Monarchie*, as his descendants in their official acts, was consciously dependent on the Old Testament. Whether he realized it or not, he was in the spiritual succession of Rehoboam. Yet if he had studied his Old Testament better, he might have found other matter more pertinent for his heirs, for one of these lost his head through his father's principles, and another, like Rehoboam, lost his kingdom.

Judah, then, by its loyalty to the House of David, was in the position of supporting despotism. And doubtless we are in a qualified way so to read Judean history, for the striking difference of its politics as over against Israel's was the stability of the dynasty. Yet this meant less than the bare fact might suggest. The depositions in the north were seldom the result of quasi-democratic agitation, the revolt of Jehu, inspired by the prophets, being a debatable exception. On the contrary, the accession of a new dynasty came about purely through personal ambition and commonly by violence. The initial impulse of liberty that rejected Rehoboam and set Jeroboam on the throne soon spent itself, and the north became even more the bauble of unprincipled and irresponsible rulers than was Judah. To the end, except for the doubtful case of Jehu's overthrow of the House of Ahab, it provided no further matter relevant to constitutional development. Likewise there is all too little on the surface of Judean history. The succession of son following father upon the throne, broken only for the interval of Athaliah's usurpation, is related in the colorless terms that he "ruled in his stead"; whatever may have been Judah's ritual counterpart of "The king is dead; long live the king," information is generally lacking. In just three cases, where the monarch had met a violent death, it is told that the people took his son and set him on the throne (II Kings 14:21; 21:24; 22:30). The relation of this to normal procedure of accession is quite uncertain; it lies wide open to guessing. But one matter at least is clear. The consciousness that final authority in selection of the monarch lay with the people was never abandoned. At most the right was merely held in abeyance, if indeed we may be certain that it was not exercised or symbolized in each case. That fact means much. After nearly four hundred years of the kingship the Judean people still refused to be regarded as pawns in the game of power politics; they had far-reaching rights, even as against their kings, which they would not surrender. And those rights, it will be observed, implied the complete democratic position. If the people were the final arbiters of who should rule over them, then authority rested, in the last recourse, not in the king, but in the people, however submissive these might at times consent to show themselves toward the court.

A jealous concern for their traditional prerogatives was kept alive among the people by various agitators, notably the prophets. Nathan's rebuke of David, as Elijah's of Ahab, was a direct denial of the assumptions of divine right and a bold affirmation of the principle that the king was amenable to the same standards of right, the same pervasive natural law as his humblest subject. Here, too, it is apparent, was the principle basic to the entire attitude of the prophets and other progressive thinkers toward the monarchy: the king ruled, not by divine right, but under divinely imposed responsibility. He was only the servant of the Lord appointed to shepherd his people Israel. His task was to rule in accord with revealed standards of equity. Samuel's opposition to the kingship, like that of Gideon, on the ground that it was a denial of the Lord's rule of his people, is probably a fiction of a later time; but at least it is true to the undertone of Hebrew political thought throughout the nation's history. The theocracy of late times, in reality the hierocracy, was in its assumptions but a perpetuation of the very ancient thought that Israel was "the people of Yahweh"; they were to be governed by him through the man of his choosing who in his office accepted heavy responsibility for the well-being of the people.

This sense of responsibility—of the high ethical demands devolving upon a ruler—is strikingly voiced in the valedictory of Samuel. The old priest-prophet politician at the end of his career, standing before the convocation of the tribes, reported upon his discharge of duties in these words: "I am old and grayheaded . . . . and I have walked before you from my youth unto this day. Here I am: witness against me before the Lord and before his anointed: whose ox have I taken? or whose ass have I taken? whom have I defrauded? whom have I oppressed? or of whose hand have I taken a bribe to blind my eyes therewith? and I will make restitution." But the witness of the people was: "Thou hast not defrauded us, nor oppressed us, neither hast thou taken aught of any man's hand" (I Sam. 12:2–5). Briefly, Israel's best thought recognized the far-reaching principle, which stirred as a ferment in the nation's political life throughout its history, that authority, specifically governmental office, was not to be regarded as an opportunity for exploitation: it was a call to service. The ruler must use his office, not for personal advantage or profit, but for the benefit of the ruled. Here is the very finest tradition of public office known to this day. Its radical nature is evident on a moment's consideration of the revolution it would effect even in our boasted modern lands if wholeheartedly accepted by all who share in city, state, and national government. Yet its persistence in Israel, if only as a hope and ideal of those who were outside the ruling class, is attested by Jeremiah's condemnation of Jehoiakim near the end of the history of the kingdom: "Did not thy father . . . . do justice and righteousness? he judged the cause of the poor and needy. . . . . But thine eyes and thy heart are not but for thy covetousness and for shedding innocent blood and for doing violence" (Jer. 22:15–17). Ezekiel, also, uttered a similar opinion relative to the official class of his time: "Woe to the shepherds of Israel who care for themselves! Should not the shepherds care for the sheep?" (Ezek. 34:2). The popularity of the theme is shown in the lengthy commentary that a succession of writers have attached to this oracle.

In this matter we come upon the very core of the uniqueness of Israel's government among the nations of the Orient. It would be a distortion to claim that such ideals were unknown elsewhere, for both Egypt and Babylonia had voiced them, the one in literature, the other in legislation. But the striking fact about Israel's thought was its dissemination and its persistence in the nation, as well as the expression it came to attain in law and, for a brief time, in institutions.

On the background of the struggles and protestations surveyed above, the progressive group in Judah, sometime apparently in the seventh century B.C., formulated their theory of government in a document which has come to us in whole or in part in our Book of Deuteronomy. Its social legislation must be held in mind as one goes on to study its regulation of the office of king—that he should be chosen by the people from among themselves, and certain restraints be placed upon his conduct. Then the document continues:

> It shall be when he sitteth on the throne of his kingdom that he shall write for himself a copy of this law in a book out of that which is before the priests, the Levites, and it shall be with him and he shall read therein all the days of his life that he may learn to fear the Lord his God, to keep all the words of this law and these statutes to do them; that his heart be not lifted up above his brethren, and that he turn not aside from the commandment to the right or to the left [Deut. 17:18–20].

In its historic setting and in its literary context this pronouncement is such as may without exaggeration be considered Israel's Magna Carta. The king was not to be exalted in self-importance above his subjects; he should be at pains to obey all the words of the Deuteronomic code with its rich social implications; and, further, the book was to be kept at hand as a sort of constitution of the kingdom that would guide and limit the monarch's rule. Here is the same defense of the common man against the arrogance of the monarchy and the same constitutional limitation of royal power as was voiced in the famous English document of some eighteen centuries later.

The Deuteronomic code was, in the reform of King Josiah in 621 B.C., made the law of the land; and it would appear that during the dozen years of reign which remained to him he accepted loyally its direction and limitation. After four centuries of struggle the liberal group had won. Their principles of human rights and their restraints upon royal misconduct had found embodiment in the nation's constitution. If once again one may be guilty of some measure of overmodernization in order to bring out the essential meaning, we may assert that the great achievement of the Hebrew people, practically unparalleled as it was in the ancient world, was the attainment of a limited monarchy.

But Josiah was succeeded by the despotic Jehoiakim, and he by Zedekiah, too weak a creature to have any influence on politics. And the end came so soon that no immediate sequel can be traced for the political principles affirmed in the reform. Still, in judging its historic significance, we must recall that after John, the unwilling agent of Magna Carta, came Henry III, whose arbitrariness and determination to nullify the charter were an unconscious reincarnation of the conduct of Jehoiakim. It was a long struggle, and at many a time uncertain of outcome except for the stubborn and independent character of the people concerned, before finally constitutional rights were fully established. Recollection of the ambitions of the Stuarts and the wilfulness of George III give us to realize how recent was the culmination of what began so notably at Runnymede on that June day in A.D. 1215. Until the damage of the government buildings by a Nazi bomb, members of the British House of Commons were proud to point to the dents on the door of their chamber made by the ring on the finger of the king's messenger sent to summon them to hear the speech from the throne; he might not enter, for this was the domain of the common Englishman; he could only stand at the door and humbly invite.

But Judah was afforded no such experience of national survival and constitutional maturing of the principle so boldly affirmed in the legislation of Josiah's reign. For the sequel we must look rather to the local councils of elders and the popular assemblies which not uncommonly some overenthusiastic writer in the Bible has exaggerated into "the whole congregation of all Israel." These two, it is clear from the frequency of the reference, constituted the real local government of ancient Israel. Indeed, it is claimed by a recent historian that the authority of the court was in large measure confined to the capital and a few more important cities and that the smaller communities, right through the period of the kings, continued to pay final loyalty to their own assemblies and elders, with little more interference from the central authority than occasional demands for military assistance and for payment of certain taxes. Our sources do not permit us, finally, to adjudicate this claim, but at least it is clear that local authority was a continuing reality in Israel's life and that the popular assembly was a potent facility for expression of the general will.

In this institution, then, persisting through the vicissitudes of national history from the earliest days of the settlement in Palestine, was nurtured that independence of spirit which marked Hebrew life throughout and could easily be fanned to violent action when age-old liberties were infringed. In this, too, lies justification of the claim that in ancient Israel there existed a genuine, if amorphous, political democracy. Such local assemblies became the expression of Jewish communal life after the destruction of the monarchy, both in Palestine and among that section of the people who went into exile. And the story of subsequent Jewish political development is to be traced, not primarily in the hierarchy of restored Palestinian Judaism and the arrogance of the House of Hasmon, but in the popular assembly with its ruling elders which continued, with local adaptations and variations, it is true, but in essential uniformity, right through the long centuries of the dispersion and into our own times. It was the schooling in local self-government and the institutions so developed back in the hills and valleys of ancient Palestine that gave the uprooted Jews immediately a social organism able to withstand the shock of exile and to support and adapt the community in its struggle to live in an alien environment. The Jews have always taken their politics seriously. The reason lies apparent in their age-old experience of individual participation in public affairs. This experience, crystallized into permanent form in the Old Testament, constitutes the most remarkable theory of government that came out of the ancient world and at the same time an ideal that rebukes and challenges the distressing imperfections of our boasted modern democracy.

But the king was by no means the sole menace to common freedom. The breakdown of the Egyptian empire and the circumstances contributory to the capture of Babylon by Cyrus, besides hosts of incidents from those days to the present, show that organized religion, strange as it appears, can be no less an obstacle to social and political advance than the reactionary policies of vested political or economic interests. The church carries an implicit threat to freedom quite as truly as the court.

An intimate relationship of church and state is traceable far back through human society. Early man's sense of dependence on the will of the gods and his belief in their immediate interference in human affairs gave high place in community counsel and action to the spiritual adviser who, by theory, could tell just what the gods wished. The transfer of this special prestige into the politics of the ancient East is a familiar story. The monarchs in general either kept conveniently available a group of spiritual advisers or else paid such respect to the views of the hierarchy as to elevate the chief priest virtually into an important minister of the state. In Israel the role of prophets as royal counselors is evident in many incidents already mentioned; notable were the existence of a body of four hundred prophets in the court of Ahab and the relations of Samuel and King Saul. Yet this situation in its logical working-out could mean little less than a subjection of the political rulers such that they might fairly be described as priest-ridden. Beyond a question, this was the ideal cherished by a considerable group in Israel —such subservience for them was a mark of piety; it was obedience to the will of God. This is the meaning of certain comments on the monarchs found in our Books of Kings; it is in large part the viewpoint of the Chronicler; it is freely expressed in the chapters added to the prophecies of Ezekiel in which the function of "the prince" is little more than one of leadership in ritual under the priests. Further, it was built into actual political institutions in later Old Testament times; the rule of the high priests represented a complete triumph of the claim that church is supreme above state. Indeed, it was more extreme than certain modern expressions of the theory, for it did not leave the secular rulers as a sort of sub-department under the princes of organized religion, but instead the hierarchy gathered into itself the functions of both. The church had swallowed the state.

What protests were voiced against this situation have left but few echoes in literature, which, we must recall, was transmitted by priestly, or pro-priestly, hands. Some of the Psalms are strangely nonritualistic for a collection that is freely recognized to have been "the hymn book of the second temple." A passage in the Fifty-first is famous:

> For thou delightest not in sacrifice; else would
> I give it;
> thou hast no pleasure in burnt offering.
> The sacrifices of God are a broken spirit,
> a broken and contrite heart, O God, thou wilt not
> despise [vss. 16–17].

In many, too, the temple appears as a house of prayer where worshipers go, independent of priestly propitiation. Yet all such expressions do not obscure the fact that the Psalter, in the large, is loyal to the ritual and the hierarchy. At times it reaches an extreme of glorification of the priestly system, as in Psalm 119. But, on the other hand, in the account of the reform of Ezra a passage of dubious translation is supposed to mention by name two individuals who withstood the proposed measures (Ezra 10:15). But the activity of Ezra was so mixed with power politics that one may not deduce too much from opposition, if actual. Similarly, the inference commonly drawn from the Books of Ruth and Jonah may not be adduced as anti-hierarchical. Somewhat earlier the prophet known as Malachi protested vigorously against the misconduct of the priests and voiced a high ideal of their responsibility:

> And now, O ye priests, this commandment is for you. If ye will not hear and lay it to heart to give glory to my name, saith the Lord of hosts, then I will send the curse upon you and will curse your blessings; yea I have cursed them already. . . . . My covenant was with him [Levi] of life and peace. . . . . The law of truth was in his mouth and unrighteousness was not found in his lips: he walked with me in peace and uprightness and turned many away from iniquity. For the priest's lips should keep knowledge, and they should seek the law at his mouth; for he is the messenger of the Lord of Hosts [2:1–7].

Yet none of this gives us quite what we seek.

In the days of the kingdoms the priesthood enjoyed secular power through its judicial functions. The legislation of the Book of Deuteronomy, in fact, elevates the priests into a supreme court of appeal, with but the possibility that a secular judge also was associated with them. Judges and officers were to be appointed in every locality, but

> if there arise a matter too hard for thee in judgment . . . . then thou shalt arise and get thee up unto the place which the Lord thy God shall choose, and thou

shalt come unto the priests, the Levites, and unto the judge that shall be in those days . . . . and they shall show thee the sentence of judgment . . . . thou shalt not turn aside from the sentence which they shall show thee, to the right hand or to the left. And the man that doeth presumptuously in not hearkening to the priest that standeth to minister there before the Lord thy God, or unto the judge, even that man shall die; and thou shalt put away the evil from Israel. And all the people shall hear and fear and do no more presumptuously [17:8-13].

The legislation had teeth in it: capital punishment for disobedience of the priests! It was a provision that centuries later was doubtless congenial to Torquemada.

However, matters were by no means as bad as this would indicate. On the contrary, Saul's bold defiance of the priest-prophet Samuel has already been cited, and Zadok and Abiathar and their sons seem to have been fully subject to David and Solomon. The leadership of Jehoiada in the overthrow of Athaliah and his rule for some years as regent may not be employed as evidence of the rise of the hierarchy to temporal power (II Kings 11:4—12:16). It was a popular movement of which the chief priest was head, evidently because of his forceful personality. Indeed, to the end the supremacy of the monarchy appears to have been undisputed; even the law-abiding Josiah gave orders to the chief priest and was obeyed (II Kings 22:3-7, 12). The prophets, too, indorsed this situation. Except for a few utterances, mainly those of Hosea, which may well relate to temporary conditions rather than to the monarchy per se, the prophets accept the kings as legitimate officials supreme in their sphere. Their demand was only that their rule must accord with the will of God. But nowhere do they suggest or imply that the hierarchy possesses secular authority to rival the monarchy. On the contrary, their stern denunciations of priestly veniality and their deprecation of the ritual imply rather that, as between king and priest, they would prefer to dispense with the latter. Even the legislation in the Book of Deuteronomy, which a moment ago we found guilty of marked favoritism toward the priests, accepts the kingship as a valid institution. The king must obey the law of God; he is to accept as the constitution of the state a copy of the Deuteronomic law from that "which is before the priests." But beyond this he rules free of interference from the hierarchy.

And such is the limit of our evidence. Certainly Israel's thought was less clarified on this than on the issue of popular rights vis-à-vis secular rulers. It appears that, subsequent to the popular protest and action which freed the government from domination by Samuel, the priesthood were never again a threat to secular power as long as the kingdoms stood. Consequently, the question of church and state did not become an issue to provoke thought such as Israel's intellectual leaders exercised elsewhere. It was the accident of history, the destruction of the monarchy and the state, and then later the unhappy events, whatever their detail may have been, which weakened the prestige and power of the Jewish governor in the days of Darius I that by consequence elevated the priests into *de facto* leadership and rule of the Palestinian community. The theocracy was a natural development from this. The situation was a remarkable anticipation of the events through which the Christian church centuries later assumed secular power in the city of Rome. Nonetheless, the Jewish theocracy, so called, was an aberration from the true national genius and tradition. Israel had been governed by secular rulers chosen, such was orthodox dogma, by the Lord himself and commissioned to "shepherd his people Israel." Of the supremacy of religious standards and restraints above the secular ruler there was no question in Israel's best thought; but until after the collapse of Zerubbabel's governorship the exercise of authority over the state by the priesthood was never a practical consideration. Israel, we may say, would have granted the supremacy of the invisible church, the custodian of the nation's best social achievements and highest idealism; but the visible church was too fallibly human to be trusted with so high responsibility.

The conclusion from our findings already is apparent; if it may be compressed into a single phrase, it is the supremacy of Israel's thinking in the ancient East.

But the astonishing feature of this supremacy is that it was attained in spite of, or, better, through, the material and military inferiority of the Hebrew people. They were far overshadowed by Egypt and Babylon; Assyria trod them down at will. But Israel has lived in the faith and thought and conduct of succeeding centuries, a heritage that grows ever richer, while her proud contemporaries are a faded memory interesting, primarily, to archeologists and historians. We have grown somewhat accustomed in recent years to a realization of Israel's literary excellence; in her poetry and prose alike she is of the modern world. But it is a much less familiar idea that Israel takes by native right her place among the creative intellectual peoples of history. In her achievements she stood head and shoulders above the best of her oriental contemporaries at their highest outreach. Their excellence is that at times they approach those attainments where Israel's thinkers lived and moved with the sure confidence of one who treads his native soil.

But a noteworthy feature is Israel's obvious and self-conscious dependence upon these other cultures. The time has gone when the uniqueness of the Old Testament is to be defended by denial of foreign influence in Israel's achievement. On the contrary, this is the glory of Israel. They were no remote and ingrown people; they stood at the crossroads of the ancient world, sensitive to all the best that was achieved within its limits. They took freely from all; their excellence is that they recognized value wherever it arose and freely appropriated it as their own. But in the process they transformed it. The mark of their distinctive genius is on all that they took, so that in the result it is Hebraic; and its difference from its foreign original is more significant than its similarity.

Yet we do Israel but half-justice if we fail to look also down the following centuries. For we have had occasion to remark again and again in the course of this discussion the direct indebtedness of the modern world to these ancient thinkers. Their basic convictions on the ultimate character of the world, their view of the nature and place of man, their social ideals, and their political principles have become so large a part of our common heritage of today—and that in general by an immediate and demonstrable line of descent—that with full recognition of the profound contributions of Greece and Rome one may well question whether any other nation has so profoundly influenced the course of human life or has contributed comparable impulse to the thought and action of our day.

SUGGESTED READINGS

ALBRIGHT, W. F. *From the Stone Age to Christianity*, chap. v. Baltimore: Johns Hopkins Press, 1940.

BERTHOLET, A. *A History of Hebrew Civilization*, Book II. London: Harrap & Co., 1926.

CAUSSE, A. *Du Groupe ethnique à la communauté religieuse*. Paris: Librairie Félix Alcan, 1937.

EICHRODT, W. *Theologie des Alten Testaments*. Leipzig: Hinrichs, 1933–39.

FEIGIN, S. I. "Solomon and Adonijah," in *Missitrei Heavar*, pp. 70–82. New York: Sepharim, 1943.

GASTER, T. H. "Divine Kingship in the Ancient Near East: A Review Article," *Review of Religions*, 1945, pp. 267–81.

KENNETT, R. H. "The Contribution of the Old Testament to the Religious Development of Mankind," in *The People and the Book*, pp. 383–402. Oxford, 1925.

MACDONALD, D. B. *The Hebrew Literary Genius*. Princeton: Princeton University Press, 1933.

————. *The Hebrew Philosophical Genius*. Princeton: Princeton University Press, 1936.

MORGENSTERN, JULIAN. "Universalism in Judaism," *Universal Jewish Encyclopedia*, X, 353–57.

NOYES, C. *The Genius of Israel*, chap. xviii. Boston and New York: Houghton Mifflin Co., 1924.

PEDERSEN, JOHS. *Israel, Its Life and Culture*. London: Humphrey Milford, 1926.

ROBINSON, H. W. "Hebrew Psychology," in *The People and the Book*, pp. 353–82. Oxford, 1925.

SMITH, SIR GEORGE ADAM. "The Hebrew Genius as Exhibited in the Old Testament," in *The Legacy of Israel*, pp. 1–28. Oxford, 1927.

CONCLUSION

H. *and* H. A. FRANKFORT

CHAPTER XII

THE EMANCIPATION OF THOUGHT
FROM MYTH

WHEN we read in Psalm 19 that "the heavens declare the glory of God; and the firmament sheweth his handiwork," we hear a voice which mocks the beliefs of Egyptians and Babylonians. The heavens, which were to the psalmist but a witness of God's greatness, were to the Mesopotamians the very majesty of godhead, the highest ruler, Anu. To the Egyptians the heavens signified the mystery of the divine mother through whom man was reborn. In Egypt and Mesopotamia the divine was comprehended as immanent: the gods were in nature. The Egyptians saw in the sun all that a man may know of the Creator; the Mesopotamians viewed the sun as the god Shamash, the guarantor of justice. But to the psalmist the sun was God's devoted servant who "is as a bridegroom coming out of his chamber, and rejoiceth as a strong man to run a race." The God of the psalmists and the prophets was not in nature. He transcended nature—and transcended, likewise, the realm of mythopoeic thought. It would seem that the Hebrews, no less than the Greeks, broke with the mode of speculation which had prevailed up to their time.

The mainspring of the acts, thoughts, and feelings of early man was the conviction that the divine was immanent in nature, and nature intimately connected with society. Dr. Wilson emphasized this fact by calling the Egyptians monophysites. Dr. Jacobsen indicated that his approach to Mesopotamian thought could not do full justice to it; but the myths and beliefs which he discussed reflect it at every turn. And in our first chapter we found that the assumption of an essential correlation between nature and man provided us with a basis for the understanding of mythopoeic thought. Its logic, its peculiar structure, was seen to derive from an unceasing awareness of a live relationship between man and the phenomenal world. In the significant moments of his life, early man

363

was confronted not by an inanimate, impersonal nature—not by an "It"—but by a "Thou." We have seen that such a relationship involved not only man's intellect but the whole of his being—his feeling and his will, no less than his thought. Hence early man would have rejected the detachment of a purely intellectual attitude toward nature, had he been able to conceive it, as inadequate to his experience.

As long as the peoples of the ancient Near East preserved their cultural integrity—from the middle of the fourth to the middle of the first millennium b.c.—they remained conscious of their close bond with nature. And that awareness remained vivid notwithstanding the conditions of city life. The efflorescence of civilization in Egypt and Mesopotamia brought with it the need for a division of labor and a diversification of life possible only when people congregate in sufficient numbers for some to be freed from preoccupation with earning a livelihood. But the ancient cities were small by our standards, and their inhabitants were not cut off from the land. On the contrary, most of them derived their sustenance from the surrounding fields; all of them worshiped gods personifying natural powers; and all of them participated in rites which marked the turning-points in the farmer's year. In the great metropolis of Babylon the outstanding annual event was the New Year's Festival celebrating the renewal of the generative force of nature. In all Mesopotamian cities the business of everyday life was interrupted several times in the course of each month when the moon completed one of its phases or other natural events called for appropriate action on the part of the community. In Egypt, too, the husbandman's preoccupations found expression in festivals at Thebes, Memphis, and other Egyptian cities where celebrations marked the rise of the Nile, the end of the inundation, or the completion of the harvest. Thus urban life in no way diminished man's awareness of his essential involvement in nature.

When we accentuate the basic conception of ancient Near Eastern thought, as we have just done, we are necessarily obscuring its richness and diversity. Within the scope of mythopoeic thought a great variety of attitudes and outlooks are possible; and contrast as well as variety become apparent when we compare the speculative myths of Egypt and Mesopotamia. It is true that the same natural phenomena were often personified in these two countries and that the same images were often used to describe them. Yet the mood of the myths and the significance of the images are most unlike.

In both countries, for instance, the existing world was believed to have emerged from the waters of chaos. In Egypt this primeval ocean was male—the god Nūn. In other words, it was conceived as a fertilizing agent, and as such it was a permanent factor in the created universe recognized in the subsoil water and in the annual flood of the Nile. In Mesopotamia the fertilizing power in water was personified as the god Enki or Ea. But he was entirely unrelated to the primordial ocean. This ocean was a female, Tiᵓamat, the mother who brought forth gods and monsters in such profusion that her unbounded fruitfulness endangered the very existence of the universe. She was killed in combat by Marduk, who formed the world from her body. Thus water was significant to both Babylonians and Egyptians as the source and also as the sustainer of life. Yet these conceptions were very differently expressed by the two peoples.

A similar contrast appears in relation to earth. Mesopotamia worshiped a beneficial Great Mother whose fertility was seen in the produce of the earth and who gained additional religious importance by a variety of associations. The earth was viewed as the counterpart (and hence the spouse) of Heaven, Anu; or of the waters, Enki; or even of Enlil, the kingly storm-god. In Egypt, on the other hand, the earth was a male—Geb or Ptah or Osiris: the ubiquitous mother-goddess was not connected with the soil. Her image was either cast in the primitive and ancient guise of the cow or projected on the sky which, as Nūt, gave birth to the sun and stars each day at dawn and dusk. Moreover, the dead entered her body to be reborn as immortals. The sustained Egyptian preoccupation with death and the hereafter, however, found no equivalent in Mesopotamia. On the contrary, death was understood there as an almost complete destruction of personality; and man's chief desires were for a worthy life and freedom from disease, with a good reputation and descendants to survive him; and the sky was not a goddess bending over her children but the most unapproachable of male gods.

The differences which we have enumerated do not merely represent a meaningless variety of images; they betray a thorough contrast between the Egyptian and Mesopotamian views as to the nature of the universe in which man lives. Throughout the Mesopotamian texts we hear overtones of anxiety which seem to express a haunting fear that the unaccountable and turbulent powers may at any time bring disaster to human society. But in Egypt the gods were powerful without being violent. Nature presented itself as an established order in which changes were either superficial and insignificant or an unfolding in time of what had been preordained from the beginning. Moreover, Egyptian kingship guaranteed stability to society. For, as Dr. Wilson explained, one of the gods occupied the throne. Pharaoh was divine, the son and image of the Creator. Thus Pharaoh insured a harmonious integration of nature and society at all times. But in Mesopotamia the assembly of the gods assigned a mere mortal to rule men, and the divine favor might at any time be withdrawn from him. Man was at the mercy of decisions he could neither influence nor gauge. Hence the king and his counselors watched for portents on earth and in the sky which might reveal a changing constellation of divine grace, so that catastrophe might be foreseen and possibly averted. In Egypt neither astrology nor prophecy ever developed to any great extent.

The contrast between the temper of the two countries was concisely expressed in their creation myths. In Egypt creation was viewed as the brilliant act of an omnipotent Creator disposing of submissive elements. Of the lasting order which he created, society formed an unchanging part. In Mesopotamia the Creator had been chosen by a divine assembly helpless before the threat of the powers of chaos. Their champion, Marduk, had followed up his victory over these antagonists by the creation of the universe. This took place almost as an afterthought, and man was especially designed as a servant of the gods. There was no permanence in the human sphere. The gods assembled on every New Year's Day to "establish (such) destinies" for mankind as they pleased.

The differences between the Egyptian and Mesopotamian manners of viewing the world are very far-reaching. Yet the two peoples agreed in the fundamental assumptions that the individual is part of society, that society is imbedded in nature, and that nature is but the manifestation of the divine. This doctrine was, in fact, universally accepted by the peoples of the ancient world with the single exception of the Hebrews.

The Hebrews arrived late upon the scene and settled in a country pervaded by influences from the two superior adjacent cultures. One would expect the newcomers to have assimilated alien modes of thought, since these were supported by such vast prestige. Untold immigrants from deserts and mountains had done so in the past; and many individual Hebrews did, in fact, conform to the ways of the Gentiles. But assimilation was not characteristic for Hebrew thought. On the contrary, it held out with a peculiar stubbornness and insolence against the wisdom of Israel's neighbors. It is possible to detect the reflection of Egyptian and Mesopotamian beliefs in many episodes of the Old Testament; but the overwhelming impression left by that document is one, not of derivation, but of originality.

The dominant tenet of Hebrew thought is the absolute transcendence of God. Yahweh is not in nature. Neither earth nor sun nor heaven is divine; even the most potent natural phenomena are but reflections of God's greatness. It is not even possible properly to name God:

And Moses said unto God, Behold, when I come unto the children of Israel and shall say unto them, The God of your fathers hath sent me unto you; and they shall say to me: What is his name? what shall I say unto them?
And God said unto Moses: I AM THAT I AM: and he said, Thus shalt thou say unto the children of Israel, I AM hath sent me unto you [Exod. 3:13-14].

The God of the Hebrews is pure being, unqualified, ineffable. He is *holy*. That means that he is *sui generis*. It does not mean that he is taboo or that he is power. It means that all values are ultimately attributes of God alone. Hence, all concrete phenomena are devaluated. Dr. Irwin has pointed out that in Hebrew thought man and nature are not necessarily corrupt; but both are necessarily *valueless* before God. As Eliphaz said to Job (and we use the Chicago translation):

Can a mortal be righteous before God
Or a man be pure before his Maker?
Even in his servants he does not trust,

And his angels he charges with error.
How much less them that dwell in houses of clay,
Whose foundation is in the dust . . . . [Job 4:17–19a].

A similar meaning lies in the words of Deutero-Isaiah (64:6a):
"We are all as an unclean thing, and all our righteousnesses are as
filthy rags." Even man's righteousness, his highest virtue, is devaluated by the comparison with the absolute.

In the field of material culture such a conception of God leads to
iconoclasm; and it needs an effort of the imagination to realize the
shattering boldness of a contempt for imagery at the time, and in
the particular historical setting, of the Hebrews. Everywhere religious fervor not only inspired verse and rite but also sought plastic
and pictorial expression. The Hebrews, however, denied the rele-
vancy of the "graven image"; the boundless could not be given
form, the unqualified could but be offended by a representation,
whatever the skill and the devotion that went into its making.
Every finite reality shriveled to nothingness before the absolute
value which was God.

The abysmal difference between the Hebrew and the normal
Near Eastern viewpoints can best be illustrated by the manner in
which an identical theme, the instability of the social order, is
treated. We have a number of Egyptian texts which deal with the
period of social upheaval which followed the great era of the pyramid builders. The disturbance of the established order was viewed
with horror. Neferrohu said:

I show thee the land in lamentation and distress. The man with a weak arm
(now) has (a strong) arm. . . . . I show thee how the undermost is turned to
uppermost. . . . . The poor man will acquire riches.[1]

The most famous of the sages, Ipuwer, is even more explicit. For
instance, he condemns as a disastrous parody of order the fact that
gold and lapis lazuli are hung about the necks of slave girls. But noble ladies walk
through the land and mistresses of houses say: Would that we had something to
eat. . . . . Behold they that possessed beds now lie upon the ground. He that
slept with dirt upon him now stuffeth for himself a cushion.

The upshot is unmitigated misery for all: "Nay but great and small
say: I wish I were dead."[2]

In the Old Testament we meet the same theme—the reversal of

established social conditions. When Hannah, after years of barrenness, had prayed for a son, and Samuel was born, she praised God:

> There is none holy as the Lord: for there is none beside thee: neither is there any rock like our God. . . . . The bows of the mighty men are broken, and they that stumbled are girded with strength. They that were full have hired out themselves for bread; and they that were hungry ceased. . . . . The Lord maketh poor and maketh rich: he bringeth low, and lifteth up. He raiseth up the poor out of the dust, and lifteth up the beggar from the dunghill, to set them among princes, and to make them inherit the throne of glory: for the pillars of the earth are the Lord's and he hath set the world upon them [I Sam. 2:2–8].

Notice that the last verses state explicitly that God created the existing social order; but, quite characteristically, this order did not derive any sacredness, any value, from its divine origin. The sacredness and value remain attributes of God alone, and the violent changes of fortune observed in social life are but signs of God's omnipotence. Nowhere else do we meet this fanatical devaluation of the phenomena of nature and the achievements of man: art, virtue, social order—in view of the unique significance of the divine. It has been rightly pointed out that the monotheism of the Hebrews is a correlate of their insistence on the unconditioned nature of God.[3] Only a God who transcends every phenomenon, who is not conditioned by any mode of manifestation—only an unqualified God can be the one and only ground of *all* existence.

This conception of God represents so high a degree of abstraction that, in reaching it, the Hebrews seem to have left the realm of mythopoeic thought. The impression that they did so is strengthened when we observe that the Old Testament is remarkably poor in mythology of the type we have encountered in Egypt and Mesopotamia. But this impression requires correction. The processes of mythopoeic thought are decisive for many sections of the Old Testament. For instance, the magnificent verses from the Book of Proverbs quoted in chapter ix describe the Wisdom of God, personified and substantialized in the same manner in which the corresponding concept of *ma͑at* is treated by the Egyptians. Even the great conception of an only and transcendent God was not entirely free from myth, for it was not the fruit of detached speculation but of a passionate and dynamic experience. Hebrew thought did not entirely overcome mythopoeic thought. It created, in fact, a new myth—the myth of the Will of God.

Although the great "Thou" which confronted the Hebrews transcended nature, it stood in a specific relationship to the people. For when they were freed from bondage and roamed in "a desert land . . . . the waste howling wilderness . . . . the Lord alone did lead (them) and there was no strange god with (them)" (Deut. 32:10–12). And God had said:

But thou, Israel, art my servant, Jacob whom I have chosen, the seed of Abraham my friend. Thou whom I have taken from the ends of the earth, and called thee from the chief men thereof, and said unto thee, Thou art my servant; I have chosen thee, and not cast thee away [Isa. 41:8–9].

Thus God's will was felt to be focused on one particular and concrete group of human beings; it was asserted to have manifested itself at one decisive moment in their history and ceaselessly and relentlessly to have urged, rewarded, or chastised the people of its choice. For in Sinai, God had said, "Ye shall be unto me a kingdom of priests and an holy nation" (Exod. 19:6).

It is a poignant myth, this Hebrew myth of a chosen people, of a divine promise made, of a terrifying moral burden imposed—a prelude to the later myth of the Kingdom of God, that more remote and more spiritual "promised land." For in the myth of the chosen people the ineffable majesty of God and the worthlessness of man are correlated in a dramatic situation that is to unfold in time and is moving toward a future where the distant yet related parallels of human and divine existence are to meet in infinity.

Not cosmic phenomena, but history itself, had here become pregnant with meaning; history had become a revelation of the dynamic will of God. The human being was not merely the servant of the god as he was in Mesopotamia; nor was he placed, as in Egypt, at a preordained station in a static universe which did not need to be—and, in fact, could not be—questioned. Man, according to Hebrew thought, was the interpreter and the servant of God; he was even honored with the task of bringing about the realization of God's will. Thus man was condemned to unending efforts which were doomed to fail because of his inadequacy. In the Old Testament we find man possessed of a new freedom and of a new burden of responsibility. We also find there a new and utter lack of *eudaimonia*, of harmony—whether with the world of reason or with the world of perception.

All this may help to explain the strange poignancy of single individuals in the Old Testament. Nowhere in the literature of Egypt or Babylonia do we meet the loneliness of the biblical figures, astonishingly real in their mixture of ugliness and beauty, pride and contrition, achievement and failure. There is the tragic figure of Saul, the problematical David; there are countless others. We find single men in terrible isolation facing a transcendent God: Abraham trudging to the place of sacrifice with his son, Jacob in his struggle, and Moses and the prophets. In Egypt and Mesopotamia man was dominated, but also supported, by the great rhythm of nature. If in his dark moments he felt himself caught and held in the net of unfathomable decisions, his involvement in nature had, on the whole, a soothing character. He was gently carried along on the perennial cosmic tides of the seasons. The depth and intimacy of man's relationship with nature found expression in the ancient symbol of the mother-goddess. But Hebrew thought ignored this image entirely. It only recognized the stern Father, of whom it was said: "he led him (Jacob, the people) about, he instructed him, he kept him as the apple of his eye" (Deut. 32:10*b*).

The bond between Yahweh and his chosen people had been finally established during the Exodus. The Hebrews considered the forty years in the desert the decisive phase in their development. And we, too, may understand the originality and the coherence of their speculations if we relate them to their experience in the desert.

The reader will remember that preceding chapters took great care to describe the Egyptian and Mesopotamian landscapes. In doing so, the authors did not succumb to an unwarranted naturalism; they did not claim that cultural phenomena could be derived from physiographical causes. They merely suggested that a relation between land and culture may exist, a suggestion we can accept the more readily since we have seen that the surrounding world confronted early man as a "Thou." We may ask, then, what was the natural setting which determined the Hebrew's experience of the world around him. Now, the Hebrews, whatever their ancestry and historical antecedents, were tribal nomads. And since they were nomads in the Near East, they must have lived, not in boundless steppes, but between the desert and the sown, between the most fertile of lands and the total negation of life, which, in this remarkable corner of the earth, lie cheek by jowl. They must, therefore, have known through experience both the reward and the cost of existence in either.

The Hebrews craved to settle for good in the fertile plains. But characteristically they dreamed of lands overflowing with milk and honey, not lands of superabundant crops like those the Egyptians imagined for their hereafter. It seems that the desert as a metaphysical experience loomed very large for the Hebrews and colored all their valuations. It is, perhaps, the tension between two valuations—between a desire and a contempt for what is desired —that may explain some of the paradoxes of ancient Hebrew beliefs.

The organized states of the ancient Near East were agricultural; but the values of an agricultural community are the opposites of those of the nomadic tribe, especially of the extreme type of nomads of the desert. The settled peasant's reverence for impersonal authority, and the bondage, the constraint which the organized state imposes, mean an intolerable lack of personal freedom for the tribesman. The farmer's everlasting preoccupation with phenomena of growth and his total dependence on these phenomena appear to the nomad a form of slavery. Moreover, to him the desert is clean, but the scene of life, which is also the scene of decay, is sordid.

On the other hand, nomadic freedom can be bought only at a price; for whoever rejects the complexities and mutual dependencies of agricultural society not only gains freedom but also loses the bond with the phenomenal world; in fact, he gains his freedom at the cost of significant form. For, wherever we find reverence for the phenomena of life and growth, we find preoccupation with the immanence of the divine and with the *form* of its manifestation. But in the stark solitude of the desert, where nothing changes, nothing moves (except man at his own free will), where features in the landscape are only pointers, landmarks, without significance in themselves—there we may expect the image of God to transcend concrete phenomena altogether. Man confronting God will not contemplate him but will hear his voice and command, as Moses did, and the prophets, and Mohammed.

When we compared the lands of origin of Hebrews, Egyptians, and Mesopotamians, we were concerned, not with the relation between group psychology and habitat, but with profound differences in pristine religious experience. The peculiar experience which we have just described seems characteristic for all the most significant figures of the Old Testament. It is important to realize this, not because it enables us to understand them better as individuals, but because we then recognize what colored and integrated their thought. They propounded, not speculative theory, but revolutionary and dynamic teaching. The doctrine of a single, unconditioned, transcendent God rejected time-honored values, proclaimed new ones, and postulated a metaphysical significance for history and for man's actions. With infinite *moral* courage the Hebrews worshiped an absolute God and accepted as the correlate of their faith the sacrifice of a harmonious existence. In transcending the Near Eastern myths of immanent godhead, they created, as we have seen, the new myth of the will of God. It remained for the Greeks, with their peculiar *intellectual* courage, to discover a form of speculative thought in which myth was entirely overcome.

In the sixth century B.C. the Greeks, in their great cities on the coast of Asia Minor, were in touch with all the leading centers of the civilized world: Egypt and Phoenicia; Lydia, Persia, and Babylon. There can be no doubt that this contact played some part in the meteoric development of Greek culture. But it is impossible to estimate the Greek indebtedness to the ancient Near East. As is usual when cultural contact is truly fruitful, simple derivations are rare. What the Greeks borrowed, they transmuted.

In the Greek mystery religions we meet well-known oriental themes. Demeter was the sorrowing mother-goddess searching for her child; Dionysus died a violent death but was resurrected. In some of the rites the participants experienced an immediate relationship with the divine in nature; and in this respect there is similarity with the ancient Near East. But it would be hard to find antecedents for the individual salvation vouchsafed to the initiates. A possible parallel would be the Osiris cult; but, as far as we know, the Egyptian did not undergo an initiation or share the god's fate during his lifetime. In any case, the Greek mysteries show several features which were without precedent. These generally amount to a diminished distance between men and gods. The initiate of the Orphic mysteries, for instance, not only hoped to be liberated from the "wheel of births" but actually emerged as a god from his union with the mother-goddess, "queen of the dead." The Orphic myths contain speculations about the nature of man which are characteristically Greek in their tenor. It was said that the Titans had devoured Dionysus-Zagreus and were therefore destroyed by the lightning of Zeus, who made man from their ashes. Man, in so far as he consists of the substance of the Titans, is evil and ephemeral; but since the Titans had partaken of a god's body, man contains a divine and immortal spark. Such dualism and the recognition of an immortal part in man are unknown in the ancient Near East outside Persia.

It is not only in the mystery religions that the Greeks placed man closer to the gods than the Egyptians or Babylonians had ever done. Greek literature names many women who had gods for lovers and bore them children, and it has been pointed out that the typical sinner in Greece was the man who had attempted to do violence to a goddess.[4] Moreover, the Olympian gods, though they were manifest in nature, had not made the universe and could not dispose of man as their creature with the same unquestioned right of ownership which the ancient Near Eastern gods exercised. In fact, the Greek claimed a common ancestry with the gods and, consequently, suffered the more acutely because of his own disabilities. Pindar's Sixth Nemean Ode, for instance, starts as follows:

> Of one race, one only, are men and gods. Both of one mother's womb we draw our breath; but far asunder is all our power divided, and fences us apart; here there is nothingness, and there, in strength of bronze, a seat unshaken, eternal, abides the heaven. [After Cornford.]

The spirit of such poetry differs profoundly from that of the ancient Near East, even though, at this time, Greece still shared many beliefs with the Orient. The common mother of gods and men to whom Pindar refers is Gaea, the earth; and the earth, as Ninhursaga, was often regarded as the Great Mother in Mesopotamia. Homer still knew of the primeval waters: "Okeanos from whom the gods are sprung."[5] Yet more important than such echoes of Near Eastern beliefs is the similarity between the Greek and the oriental methods of interpreting nature: an ordered view of the universe was obtained by bringing its elements in a genealogical relationship with one another. In Greece this procedure found monumental expression in Hesiod's Theogeny, written probably about 700 B.C. Hesiod starts his account with Chaos and proclaims Sky and Earth the parents of gods and men. He introduces numerous personifications which recall Egyptian ma^{c}at or the "Wisdom of God" in the Book of Proverbs. " . . . . Next he (Zeus) wedded bright Themis who bare the Horai, even Eunomia (Good Government) and Dike (Justice) and blooming Eirene (Peace) who care for the works of mortal man" (ll. 901–3).[6]

Associations and "participations" typical of mythopoeic thought appear often. A particularly clear example is: "And Night bare hateful Doom; and black Fate and Death and Sleep she bare, and she bare the tribe of dreams; all these did dark Night bare, albeit mated unto none" (ll. 211 ff.). The natural process of procreation thus supplied Hesiod with a scheme which allowed him to connect the phenomena and to arrange them in a comprehensible system. The Babylonian Epic of Creation and the An-Anum list use the same device; and we meet it in Egypt when Atum is said to have begotten Shū and Tefnūt (Air and Moisture), who, in their turn, brought forth Geb and Nūt (Earth and Sky).

And yet Hesiod is without oriental precedent in one respect: the gods and the universe were described by him as a matter of private interest. Such freedom was unheard of in the Near East, except among the Hebrews, where Amos, for instance, was a herdsman. In Egypt and Mesopotamia religious subjects were treated by members of the established hierarchy. But Hesiod was a Boeotian farmer called by the Muses, "which time he tended his flocks under holy Helicon." He says: "(The Muses) breathed in me a voice divine that I might celebrate the things that shall be and the things that were aforetime. They bade me sing the race of the Blessed Ones that are forever" (ll. 29 ff.). Thus a Greek layman recognized his vocation and became a singer who took the gods and nature as his theme, although he continued to use the traditional forms of epic poetry.

The same freedom, the same unconcern as regards special function and hierarchy, is characteristic for the Ionian philosophers who lived a century or more after Hesiod. Thales seems to have been an engineer and statesman; Anaximander, a mapmaker. Cicero stated: "Almost all those whom the Greeks called the Seven Sages, you will see to have been engaged in public life" (*De Rep.* i. 7). These men, then, in contrast to the priests of the Near East, were not charged by their communities to concern themselves with spiritual matters. They were moved by their own desire for an understanding of nature; and they did not hesitate to publish their findings, although they were not professional seers. Their curiosity was as lively as it was unhampered by dogma. Like Hesiod, the Ionian philosophers gave their attention to the problem of origins; but for them it assumed an entirely new character. The origin, the ἀρχή, which they sought was not understood in the terms of myth. They did not describe an ancestral divinity or a progenitor. They did not even look for an "origin" in the sense of an initial condition which was superseded by subsequent states of being. The Ionians asked for an immanent and *lasting* ground of existence. 'Αρχή means "origin," not as "beginning," but as "sustaining principle" or "first cause."

This change of viewpoint is breath-taking. It transfers the problems of man in nature from the realm of faith and poetic intuition to the intellectual sphere. A critical appraisal of each theory, and hence a continuous inquiry into the nature of reality, became possible. A cosmogonic myth is beyond discussion. It describes a sequence of sacred events, which one can either accept or reject. But no cosmogony can become part of a progressive and cumulative increase of knowledge. As we said in our first chapter, myth claims recognition by the faithful, not justification before the critical. But a sustaining principle or first cause must be comprehensible, even if it was first discovered in a flash of insight. It does not pose the alternative of acceptance or rejection. It may be analyzed, modified, or corrected. In short, it is subject to intellectual judgment.

Yet the doctrines of the early Greek philosophers are not couched in the language of detached and systematic reflection. Their sayings sound rather like inspired oracles. And no wonder, for these men proceeded, with preposterous boldness, on an entirely unproved assumption. They held that the universe is an intelligible whole. In other words, they presumed that a single order underlies the chaos of our perceptions and, furthermore, that we are able to comprehend that order.

The speculative courage of the Ionians is often overlooked. Their teachings were, in fact, predestined to be misunderstood by modern—or rather, nineteenth-century—scholars. When Thales proclaims water to be the first cause, or Anaximenes air; when Anaximander speaks of the "Boundless," and Heraclitus of fire; when, moreover, Democritus' theory of atoms can be considered the outcome of these earlier speculations; then we need not be astonished that commentators in a positivistic age unwittingly read familiar connotations into the quasi-materialist doctrines of the Ionians and regarded these earliest philosophers as the first scientists. No bias could more insidiously disfigure the greatness of the Ionian achievement. The materialist interpretation of their teachings takes for granted what was to be discovered only as a result of the labors of these ancient thinkers—the distinction between the objective and the subjective. And only on the basis of this distinction is scientific thought possible.

In actual fact the Ionians moved in a curious borderland. They forefelt the possibility of establishing an intelligible coherence in the phenomenal world; yet they were still under the spell of an undissolved relationship between man and nature. And so we remain somewhat uncertain of the exact connotations of the Ionian sayings which have been preserved. Thales, for instance, said that water was the ἀρχή, the first principle or cause of all things; but he also said: "All things are full of gods. The magnet is alive for it has the power of moving iron."[7] Anaximenes said: "Just as our soul, being air, holds us together, so do breath and air encompass the whole world."

It is clear that Anaximenes did not consider air merely as a physical substance, although he did consider it, among other things, a substance whose properties changed when it was either condensed or rarefied. But at the same time air was mysteriously connected with the maintenance of life itself: it was an agent of vitality. Anaximenes recognized in air something variable enough to make it seem possible to interpret the most diverse phenomena as its manifestations. Thales had preferred water, but he, too, did not consider his first cause merely as a neutral, colorless liquid. We must remember that seeds and bulbs and the eggs of insects lie lifeless in the rich soil of Eastern Mediterranean lands until the rains come—remember, also, the preponderant role of watery substances in the processes of conception and birth in the animal kingdom. It is possible that the ancient oriental view of water as a fertilizing agent had retained its validity for Thales. It is equally possible that he indorsed the oriental conception of a primeval ocean from which all life came forth. Homer, as we have seen, called Okeanos the origin of gods and men. Thales' pupil, Anaximander, stated explicitly: "the living creatures came forth from the moist element." There are many other symbolic meanings which we can impute to Thales' theory; for, after all, the sea exercises its magic even today. Thus it has been supposed (by Joël) that Thales regarded the sea as the epitome of change, as many poets since have done.

Now to claim, on any or all of these analogies, that water is the first cause of all things is to argue in the manner of mythopoeic thought. But observe that Thales speaks of *water*, not of a water-god; Anaximenes refers to *air*, not to a god of air or storms. Here lies the astonishing novelty of their approach. Even though "all things are full of gods," these men attempt to understand the coherence of the *things*. When Anaximenes explains that air is the first cause, "just as our soul, being air, holds us together," he continues to specify how air can function as such a sustaining principle: "It [air] differs in different substances in virtue of its rarefaction and condensation." Or, even more specifically:

When it [air] is dilated so as to be rarer it becomes fire; while winds, on the other hand, are condensed air. Cloud is formed from air by felting; and this, still further condensed, becomes water. Water, condensed still more, turns to earth; and when condensed as much as it can be, to stones.

There is nowhere a precedent for this type of argument. It shows a twofold originality. In the first place, early Greek philosophy (in Cornford's words) "ignored with astonishing boldness the prescriptive sanctities of religious representation."[8] Its second characteristic is a passionate consistency. Once a theory is adopted, it is followed up to its ultimate conclusion irrespective of conflicts with observed facts or probabilities. Both of these characteristics indicate an implicit recognition of the autonomy of thought; they also emphasize the intermediate position of early Greek philosophy. The absence of personification, of gods, sets it apart from mythopoeic thought. Its disregard for the data of experience in its pursuit of consistency distinguishes it from later thought. Its hypotheses were not induced from systematic observations but were much more in the nature of inspired conjectures or divinations by which it was attempted to reach a vantage point where the phenomena would reveal their hidden coherence. It was the unshakable conviction of the Ionians, Pythagoreans, and early Eleatics that such a vantage point existed; and they searched for the road toward it, not in the manner of scientists, but in that of conquistadors.

Anaximander, a pupil of Thales, made an important new advance. He realized that the sustaining principle of all determinate phenomena could not be itself determinate. The ground of all existence had to be essentially different from the elements of actuality; it had to be ἕτερα φύσις—of another nature—while yet containing all contrasts and specific qualities. Anaximander called the ἀρχή the ἄπειρον, the "Infinite" or "Boundless." It is reported by Theophrastos that Anaximander "said that the material cause and first element of things was the Infinite. . . . . He says it is neither water nor any other of the so-called elements but a substance different from them which is infinite, from which arise all the heavens and the worlds within them."[9] Notice that Anaximander submits to the substantializing tendency of mythopoeic thought by calling the ἄπειρον a substance—or, in the following quotation, a body: "He did not ascribe the origin of things to any alteration in matter, but said that the oppositions in the substratum, which was a boundless body, were separated out."

The opposites which Anaximander found in actuality were the traditional ones: warm and cold, moist and dry. When he stated that these opposites "separated out" from the Boundless, he did not refer (as we would expect) to a mechanistic process. He put it as follows: "And into that from which things take their rise they pass away once more, as is meet; for they make reparation and satisfaction to one another for their injustice according to the ordering of time." In the winter, cold commits an injustice to heat, etc. Again we meet the marvelous blend of imaginative, emotional, and intellectual vigor which was characteristic of the sixth and fifth centuries B.C. in Greece. Even that most abstract of notions, the Boundless itself, is described by Anaximander as "eternal and ageless"—ἀθάνατος καὶ ἀγήρως—words which serve as a stock phrase in Homer to characterize the gods. Yet Anaximander, like Thales and Anaximenes, describes the universe in purely secular terms. We happen to know a good deal of his cosmography. Let us quote, as characteristic samples, his statement that "the earth swings free, held in its place by nothing. It stays where it is because of its equal distance from everything." The heavenly bodies are described as "wheels of fire": "And there are breathing-holes, certain pipe-like passages, at which the heavenly bodies show themselves." Thunder and lightning are blasts of the winds—a theory broadly parodied in Aristophanes' clouds—and, as to living beings, we find this curious anticipation of phylogenetics: "Living creatures arose from the moist element as it was evaporated by the sun. Man was like another animal, namely, a fish in the beginning." Again, Anaximander presents a curious hybrid of empirical and mythopoeic thought. But in his recognition that the ground of all determinate existence could not itself be determinate, in his claim that not water nor air nor any other "element" but only the "Boundless" from which all opposites "separated out," could be the ἀρχή, he showed a power of abstraction beyond anything known before his day.

With Heraclitus of Ephesus philosophy found its *locus standi*. "Wisdom is one thing. It is to know the *thought* by which all things are steered through all things."[10] Here, for the first time, attention is centered, not on the thing known, but on the knowing of it. Thought, γνώμη (which may also be translated "judgment," or "understanding"), controls the phenomena as it constitutes the thinker. The problem of understanding nature is moved once more to a new plane. In the ancient Near East it had remained within the sphere of myth. The Milesian school of philosophers had moved it to the realm of the intellect in that they claimed the universe to be an *intelligible* whole. The manifold was to be understood as deriving from a sustaining principle or first cause, but this was to be looked for in the phenomena. The question of how we can know what is outside us was not raised. Heraclitus asserted that the universe was intelligible because it was ruled by "thought" or "judgment" and that the same principle, therefore, governed both existence and knowledge. He was conscious that this wisdom surpassed even the loftiest conception of Greek mythopoeic thought: "The wise is one only. It is unwilling and willing to be called by the name of Zeus."[11]

Heraclitus calls this wisdom *Logos*, a term so heavily laden with associations as to be an embarrassment whether we translate it or not. "Reason" is perhaps the least objectionable rendering. "It is wise to hearken, not to me, but to the Logos and to confess that all things are one."[12] All things are one. Things that are distinct from one another, or qualities that are each other's opposites, have no permanent existence. They are but transitory stages in a perpetual flux. No static description of the universe is true. "Being" is but "becoming." The cosmos is but the dynamics of existence. The opposites which Anaximander saw "separating out" from the Boundless are for Heraclitus united by a tension which causes each of them ultimately to change into its opposite. "Men do not know how what is at variance agrees with itself. It is an attunement (αρμονία) of opposite tensions, like that of the bow and the lyre."[13]

But if the universe changes continually according to the tensions between opposites, it is senseless to ask for its origin in the manner of myth. There is no beginning and no end; there is only existence. Heraclitus states magnificently: "This world (κόσμος) which is the same for all, no one of the gods or men has made; but it was ever, is now, and ever shall be an ever-living fire, with measures of it kindling, and measures going out."[14] Fire is the symbol for a universe in flux between tensional opposites. As Burnet says: "The quantity of fire in a flame burning steadily appears to remain the same, the flame seems to be what we call a 'thing.' And yet the substance of it is continually changing. It is always passing away in smoke, and its place is always taken by fresh matter from the fuel that feeds it."[15]

Heraclitus takes pains to stress that it is only the total process that is lasting and, hence, significant: "The way up and the way down is one and the same,"[16] or "it rests by changing,"[17] or, more metaphorically, "fire is want *and* surfeit,"[18] or one "cannot step twice in the same river, for fresh waters are forever flowing in upon you."[19]

No momentary phase in this perpetual change is more important then any other; all opposites are transitory: "Fire lives the death of air and air lives the death of fire; water lives the death of earth, earth that of water."[20] This fragment might startle us, for here fire appears as one of the "elements" on a par with earth, air, and water; and we would seem to be back on the level of Thales and Anaximenes. Heraclitus is using fire here as one of the traditional four elements in order to insist on the impermanence of the distinction among them. In another fragment the emergence and resorption of all determinate things in the one lasting flux of change is expressed as follows: "All things are an exchange for fire and fire for all things, even as wares for gold and gold for wares."[21] Here the symbolical significance of fire is obvious.

In the writing of Heraclitus, to a larger degree than ever before, the images do not impose their burden of concreteness but are entirely subservient to the achievement of clarity and precision. Even for Thales and Anaximenes, water and air are no mere constituents of the material world; they also possess a symbolical connotation, if only as agents of vitality. But for Heraclitus fire is purely a symbol of reality in flux; he calls wisdom "to know the thought by which all things are steered through all things."

Heraclitus gives the sharpest and profoundest expression to the Ionian postulate that the universe is an intelligible whole. It is intelligible, since *thought* steers all things. It is a whole, since it is a perpetual flux of change. Yet in this form the doctrine retains one contradiction. Mere change and flux cannot be intelligible, for they achieve not cosmos but chaos. Heraclitus solved this difficulty by recognizing in the flux of change an inherent dominant measure. We remember that the world was "an ever-living fire, with measures of it kindling and measures going out." The continuous transition of everything into its opposite was regulated by this measure. It was, as we have also seen, "an attunement of opposite tensions, like that of the bow and of the lyre." For this reason Heraclitus rejected the doctrine of Anaximander according to which the opposites had to make reparation to one another for their injustice. He held that it was in the nature of things that they should be continually replaced by their opposites:

> We must know that war is common to all and strife is justice and that all things come into being and pass away (?) through strife.[22]

> War is the father of all and the king of all, and some he has made gods and some men, some bond and some free.[23]

> Homer was wrong in saying "Would that strife might perish from among gods and men." He did not see that he was praying for the destruction of the universe, for, if his prayer were heard, all things would pass away.[24]

Heraclitus did not mean to equate existence with a blind conflict of opposing forces, but he called war the dynamics of existence which necessarily involved "the hidden attunement (which) is better than the open."[25] This attunement is of the essence of existence; it is valid in the same manner in which we claim the laws of nature to be valid: "The sun will not overstep his measures; if he does the Erinyes, the handmaids of justice, will find him out."[26] This reference to the sun indicates, perhaps, that the regularity of the movements of the heavenly bodies suggested to Heraclitus that all change was subject to a "hidden attunement." If this surmise were correct, it would link him appropriately with both mythopoeic and Platonic thought.

The philosophy of Heraclitus shows both parallels and contrasts to that of his older contemporary Pythagoras. According to Pythagoras, also, a hidden measure dominated all the phenomena. But, while Heraclitus was satisfied with proclaiming its existence, the Pythagoreans were anxious to determine it quantitatively. They believed a knowledge of essentials to be a knowledge of numbers, and they attempted to discover the immanent proportionality of the existing world. The starting-point for their enterprise was a remarkable discovery by Pythagoras. Measuring the lengths on the string of the lyre between the places where the four principal notes of the Greek scale were sounded, he found that they had the proportion 6:8:12. This harmonic proportion contains the octave (12:6), the fifth (12:8), and the fourth (8:6). If we attempt to regard the discovery naïvely, we shall admit that it is astonishing. It correlates musical harmonies, which belong to the world of the spirit no less than to that of sensual perception, with the precise abstractions of numerical ratios. It seemed legitimate for the Pythagoreans to expect that similar correlations would be discovered; and, with the truly Greek passion for following up a thought to its ultimate consequences, they maintained that certain arithmetical proportions explained every facet of actuality. Heraclitus said contemptuously: "The learning of many things teacheth not understanding, else it would have taught Hesiod and Pythagoras."[27]

Moreover, the Pythagoreans were far from sharing Heraclitus' views. While he had said proudly, "I have sought for myself,"[28] the Pythagoreans indorsed much traditional lore. While Heraclitus stated that all being was but a becoming, the Pythagoreans accepted the reality of the opposites and shared the common preference for the light, static, and unified aspects of existence, assigning the dark, the changing, and the manifold to the side of evil. Their dualism, their belief in the transmigration of souls, and their hope of liberation from the "wheel of births" connected the Pythagorean doctrine with Orphism. In fact, the teachings of Pythagoras belong preponderantly to the sphere of mythopoeic thought. This can be explained if we remember his orientation. Pythagoras was not concerned with knowledge for its own sake; he did not share the detached curiosity of the Ionians. He taught a way of life. The Pythagorean society was a religious fraternity striving for the sanctification of its members. In this, too, it resembled the Orphic societies; but its god was Apollo, not Dionysus; its method comprehension, not rapture. For the Pythagoreans, knowledge was part of the art of living; and living was seeking for salvation. We saw in the first chapter that man, when thus involved with the whole of his being, cannot achieve intellectual detachment. Therefore, Pythagorean thought is steeped in myth. Yet it was a member of the Pythagorean society, who after his apostasy, destroyed the last hold of myth on thought. This man was Parmenides, the founder of the Eleatic School.

Parmenides once more interpreted the Ionian postulate that the world forms an intelligible whole. But, as Burnet puts it, "he showed once and for all that if you take the One seriously you are bound to deny everything else."[29] Parmenides saw that not only each theory of origin, but even each theory of change or movement, made the concept of being problematical. Absolute being cannot be conceived as coming into existence out of a state of nonexistence.

How, then, can what *is* be going to be in the future? Or how could it come into being? If it came into being, it is not; nor is it, if it is going to be in the future. Thus is becoming extinguished and passing away not to be heard of.[30]

Parmenides' conclusion that this is so is a purely logical one, and hence we may say that the autonomy of thought was definitely established by him. We have seen that Heraclitus went far in this direction, claiming the congruity of truth and existence when he said: "Wisdom is one thing. It is to know the thought by which all things are steered through all things."

When Parmenides restated this thesis, he eliminated the last vestige of mythical concreteness and imagery which had survived in the "steered" of Heraclitus' saying and also in his symbol of fire. Parmenides said: "The thing that can be thought, and that for the sake of which the thought exists, is the same; for you cannot find thought without something that is, as to which it is uttered."[31] But since Parmenides considered "becoming extinguished and passing away not to be heard of," he assumed an entirely new position. The Milesians had attempted to correlate *being* (as the static ground of existence) and *becoming* (observed in the phenomena). Heraclitus had declared *being* a perpetual *becoming* and had correlated the two concepts with his "hidden attunement." Now Parmenides declared the two to be mutually exclusive, and only *being* to be real.

Come now, I will tell thee—and do thou hearken to my saying and carry it away—the only two ways of search that can be thought of. The first, namely, that *It is*, and that it is impossible for it not to be, is the way of conviction,[32] for truth is its companion. The other, namely, that *It is not*, and that it must needs not be—that, I tell thee, is a path that none can learn of at all. For thou canst not know what is not—that is impossible—nor utter it; for it is the same thing that can be thought and that can be.[33]

And again:

One path only is left for us to speak of, namely, that *It is*. In this path are very many tokens that what is is uncreated and indestructible; for it is complete, immovable and without end. Nor was it ever, nor will it be; for now *it is*, all at once, a continuous one. For what origin for it wilt thou look for? In what way and from what source could it have drawn its increase ? . . . . I shall not let thee say nor think that it came from what is not; for it can neither be thought nor uttered that anything is not.[34]

Here, in what Parmenides calls "the unshaken heart of well-rounded truth," we meet a philosophical *absolute* that reminds us of the religious absolute of the Old Testament. In the strictly idealistic position of Parmenides the autonomy of thought is vindicated, and every concrescence of myth is stripped off. Yet Parmenides is strongly connected with his predecessors in one respect. In his denial of the reality of movement, change, and distinctiveness, he reached a conclusion which, like theirs, was oddly at variance with the data of experience. He was aware of this and appealed to reason in defiance of the testimony of the senses: "But do thou restrain thy thought from this way of inquiry, nor let habit by its much experience force thee to cast upon this way a wandering eye or sounding ear or tongue; but judge by reason[35] the much disputed proof uttered by me."[36]

This same attitude was, implicitly or explicitly, adopted by all Greek thinkers of the sixth and fifth centuries b.c. For neither their basic assumption—that the world is an intelligible whole—nor their further explanation—that it unfolds in opposites—nor any of their other theses can be proved by logic or by experiment or by observation. With conviction they propounded theories which resulted from intuitive insight and which were elaborated by deductive reasoning. Each system was based upon an assumption held to be true and made to bear a structure erected without further reference to empirical data. Consistency was valued more highly than probability. This fact in itself shows that throughout early Greek philosophy *reason* is acknowledged as the highest arbiter, even though the Logos is not mentioned before Heraclitus and Parmenides. It is this tacit or outspoken appeal to reason, no less than the independence from "the prescriptive sanctities of religion," which places early Greek philosophy in the sharpest contrast with the thought of the ancient Near East.

As we have said before, the cosmologies of mythopoeic thought are basically revelations received in a confrontation with a cosmic "Thou." And one cannot argue about a revelation; it transcends reason. But in the systems of the Greeks the human mind recognizes its own. It may take back what it created or change or develop it. This is true even of the Milesian philosophies, although they have not entirely shed the concrescence of myth. It is patently true of the doctrine of Heraclitus, which established the sovereignty of thought, rejected Anaximander and Pythagoras, and proclaimed an absolute *becoming*. It is equally true of the teaching of Parmenides, who confounded Heraclitus and proclaimed an absolute *being*.

One question remains to be answered. If mythopoeic thought took shape in an undissolved relationship between man and nature, what became of that relationship when thought was emancipated? We may answer his question with a quotation to balance the one with which we began this chapter. We saw that in Psalm 19 nature appears bereaved of divinity before an absolute God: "The heavens declare the glory of God and the firmament sheweth his handiwork." And we read in Plato's *Timaeus*, in Jowett's translation (47c):

.... had we never seen the stars, and the sun, and the heaven, none of the words which we have spoken about the universe would ever have been uttered. But now the sight of day and night, and the months and the revolutions of the years, have created number, and have given us a conception of time; and the power of enquiring about the nature of the universe; and from this source we have derived philosophy, than which no greater good ever was or will be given by the gods to mortal man.

NOTES

1. Blackman's translation of Erman, *Literature of the Egyptians*, p. 115.
2. After Blackman, *ibid.*, pp. 94 ff.
3. Johannes Hehn, *Die biblische und die babylonische Gottesidee* (1913), p. 284.
4. F. M. Cornford, *From Religion to Philosophy* (London, 1912), 119–20.
5. *Iliad* xiv. 201, 241.
6. This and the following quotations are taken from A. W. Mair, *Hesiod, the Poems and Fragments* (Oxford: Clarendon Press, 1908).
7. This and the following quotations are taken from J. Burnet, *Early Greek Philosophy* (4th ed.; London, 1930).
8. *Cambridge Ancient History*, IV, 532.
9. Burnet, *op. cit.*, p. 52.
10. Burnet, Frag. 19.

11. Burnet, Frag. 65. This statement gains in pregnancy if we remember that Heraclitus was a contemporary of Aeschylus.

12. Burnet, Frag. 1. Burnet translates "my word."

13. Burnet, Frag. 45.

14. Burnet, Frag. 20.

15. *Op. cit.*, p. 145.

16. Burnet, Frag. 69.

17. Burnet, Frag. 83.

18. Burnet, Frag. 24.

19. Burnet, Frags. 41–42.

20. Burnet, Frag. 25.

21. Burnet, Frag. 22.

22. Burnet, Frag. 62.

23. Burnet, Frag. 44.

24. Burnet, Frag. 43.

25. Burnet, Frag. 47.

26. Burnet, Frag. 29.

27. Burnet, Frag. 16.

28. Burnet, Frag. 80.

29. *Op. cit.*, p. 179.

30. *Ibid.*, p. 175, ll. 19–22.

31. *Ibid.*, p. 176, ll. 34–36.

32. Burnet (*ibid.*, p. 173) translates "belief."

33. *Ibid.*, p. 173; Frags. 4 and 5.

34. *Ibid.*, p. 174; Frag. 8, ll. 1–9.

35. Burnet (*ibid.*, p. 173 n.) defends a translation of *logos* by "argument."

36. *Ibid.*, ll. 33–36.

SUGGESTED READINGS

BURNET, JOHN. *Early Greek Philosophy*. London, 1930.

CASSIRER, ERNST. "Die Philosophie der Griechen von den Anfängen bis Platon," in MAX DESSOIR, *Handbuch der Philosophie*, I, 7–140. Berlin, 1925.

CORNFORD, F. M. *From Religion to Philosophy*. London, 1912.

JOËL, KARL. *Geschichte der antiken Philosophie*, Vol. I. Tübingen, 1921.

MYRES, J. L. "The Background of Greek Science," *University of California Chronicle*, Vol. XIV, No. 4.

INDEX

INDEX